SENSATION & SENSIBILITY

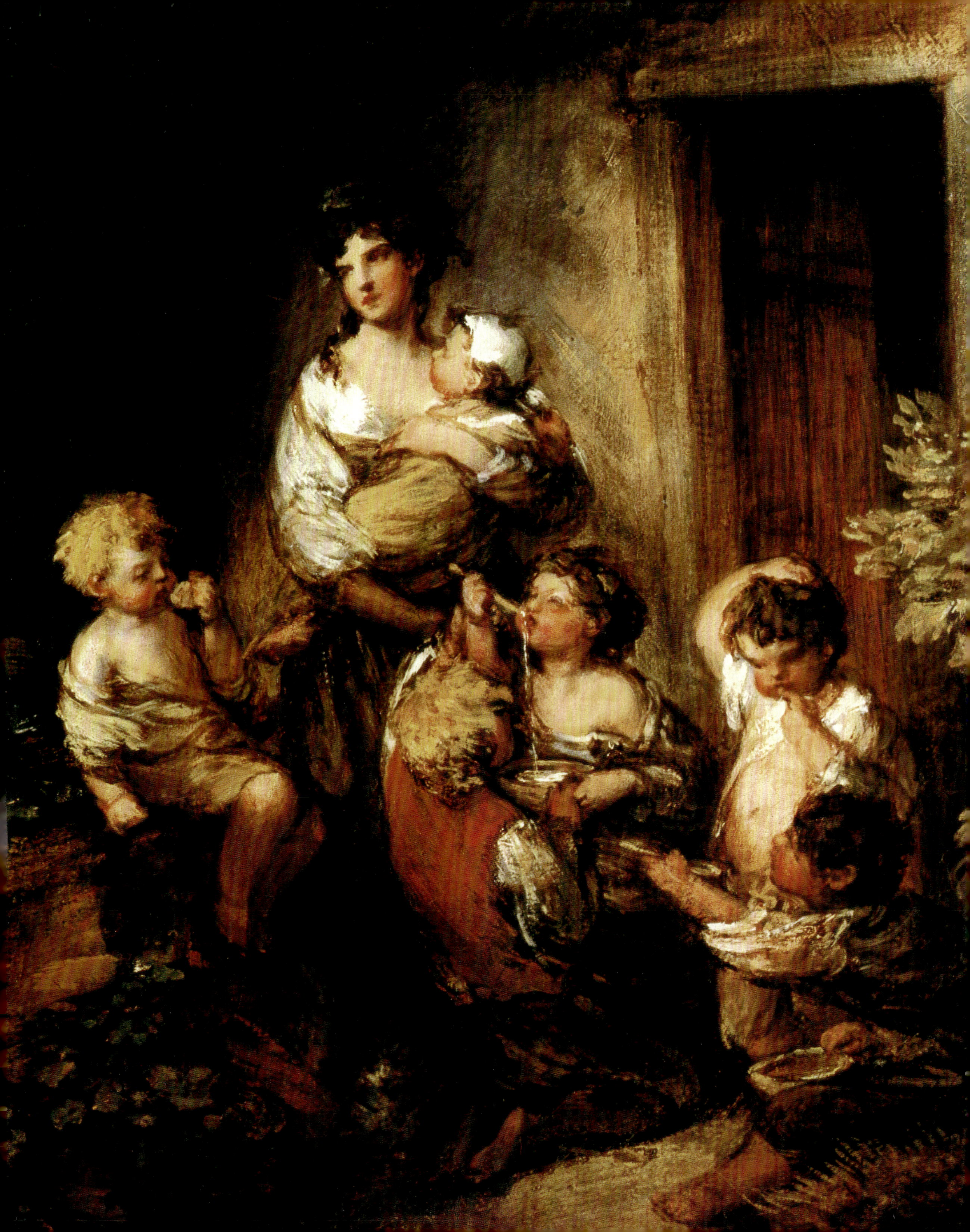

SENSATION & SENSIBILITY

VIEWING GAINSBOROUGH'S *COTTAGE DOOR*

Edited by

ANN BERMINGHAM

YALE CENTER FOR BRITISH ART

THE HUNTINGTON LIBRARY, ART COLLECTIONS, & BOTANICAL GARDENS

YALE UNIVERSITY PRESS, NEW HAVEN & LONDON

This publication accompanies the exhibition
Sensation and Sensibility: Viewing Gainsborough's Cottage Door,
co-organized by the Yale Center for British Art (YCBA) and
The Huntington Library, Art Collections, and Botanical Gardens in San Marino, California.
Exhibition dates: at the YCBA from 6 October to 31 December 2005
and at the Huntington from 11 February to 14 May 2006.

Major support for this project was provided by a grant from the National Endowment for the Humanities. Any views, finding, conclusions, or recommendations expressed in this publication do not necessarily represent those of the National Endowment for the Humanities.

Additional support was provided by the Samuel H. Kress Foundation; the Essick Foundation, Inc.; and Melvin R. Seiden in honor of Robert F. and Lois Erburu.

Printed and bound in Italy by Conti Tipocolor

Library of Congress Cataloging-in-Publication Data

Sensation and sensibility : viewing Gainsborough's cottage door / edited by Ann Bermingham.
p. cm.
Includes bibliographical references and index.
ISBN 0-300-11002-2 (cl : alk. paper)
ISBN 0-930606-99-x (cl : alk. paper)
1. Gainsborough, Thomas, 1727–1788–Criticism and interpretation. 2. Rural poor in art.
3. Genre painting, English–18th century. 4. Art–Exhibition techniques–History–18th century.
I. Bermingham, Ann.
ND497.G2S45 2005
759.2–dc22

2005009022

Frontispiece Thomas Gainsborough, *The Cottage Door*, 1780, oil on canvas, 147.3 × 119.4 cm (58 × 47 in.), Henry E. Huntington Library, Art Collections, and Botanical Gardens, San Marino, California. Detail of pl. III

Contents

Directors' Foreword

THIS VOLUME RESULTS FROM AN EXHIBITION ENTITLED "Sensation and Sensibility: Viewing Gainsborough's *Cottage Door*," a joint collaboration between The Huntington and the Yale Center for British Art. Organized by Ann Bermingham, guest curator of the exhibition and editor of the publication, this important project has taken as its focal point Thomas Gainsborough's great landscape painting *The Cottage Door* (c. 1780), now in the Huntington Art Collections, and has situated it for the first time in the context of a group of paintings, prints, and drawings related to the artist's pictorial treatment of the cottage and cottage life. As Ann Bermingham has shown, these works were among the first by a British artist to embody the eighteenth-century cult of sensibility, a movement that celebrated the artless beauty of nature and idealized the life of the countryside and rural peasantry. Taken together, they form a vision of a rustic idyll that resonated powerfully with the metropolitan culture of late eighteenth-century Britain. The works exhibited in this show also made a real impact on new modes of thinking about vision and visual perception at the time when they were first viewed. The exhibition thus includes displays that have aimed to recreate the actual viewing circumstances of early audiences, among them, reconstructions of an eighteenth-century sound-and-light show called an Eidophusikon, and of the "tent room" in Sir John Leicester's Hill Street Gallery, in which – surrounded by fabric, tenting, mirrors, and glowing oil lamps – *The Cottage Door* was shown to great fanfare.

The exhibition has benefited from the ideas, advice, and expertise of Shelley Bennett, Curator of British and European Art at the Huntington, from her research assistant, Melinda McCurdy, and, at Yale, from Associate Director of Programmatic Affairs, Julia Marciari Alexander, her administrative assistant, Diane Bowman, and her research assistant, Lucinda Stamm. The imaginative work of the Yale Center's installation and design team led by Richard F. Johnson – working collaboratively with Huntington preparator Gregg Bayne, independent designer Stephen Saitas, lighting historian Stephen Cannon-Brookes, fabric designer Tina Menchetti, and Robert Poulter, who designed the Eidophusikon on view in the exhibition – has allowed the historical displays of the tent room and the Eidophusikon to come to life for modern audiences with extraordinary effectiveness.

The exhibition has also given form to this excellent collection of essays, which under Ann Bermingham's editorial guidance will advance our understanding of the English landscape tradition in significant ways. The essays take up four major issues raised by the exhibition. They are: the cultural significance of the cottage and Gainsborough's series of cottage-door paintings; the meaning of the theme for Gainsborough and his reputation; the collection and exhibition of these paintings in the eighteenth and nineteenth centuries; and, finally, the intersection of these paintings with popular landscape spectacles and the growing array of special visual effects in the second half of the eighteenth century. As this suggests, the essays explore the style and imagery of the cottage-door paintings by assuming that vision is a historically specific experience dependent on period technologies and ways of seeing, whether they be sensibility, theatrical effects, or the dynamism of Gainsborough's own brushwork. We are indebted to the distinguished team of essayists who have contributed to the book, to Katharine R. Ridler who has edited the text and to Gillian Malpass of Yale University Press who has overseen the design and production of this beautiful book.

We were fortunate to receive funding for the exhibition and this accompanying volume from the National Endowment for the Humanities, the Samuel Kress Foundation, and the Essick Foundation, Inc. We are grateful to our friends and colleagues in both the United States and the United Kingdom who lent precious works so generously from their own institutional and private collections to make the exhibition possible. We also give special thanks to those who helped in securing several of these loans, including Susan Sloman, Deborah Gage, and Andrew Wyld.

As representatives of the two great collections for the study of British art in the United States, we are pleased to sponsor important joint projects such as this to further study within our field in the most productive ways. Indeed, we hope that this exhibition and associated publication will stimulate many future collaborations between our two institutions, further emphasizing the important position held by scholarship in British art in the broader field of British Studies, as well as in the study of art history from a global vantage point.

Amy Meyers	*John Murdoch*
Director	*Hannah and Russel Kully Director of*
Yale Center for British Art	*the Huntington Art Collections*

Ann Bermingham

Acknowledgments

The essays for this volume accompany an exhibition "Sensation and Sensibility: Viewing Gainsborough's *Cottage Door*" held at the Yale Center for British Art in New Haven and the Huntington Library, Art Collections, and Botanical Gardens in San Marino. The exhibition examines Gainsborough's theme of the cottage door in relation to eighteenth-century ideas of sensibility. In addition to bringing together the major cottage-door paintings, the exhibition includes comparative and contextual material that expands on the theme of the cottage and cottage scenery. Like the exhibition, this volume of essays resituates Gainsborough's cottage-door paintings in the light of recent scholarship and critical debates having to do with rural genre painting, sentimentalism, collecting, eighteenth-century popular visual culture, and issues of visual reception.

Both the exhibition and the volume were major undertakings, and their complexities went well beyond my limited experience and capabilities. A number of people therefore are owed a large debt of thanks. I would like to begin by thanking Shelley Bennett, Curator of British and European Art at the Huntington, for first conceiving the idea of an exhibition recreating Sir John Leicester's 1818 installation of the *Cottage Door*. Shelley devoted four years to the exhibition and played an absolutely central role in its development at every stage. It would never have happened without her, and I am deeply indebted to her for everything she did to bring it about. Her knowledgeable expertise and administrative competence are reflected in every aspect of the exhibition. I owe a large debt of gratitude to her skilled and tireless Assistant Curator, Melinda McCurdy, for her attention to all the details of the loans and other important aspects of the exhibition. John Murdoch, Director of the Art Collections at the Huntington, kindly encouraged this volume and helped to bring it to the attention of Yale University Press. Amy Meyers, Director of the Yale Center for British Art, contributed the extraordinary resources of the Center to the production of the volume and the exhibition. Her faith in the project and her enthusiasm and support for all aspects of it are deeply appreciated. Julia Marciari Alexander, Associate Director of Programmatic Affairs, did a heroic job of coordinating the Center's portion of the exhibition, and her assistants, Diane Bowman and Lucinda Stamm, had the daunting task of overseeing the collection of all the photographic material for the volume. Julia's timely and professional assistance to me at critical points in the exhibition's planning and development was invaluable. I am grateful to her and her assistants for their help, advice, care, and expertise. At the Yale Center for British Art I also benefited from the connoiseurial knowledge and judgement of Elisabeth Fairman, Scott Wilcox, Gillian Forrester, Angus Trumble, and Cassandra Albinson. Under the direction of Richard Johnson the Center's installation team did a superlative job realizing Stephen Saitas's brilliant designs for the exhibition and the "tent room" and Robert Poulter's recreation of the Eidophusikon. Thanks are owed to Michael Hatt, my collaborator in arranging a symposium to open the exhibition at the Center, and to Robert Richie who did the same for the opening at the Huntington. This book was beautifully designed and produced by Gillian Malpass of Yale University Press and skillfully edited by Katharine Ridler. Colleagues in the United Kingdom, Susan Sloman, Michael Rosenthal, Martin Myrone, Andrew Wyld, Peter Cannon-Brooke, Leslie Edwards, Hugh Belsey, John Styles, and Deborah Gage, were generous in helping with the exhibition and volume at various crucial stages. Stateside I owe a huge debt of thanks to Robert Essick and to Timothy Standring of the Denver Art Museum.

Finally I wish to thank the authors who contributed such brilliant and provocative essays. All of them engaged in this project with enthusiasm, dedication, and the highest professional standards. They made my task as editor a pleasant one, and I can hope only that they in turn are pleased with the results of their effort. As is clear to all the contributors, the work of many art historians who are not represented in this volume has been essential to our understanding and appreciation of Thomas Gainsborough. The scholarship, in particular, of John Hayes, Hugh Belsey, Martin Myrone, Marcia Pointon, Martin Postle, Mary Woodall, and Ellis Waterhouse has been most influential in helping us to arrive at our conclusions.

Notes on Contributors

ANN BERMINGHAM is a professor of the history of art and architecture at the University of California, Santa Barbara. She is the author of *Landscape and Ideology: The English Rustic Tradition, 1760–1860* (University of California Press, and Thames and Hudson, 1986) and *Learning to Draw: Studies in the Cultural History of a Polite and Useful Art* (Yale University Press, 2000), and co-editor with John Brewer of *The Consumption of Culture 1600–1800: Image, Object, Text* (Routledge, 1995).

AMAL ASFOUR AND PAUL WILLIAMSON have written and lectured on many aspects of British art and culture in the eighteenth century. Their publications on Gainsborough include *Gainsborough's Vision* (Liverpool University Press, 1999). They live and work in London.

JOHN BARRELL is a member of the Centre for Eighteenth Century Studies at the University of York, England. He has written a number of books on eighteenth-century literature, history, and art, most recently *Imagining the King's Death: Figurative Treason, Fantasies of Regicide, 1793–1796* (Oxford University Press, 2000) and *The Spirit of Despotism: Invasions of Privacy in the 1790s*, soon to be published by Oxford University Press.

DONGHO CHUN is a part-time lecturer in art history at Seoul National University, South Korea. He is a specialist on patronage of British art and currently completing a book-length study on aristocratic patronage of visual arts in England.

IAIN MCCALMAN is Professor of History and Federation Fellow at the Australian National University, in Canberra, Australia, and a Visiting Mellon Research Fellow at California Institute of Technology, Los Angeles. A specialist in eighteenth-century British and European cultural history, his recent publications include *The Last Alchemist: Count Cagliostro, Master of Magic in the Age of Reason* (Harper Collins, New York and Sydney, and Random House, London, 2003), as co-editor, *The Enlightenment World* (Routledge, 2004), and, as general editor, *The Romantic Age: An Oxford Companion to British Culture, 1776–1832* (Oxford University Press, 2001). He is currently researching a study of special effects in eighteenth-century Britain.

MICHAEL ROSENTHAL teaches the history of art at the University of Warwick. He is the author of the book *The Art of Thomas Gainsborough: "a little business for the Eye*" (Yale University Press, 1999), and he was lead curator for the Gainsborough exhibition held at Tate Britain in 2002 which traveled to Washington and Boston in 2003. He is currently working on the art of early colonial Australia.

SUSAN SLOMAN is the author of *Gainsborough in Bath* (Yale University Press, 2002) and has published a number of articles on the artist in the *Gainsborough's House Review* and the *Burlington Magazine*. She is now working on a new book on Gainsborough's life in London. Her career has been divided between museums and the commercial world, with the last six years spent at Agnew's in London.

WILLIAM VAUGHAN is Professor Emeritus in the history of art at Birkbeck College, University of London. He has published widely on romanticism and on British and German art of the eighteenth and nineteenth centuries. His recent publications include *Romanticism and Art* (Thames and Hudson, 1994) and *Gainsborough* (Thames and Hudson, 2002). He has co-edited with Laura Morowitz *Artistic Brotherhoods in the Nineteenth Century* (Ashgate, 2001) and with Christiana Payne *English Accents: Interactions with British Art c.1776–1855* (Ashgate, 2004). He is currently completing a study on the concept of the British School, to be published in 2005, and is preparing an exhibition on the works of Samuel Palmer, to be held at the British Museum in 2005.

Gallery of Images

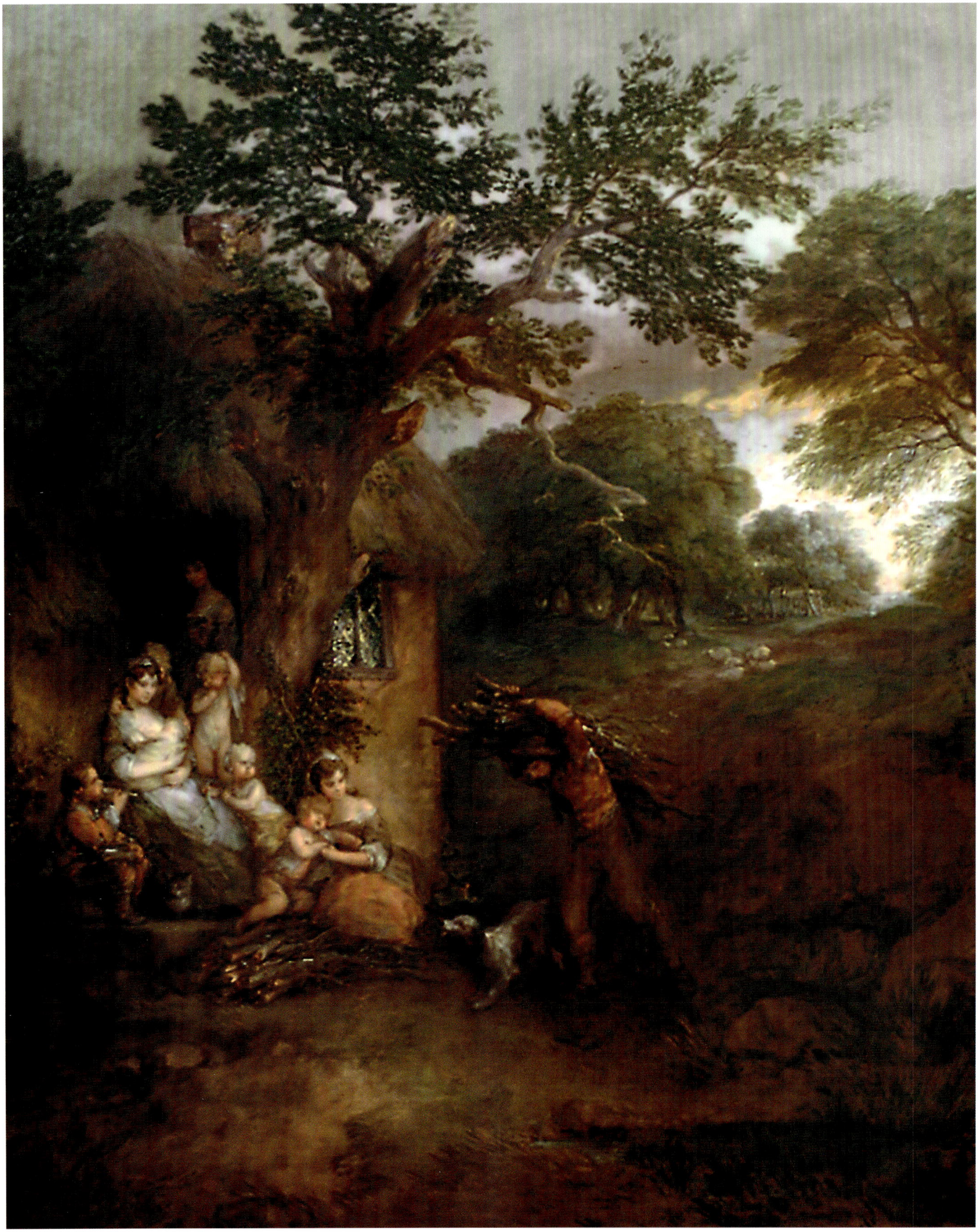

Plate 1 Thomas Gainsborough, *The Woodcutter's Return*, c. 1772–3, oil on canvas, 147.3 × 123.2 cm (58 × 48½ in.), Duke of Rutland, Belvoir Castle, Leicester

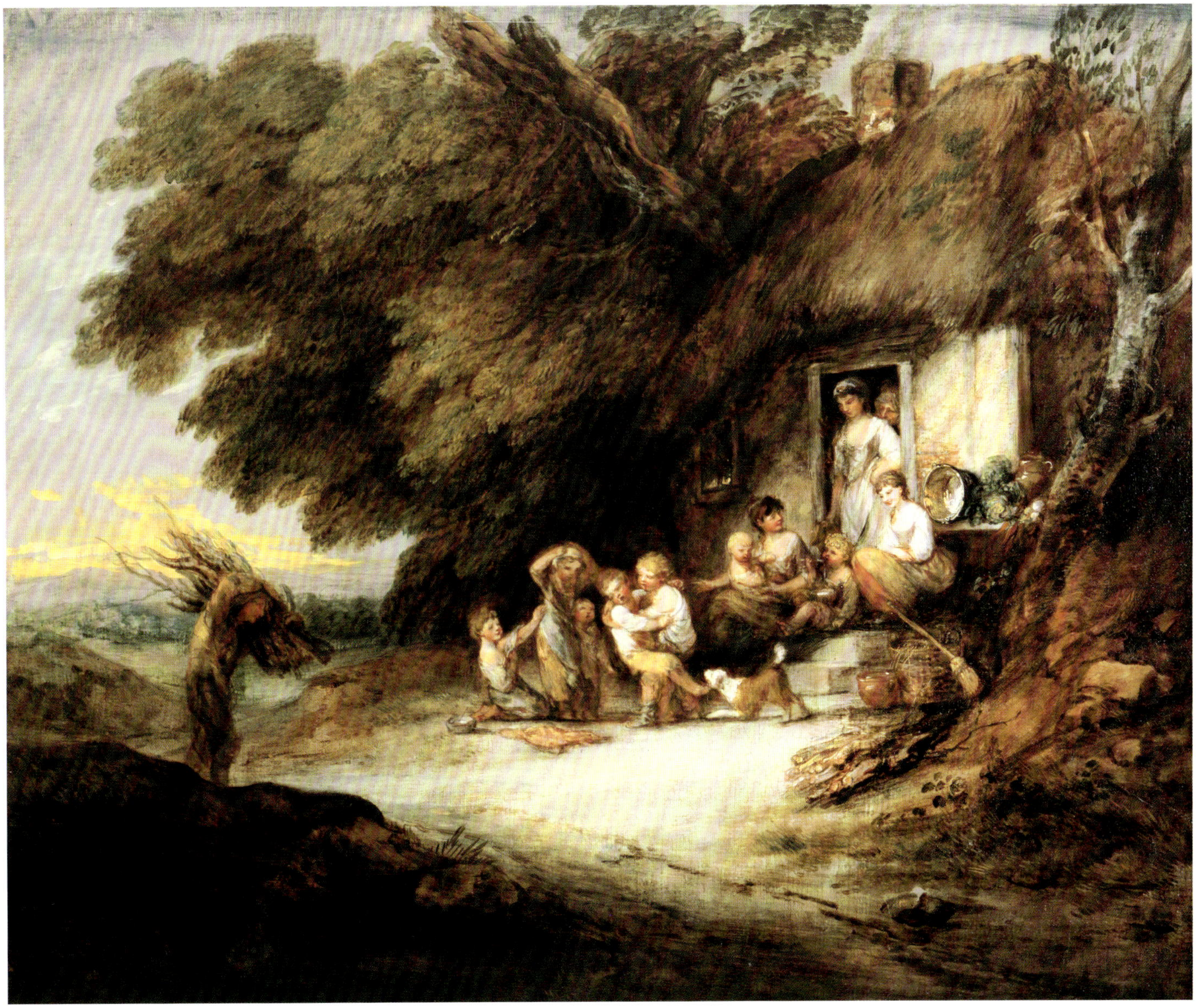

Plate II Thomas Gainsborough, *Cottage Door with Children Playing*, 1777–8, oil on canvas, 122.5 × 149.2 cm ($48\frac{1}{4} \times 58\frac{3}{4}$ in.), Cincinnati Art Museum. Gift in honor of Mr. and Mrs. Charles F. Williams by their children

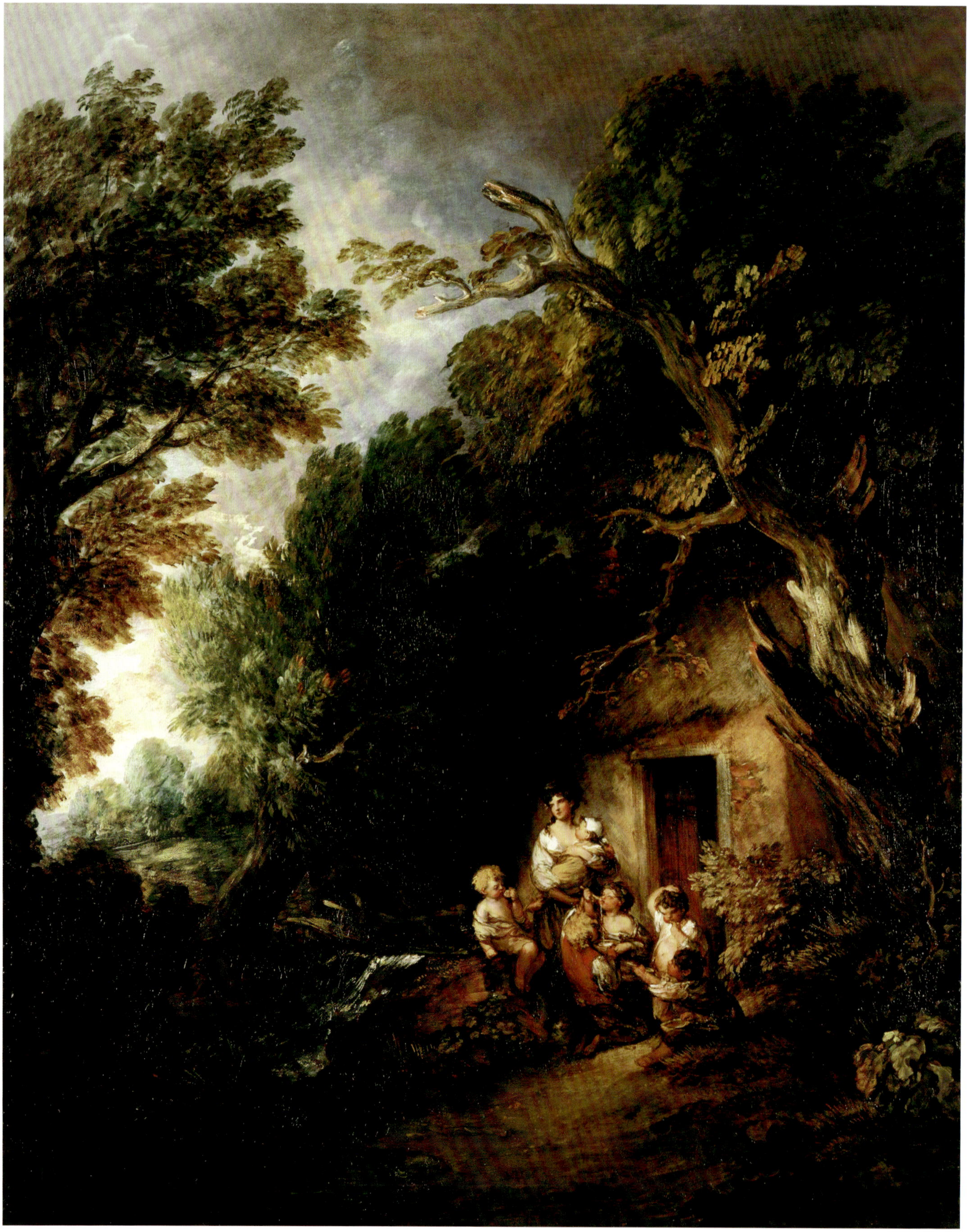

Plate III Thomas Gainsborough, *The Cottage Door*, 1780, oil on canvas, 147.3 × 119.4 cm (58 × 47 in.), Henry E. Huntington Library, Art Collections, and Botanical Gardens, San Marino, California

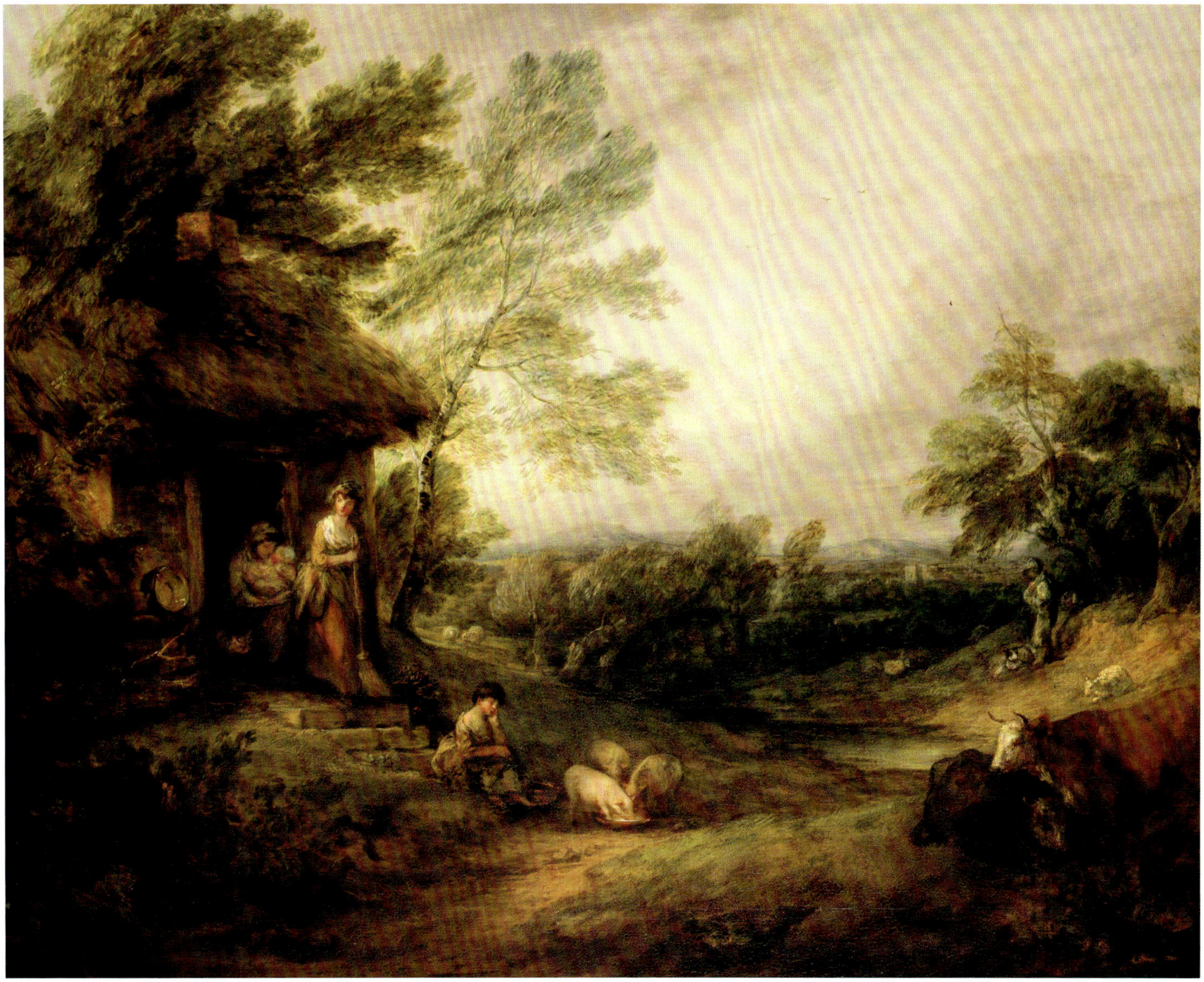

Plate IV Thomas Gainsborough, *Cottage Door with Girl and Pigs*, 1786, oil on canvas, 96.5 × 121.9 cm ($38\frac{3}{4}$ × $48\frac{3}{4}$ in.), Ipswich Borough Council Museums and Art Galleries, Ipswich

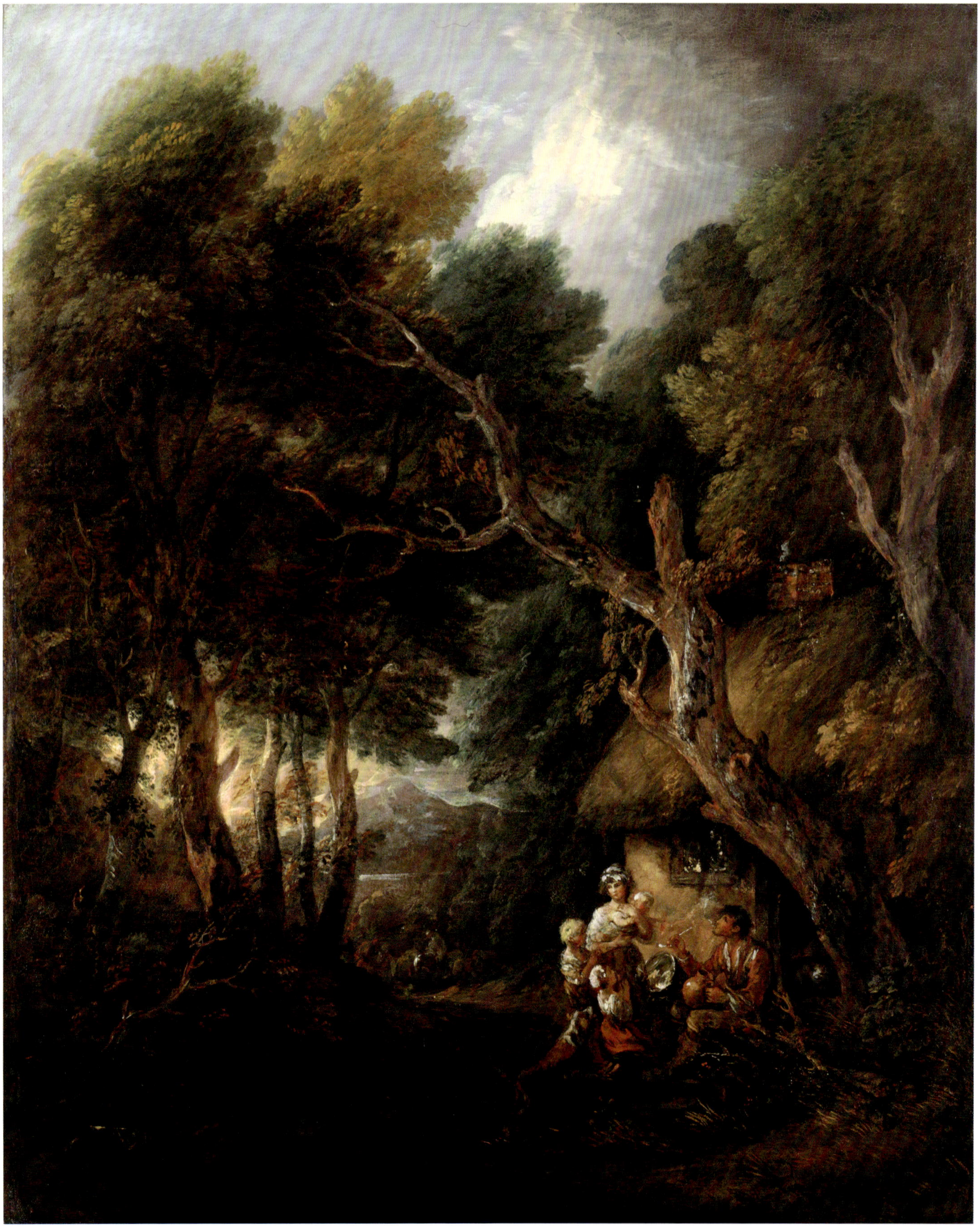

Plate v Thomas Gainsborough, *Peasant Smoking at a Cottage Door*, 1788, oil on canvas, 195.6 × 157.5 cm. (77 × 62 in.), Collections of the University of California, Los Angeles, Hammer Museum, Los Angeles. Gift of Mrs. James Kennedy

Ann Bermingham

Introduction
Gainsborough's Cottage Door*: Sensation and Sensibility*

"Nothing is little," Samuel Johnson wrote to his friend Joseph Baretti, "to him that feels it with great sensibility, a mind able to see common incidents in their real state, is disposed by very common incidents to very serious contemplations."[1] Johnson suggests that sensibility was not only a mode of feeling but also a way of seeing that found in ordinary scenes and events occasions for deep reflection. In valuing the insignificant, sensibility saw little things as large, perceived meaning in the meaningless, and was moved with profound feeling in the presence of the ordinary. Such aggrandizement of the negligible might be regarded as foolish today; nevertheless, in the eighteenth century the doctrine of sensibility opened men and women to life's experiences in new ways, ways that had the power to move, to wound, and to transform.

Nowhere is this eighteenth-century way of seeing and feeling more intensely evoked than in Thomas Gainsborough's "cottage-door" paintings. As exemplars of the rustic idyll, Gainsborough's cottage doors are some of the first works of British landscape painting to embody the aesthetics of sensibility as well as to treat the subject of the cottage and cottage life. Before Gainsborough, such humble subjects were too insignificant to merit an artist's attention; as such they fell below the period's threshold of visibility, not so much ignored as not seen. What made Gainsborough notice these humble subjects, and the significance of what he did once he noticed them, is the subject of this volume.

The image of the cottage door was one to which Gainsborough returned again and again. As early as 1768 it emerges in one of Gainsborough's most majestic paintings of his Bath period. Known as *Peasants Returning from Market* and hung today in Kenwood, London, this large horizontal landscape depicts peasants on horseback moving through a misty landscape that is warmed by the glow of the setting sun (fig. 1). In the distance, cottagers rest outside their cottage enjoying the early evening. As John Hayes and others have observed, Gainsborough extracted the motif of the cottage door from this landscape, and went on to develop it in five major paintings. His first full-scale treatment of the theme dates from the Bath period (c. 1772–3) and is entitled *The Woodcutter's Return* (pl. 1). The painting includes all the elements that made up the other variations: evening, a cottage secluded in a forest, its doorframe filled with young nursing women and small children, a woodcutter laden with faggots returning or resting on the doorstep. This first painting was bought by Charles Manners, the fourth Duke of Rutland. Although never exhibited publicly it was well enough known

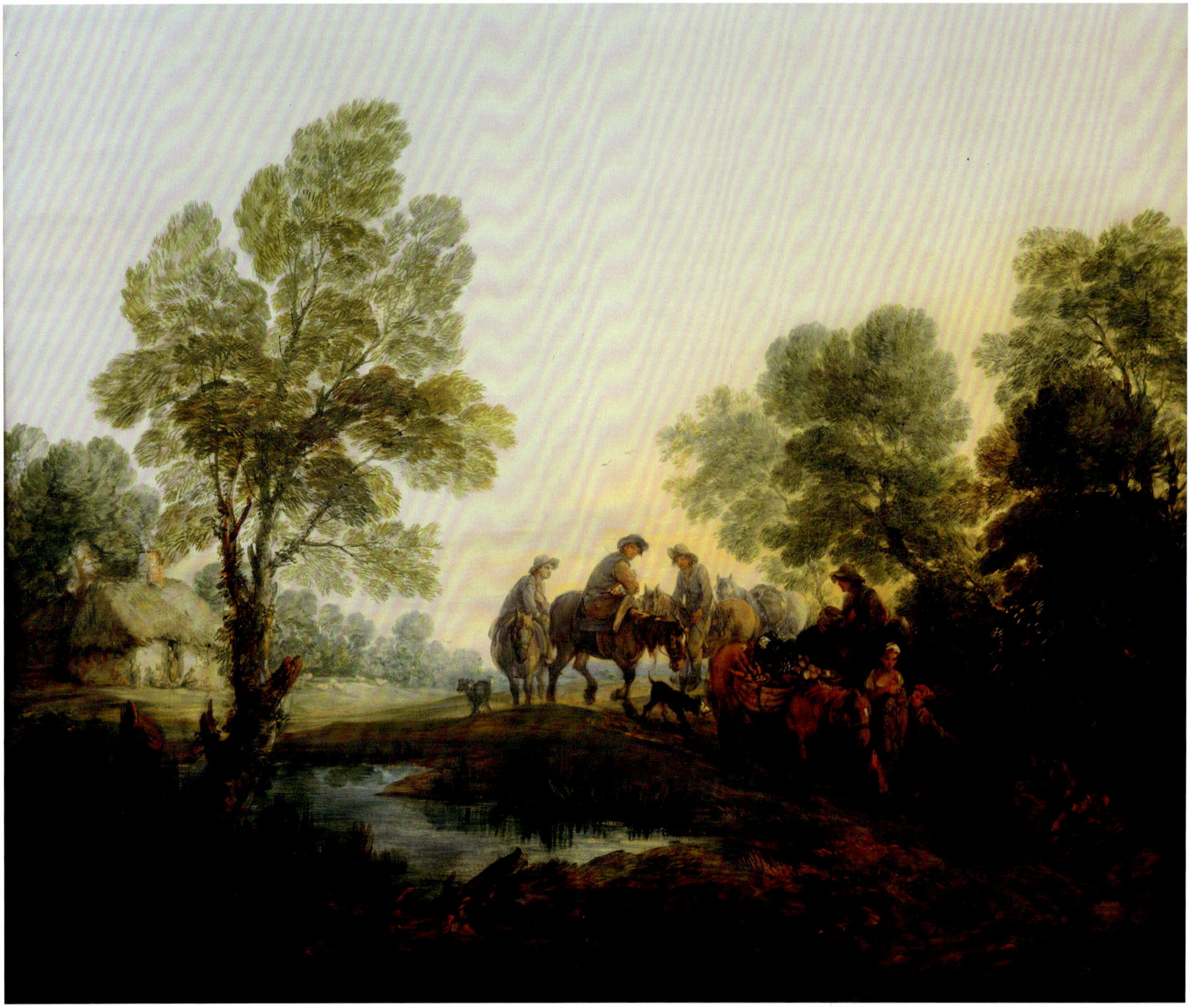

1 Thomas Gainsborough, *Peasants Returning from Market*, c. 1768–71, oil on canvas, 122.3 × 150 cm ($48\frac{1}{8}$ × 59 in.), Iveagh Bequest, Kenwood, London

to have inspired an anonymous poem, which described it as "a scene of beauty and domestic love."[2] Gainsborough's musical friend, Felice de' Giardini, so admired the painting that he commissioned the artist to make for him an exact copy (fig. 2). The second treatment of the theme came after Gainsborough had moved from Bath to London. This horizontal composition, known as *Cottage Door with Children Playing*, again takes up the subject of the woodcutter returning to his cottage, home now to a host of boisterous, cheerful children (pl. II). This painting was probably exhibited at the Royal Academy in 1778. The painting known today as simply *The Cottage Door* was Gainsborough's third treatment of the theme (pl. III). It was exhibited at the Royal Academy in 1780 and was described by the *Morning Chronicle* as a "beautiful scene where serenity and pleasure dwell in every spot . . . a scene of happiness that may truly be called Adam's paradise."[3] Unlike the first two cottage-door paintings, this version does

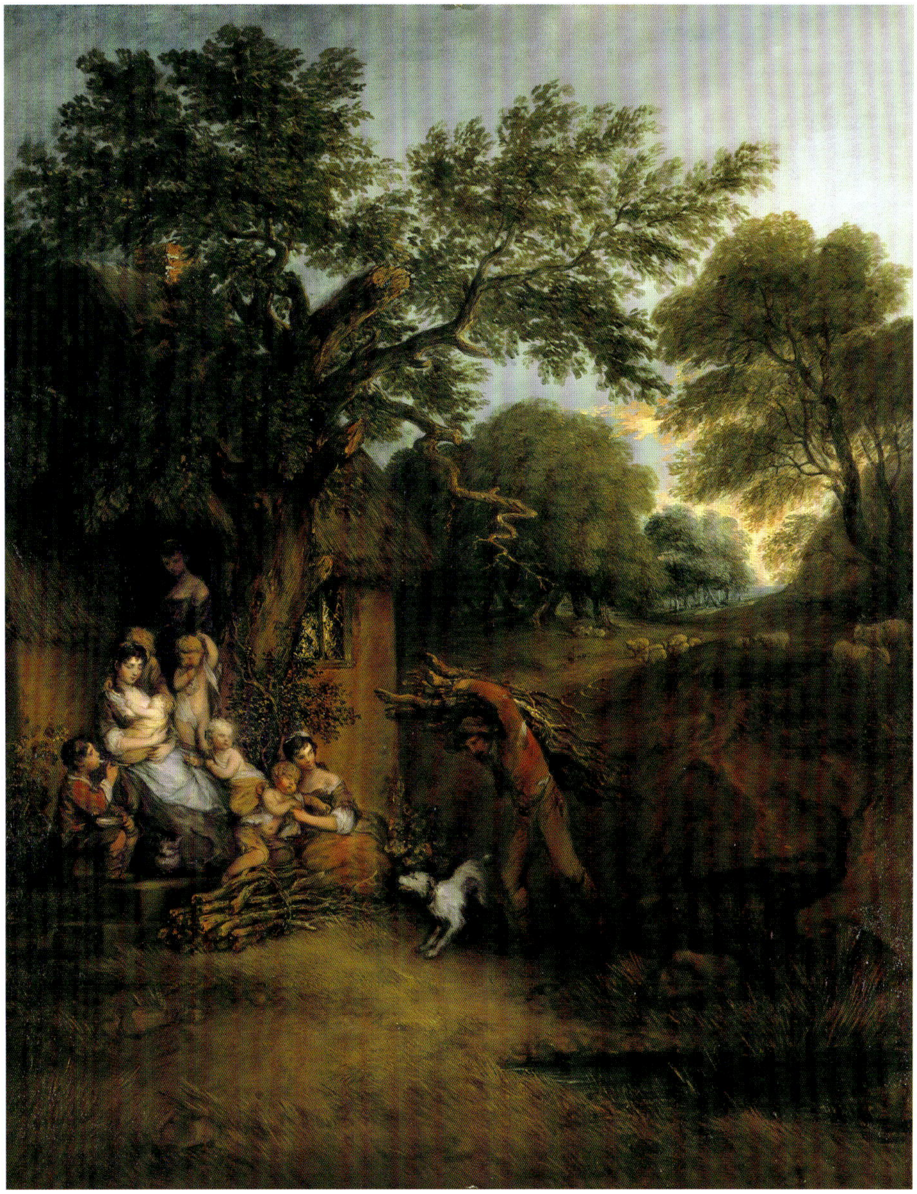

2 Thomas Gainsborough, *The Woodcutter's Return*, c. 1773, oil on canvas, 147.3 × 123.2 cm (58 × 48½ in.), Fuji Museum, Tokyo

not include a woodcutter, but focuses on the lush landscape setting and the women and children gathered before the cottage door. A copy of this painting attributed to Gainsborough depicts the same subject exactly but in a style characterized by more luminous color and looser handling (see fig. 21). Another, smaller cottage subject, exhibited in 1786 and depicting a woman with a broom at the door of a cottage and a girl seated with pigs at the foot of its steps, is Gainsborough's fourth essay on the theme (pl. IV). This painting is of particular interest for it combines in one image motifs from two other Gainsborough paintings: the Tate Gallery's *Housemaid* (c. 1782–6) and the painting originally owned by Sir Joshua Reynolds and known as *Girl with Pigs* (1782; figs. 3 and 5). Gainsborough's final treatment of the cottage-door theme came in the late 1780s. Entitled *Peasant Smoking at a Cottage Door*, it was found in Gainsborough's studio after his death in 1788 (pl. V). Its high price of 500 guineas may be the

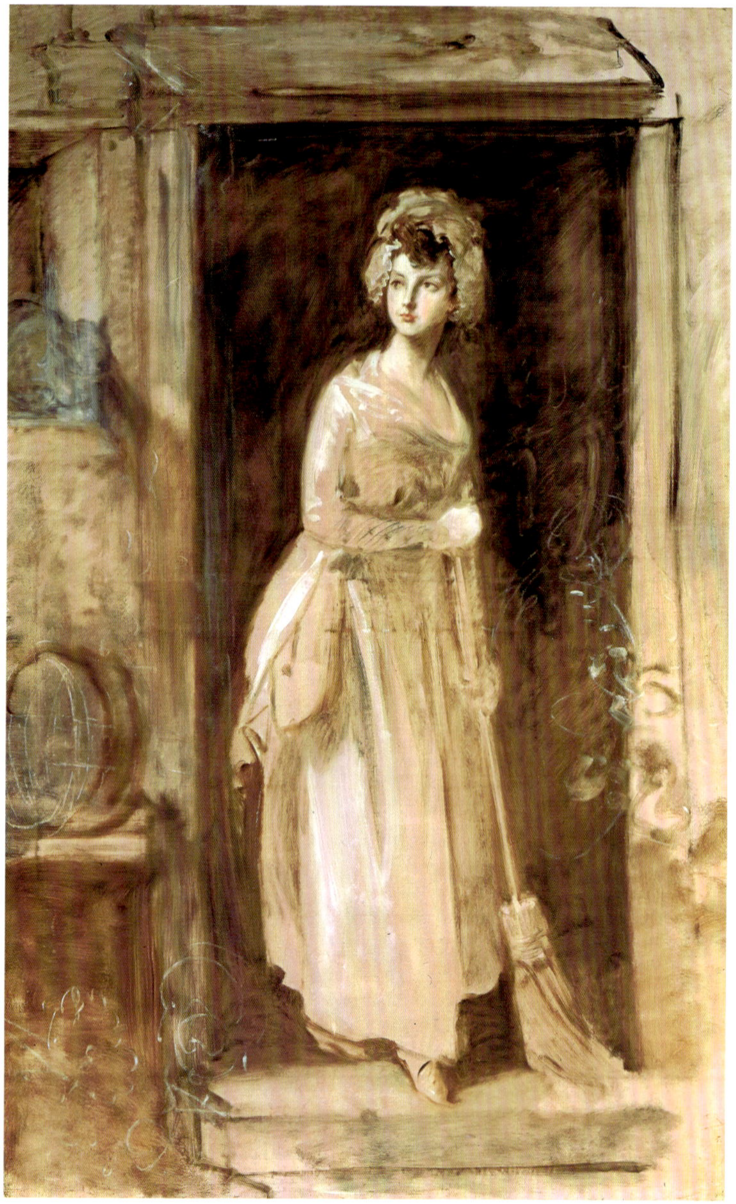

3 Thomas Gainsborough, *The Housemaid*, c. 1782–6, oil on canvas, 3.96 × 2.74 m ($12'11\frac{3}{4}$ × $8'11\frac{1}{2}$), Tate, London

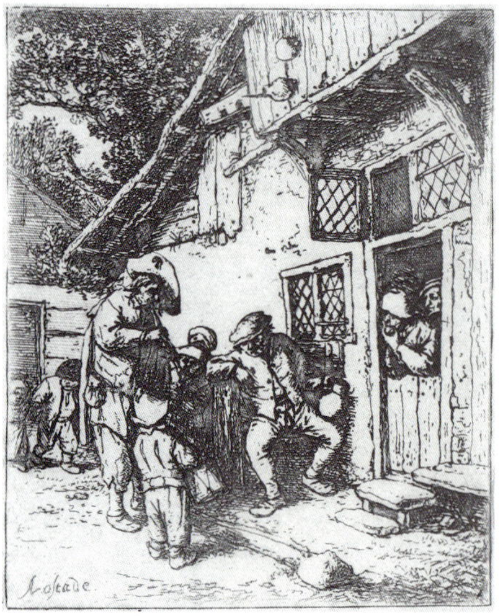

4 Adriaen van Ostade, *The Wandering Musicians*, 1642, etching, 16.7 × 14.2 cm ($6\frac{1}{2}$ × $5\frac{1}{2}$ in.), Los Angeles County Museum

reason it was left unsold at the auction of his effects. Eventually the painting was bought by Sir George Beaumont, the friend and mentor of John Constable.

Gainsborough derived his treatment of cottage scenes from the examples of Dutch and Flemish artists of the seventeenth century. Uvedale Price, a friend with whom Gainsborough went riding while in Bath, remarked in his essay *On the Picturesque* (1794) that cottage scenery was highly picturesque and singled out the landscapes by the Dutch artist Adriaen van Ostade as particularly fine examples of the genre (fig. 4).[4] Gainsborough's fondness for "little Dutch landskips" such as those by Ostade, but also Jacob van Ruisdael, Meyndert Hobbema, Jan Wijnants, and Antoine Waterloo, is well known. Dutch landscape paintings and prints circulated in London and Gainsborough collected them. In later life he attributed his own early style of landscape painting to the influence of these Dutch examples.

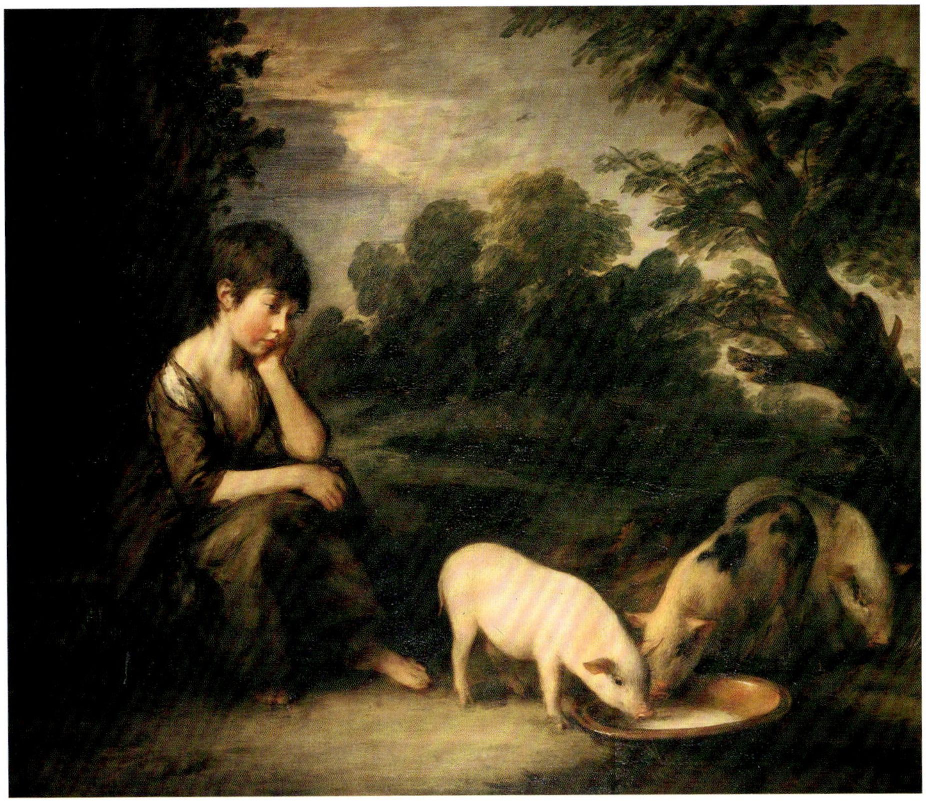

5 Thomas Gainsborough, *Girl with Pigs*, 1782, oil on canvas, 125.6 × 148.6 cm ($49\frac{1}{2} \times 58\frac{1}{2}$ in.), Castle Howard, Yorkshire

The work of the seventeenth-century Netherlandish artists Adriaen Brouwer and David Teniers who specialized in peasant scenes (fig. 6) may also have been known by Gainsborough. Their clumsy boorish peasants, however, differ sharply from the refined and appealing figures found in Gainsborough's cottage doors. Upon the artist's death, *The World* published an elegy likening his cottage scenes to the beauty of Milton's *Lycidas* and Gray's *Elegy*, and Kenneth Clark later made a similar association when he described Gainsborough's peasant figures as arranged into "groups as elegant as Gray's diction."[5] In his fourteenth discourse,

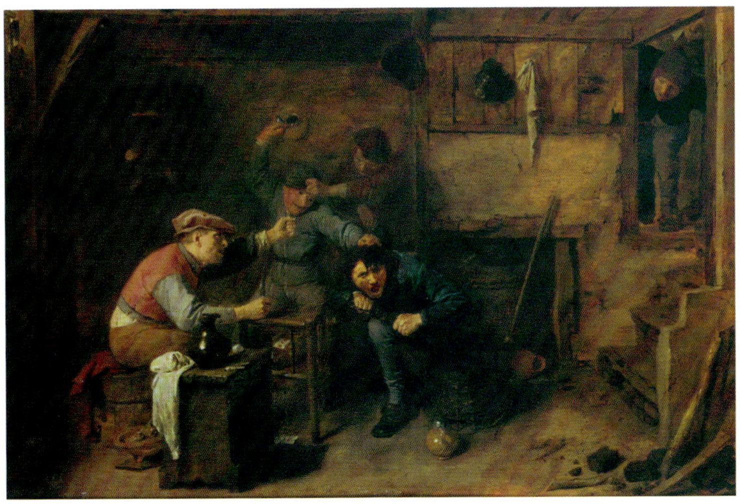

6 Adriaen Brouwer, *Fighting Card Players*, c. 1630–35, oil on canvas, 33 × 49 cm ($13 \times 19\frac{1}{4}$ in.), Alte Pinakothek, Munich

8 (*right*) Thomas Gainsborough, *Young Hobbinole and Ganderetta*, 1788, oil on canvas, 125.7 × 100.3 cm ($49\frac{1}{2} \times 39\frac{1}{2}$ in.), Henry E. Huntington Library, Art Collections, and Botanical Gardens, San Marino, California

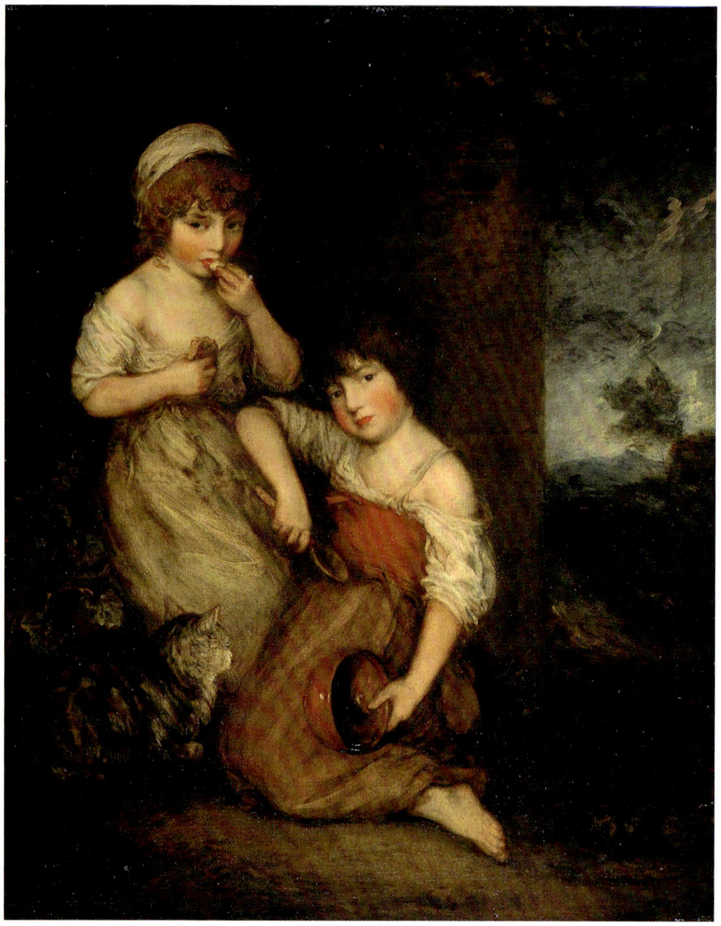

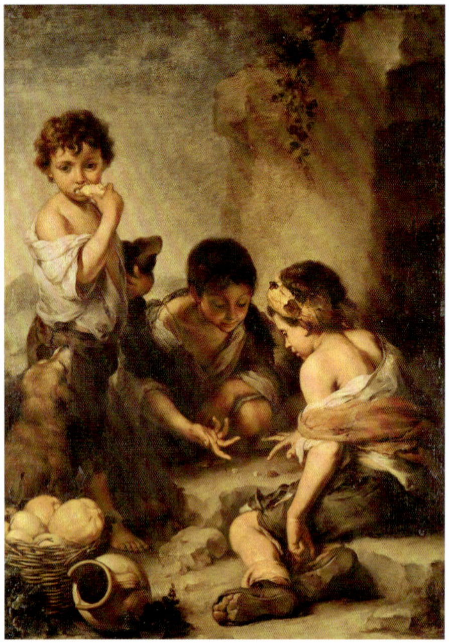

7 Bartolomé Esteban Murillo, *Beggar Boys Playing Dice*, c. 1675, oil on canvas, 146 × 108.5 cm ($57\frac{1}{2} \times 42\frac{3}{4}$ in.), acquired by Duke Max Emanuel, Alte Pinakothek, Munich

9 (*facing page*) Thomas Gainsborough, *The Woodgatherers*, 1787, oil on canvas, 147.6 × 120.3 cm ($58\frac{1}{8} \times 47\frac{3}{8}$ in.), The Metropolitan Museum of Art, Bequest of Mary Sillman Harkness, 1950

Reynolds remarked that Gainsborough's peasant figures had "such a grace" and "such an elegance . . . as are more frequently found in cottages than in courts."[6] The unreality of Gainsborough's peasants was not to everyone's taste and came in for harsh treatment at the hands of the nineteenth-century critic William Hazlitt who accused the artist of introducing the "masquerade style" into landscape painting, in which the driver of a hay-cart is given the "air of Adonis" and the features of a milkmaid are "modeled on the antique."[7] As this suggests, unlike the images of cottagers and peasant life which followed, Gainsborough's depictions are conspicuously idealized and artificial and were not intended, as the watercolorist Thomas Hearne said, to excite any idea of "dirt or wretchedness."[8]

Gainsborough's sympathetic treatment of the rural poor departs from the realist tradition of seventeenth-century Northern artists; it derives, in part, from his study of the work of the seventeenth-century Spanish artist Bartolomé Esteban Murrillo (fig. 7). As an admirer of Murillo Gainsborough made a copy of *Christ Child as Good Shepherd* (itself a copy of a painting by Murillo), which he saw in Christie's auction room. Murillo's images of beggar children inspired Gainsborough; the result was the exploration of a genre of painting known as "fancy pictures," which consisted of large-scale images of cottage children like the *Woodgatherers* and *Young Hobbinole and Ganderetta* (figs. 9 and 8). In both images,

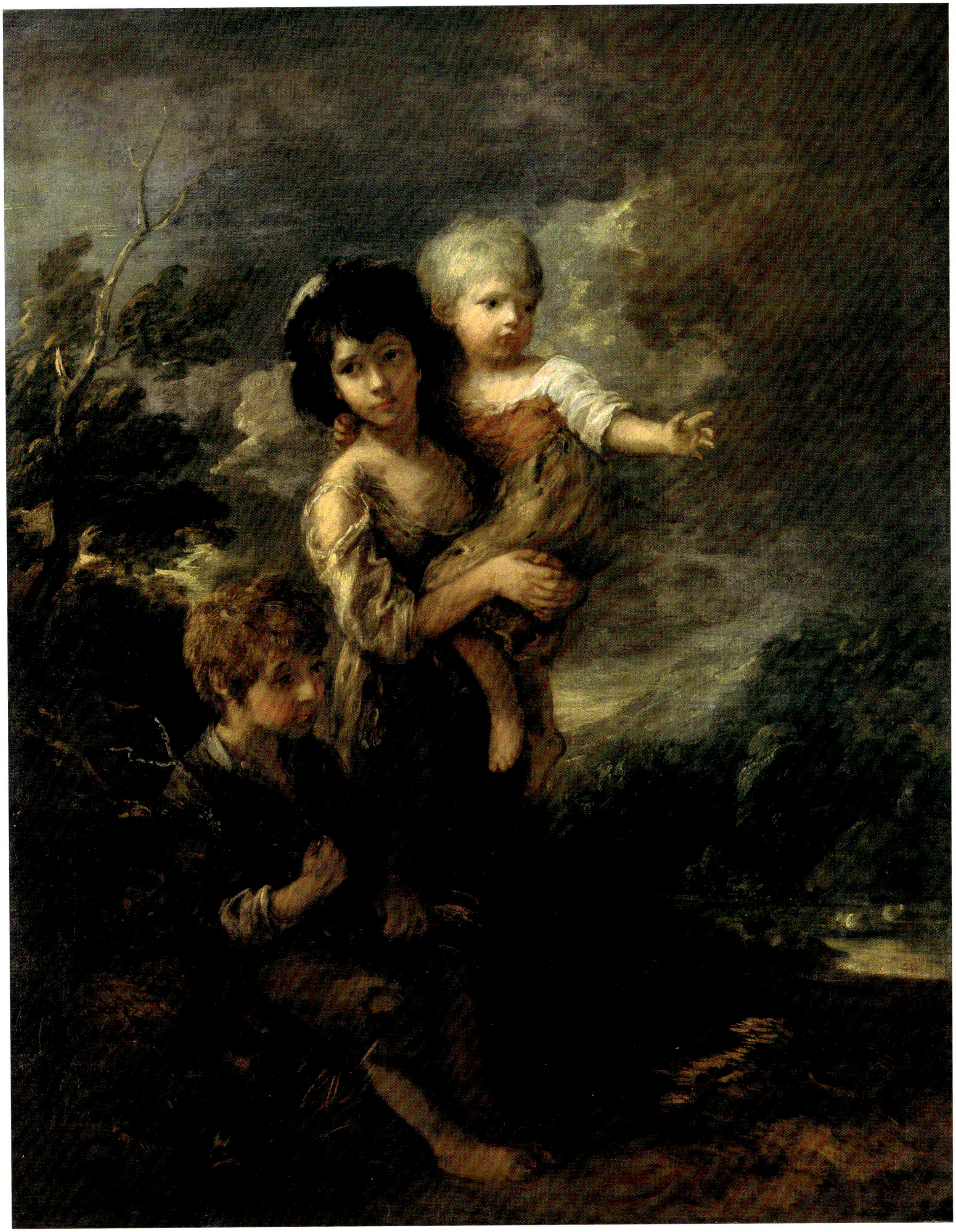

the sweet, wistful sentiment of the children is striking, when compared with the more robust expressions typical of Murillo's children. Moreover, unlike the French artist Jean-Baptiste Greuze's contemporaneous images of children, Gainsborough's are notable for their quiet inwardness, rather than the display of emotion.

* * *

In certain respects sensibility can be understood in terms of modern notions of sympathy; that is, as an intensified awareness of another's feelings and an ability to enter into them. "Nature," said Lord Kames, "which has designed us for society, has connected us together by a participation in the joys and miseries of our fellow creatures."[9] It was precisely this ability to feel with another, that Adam Smith believed was natural to humankind and aroused our moral sentiments. Smith began his *Theory of Moral Sentiments* with the proposition that, "how selfish soever man may be supposed, there are evidently some principles in his nature, which interest him in the fortune of others, and render their happiness necessary to him, though he derives nothing from it except the pleasure of seeing it."[10] David Hume argued that it was emotion not reason that made people act in benevolent and altruistic ways. As these moral philosophers realized, sympathy had important civic and political implications. Emotion, when it took the form of sympathy and fellow feeling, was the foundation for social life. "It appears," Hume observed, "that a tendency to public good, and to the promoting of peace, harmony, and order in society does always, by affecting benevolent principles of our frame, engage us on the side of social virtues."[11] Cultivated as an improving moral value, sensibility, it was argued, produced and sustained civil society.[12]

Whereas moral philosophers saw sensibility as a positive human trait to be cultivated universally, the physician Dr. George Cheyne identified sensibility as a "malady" and a peculiarly English one. Thinking of it perhaps as the successor to melancholy, sensibility at its most virulent, Cheyne believed, left one susceptible to a whole host of nervous disorders.[13] In Cheyne's account a weakened state of the nerves' fibers made one vulnerable to oppressed spirits and imagined ills and complaints. The susceptibility of the English to sensibility could be attributed to the dampness of the English climate and to the rich food and soft sedentary life that attended the progress of civilization. To Cheyne's mind, and to the minds of his medical colleagues, sensibility in excess was the disease of an overly refined society and unchecked luxury.[14]

As the index of civilization, sensibility could also be seen as the social quality that made modern life superior to the past, even to classical antiquity. "The ancient Greeks and Romans were the most civilized people on earth," wrote Visecimus Knox, yet, "they . . . were unacquainted with that extreme delicacy of sentiment which is become universally present in modern times."[15] As Knox suggests, sensibility was a contemporary phenomenon and went hand in hand with the growth of a polite commercial society. Men who no longer had to struggle for survival were now expected to "feel for others as for themselves" and to unite "mildness" with "fortitude" in their conduct.[16] The most immediate benefit of modern sensibility, Knox argued, could be seen in the treatment of women. "This [modern] deference to women refines the manners and softens the temper; and it is no wonder that the ancients, who admitted not women to their social conversations, should acquire a roughness of manners incompatible with Delicacy of Sentiment."[17] As this suggests, women were already imagined to be creatures of sensibility, and as such were to be socially valued. It was not until the end of the eighteenth century, when feminists including Mary Wollstonecraft indicted the cult of sensibility for keeping women in a weak and infantile state, and politicians condemned it for leaving the body politic vulnerable to French ideas of liberty, equality, and fraternity, that moral reformers began to question sensibility's social effects.[18] The consequence was that sensibility came to be associated primarily with women and the ignorant rabble, the middle-class "man of feeling" having vanished from the social stage.

Despite the many claims made for the Englishness of sensibility, the cult of feeling depended heavily on the ideas of the French philosopher Jean-Jacques Rousseau, and the high value he placed on nature for its unspoiled innocence and simplicity. In France, as in England, *sensibilité* was embraced by intellectuals, aristocrats, and bourgeoisie. In sensitizing their readers to the beauty of nature, Rousseau's essays and novels awakened a desire for the "simple life" and for a new emotional and expressive openness to accompany it. Rousseau's stature, and his popularity in England and among moral philosophers including Hume, helped to spread the ideals of sensibility, particularly as it related to the love of nature, throughout British society.

The beauties of nature and their soothing and ennobling effects on the mind became one of the most enduring tropes of the cult of sensibility and can be found in the poetry of Gray, Cowper, and Thomson. As a landscape painter Gainsborough was certainly not immune to the appeal of sentimental nature. Writing to his friend William Jackson from Bath, Gainsborough complained, "I am sick of portraits and wish very much to take my Viol da Gam and walk off to some sweet Village where I can paint Landskips and enjoy the fag End of life in quietness and ease."[19] To Sir William Chambers he wrote, "If I can pick pockets . . . in the portrait way two or three years longer I intend to sneak into a cot & turn a serious fellow."[20] These oft-quoted remarks have served as evidence of Gainsborough's fondness for landscape, music, and the pastoral dream of rural retirement to a cottage.[21] Such assumptions are supported by the fact that some time after moving from Bath to London, Gainsborough purchased a cottage near Richmond Hill. Other accounts, such as Walter Armstrong's, have him purchasing a cottage at Kew, while John Thomas Smith wrote that he had lodgings in Hampstead. Finally, there is a drawing by Thomas Rowlandson of a cottage in Essex that Rowlandson identifies as belonging to Gainsborough. This fondness for the countryside extended to its poorest inhabitants. Uvedale Price recalled that when Gainsborough came upon "cottage or village scenes, to groups of children, to any objects of that kind which struck his fancy, I have often remarked in his countenance an expression of particular gentleness and complacency."[22] If all this were not enough to convince one of Gainsborough's intense attachment to the rural pastoral, there is the pictorial evidence of the cottage-door paintings themselves.

The major cottage-door compositions all show young, elegant-looking women and cherubic children clustered at the door of a cottage. The children feed themselves from bowls or are suckled at the breast. Nourishment, as Amal Asfour and Paul Williamson note in their essay here, is an ever-present theme in these paintings. In several compositions (pls. I, II, and V) single male figures either return home from gathering wood or take their ease before the cottage.[23] In all the compositions, the cottage melts imperceptibly into its landscape setting; its roughcast blends with the soil and rocks of the landscape, its thatch seems an extension of the leafy tree branches that shelter it, and in the case of *The Woodcutter's Return* a tree appears to spring up from the doorstep where the women and children gather, becoming a virtual structural element in the cottage's design (see detail of fig. 2 on facing page). In these paintings the cottage is not just an extension of nature into culture but a remaking of nature as culture. It is a nature made wholly domestic, a nature made home.

This fusion of culture and nature exists at the level of composition where the placement of the women at the door of the cottage links them to its recessed interior, while the laboring man suggests the wider world beyond. The powerful maternal presence in the cottage doors, so powerful that the young women attending the children number three in the Rutland and Cincinnati versions (see pls. I and II), and the emphasis on nourishment (food) and comfort (fuel) suggests the Freudian notion of the *heimlich*, that is to say, the home-like with all its connotations of shelter, comfort, intimacy, safety, quiet content, and the inevitable association of these qualities with the maternal body.[24] Seen in these terms the image becomes a powerfully charged trope of infantile desire. In this volume Susan Sloman argues convincingly that with the exception of the last of the series, *Peasant Smoking at a Cottage Door* (see pl. V), these are not images of families but of wet-nursing, and as such reflect Gainsborough's concern with the care of children and his connections to the London Foundling Hospital. This helps to explain the numerous children and multiple women in the paintings. Instead of images of home and mother they become in this reading uncanny images, examples of the *unheimlich*. For what at first glance appears to be a welcoming retreat from the world of labor and commerce, becomes its opposite, that is, a place of labor and commerce. In assessing the thematics of the series, Michael Rosenthal in his essay here argues that the cottage-door paintings are comments on poverty in the countryside caused by agricultural improvement, while Asfour and Williamson see *Peasant Smoking at a Cottage Door* as emblematic of an ideal of domestic felicity that escaped Gainsborough in real life.[25] The power of the cottage-door paintings is that they pose questions of meaning that are not easily resolved, inviting one instead to reflect in an ever deepening way on their interpretive possibilities.

As John Hayes has observed, the cottage-door paintings form a link between Gainsborough's landscape paintings and his later "fancy pictures" of rural children.[26] They are thus neither landscape paintings proper nor fancy pictures but something in between that takes advantage of the expressive power of both genres. Hayes notes that the figures in his cottage-door paintings provide more than just, as Gainsborough would have said, "a little business for the Eye."[27] They are instead *dramatis personae* who amplify the mood of the landscape and give it

facing page Thomas Gainsborough, *The Woodcutter's Return* (detail of fig. 2)

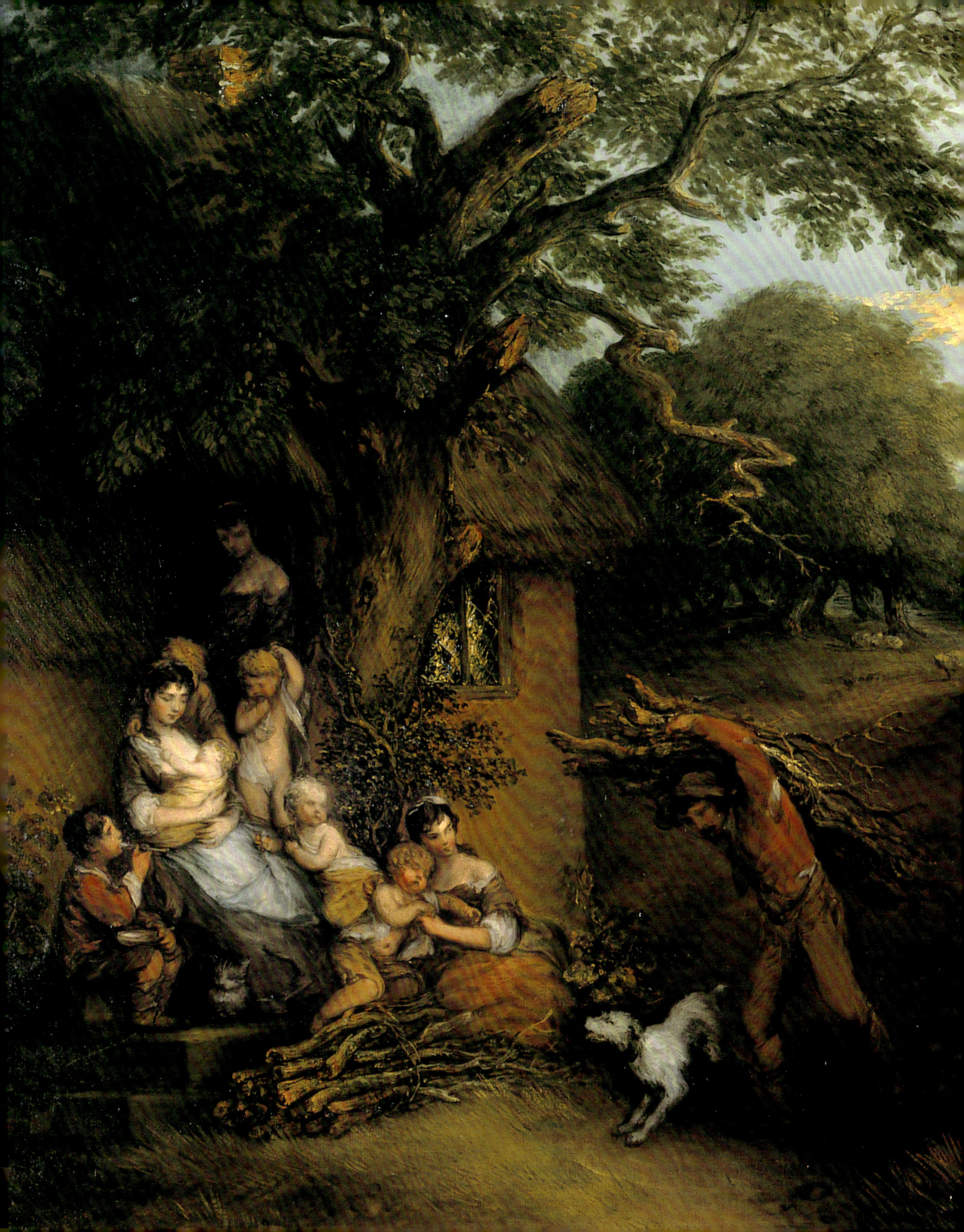

meaning through the way in which they abide in it. They propel the landscape toward narrative. In his essay Rosenthal argues that these paintings should be seen as a kind of history painting, as modern moral subjects that posed an alternative to the abstract style and idealized subject matter recommended by Sir Joshua Reynolds in his third and sixth *Discourses*. Seen in this way, what Gainsborough jokingly called his "dirty little subjects" become challenges to Reynolds's ideas of history painting.[28]

* * *

Along with the new cult of feeling came an interest in the nature of touch and visual perception. The science of sensibility was founded on the popularization of the sensationalist psychology of John Locke and the optics of Isaac Newton. Both made vision a potent source of knowledge of the world. Similarly, eighteenth-century theorists of sensibility saw vision as the prime organ of feeling. Sense stimuli striking the optic nerve, they believed, resonated deeply in the emotional core of the observer. "The eye," wrote Lawrence Sterne, "has the quickest commerce with the soul."[29] Adam Smith is particularly interesting in this regard. His theory of moral sentiments depends on vision and spectatorship for, as he explains, it is in observing the pain of others that we begin the process of imagining how we might feel in their situation and thus we eventually come to sympathize with their suffering.[30] Sympathy therefore depends on an act of imagination, which is in turn largely dependent on vision.

If natural scenes could have such effects, how much more powerful were images constructed to move the viewer. Vicesimus Knox observed that "the imitative arts are capable of conveying moral instruction in the most effectual manner . . . by appealing to the senses . . . they strike immediately and irresistibly on the susceptible heart."[31] The eighteenth-century idea of sensibility, therefore, imagines sight as a sensory portal through which images enter the imagination and touch the heart. In his *Cours de peinture* (1708, translated 1743) the French academician Roger de Piles argued that painting was more moving than words:

> The very men, whose profession it was to persuade, have often called in the assistance of painting, in order to touch the heart; because the mind . . . is sooner and more lively moved by what strikes the eye, than by what enters at the ears. . . . The reason is plain: Words are only the signs of things, whereas painting shews truth in a more lively manner, and moves and penetrates the heart more strongly, than can be done by discourse.[32]

De Piles not only announces the superiority of painting to poetry but also argues that the role of painting is to persuade and move the viewer through its visual effects. The eloquence of a work of art is not in what it represents but in how it touches the viewer. Circulating as they did in eighteenth-century artistic circles, such ideas were confluent with the doctrine of sensibility, which judged images, objects, texts, and experience in terms of their emotional effects.

Also pertinent to eighteenth-century artists was the link made in optics and perceptual psychology between sight and touch. From Euclid on there had been a notion that the eye perceived things by sending out beams or rays that in touching the surfaces of objects conveyed back to the viewer an idea of their distance, shape, color, and texture. This theory of what Martin Kemp has called "extramission," which proposed that seeing was a form of touch, was popular among Renaissance artists. Lomazzo in his treatise on painting speaks of "rays of sight" which "adopt all the particulars of the object" and then return "to the eye by the direct path whence they departed."[33] For the portrait painter extramission held particular perils. The Elizabethan miniaturist Nicholas Hilliard, a reader of Lomazzo, warned of the "stolen glances" between artist and subject which "suddenly like lightening pass."[34] Eye beams were a form of touch; they could caress or, as Hillard suggests, pierce like a lighting bolt. The notion of eye beams was revived in the eighteenth century by the French professor of geometry at the Académie in Paris, Sébastien Le Clerc (1637–1714).[35] This may explain why the idea had particular resonance for novelists of sensibility such as Samuel Richardson, who imagines Clarissa's eye beams as powerful enough to "dart through [Captain Tomlinson's] shivering reins" or to pierce Lovelace's soul.[36] Such a notion may also account, in part, for Gainsborough's remark to James Unwin that he was teaching his daughters to paint landscape because it was "not so apt to lay snares in their way as Portrait or Miniature Painting."[37]

The theory of extramission had been challenged by seventeenth-century optics. In Britain, Newton's observation that color was a function of light rays striking the retina and Locke's notion that the eye was like a *camera obscura* proposed a model of vision that did not depend on the viewer's eye beams. Instead images were produced by light reflected from objects. Reflected light entered the eye and created images on the retina, which in turn conveyed visual images to the brain.

Nevertheless, the idea of vision as linked to touch is not absent from Locke and Newton's accounts. In addition to imagining the mind as a *camera obscura*, Locke also proposed that ideas formed from experience impressed themselves on the mind in the way that a seal impresses itself on a wax tablet. Similarly, if one accepted Newton's ideas of sight as the result of imperceptible rays touching the receptors in the eye, one again found vision and touch linked in the science of perception. The viewer then was imagined as a receptor of visual stimuli, rather than the initiator of perception in the form of eye beams. The reception of visual stimuli, color and light in particular, and the ways in which they touched or imprinted themselves in the eye and imagination was a subject of ongoing scientific interest and one that appeared in popular as well as scientific accounts of vision and perception.[38] This increased interest in perception, as a way of being touched by the world, stimulated some artists to find visual equivalents in paint, pencil, ink, and chalk for this experience of vision.

Therefore sensibility depended on a mode of vision that in turn depended on touch. Early in the century there had been a lively debate as to which sense – touch or vision – was primary in enabling one to gain knowledge of the world. The Abbé de Condillac in his *Traité des sensations* (1754) imagined a marble statue, endowed successively with each of the five senses. Only the sense of touch allows the statue to experience itself and thus distinguish itself from others (the basic distinction for processing external stimuli). Thus touch emerges as the most essential of the senses. In locating perception in touch, Condillac located the

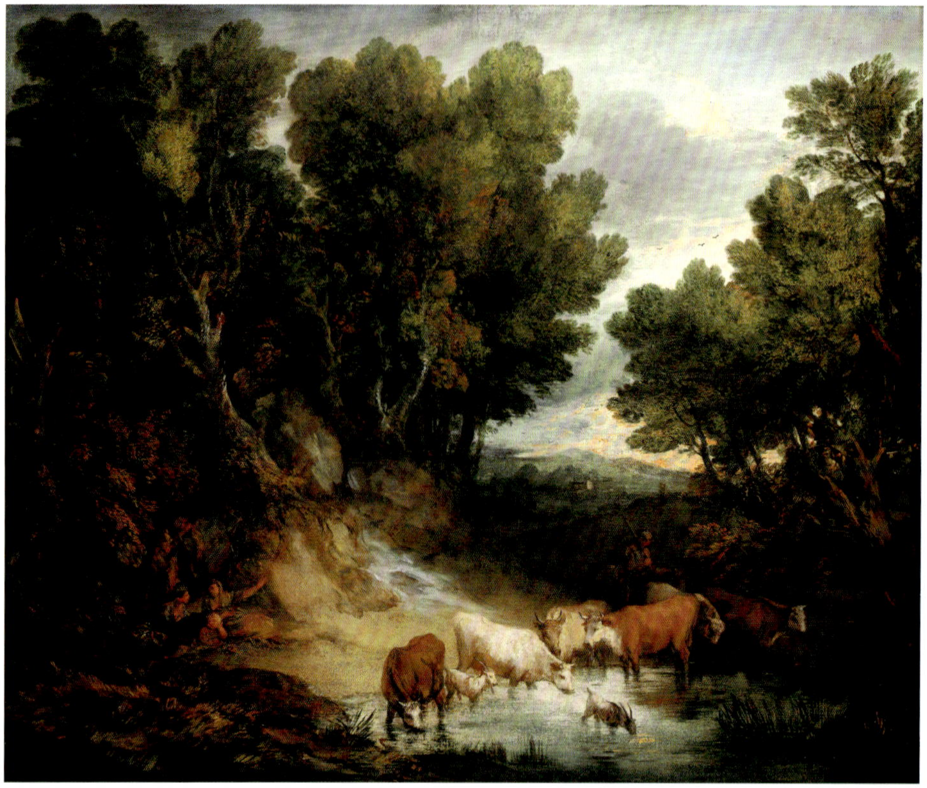

10 Thomas Gainsborough, *The Watering Place*, R.A. 1777, oil on canvas, 147.3 × 180.3 (58 × 71 in.), National Gallery, London

experience of perception in the body rather than the mind.[39] Hence Cheyne and other physicians took the logical step of proposing that disease (particularly imaginary or psychological disorders, that is, distortions in perception) originated not in the mind but in the nerves of the body and the way in which they responded to external stimuli. He saw that both the psychological perception of experience and the body's sensitivity to experience that made up the English malady known as sensibility had their origin in touch.

The notion of vision as a mode of touching needs exploring in relation to Gainsborough's painting technique. In his discourse on Gainsborough, Reynolds referred to the artist's "odd scratches and marks" and noted that Gainsborough himself considered this lively brushwork "the beauty of his art."[40] Gainsborough's contemporaries, however, were not sure what to make of his technique. A reviewer for the *St James Chronicle* in 1777 wrote of *The Watering Place* (fig. 10),

> But what shall I say of the Pencilling [brushwork]? I really do not know; it is so new, so very original, that I cannot find words to convey an Idea of it. I do not know of any Artists living or dead who have managed their pencil in that Manner, and I am afraid that any attempt to imitate it will be attended with little success.[41]

Clearly, Gainsborough's loose brushwork with its abstract economy of means, which resulted in daring calligraphic flourishes, looked "odd" to his contemporaries (fig. 11).

It is tempting to imagine that Gainsborough's handling is a literal trace of the perceptual moment of the artist in the presence of the motif – of his having been

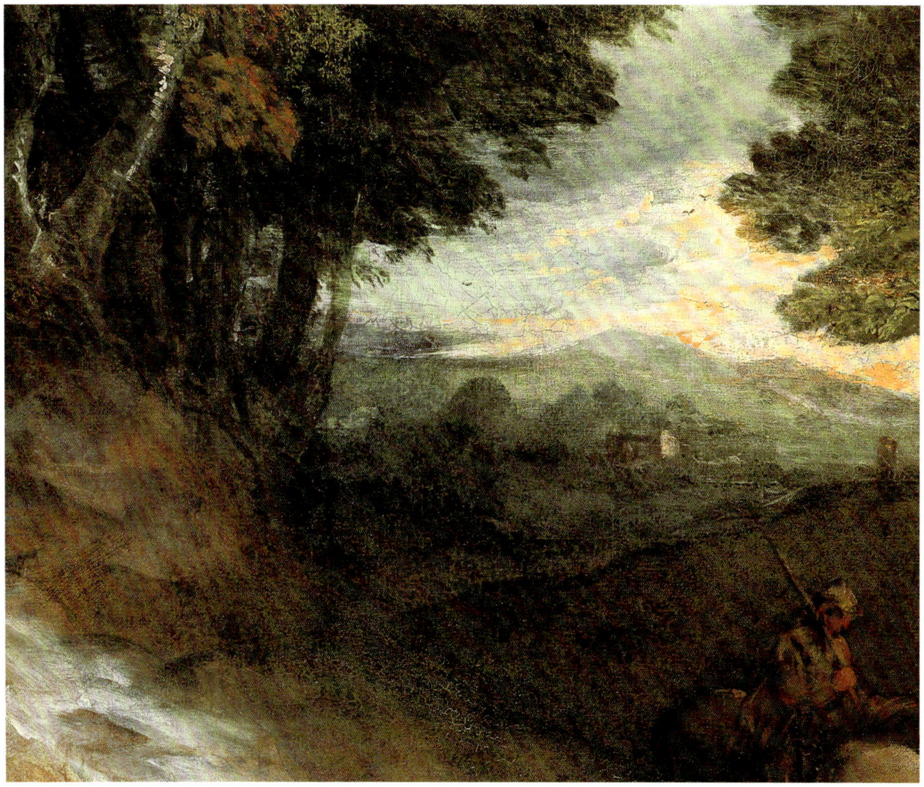

11 Thomas Gainsborough, *The Watering Place* (detail of fig. 10)

touched by the objects of vision – a touching that is highly personal and thus inimitable. Similarly the "slightness" that Reynolds observed in the rendering in some of Gainsborough's works may be due to a kind of selective focus, a record of the artist's moments of optical attention and inattention. As tempting as these ideas are, I think they are not quite accurate. Gainsborough's brushwork is not so much a passive record of visual stimuli as an active communicative gesture of touch, a calculated attempt to affect the viewers, to imprint itself and its vision on them. The conspicuous artificiality of Gainsborough's works, particularly the later works, the way they call attention to their own status as paintings through a brushwork that is a theatrical *tour de force*, signals their separateness from the natural world of vision. They are artificial worlds, full of new visual stimuli intended, in the spirit of de Piles, to touch and move one in new ways.[42]

To understand how Gainsborough may have intended viewers to be touched, it is useful to recall Reynolds's observation that Gainsborough's brushstrokes, his "chaos" of unmeaning marks, assumed "form" at the proper distance so that "all the parts seem to drop into their proper places."[43] The necessity of looking at the composition from the proper distance in order to make the brushstrokes cohere would explain the fact noted by some contemporaries that Gainsborough painted with brushes six feet long.[44] This suggests that Gainsborough painted his works at the distance from which he wished them to be seen, and would explain why his brushwork is loose and seemingly negligent when viewed close up.

The perception of Gainsborough's paintings thus depends on the viewer's powers of optical fusion.[45] Just as Locke acknowledged that the mental patterns of custom and habit as derived from experience enable one to order the chaos of visual images entering the brain by filling in missing bits of visual information and linking them into an imagistic whole, Reynolds acknowledged that the viewer's imagination supplied what was missing in Gainsborough's works, and did so in a way that was "more satisfactory to himself."[46] In this sense, Gainsborough's paintings are invitations to experience and perceive the artist's process of making form from chaos. Thus the viewer becomes a sympathetic collaborator with the artist or, alternatively, the sensibility of the artist invites the sensibility of the viewer to participate in creating a work of art. The final work becomes the fusion of the artist's sensibility with the viewer's.[47] Just as his subjects call upon viewers' interpretive powers, Gainsborough's handling calls upon viewers' perceptual powers. In both cases one is asked to feel with the artist and sympathize with his vision.

* * *

Given this invitation to experience the creation of an ideal world of vision and touch, it is not surprising to find that Gainsborough was drawn to the performative arts of music and theater. To some degree Gainsborough invites one to imagine painting as a performative art, an art that seeks to move by staging a spectacle of emotive visual effects. Much has been written of Gainsborough's love of music and of his own amateur performances; less, however, has been said of his interest in the theater.[48]

Gainsborough was a friend of David Garrick and took a lively interest in the actor's projects (fig. 12). Garrick, famous for his supposedly "natural" style of acting, was a phenomenon in the world of eighteenth-century theater. He was reputed to act instinctually, allowing himself to be carried away and lose himself in his role.[49] An English pamphlet identified Garrick as a man of sensibility, that is, as an actor who obeyed "the impulse of nature, and gives nothing more or less than the cry of his very heart."[50] The French *philosophe* Denis Diderot objected to this image of Garrick. Such emotion if really felt by Garrick could not be acting but simply emotion; acting, Diderot insisted, was the power of imitation, the ability to counterfeit all emotions.[51] Garrick's own *Essay on Acting* (1744) refutes the notion of instinctive artlessness, revealing the careful way Garrick constructed his roles. Nevertheless, the image of Garrick as the instinctive actor persisted. Diderot's distinction between true acting and mere emotion did not mean that Garrick was not a man of sensibility or that his parts were not masterpieces of emotional nuance. What it suggests is something akin to the notion of the performative that one finds in Gainsborough's paintings – the fabrication of an emotion intended to move the viewer and to invite a sympathetic response.

As the manager of the Drury Lane Theatre, Garrick had hired the Strasbourg artist and scenographer, Philippe-Jacques de Loutherbourg in 1772 (fig. 13). As Iain McCalman explains here, de Loutherbourg's revolutionary innovations transformed the dark, candle-lit stage of the eighteenth century into a bright luminous one. Traditional stage lighting had been achieved by candle loops at the front of the stage, and the use of candles or lamps placed at the foot of the stage. De Loutherbourg removed the footlights and added head and border lights. He

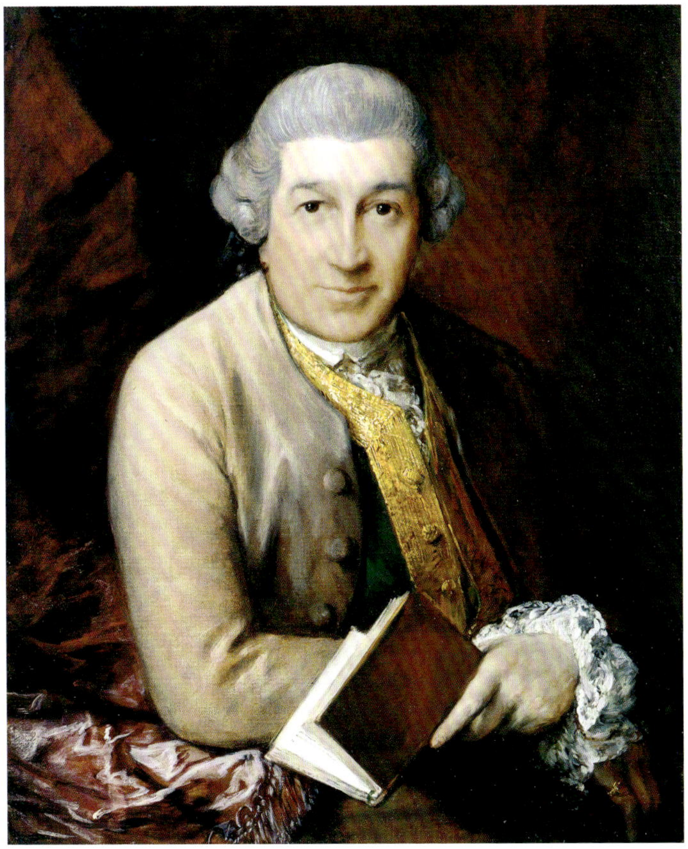

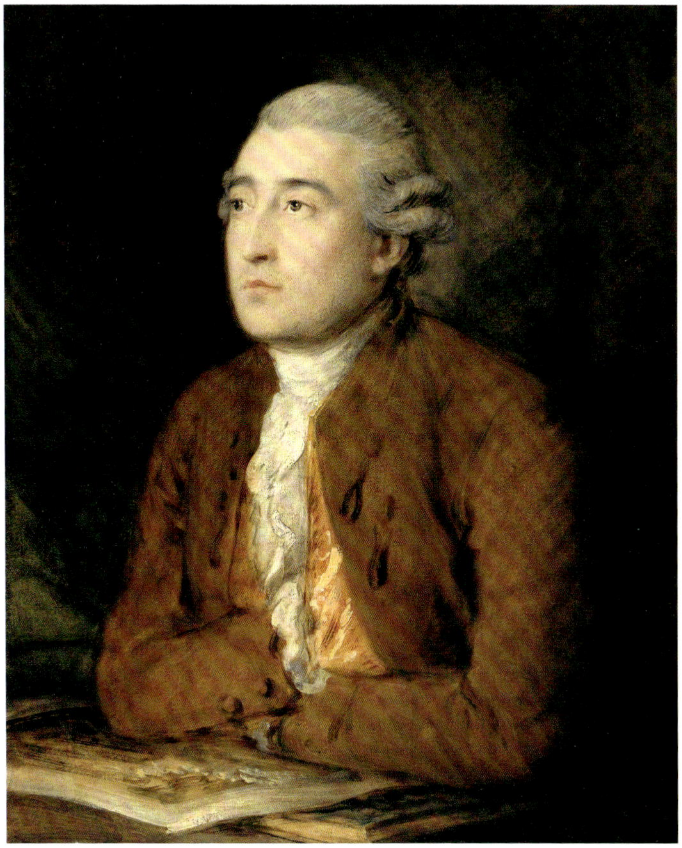

12 (*above left*) Thomas Gainsborough, *David Garrick*, R.A. 1770, oil on canvas, 76.2 × 63.5 cm. (30 × 25 in.), National Portrait Gallery, London

13 (*above right*) Thomas Gainsborough, *Philip James de Loutherbourg*, R.A. 1778, oil on canvas, 76.5 × 63.2 cm ($30\frac{1}{8} \times 24\frac{7}{8}$ in.), The Trustees of Dulwich Picture Gallery, London

also had lamps in the back of the stage so that they could shine through transparent scrims to create back lighting. This increased illumination on the stage integrated the actor into the stage picture and made the scenery more visible and more important.[52] De Loutherbourg also created illusionistic effects through the use of colored light. These effects were created by lamps – that were fitted with lenses and colored filters of red, blue, and yellow silk. Colored light on the stage created psychological mood and spatial depth, and further made it possible to animate the set by simulating natural changes of the seasons, weather, and times of day. Henry Angelo recalled that in one pantomime the audience was astonished by a "sudden transition in a forest scene, where foliage varies from green to blood colour," and noted that this was achieved by de Loutherbourg through the use of colored lights.[53]

As early as the seventeenth century artists were thinking of color as light. De Piles for instance had divided color into three types: the color of objects (local color), reflected color (shadows and highlights), and the color of ambient light.[54] From Newton on there had been a growing scientific and artistic preoccupation with transparent color and prismatic light, and with the properties of each color of the spectrum.[55] De Loutherbourg may have been interested in the properties of light not only as outlined by de Piles or Newton in his *Optics* but also, as McCalman explains, with regard to the central role light played in Masonic mysticism and alchemy. In Masonry light is the sign of enlightenment and in alchemy color is of major importance to the properties and transformation of matter. The three primary colors, red, blue, and yellow, are particularly significant, and they played a major role in de Loutherbourg's set lighting. Alchemical observations of how the color of matter is transformed when subjected to heat or water may also account for de Loutherbourg's fascination with and understanding of arial effects and his use of color progressions on stage. Transmutations of one color into another such as that described by Angelo were de Loutherbourg's specialty at Drury Lane. To create them de Loutherbourg devised a machine whereby colored silk screens turning on pivots in front of lamps projected changing color onto the set.[56] Most often these progressions took place in landscape scenes and mimicked the look of the changing seasons, weather, or times of day, as when the artist composed sets that created the illusion of silvery moonlight gradually yielding to the delicate tints of the rising sun and then in turn to the brilliance of noon.[57] Contemporary accounts reveal that de Loutherbourg believed that color was tonal and composed of a harmony of opposites. At one point in his experiments, Joseph Farington reports, de Loutherbourg had reduced the three primaries to blue and yellow.[58] One suspects that it was the confluence of color ideas gathered from Masonic mysticism, alchemy, art theory, and Newtonian optics rather than any one system that spurred de Loutherbourg to work his stage magic with colored light.

In the first season that Garrick hired de Loutherbourg, Gainsborough wrote to his friend to complain of the garishness of the new stage. "When the streets are paved with brilliants," he joked, "and the Skies made of Rainbows I suppose you'l be contented, and satisfied with Red blue & yellow."[59] Gainsborough's remark suggests that for his taste de Loutherbourg relied too much on the three primaries to create his dazzling light effects. A painting by de Loutherbourg showing Garrick in Beaumont and Fletcher's *The Chances* gives some idea of what the new stage may have looked like in 1773 (fig. 14). A deep blue evening sky contrasts with the warm yellow glow of a lamp set inside an open doorway in the left foreground. Garrick as Don John appears dressed in white holding a baby swaddled in a bright red cloth. The warm hues of the foreground make the sky and view of the Bay of Naples appear distant, and these distant objects provide a blue screen against which the warm tones of the foreground contrast and project sharply. The touch of red surrounded by the white of Garrick's costume is the brightest spot in the painting and glows with a fiery intensity in the center of the composition.

Scientists interested in optics were aware of the spatial effects of color and the effects produced when colored objects were seen under different colored lights. Yellow light made blue appear green and white appear yellow. Red light when cast on blue objects gave the blue a deeper cast and made white objects appear ruddy. These warm-colored objects cast bluish shadows, which in turn intensified the green and blue objects near them.[60] Such experiments in colored light were no doubt known to de Loutherbourg, who had studied painting and scenography in Paris with Carle van Loo and Giovanni Servandoni respectively.[61] De Loutherbourg's use of the three primaries in his stage lighting allowed him to change and intensify the colors of the set with an economy of means. Using the three pigment primaries de Loutherbourg demonstrated how to paint on stage with colored light.[62]

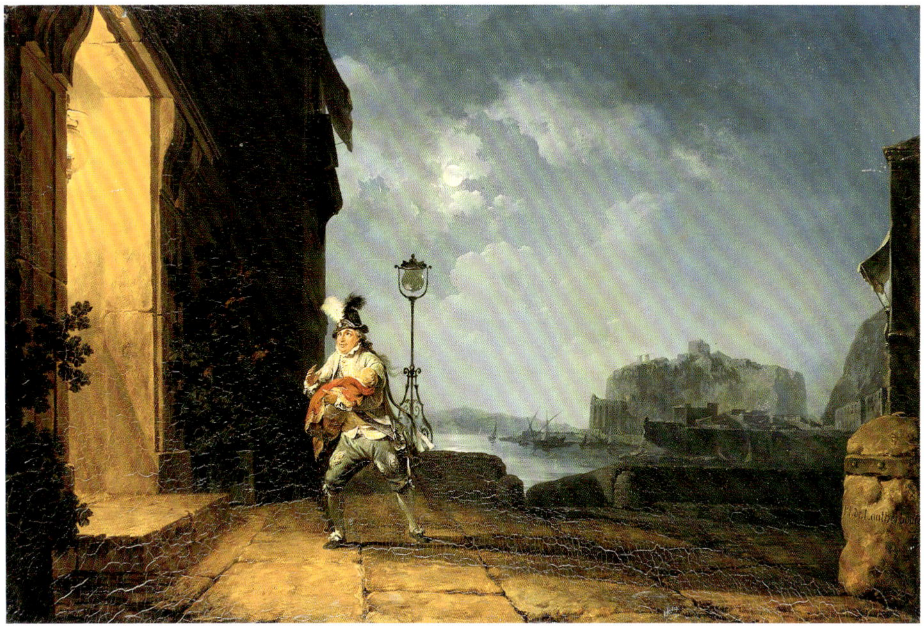

14 Philippe-Jacques de Loutherbourg, *David Garrick in Beaumont and Fletcher's "The Chances,"* 1774, oil on canvas, 57 × 78.6 cm ($22\frac{3}{8}$ × 31 in.), Dyce 70, Theatre Museum, Victoria and Albert Museum, London

In addition to the effects produced by using colored light, the coloristic effects of candlelight and daylight were also of interest, and not just to scientists and set designers but to artists. Philippe de La Hire, a mathematician who had trained as a painter, had noted in 1685 that candlelight was yellow whereas daylight was white; this meant, he said, that painters should choose their pigments according to the light in which the works would be seen. La Hire had a knowledge of pigments and could speak directly to artists' concerns. For instance, La Hire noted, "those ash pigments one describes as either green or blue appear by candlelight to be an extremely beautiful blue. The reds, which contain lake appear by candlelight as very bright, and others like carmine and vermilion seem dull."[63] It is interesting to note that Gainsborough was particularly fond of the red and yellow lakes (red and yellow organic dyes attached to transparent particles of chalk or alum) and used them extensively despite their fugitive nature.[64] He was also known to work by candlelight. The artist Ozias Humphry (1742–1810) remarked that Gainsborough's landscapes were frequently "wrought by candlelight," and his friend Henry Bate-Dudley noted that the painting *Peasant Smoking at a Cottage Door* (see pl. v) was painted entirely by candlelight.[65] Reynolds too remarked about Gainsborough's custom of painting at night by candlelight. Candlelight, Reynolds explained, made objects "appear more beautiful, from their being in a greater breadth of light and shadow, as well as having a greater breadth and uniformity of colour, nature appears in a higher style; and even flesh seems to take a higher and richer tone of colour."[66] Reynolds had already complimented Gainsborough on being a great colorist and he went on to say that, like Gainsborough, the great Italian colorists Titain and Correggio must have formed their ideas of coloring from observing objects by candlelight. Such accounts reveal Gainsborough's concern with the coloristic effects of ambient light on his paintings, and suggest that he preferred his pictures to be seen in candlelight. This may explain, in part, why he was more comfortable exhibiting his works in the subdued light of his studio than in the natural light of the Great Room at Somerset House where the Royal Academy held its annual exhibition.[67]

In the Bath period Gainsborough had embarked on his own study of color in relation to Rubens's method of coloring. De Piles had noted how Rubens kept his "bloom tints bright, separate and distinct," that is, he did not mix color on his pallet but rather applied pure strokes of color on the canvas in the knowledge that they would fuse when seen at a distance. De Piles praised Rubens's mastery of color as tone, but noted that in "pencilling" (brushwork) van Dyck was his superior.[68] As Reynolds remarked, in Gainsborough's case color "absorbed every other consideration" and he "cultivated those effects of the art [of painting] which proceed from colours."[69] This included laying down his colors separately in a style of brushwork derived from Rubens and van Dyck. This method of handling where two pure hues are laid side by side to produce optically the effect of a third color, or where a stroke of a second color is placed on top of a dominant color in order to modify it, has been observed in portraits such as Gainsborough's double portrait of the Linley sisters, as well as in his landscapes, fancy pictures, and cottage doors.[70] What de Loutherbourg may have added to Gainsborough's study of Rubens was the particular science of primary and secondary colors and the way in which they could heighten each other when placed in certain combinations and proximities, and also the use of color to create depth.

Technical analyses of Gainsborough's paintings have revealed that as early as the 1740s the artist was searching for ways to apply his colors in transparent glazes.[71] In the early Suffolk period he resorted to using ground glass in his pigments to achieve transparency. Then in the Bath period he occasionally used chalk, which becomes transparent in oil, in his grounds and his white pigments. Later, after he had mastered the art of glazing in oil paint thinned with turpentine, he even went so far as to experiment with an oleo-resinous material (which has sometimes been confused with bitumen) to give his glazing a translucent depth.[72] The artist's daughter Margaret remarked that her father's paints were so thin that they would run off his palette if he did not keep it level. As Helen Glanville has observed, this use of turpentine-thinned pigments not only gave his glazes a transparency but also allowed him to use oil as if it were watercolor, and to work up rapidly all parts of the canvas at once in a sketchy manner.[73] Gainsborough's obsession with transparency of color must have made de Loutherbourg's experiments in colored light of interest. As these analyses indicate, the expressiveness of Gainsborough's paintings, their luminous depth of coloring, and their calligraphic energy begin at the most basic level of materials – with pigments, binders, and thinners.

Gainsborough later became friends with de Loutherbourg and admired, in particular, his miniature mechanical theater, the Eidophusikon, which opened in London in 1781. De Loutherbourg's spectacle presented a series of scenic illusions made up of three-dimensional foregrounds, painted flats, moving parts (to mimic the motion of natural phenomena like ocean waves and fire), and changing light effects (again colored filters placed over lamps) to simulate seasons, times of day, and different weather conditions. All the scenes were accompanied by sound effects and music. In all respects the Eidophusikon was the eighteenth-

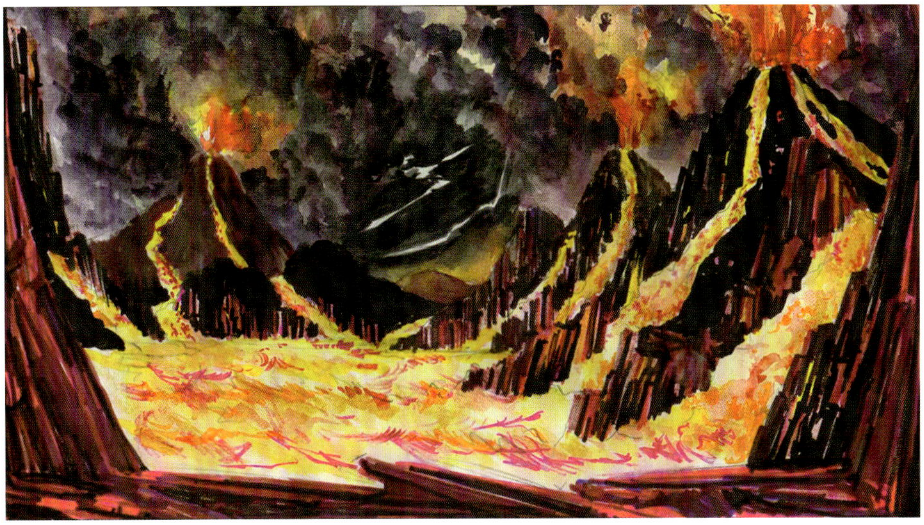

15 Robert Poulter, *Burning Fiery Lake*, 2005, working drawing for reconstruction of Milton's Pandemonium from de Loutherbourg's Eidophusikon, pen and colored ink, 14.2 × 26 cm ($5\frac{1}{2}$ × $10\frac{1}{4}$ in.)

century forerunner of Louis-Mande Daguerre's diorama of the 1820s.[74] The magic of this spectacle was such that the *London Courant* claimed that had de Loutherbourg lived at the time of Galileo he might have been charged with "conjuration" as one who "by the black arts, had captivated the sun, moon, and stars, and collected clouds, thunder, and lightning, by the aid of the Devil."[75]

The first season of the Eidophusikon included five scenes, four showing the times of day (these recalled the illusions de Loutherbourg created at Drury Lane) and a fifth portraying a storm at sea. The scenes were described in the press as: "Aurora, or the effects of the dawn, with a view of London from Greenwich Park"; "Noon, the Port of Tangier in Africa, with the distant view of Gibraltar and Europa Point"; "Sunset, a view over Naples"; "Moonlight, a view of the Mediterranean"; and "A Storm, and Shipwreck." "Moonlight" was singled out by the *Whitehall Evening Post* as "beyond every idea that can be formed from description. In the foreground of the scene a group of peasants appear sitting round a fire, the reflection of which produces the most beautiful contrast to the reflection of the moon, which rising, sheds her silvered tints over the landscape."[76] The opening season of fifty-nine performances ended May 1781 followed in January 1782 by a second with new scenes including the "Rising of the Palace of Pandemonium" from *Paradise Lost*. Pandemonium was immortalized by Edward Francis Burney in his drawing of the Eidophusikon (figs. 15 and 124). As McCalman has noted, the Eidophusikon was not a trivial attraction. The best seats cost 3 shillings, the rest 2 shillings (this while admission to the annual Royal Academy exhibition was only 1 shilling). Doors opened at half-past seven and the spectacle began precisely at eight.[77]

As at Drury Lane, light was once again the essential ingredient in the illusionist effects of the Eidophusikon. From newspaper accounts we learn that each scene was composed of many detached pieces, which enabled de Loutherbourg to vary the light throughout the set and to control the "keeping," the use of color (not white and black), to create light and shade. Scenes were built up from rows of cut-out pasteboard. For the Greenwich set the foreground was created from pieces of cork cut to suggest a sandpit covered in moss and lichen, and the trees of the park were each built separately. In the foreground were model ships and beyond them the view of London and St. Paul's. Each mass was cut out in pasteboard and diminished in size to suggest distance. The clouds were created on a linen roll stretching more than twenty times the width of the stage and painted in semi-transparent colors. This was gradually unrolled (by a winding machine) to suggest moving clouds that cast shadows over the landscape set. Changing light playing over the clouds supplied the transition from early dawn to bright morning.[78]

Between the scenes de Loutherbourg provided music but also transparencies. Transparencies were continuous designs painted on thin paper, which, when passed before a lamp, revealed a procession of figures in landscapes. The transparencies seem not to have been keyed to the major set scenes. In the first season they consisted of "an incantation"; "a seaport, a conversation of sailors of different nations"; "a view of the alps"; "a woodcutter attacked by wolves"; "a summer evening, with cattle and figures."[79]

De Loutherbourg's spectacle turned nature's ephemeral and evanescent atmospheric effects into a visual narrative. In his hands, landscape became a changing event rather than a static object, an experience more like that of music than ordinary painting. This had implications for landscape painting in the nineteenth century, in so far as it revealed that the depiction of atmospheric effects could be as compelling as the depiction of a famous view or monument. The incidental and transient – the changing effects of time and weather, for example – suddenly became the center of interest and the essence of the landscape experience. The Eidophusikon demonstrated that the conditions under which an object was seen determined how the object appeared and how one responded to it. Appearances, it showed, were relative, and light and color had central roles to play in the depiction of nature's moods and in the viewer's visual and emotional experience. Thus the Eidophusikon brought landscape art into sympathy with the cult of feeling by linking sensation, and even sensationalism, to an appeal to the viewer's sympathetic imagination.

One must suppose that in the decade between Gainsborough's letter to Garrick, complaining of the garishness of de Loutherbourg's stage, and the debut of the Eidophusikon, de Loutherbourg either modified his coloristic light effects or Gainsborough became more tolerant of them. Whatever may have been the case, by the 1780s de Loutherbourg's stage effects, particularly as managed in the Eidophusikon, were of interest to the painter. W. H. Pyne noted that

> Gainsborough was so wrapt in delight with the Eidophusikon, that for a time he thought of nothing else – he talked of nothing else – and passed his evenings at that exhibition in long succession. Gainsborough himself a great experimentalist could not fail to admire scenes wrought to such perfection by the aid of so many collateral inventions.[80]

Some of these inventions may have been the small-scale model landscapes that Reynolds and Humphry say that Gainsborough assembled in his studio from bits of rock, bark, coal, and plants, which seem similar to the foregrounds de Loutherbourg created for the Eidophusikon sets. Another may have been his "showbox" or peepbox and the transparencies he made for it.[81] Gainsborough was familiar with transparencies used in the theater and had seen Thomas Jervais's exhibition of paintings on glass.[82] Several of Gainsborough's glass transparencies survive along with his showbox in the collection of the Victoria and Albert Museum, London. His transparencies are all landscapes: a scene of a mountainous landscape with sheep; an estuary with sailing boats and figures on the shore; a woodland scene with a pond; cattle and a drover; a cottage with sheep and cattle; and a cottage by moonlight (figs. 16–20). This last scene when exhibited in 1824 was particularly admired and one critic noted that it "excite[s] the most pleasing associations of mind."[83] Some of Gainsborough's interest in de Loutherbourg seems evident in the way the transparencies evoke the varying light effects of different times of day and weather conditions.

While perhaps inspired by those shown at the Eidophusikon, Gainsborough's transparencies nevertheless differ from de Loutherbourg's in significant ways.

16 (*below left*) Thomas Gainsborough, *Landscape with Herdsman and Cattle by a Pool*, c. 1781–2, oil on glass, 27.9 × 33.7 cm (11 × 13¼ in.), Victoria and Albert Museum, London

17 (*below right*) Thomas Gainsborough, *Coastal Scene with Sailing Ships*, c. 1781–2, oil on glass, 27.9 × 33.7 cm (11 × 13¼ in.), Victoria and Albert Museum, London

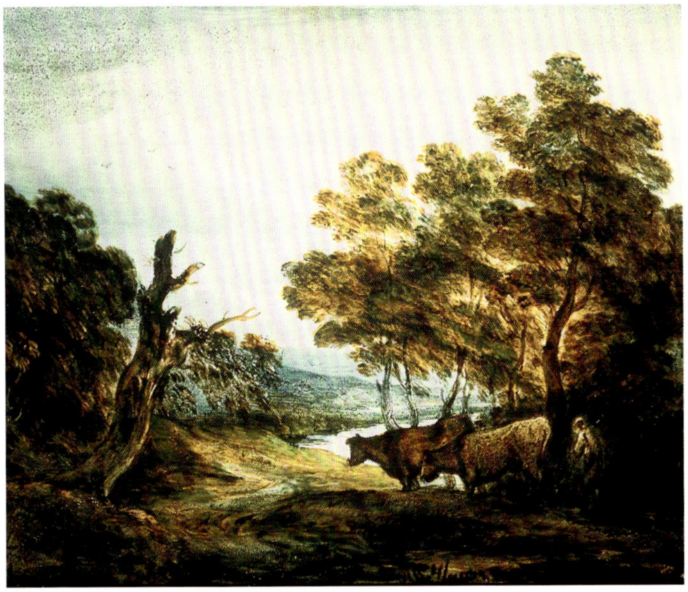

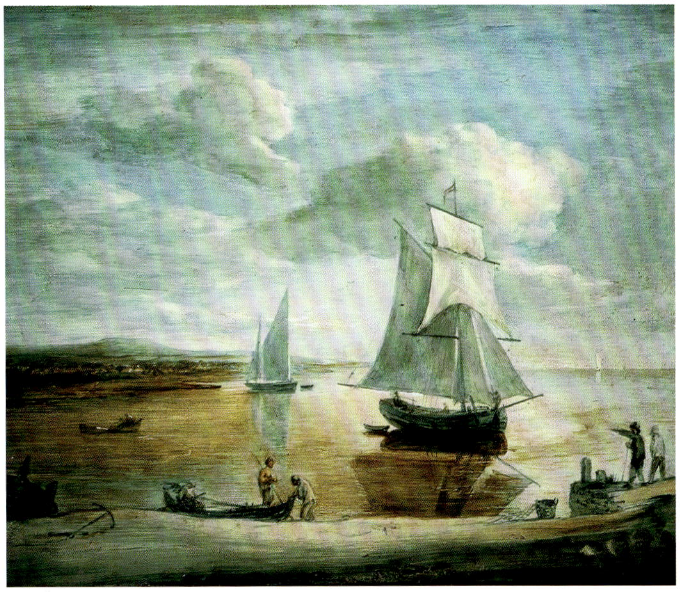

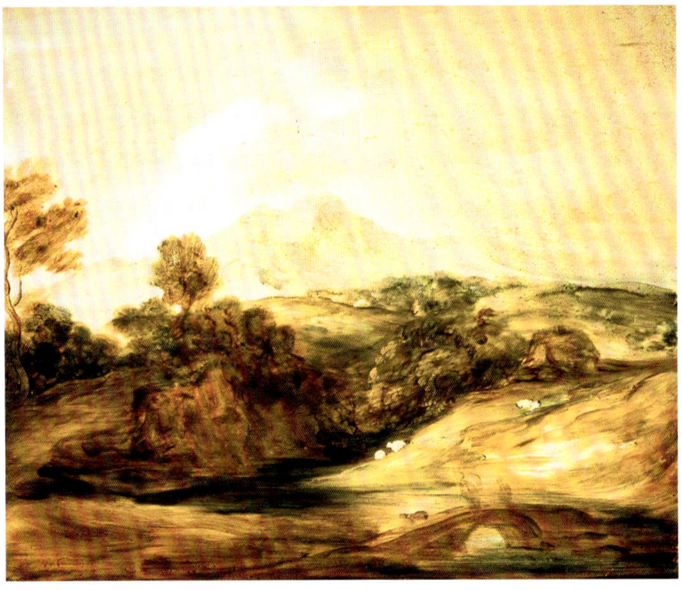

18 (*right*) Thomas Gainsborough, *Mountain Scene with Sheep*, c. 1781–2, oil on glass, 27.9 × 33.7 cm (11 × 13¼ in.), Victoria and Albert Museum, London

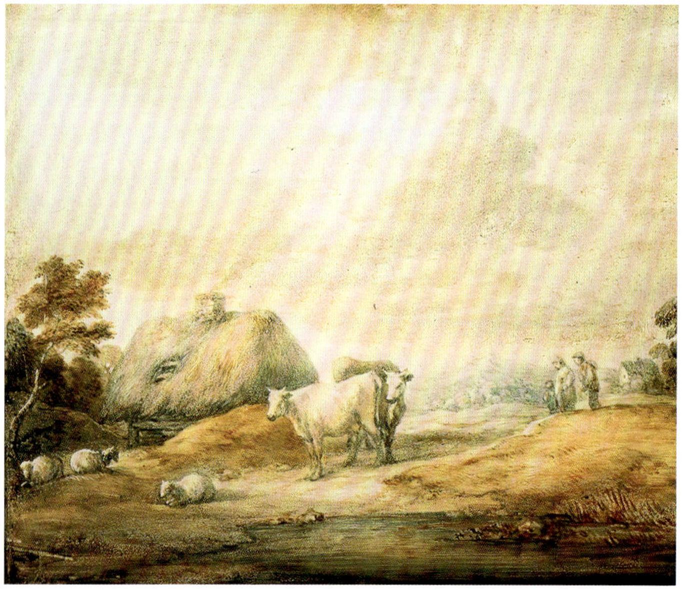

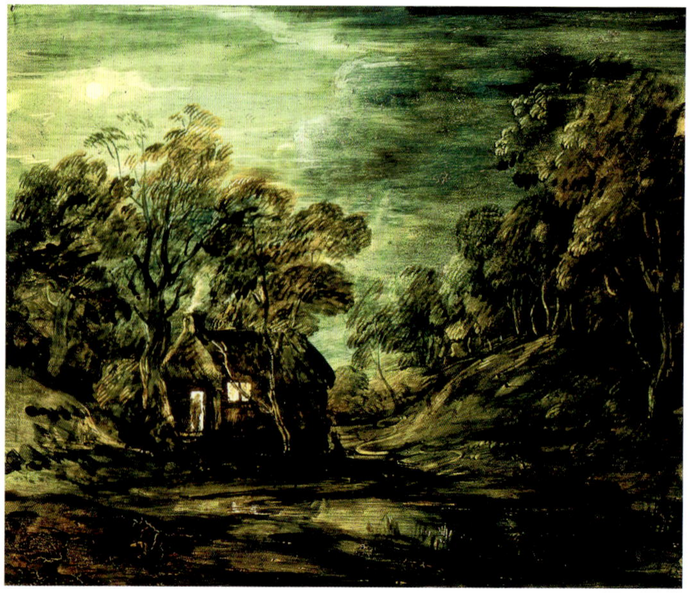

19 (*above left*) Thomas Gainsborough, *Landscape with Cottage, Sheep and Cows*, c. 1781–2, oil on glass, 27.9 × 33.7 cm (11 × 13¼ in.), Victoria and Albert Museum, London

20 (*above right*) Thomas Gainsborough, *Cottage Scene by Night*, c. 1781–2, oil on glass, 27.9 × 33.7 cm (11 × 13¼ in.), Victoria and Albert Museum, London

De Loutherbourg's were painted on paper, Gainsborough's on glass slides. De Loutherbourg's were displayed on stage, Gainsborough's were viewed in his showbox. Presumably, de Loutherbourg's paper transparencies were painted in his tight and highly illusionistic style.[84] Gainsborough's, by contrast, partake of the loose handling of his later painting style. And, while de Loutherbourg's scenes were often conspicuously sublime and involved the illusion of moving figures, Gainsborough's were less dramatic and calculated, as William Vaughan observes, to encourage "poetic thoughts about the transformative effects of colour and light."[85] As Vaughan and Asfour and Williamson note in their essays, viewing such scenes in the peep box made the visual experience of the transparencies all the more intimate and meditative.

Vaughan argues that Gainsborough's showbox enabled the viewer to withdraw from the world of experience and be absorbed into the luminous phantasmagoria of the work of art. Similarly, as I show in my essay here on the tent room built in Sir John Leicester's London town house for Gainsborough's *Cottage Door*, the creation of new exhibition spaces invited new protocols of viewing. In this case a purpose-built space was created in which certain key elements of Gainsborough's style, in particular its technical brilliance and its formal beauty, could be carefully and minutely examined. As Asfour, Williamson, and I observe, the tent room evoked the experience of the showbox. Given Gainsborough's fascination with formal technique and his reputation as a brilliant technician it is not surprising that such unusual viewing practices should emerge in the context of his work.

The importance of Gainsborough's glass transparencies for the development of his late style was recognized almost immediately. Robert Smirke told Joseph Farington that "he thought they must have been of great use to Gainsborough in his painting."[86] Pyne echoed this opinion, saying that he believed that Gainsborough "emulated their splendour in his pictures. It is owing to this practice, that some of his latest works are remarkable for violent contrasts, and wanting in that stillness and harmony which characterized his earlier labours."[87] According to these accounts the experience of transparency painting enhanced the color and light effects of Gainsborough's later paintings. Recently a full-size rendition of *The Cottage Door* has emerged on the London art market (fig. 21).[88] It has been attributed to Gainsborough by John Hayes and appears to be a hitherto unknown autograph variant of the Huntington painting possibly done in the mid-1780s while the original remained unsold in the artist's studio. What is interesting about this version is its sketch-like handling and light-gold color harmonies, both of which bear striking resemblances to the handing and color found in the glass transparencies. It seems to confirm Pyne's statement that the transparencies inspired the style of his later works. This second *Cottage Door* points to the Rubensian color and sketch-like brushwork of Gainsborough's last style.[89] Could it be that, free from the norms of finish for exhibition, Gainsborough was experimenting to see if the coloristic intensity, luminosity, and graphic immediacy of the transparencies could be translated into a full-scale oil painting? Was this a way to compare the effects to be gained by incorporating into his painting the look of the transparencies? Or, was this simply a sentimental gesture, an attempt to cling to a beloved image that was about to be sold?

The fact that Gainsborough employed in his later paintings and drawings the same kind of loose handling that he used in his transparencies suggests that he was not interested in de Loutherbourg's illusionism. Instead, Gainsborough's transparencies and later paintings, among them *The Cottage Door*, look conspicuously artificial. They announce themselves as dazzling feats of painterly imagination and technique, and in doing so they call attention to their own making and to their maker.

★ ★ ★

John Hayes has observed that Gainsborough was the first British artist to treat the theme of the cottage and cottage life. This is not to say that cottages do not appear in the work of other British artists such as George Smith of Chichester and Joseph Wright, but rather that it was Gainsborough who opened the subject up to all its compositional and thematic possibilities.[90] For this reason Gainsborough's cottage-door paintings are of particular importance to the history of British landscape and rural genre painting. To understand why, one must look at the physical history of the paintings in the late eighteenth and early nineteenth centuries. The Duke of Rutland's painting went into the collection at Belvoir Castle soon after it was finished (see pl. I). The next two cottage-door paintings, the Cincinnati and Huntington paintings, had more public lives (see pls. II and III). Both were exhibited at the Royal Academy (the Cincinnati in 1778 and the Huntington in 1780), and at the 1814 retrospective exhibition of Gainsborough's works at the British Institution. The Cincinnati painting was in the hands of Gainsborough's daughter Margaret, who by 1814 had sold it to Henry, first Earl of Mulgrave. The Huntington painting has a more significant history. It remained in the artist's studio until 1786 when it was purchased from the artist by Thomas Harvey of Catton House (1748–1819). Harvey lived in Norwich and was a collector of English and Dutch landscapes. He was not only on familiar terms with

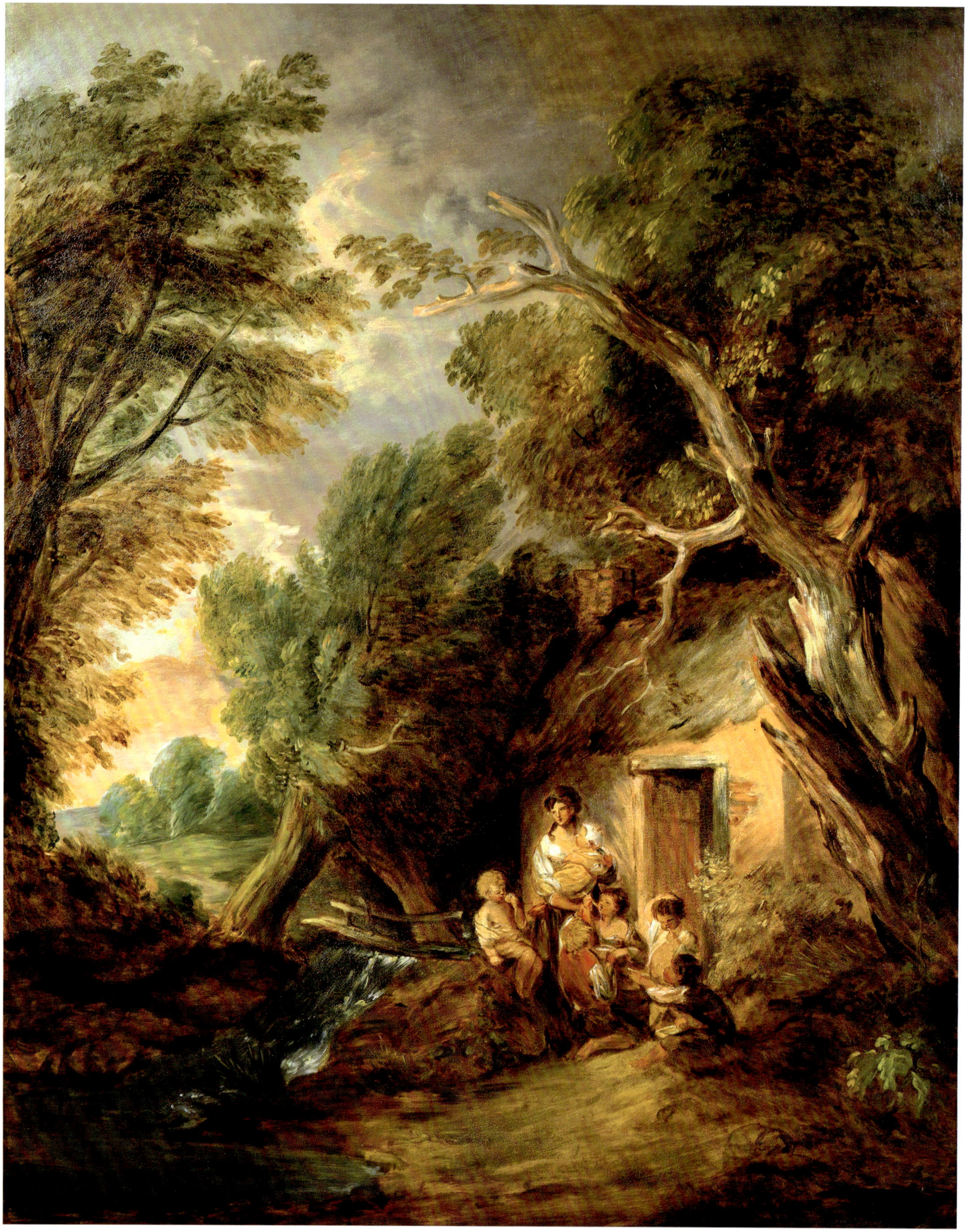

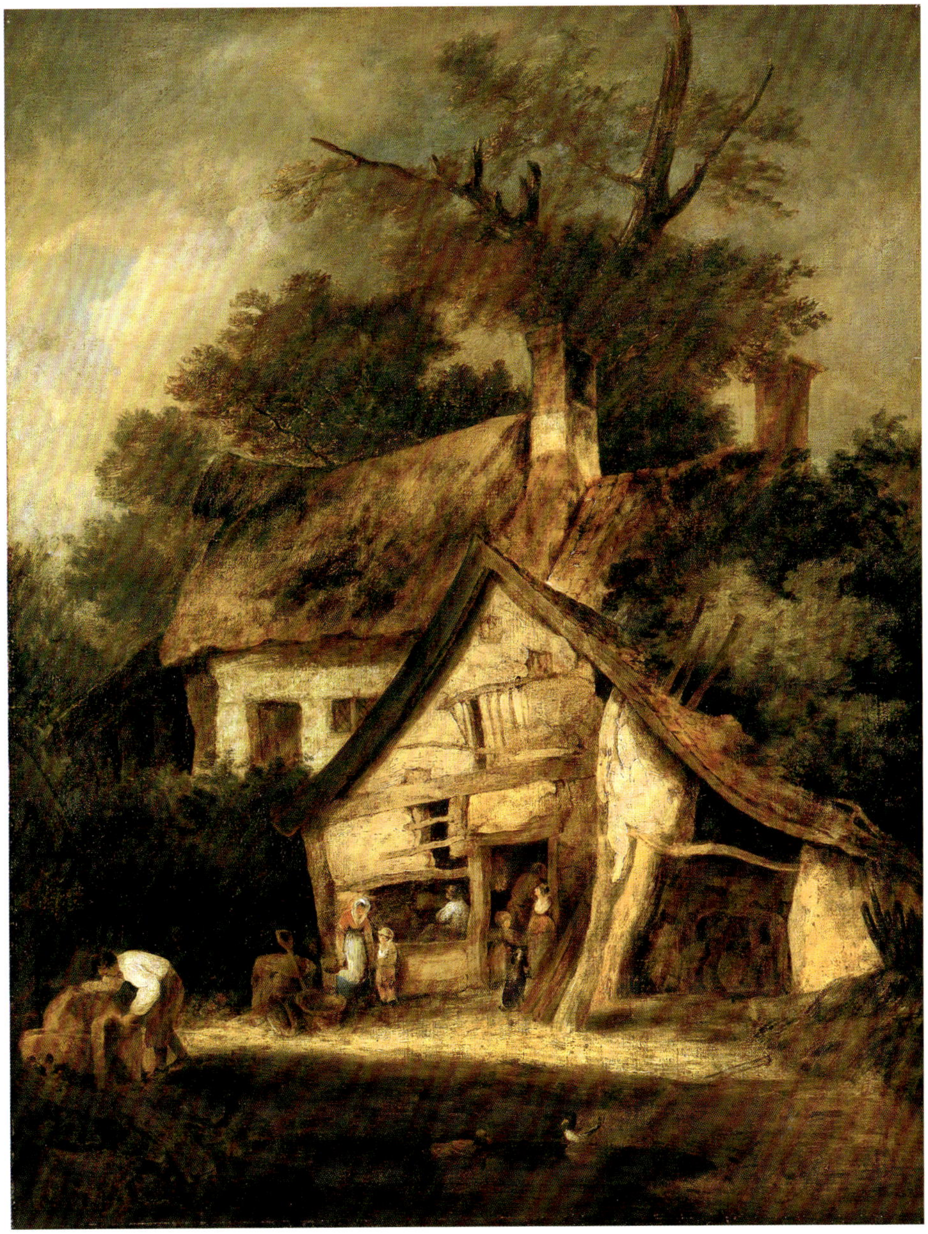

22 John Crome, *Blacksmith's Shop near Hingham, Norfolk*, R.A. 1808, oil on canvas, 153.9× 121.9 ($60\frac{1}{2}$ × 48 in.), Philadelphia Museum of Art. The John Howard Mc Fadden Collections, 1928

Gainsborough but also with John Crome, and at Harvey's suggestion Crome copied *The Cottage Door*. This copy (now lost), entitled *Cottage at Hunstanton, Norfolk*, was in the collection of Dawson Turner, a patron of both Crome and John Sell Cotman. Throughout 1807–9, Crome continued to paint subjects such as the *Blacksmith's Shop near Hingham, Norfolk* in a way that strongly evokes Gainsborough's cottage doors (fig. 22). Cotman also embarked on a series of ruined cottage paintings around the same time. This suggests that, as important as the examples of Dutch painters like Ostada and Hobbema were for the Norwich school painters, they were also influenced by Gainsborough's cottage doors.

21 (*facing page*) Thomas Gainsborough (attributed), *The Cottage Door*, 1780–86, oil on canvas, 149.85 × 121.3 cm (59 × $47\frac{3}{4}$ in.), private collection

In 1807 the Huntington painting was in the hands of a Mr. Coppin (possibly an agent for Mr. Catton) who showed it to the antiquarian John Britton. Britton, who illustrated the painting in his book, *The Fine Arts of the English School* (1812),

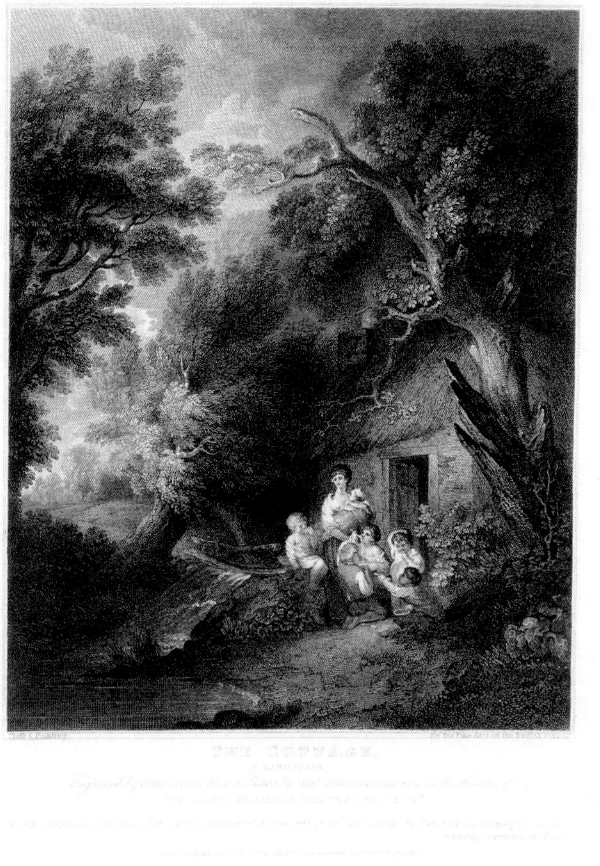

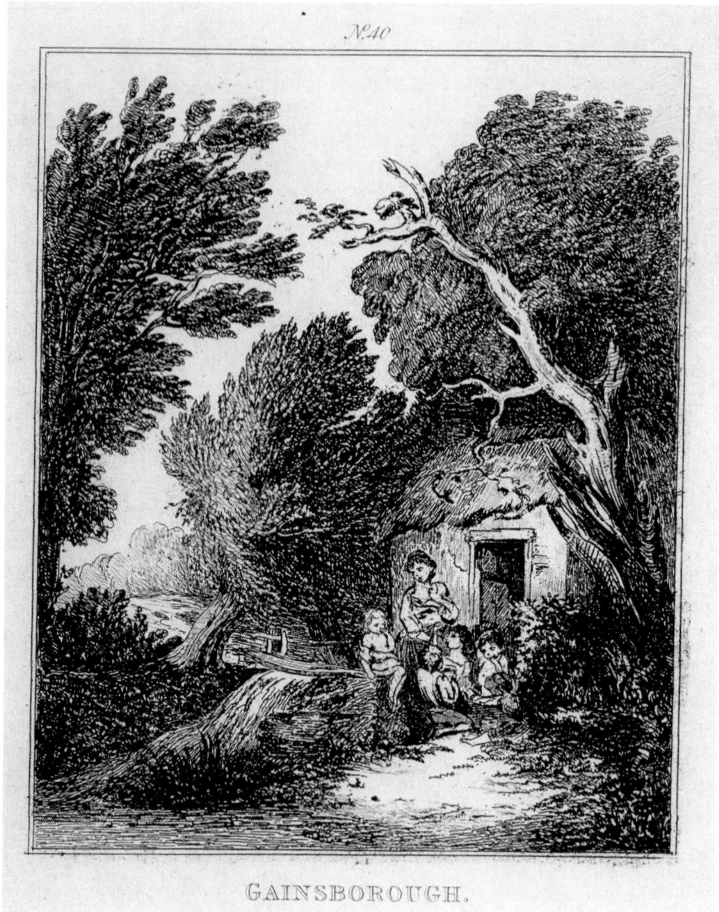

23 (*above left*) John Scott after Thomas Gainsborough, *The Cottage Door*, etching from John Britton's *The Fine Arts of the English School*, London, 1812

24 (*above right*) Artist unknown after Thomas Gainsborough, *The Cottage Door*, engraving from John Young's *A Catalogue of Pictures by British Artists, in the Possession of Sir John Fleming Leicester, Bart. With Engravings from the Whole Collection*, London, 1821

encouraged Sir John Leicester to purchase the painting, describing it to him as "the *very first* picture by this artist I ever saw."[91] Leicester bought the painting for his growing collection of British art, which was frequented by artists and was opened to the public in 1818. The illustration by John Scott of *The Cottage Door* that appeared in Britton's catalogue was the first print reproduction made of the painting; it was followed in 1821 by the illustration that appeared in John Young's catalogue of Sir John's collection (figs. 23 and 24). The reproduction of the painting is important for in the nineteenth century it was in reproduction rather than art criticism that the fame of an artist or a painting largely rested. Britton coincidentally presided over the sad demise of de Loutherbourg's Eidophusikon after the artist sold it in 1799 to Chapman's theater in Panton Street, Haymarket. As a young man Britton worked for Chapman, and he tells us that the showman added acts to de Loutherbourg's spectacle that included a "learned dog, musical glasses" and a monologue by Britton.[92] In 1800 Britton noted that the theater and all its contents were consumed by a fire that had started in a nearby brothel.

The story of Sir John Leicester and his collection is told here by Dungho Chun who examines the growing reputation and market value of *The Cottage Door* as it passed through the hands of various eighteenth- and nineteenth-century collectors. The painting was given a place of honor in Sir John's collection as one of the finest examples of British painting. While there it was cleaned by William Redmore Bigg, an artist who became known for his own rural genre scenes, in particular his cottage interiors (fig. 25). After Sir John's death the painting entered the Grosvenor collection where again it was accessible to the public.

The Ipswich painting was exhibited in the Gainsborough retrospective of 1814 at the British Institution and four other times in the nineteenth century (see pl. IV). It was bought from the artist by Wilbraham Tollemache, later the sixth Earl of Dysart, in 1786. John Constable, who was on good terms with the Tollemache family, took Sir George Beaumont to see the painting in 1812.[93] Beaumont may have wanted to see how this painting compared to his own painting, the UCLA cottage door (see pl. V). Beaumont had purchased his cottage-door painting from Margaret Gainsborough in 1799. He was a great collector and connoisseur as well as a friend and patron of Constable. His collection, like Sir John Leicester's, was frequented by artists who, as did Constable, studied it. As in the case of Crome and the Norwich School, Constable was enamored of Gainsborough's rustic scenes such as *The Cottage Door.* His own first essays in landscape were drawings of cottages made for John Thomas Smith and his later oil painting, exhibited at the Royal Academy in 1817, *A Cottage in a Corn Field* (fig. 26), is both an homage to, as well as a more naturalistic rendition of, Gainsborough's picturesque cottage scenery. The more immediate impact of the cottage-door paintings can be found in the rural genre scenes of Francis Wheatley and George Morland (figs. 28 and 29). By the beginning of the nineteenth century, cottage-door subjects appear also to have preoccupied Thomas Rowlandson (fig. 27).

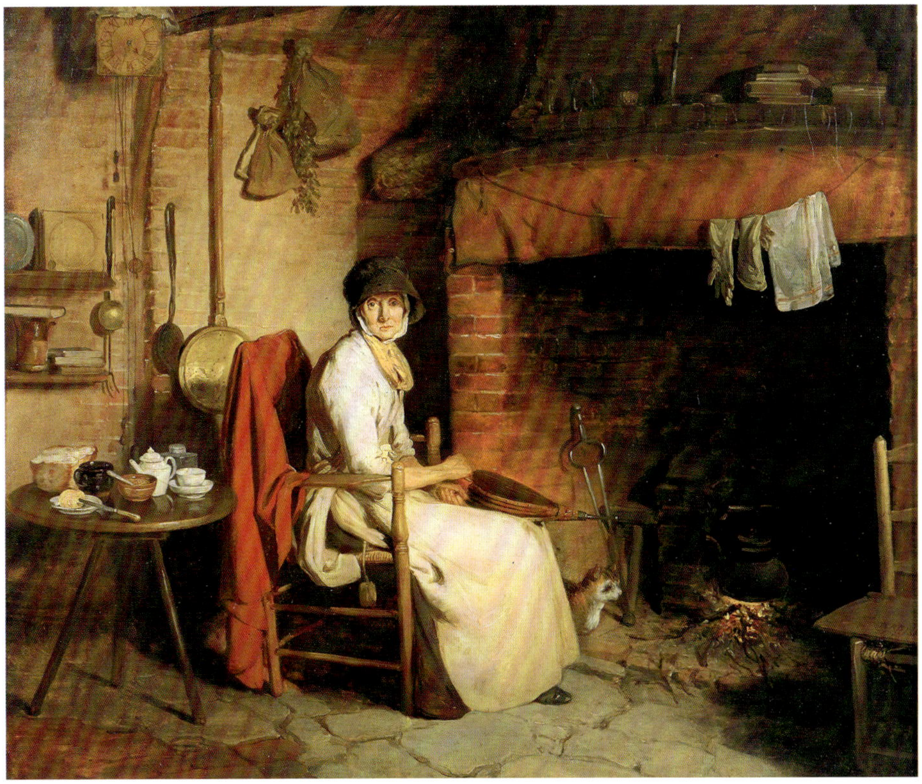

25 William Redmore Bigg, *A Cottage Interior: Woman by a Fireside*, c. 1793, 101.6 × 127 cm ($40\frac{1}{4} \times 50\frac{1}{8}$ in.), Victoria and Albert Museum, London

26 John Constable, *A Cottage in a Corn Field*, R.A. 1817, oil on canvas, 314 × 264 cm ($12\frac{3}{8}$ × $10\frac{3}{8}$ in.), Amgueddfeydd ac Orielau Cenedlaethol Cymru, National Museums and Galleries of Wales, Cardiff

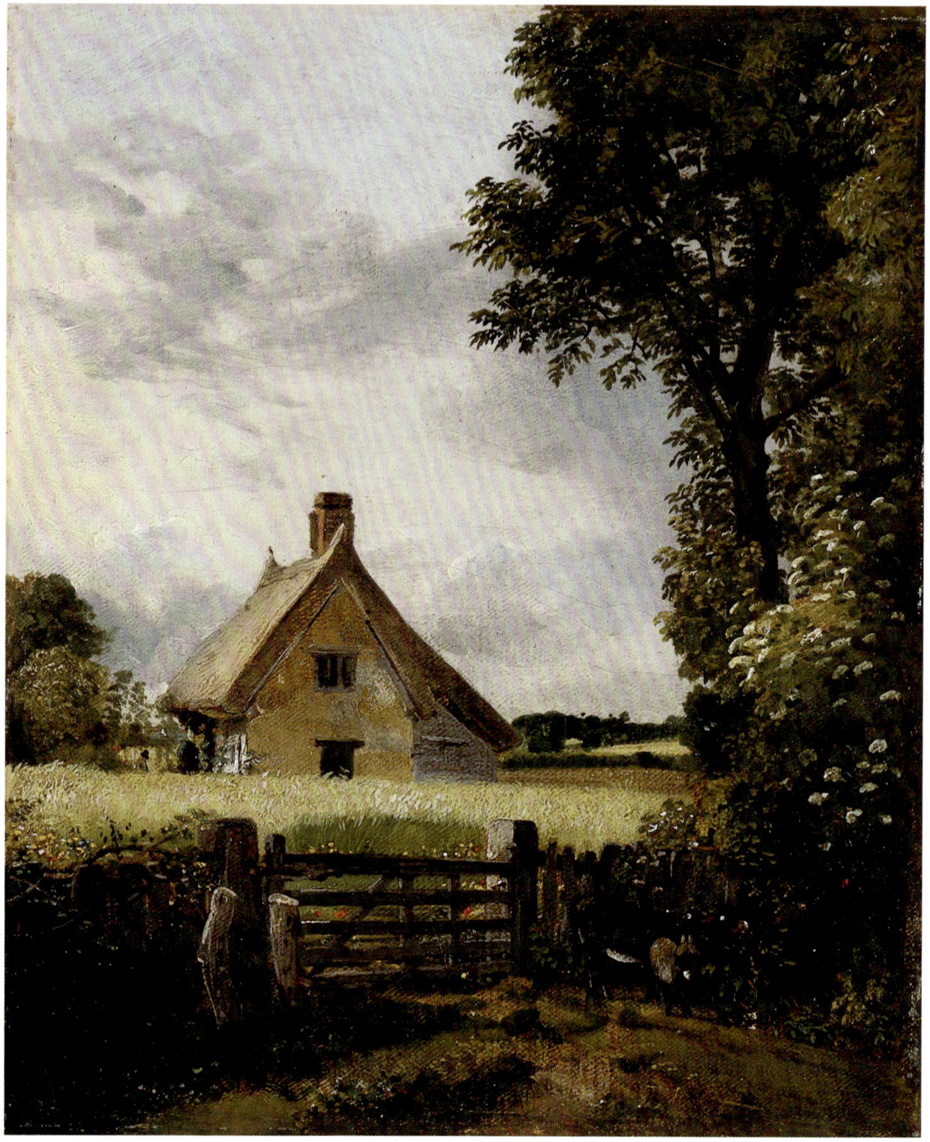

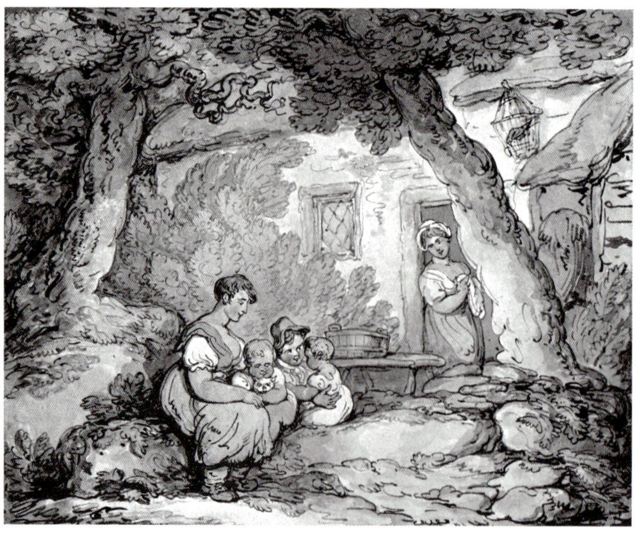

27 Thomas Rowlandson, *The Cottage Door*, c. 1805, pen and watercolor, 18.1 × 20.6 cm ($7\frac{1}{8}$ × $8\frac{1}{8}$ in.), Henry E. Huntington Library, Art Collections, and Botanical Gardens, San Marino, California

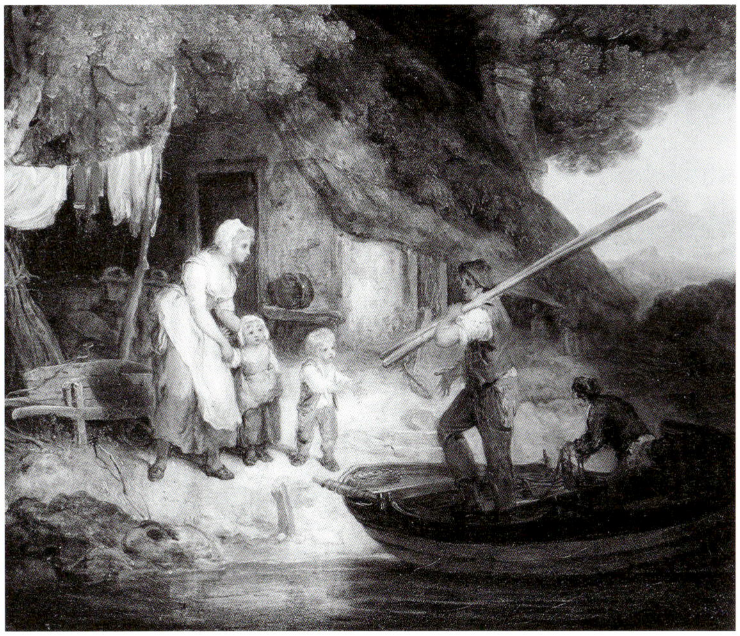

28 Francis Wheatley, *The Fisherman's Return*, c. 1795, oil on canvas, 45.8 × 55.9 cm (18 × 22 in.), Philadelphia Museum of Art: The william L. Elkins Collection, 1924

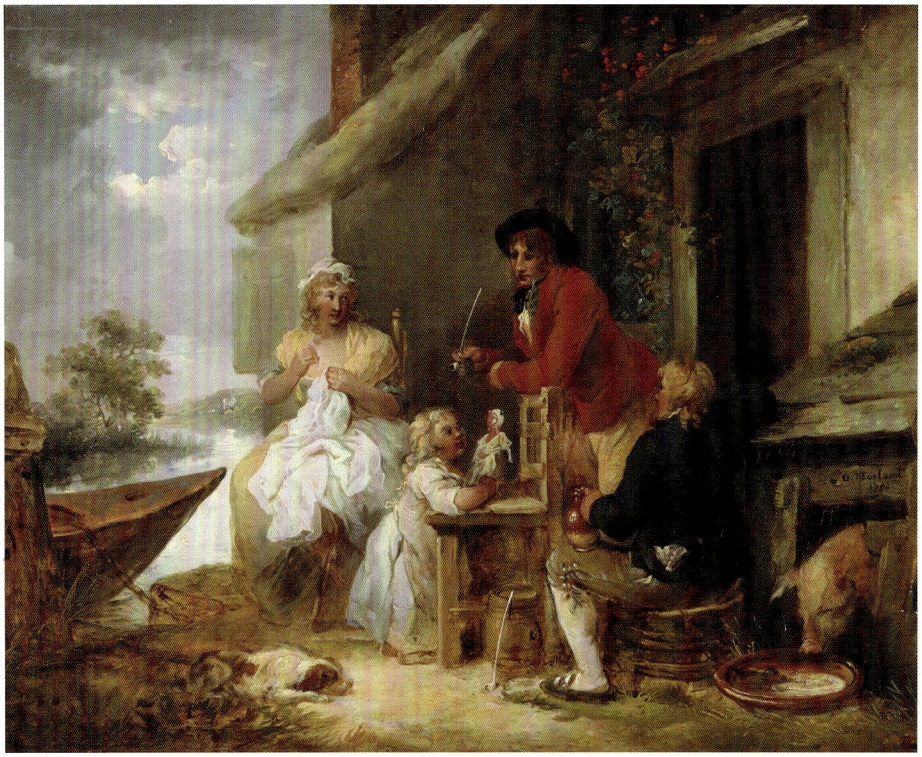

29 George Morland, *Cottage Door*, c. 1790, oil on canvas, 35.5 × 45.7 cm (14 × 18 in.), Royal Holloway College Art Gallery, University of London, Egham, Surrey

Later artists such as William Collins, known for his rustic genre scenes, also found rich material in Gainsborough's cottage doors. His popular *The Sale of the Pet Lamb* (fig. 30, 1837) owes much to the compositional formula of Gainsborough's *Cottage Door with Children Playing* (see pl. II).[94]

That the cottage-door paintings were known and admired by Gainsborough's contemporaries and by later artists is indicated not only by the fact that they

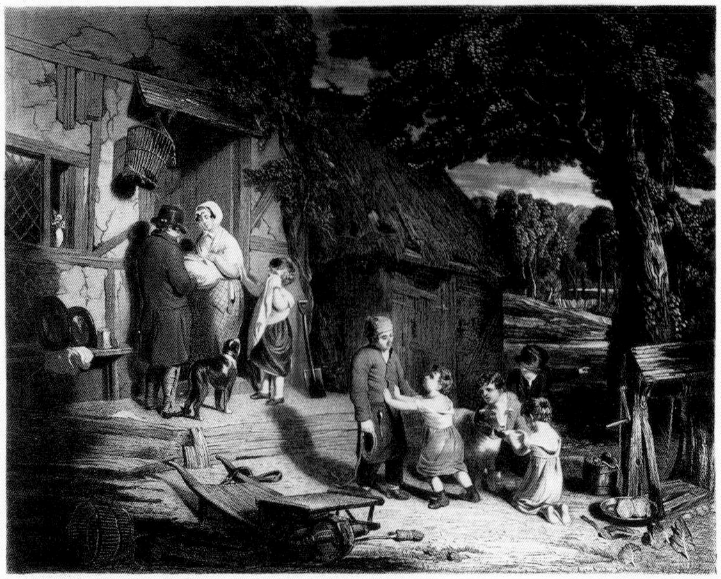

30 Samuel William Reynolds after William Collins, *The Sale of the Pet Lamb*, 1837, engraving, 47 × 51 cm ($18\frac{1}{2}$ × 20 in.), The Trustees of the British Museum, London, 1853-1-12-82

inspired subsequent works, and found their way into major collections, but also by the fact that they appear in exhibitions celebrating British art. Three cottage-door subjects were chosen to represent Gainsborough's work in the 1814 retrospective at the British Institution of Gainsborough, Reynolds, Zoffany, and Wilson, and two, the Huntington and Ipswich paintings, were exhibited at the 1857 "Art Treasures of the United Kingdom" at Manchester. Both exhibitions were intended to celebrate the masterpieces of British painting and in that sense they represent an effort to establish a canon of British works.

Looking at the treatment of cottage subjects in the nineteenth century, one finds a shift in focus from the exterior to the interior of the cottage. This is in large part because the later painters of cottage scenes drew inspiration not only from Gainsborough but also from the French artist Jean-Baptiste Greuze and David Teniers, among other Netherlandish artists. These French and northern artists depicted cottage interiors as settings for the comedies and tragedies of peasant life. David Wilkie, for instance, was known for his Teniers-like treatment of Scottish and English peasant subjects (fig. 31). These are no longer cottage doors but rural genre paintings proper. Perhaps because of their sources, in particular the examples of Greuze's work, nineteenth-century cottage subjects like Wilkie's have a pronounced moralizing tone. What had been an appeal to feelings of sympathy and benevolence in Gainsborough becomes instead a sermon on piety and dutiful domesticity. As John Barrell demonstrates here, the cottage scene as early as the 1790s was thoroughly embedded in conservative political notions of how the poor "should behave."

This is not to say that the cottage doors lost their appeal, but that their quiet meditations on rural retirement and pastoral simplicity were, as Barrell shows, overtaken by a counter-revolutionary politics that sought out unambiguous messages of moral reform. Nevertheless, to those who retained a feeling for the world evoked by Gainsborough, the cottage-door paintings radiated a nostalgic inten-

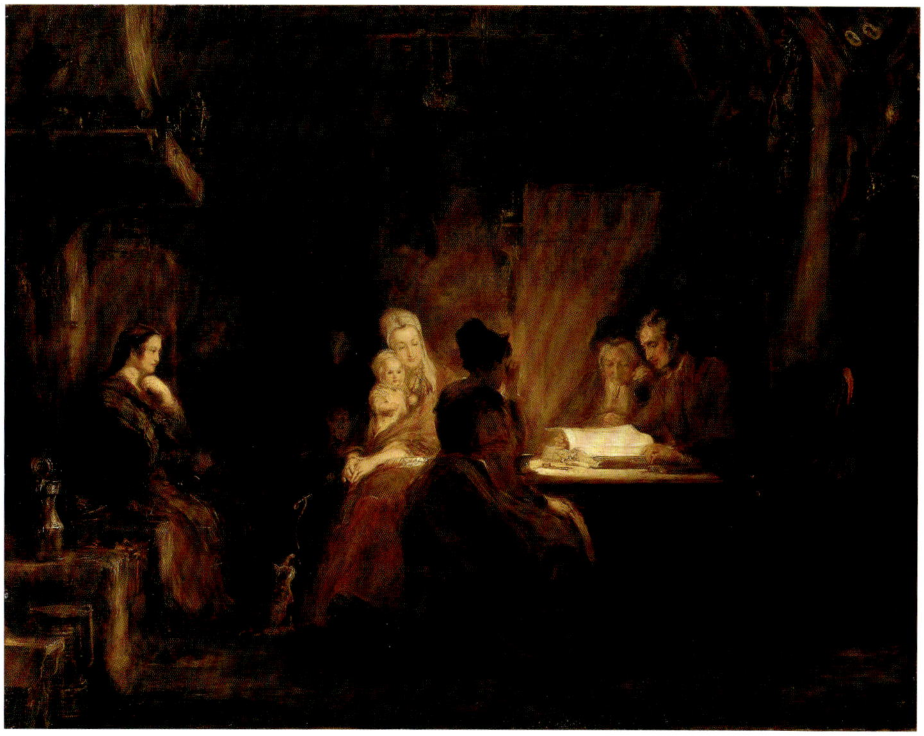

31 David Wilkie, *The Cotter's Saturday Night*, 1832–7, oil on panel, 83.8 × 108 cm (33 × 42½ in.), Glasgow Museums, Art Gallery and Museum, Kelvingrove

sity. In this regard, it is worth recalling what Constable told a London audience a year before his death in 1837:

> The landscape of Gainsborough is soothing, tender, and affecting. The stillness of noon, the depths of twilight, and the dews and pearls of the morning are all to be found on the canvases of this most benevolent and kind-hearted man. On looking at them, we find tears in our eyes, and know not what brings them. The lonely haunts of the solitary shepherd, – the return of the rustic with his bill and bundle of wood, – the darksome lane or dell, – the sweet little cottage girl at the spring with her pitcher, – were the things he delighted to paint, and which he painted with exquisite refinement, yet not refinement beyond nature.[95]

Constable's mention of the "return of the rustic with his bill and bundle of wood" indicates that some of the paintings he was thinking of were the cottage doors.

Constable's tears are evidence of the power of Gainsborough's paintings to touch and to move. They are in this sense the embodiment of sensibility. These paintings give visual expression to a movement that is most often discussed as a literary phenomenon. They show what sensibility looked like. Moreover, in its power to move, sensibility makes painting rhetorical. It gives painting work to do in the world. As Roger de Piles argued, the eloquence of painting seizes and transports the viewer. "True painting," he wrote, "not only surprises, but, as it were, calls to us; and has so powerful an effect, that we cannot help coming near it, as if it had something to tell us."[96] Rather than simple objects, treasured for their formal beauty and commercial value, paintings that embody sensibility call and reach out to their viewers. They are acts not objects. At a time when art, and Gainsborough's art in particular, was being collected and appreciated for the first time in a serious way by connoisseurs, collectors, and the British public, sensibility offered a role for art beyond that of mere commodity. In their vigorous brushwork, their reliance on optical fusion, and their poignant yet open-ended subjects, Gainsborough's cottage doors still challenge us today to respond sympathetically, to feel as they ask us to feel, and therefore to be in some degree changed by them.

Part One Cottages and *The Cottage Door*'s Cultural Significance

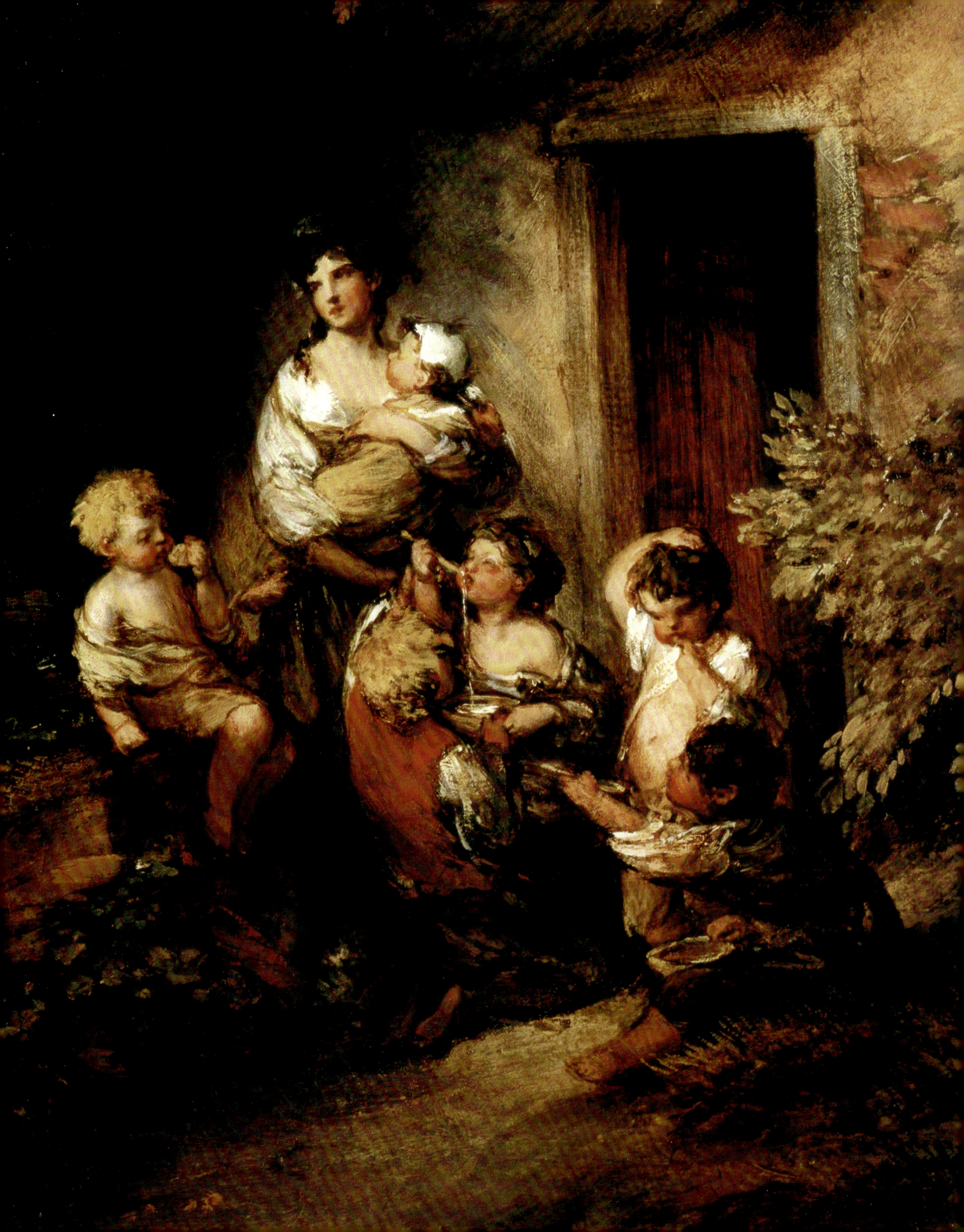

Susan Sloman

"Innocence and health": Nursing Women in Gainsborough's Cottage-door Paintings

Innocence and health, claimed Oliver Goldsmith in his poem *The Deserted Village*, are the "best companions" of the traditional laboring peasant.[1] Gainsborough's great series of cottage-door pictures, begun in Bath in the early 1770s, are possibly the most potent visual representations of innocence and health created in the eighteenth century. The canvases feature groups of young women watching over small children in the doorways of modest, but not ramshackle, country dwellings. The children are well-nourished (several are shown eating) and the women good-looking. The cottages are brick-built with glazed windows and smoke can be seen rising from the chimneys. In two of the four compositions a woodman carries home a bundle of fuel for the fire. Shiny cooking pots, brooms, piles of vegetables and contented family pets underline the impression that these households are efficiently managed.

It can be argued that these pictures represent a disappearing golden age (Goldsmith's "time . . . ere England's griefs began"), but here I suggest that they have more to do with events of Gainsborough's own day and that, although idealistic, they are not exclusively nostalgic in tone. They seem to represent the model environment for healthy child-rearing as envisaged by social reformers of the period.[2]

During the painter's lifetime the Foundling Hospital was set up to care for abandoned babies and the Parish Poor Act imposed new duties of care on London parishes (fig. 33). Both the Foundling Hospital and the parishes established schemes whereby infants were raised in the countryside with the benefits of fresh air, wholesome food, and, most importantly of all, healthy and responsible nurses. At the same time a "natural" approach to child-rearing became fashionable among the professional and moneyed classes. This is often associated with Rousseau, and the publication of *Emile*, but it is not hard to show that advice provided by London-based physicians for the charitable care of infants had a widespread effect, far beyond the bounds of the Foundling Hospital and the parishes. Dr William Cadogan, for example, Physician to the Foundling Hospital, advocated a natural style of upbringing in his *Essay upon Nursing and the Management of Children*. This sold so well that seven editions were printed between 1748 and 1757, all well before the arrival of *Emile* in 1762. Cadogan particularly recommended that "children should be kept clean and sweet, tumbled and tossed about a good deal, and carried out every day in all weathers . . ."[3] He believed that the healthiest infants "will from the impulse of

32 Thomas Gainsborough, *The Cottage Door* (detail of pl. III)

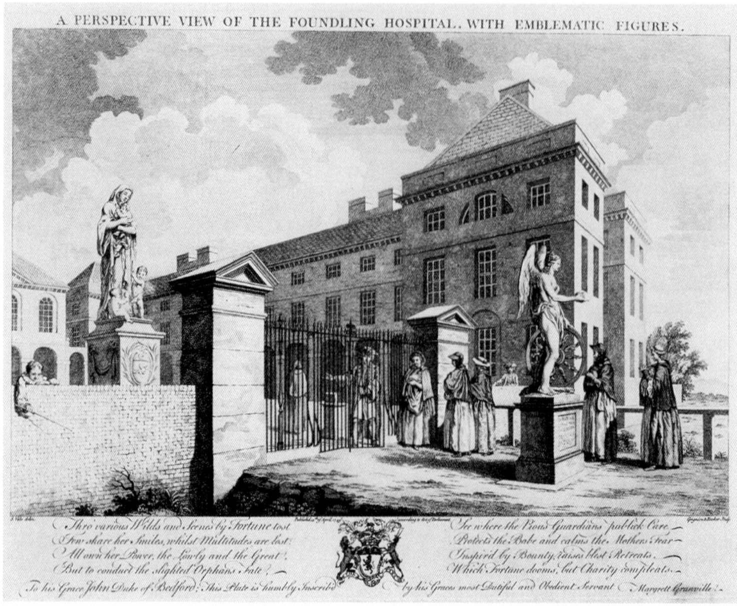

33 Charles Grignion after Samuel Wale, *A Perspective View of the Foundling Hospital, with Emblematic Figures of Fortuna* and *Charity*, 1749, engraving, 35.7 × 43.5 cm (14 × 17⅛ in.), Guildhall Library, London

their own active vigour, be found running, leaping, and playing, all day long."[4] Cadogan's advice follows that of an earlier physician, Dr George Cheyne (1671–1743), who wrote in 1724, "Tis beautiful to observe that earnest *Desire*, planted by *Nature*, in *Young* Persons, *to romp, jump, wrestle*, and *run*, and constantly to be pursuing *Exercises* and Bodily *Diversions*, that require *Labor*, even till they are ready to drop down . . ."[5] The Cincinnati cottage door painting might almost have been designed to illustrate this point (fig. 34 and pl. II).

Before examining the iconography of the cottage door pictures in more depth, it may be useful to consider the subject of Gainsborough's own health in relation to his career as a landscape painter. There are grounds for believing that the artist's observation of the countryside was connected with a personal quest for good health. The paintings, in turn, may have been conceived as illustrations of health that, when hung on people's walls, rewarded the receptive viewer with a sense of wellbeing.[6]

When Gainsborough decided to move to Bath in the late 1750s he was well aware of the city's reputation as a health spa, and the consequent advantages for his family and his career. The Gainsboroughs had suffered the death of their first child while living in London and the artist, who appears to have been a doting parent, was protective of his remaining two daughters. In a number of letters written from Bath in the 1760s, he also refers to his own physical frailty, even claiming in 1765, "my Ill Health forbids my following Business in London."[7] In fact, by 1765 Gainsborough's health seems to have been good, or at least much better than it had been in the autumn of 1763 when a severe illness, prompted by an injudicious encounter with a London prostitute, left the artist with what he described as a "Nervous complaint in the back part of my Head."[8] At its worst he found even the minimal mental exertion of writing a letter caused his head to throb.[9] On March 1, 1764 Gainsborough wrote to his friend James Unwin (who had been out of touch), "I really began to fear that your Nerves

34 (*facing page*) Thomas Gainsborough, *Cottage Door with Children Playing* (detail of pl. II)

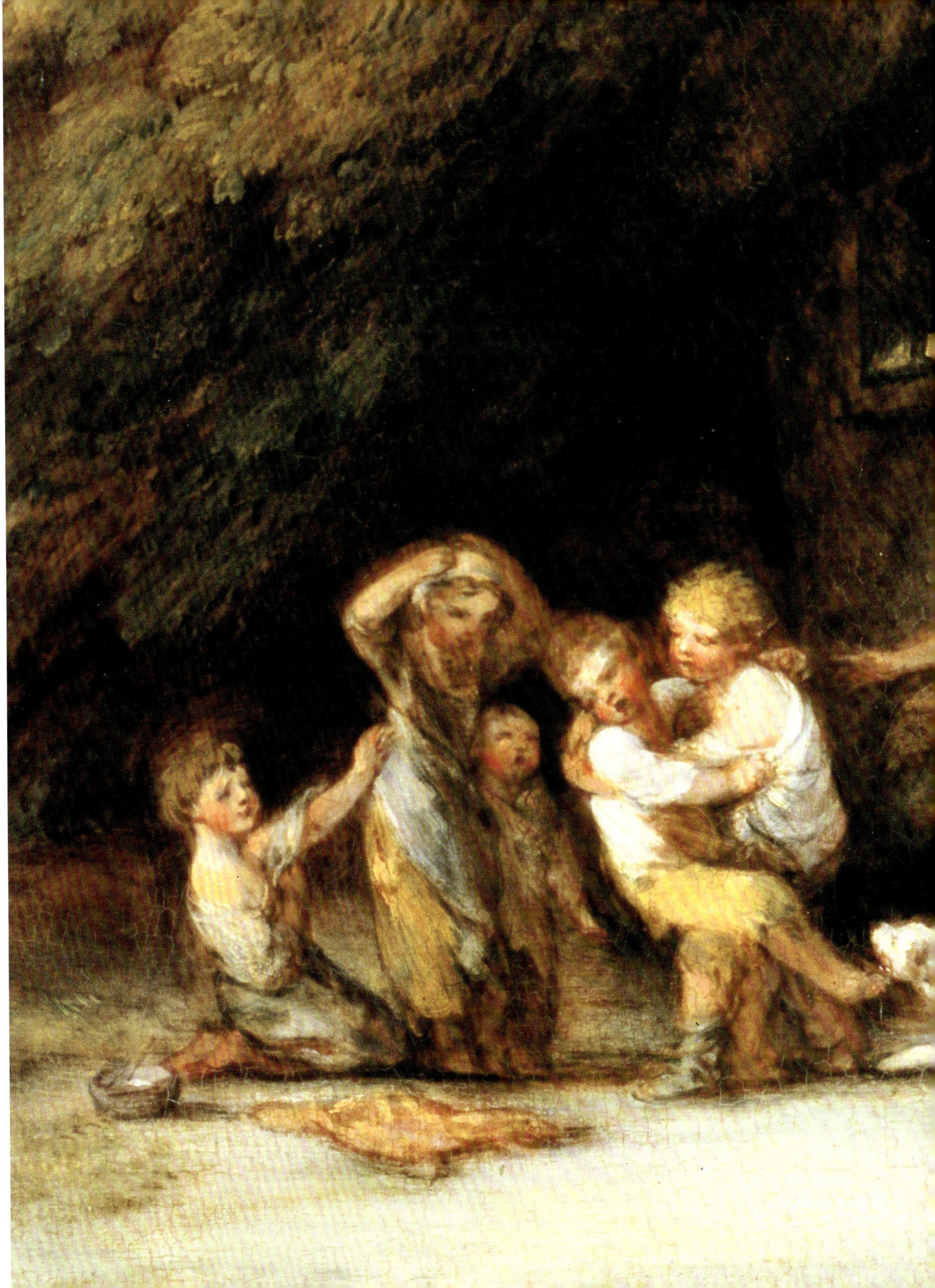

were bad too," adding that he himself was now much improved.[10] By July 1764 he reported to Unwin "Thank God I have got the better of all my Complaints both real & imaginary; I don't remember to have enjoy'd better health & spirits any part of my life than at present."[11] Bouts of illness did, however, recur. In August 1768 Gainsborough reported to David Garrick that he was now restored to health, but at the end of October 1771 his attention to his sick daughter Mary rendered him "very indifferent."[12] After the artist's death his other daughter Margaret told Joseph Farington her father "had not strong health and frequently complained."[13]

Following his near-fatal illness of 1763 Gainsborough took two important steps to hasten his recovery. He rented a new family home in the fresh air of Lansdown Hill, keeping his town-center house for painting and displaying his work. He also embarked on a regime of vigorous physical exercise that involved riding on horseback for long periods every day. He described this arrangement to Unwin: "I have taken a House about three quarters of a mile in the Lansdown Road. tis sweetly situated. . . . I Ride every minute in the Day unless it rains pouring; and do intend when I can, to be down from eleven to one o'clock, in my office, but not a moment longer for the King."[14] Gainsborough seems to have continued riding as much as possible throughout his residence in Bath. In August 1767 he reported "I have been riding out with [John Palmer] this Morn[g]," and it was also in the 1760s that Ozias Humphry and Uvedale Price regularly accompanied him on country rides. Gainsborough's horse had been given to him by his friend and patron Sir William St Quintin and was affectionately described by the painter as "not handsom but perfectly sure footed & steady upon the Road."[15] Sir William was well qualified to select a suitable animal, having been the owner of a famous racing stable and stud in Yorkshire, an establishment that contributed to the Duke of Cumberland's successful racing stock.[16]

Gainsborough's exercise regime is most likely to have been inspired by the same George Cheyne who wrote with such perspicacity on the joys of unfettered childhood (fig. 35). Cheyne, originally from Aberdeen, settled in Bath in 1718 and his influence in the city outlasted the century. He was a scholar, a follower of Newton who wrote a number of scientific treatises, but it was through his self-help medical books that he was best remembered.[17] These were based on personal experience – he suffered from depression linked to obesity – and his larger-than-life personality made an impression on countless Bath residents and visitors. He was described by one of his patients, the poet Alexander Pope, as "so very a child in true Simplicity of Heart," and his writings lie at the root of eighteenth-century sensibility.[18] The Bath poet Mary Chandler (1687–1744) died of "extreme sensibility," partly caused by an over-zealous devotion to Dr Cheyne's ascetic diet.[19] Cheyne had reversed his own physical and mental decline by ceasing to live permanently in London, becoming a vegetarian and riding "on Horseback, ten or fifteen Miles a Day, both Summer and Winter."[20] According to Cheyne, of all forms of exercise, riding was "certainly the most *Manly*," and "To those who have weak *Nerves* and *Digestion*, and to those who are much troubled with *Head-aches*," he recommended "riding on *Horseback* as much as

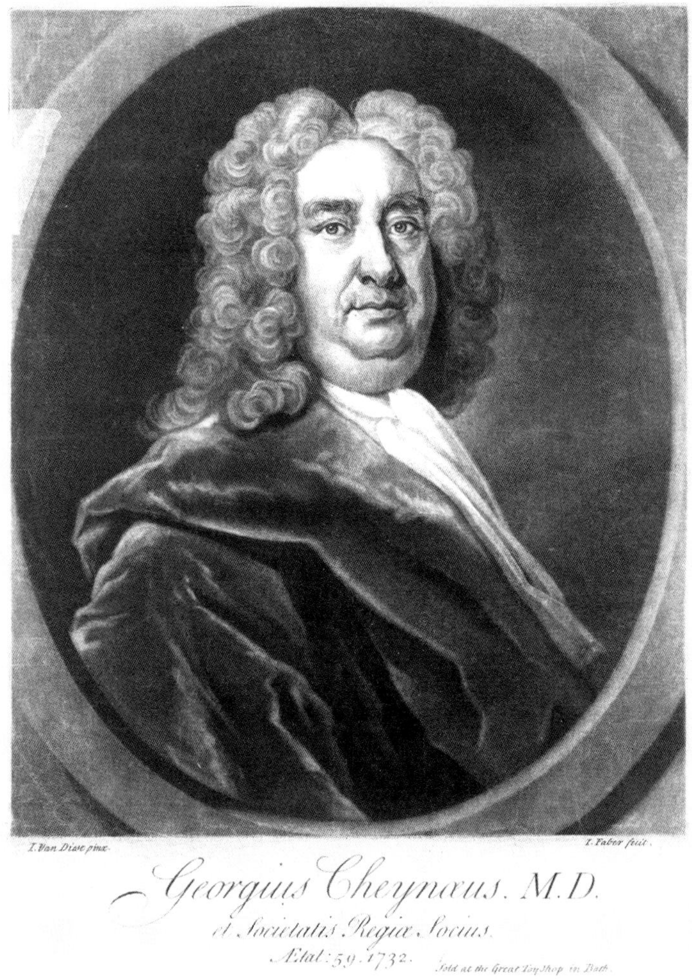

35 John Faber the Younger after Johann Baptiste Van Diest, *Dr George Cheyne*, 1732, mezzotint, 35 × 23.8 cm ($13\frac{3}{4} \times 9\frac{3}{8}$ in.), Wellcome Library, London

possibly they could."[21] He classified the "nervous distempers" that required this form of cure as diseases of the educated and the wealthy. In Cheyne's experience he "seldom ever observ'd a *heavy, dull, earthly, clod-pated Clown*, much troubled with *nervous* Disorders."[22] Riding in the countryside had the benefits of "variously twitching the Nervous Fibres, to brace and contract them, as new Scenes amuse the mind" and bodily movement in an upright posture, which he believed to be the most "natural Motion of all the Organs."[23] For those physically unable to ride he recommended they should be carried in a coach or litter; those unable to go out of doors could improve their health by riding an artificial horse in their lodgings. Samuel Richardson was one such patient who claimed to have found his daily hour of bouncing on a "chamber-horse" to be of "great Benefit."[24]

George Cheyne appears to have been admired and laughed at in equal measure. Oliver Goldsmith described him as "a man of some wit and breeding" but took great delight in recording Beau Nash's alleged reaction to a consultation:

> Doctor *Cheney* [*sic*] once, when *Nash* was ill, drew up a prescription for him, which was sent in accordingly. The next day the Doctor coming to see his patient found him up and well; upon which he asked, if he had followed his prescription? Followed your prescription, cried *Nash*, No. – Egad, if I had, I should have broke my neck, for I flung it out of the two pair of stairs window.[25]

Gainsborough seems to have been making a joke about riding as a remedy for all ills when he endorsed a recipe for a cough cure: having written out the method of concocting the medicine (presumably for a friend), he signed the note, "This Cured Mr Gainsbro: of a galloping/Consumption witness my Hand /TG./Riding is included!."[26]

Joking aside, there is no doubt that Cheyne's publications on diet and health were among the most widely read books of the century.[27] Gainsborough's friend the Reverend Richard Graves attributed his own recovery from a nervous fever and persistent headaches to reading Cheyne, and as late as 1790 Dr William Falconer declared that "exercise . . . principally on horseback, is absolutely necessary to be joined with [the Bath waters]."[28] Goldsmith's *Life of Richard Nash*, which assumes a knowledge of Cheyne, was published during Gainsborough's residence in Bath, in 1762. There is even evidence that Bath's premier pastry-cook, Charles Gill, famous for his cooked meats and pies, applied Cheyne's principles when it came to the health of his own family. Gill's artist son Charles, a pupil of Joshua Reynolds, fell ill in London in 1772, though only mildly ill according to his fellow pupil James Northcote. The response of young Gill's parents was to withdraw him from Reynolds's studio and send him "to live in the country and drink milk," a classic Cheyne-inspired cure.[29] When, in the midst of his illness, Gainsborough mentioned observing the exact quantity of food and exercise best for him, he must have been referring directly to the advice of his personal physician Rice Charleton, but Charleton too followed in Cheyne's footsteps.[30] At this same time Charleton was giving the artist cinchona bark, Dr Cheyne's favourite eliminative cure, believed to deal with clogging of the "fibres" of the body and the last element (after exercise and diet) in his three-pronged attack on nervous complaints.[31]

One cannot tell whether Gainsborough benefited physically from the stimulation of his optic "fibres" on his country rides, but he certainly used the occasions to gather into his visual memory a store of images that lasted a lifetime. Uvedale Price recalled the frequent excursions he made with the artist in the 1760s, and how Gainsborough reacted with "particular gentleness" to "cottage or village scenes, to groups of children, or to any objects of that kind that struck his fancy."[32] Writing with the benefit of hindsight, Ozias Humphry claimed that the greater part of Gainsborough's landscapes owed their origin to his rides around Bath.[33] Certainly the cottage-door composition, first committed to canvas in 1772–3, never wavered far from its original conception, although changes of emphasis and detail are worked out through a large number of drawings, and the paintings vary between a portrait and a landscape format.

The earliest cottage door was the subject of a poem published in the *Gentleman's Magazine* in December 1773 (pl. 1).[34] It was replicated by Gainsborough

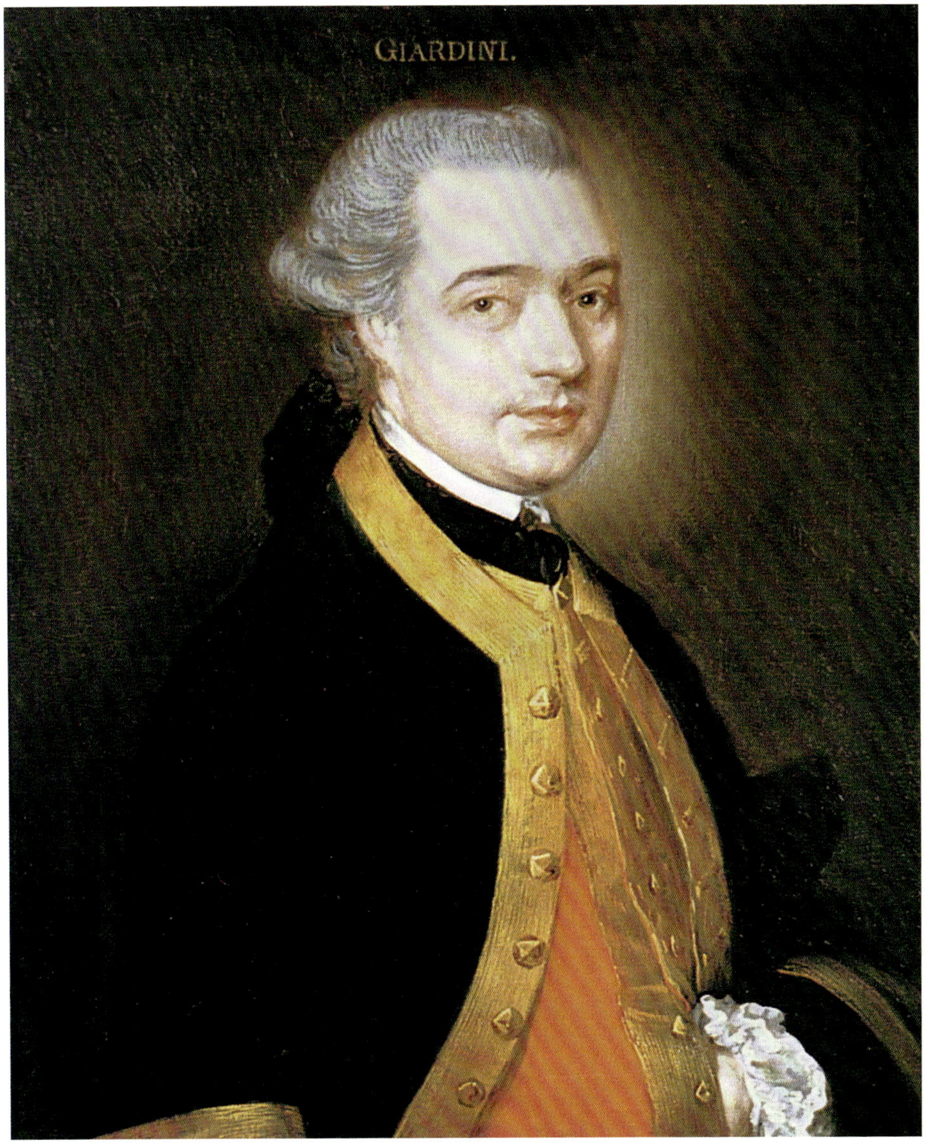

36 Thomas Gainsborough, *Felice de' Giardini*, early 1760s, oil on canvas, 76.2 × 63.5 cm (30 × 25 in.), private collection

for the musician Felice de' Giardini some time before February 1774, at which time the artist referred to it as a "Cottage & ragged Family" (fig. 36).[35] Giardini had been a governor of the Foundling Hospital since 1770 and assisted in its musical programs. In 1773–4 he was actively involved in trying to set up a national music school at the Hospital.[36] The second cottage-door composition (now in Cincinnati) is generally believed to be the picture exhibited at the Royal Academy in 1778, and the Huntington picture was that shown at the Academy in 1780 (pls. II and III). The final and largest canvas, now the property of the University of California, dates from 1788, the year of the artist's death (pl. V). The Cincinnati canvas was offered for sale by Miss Margaret Gainsborough in February 1799 for 180 guineas: Joseph Farington, who viewed it at the time, called it "Cottage – Boys wrestling" to distinguish it from the 1788 painting which was priced at 250 guineas, and which he called "Upright Cottage – man smoaking."[37]

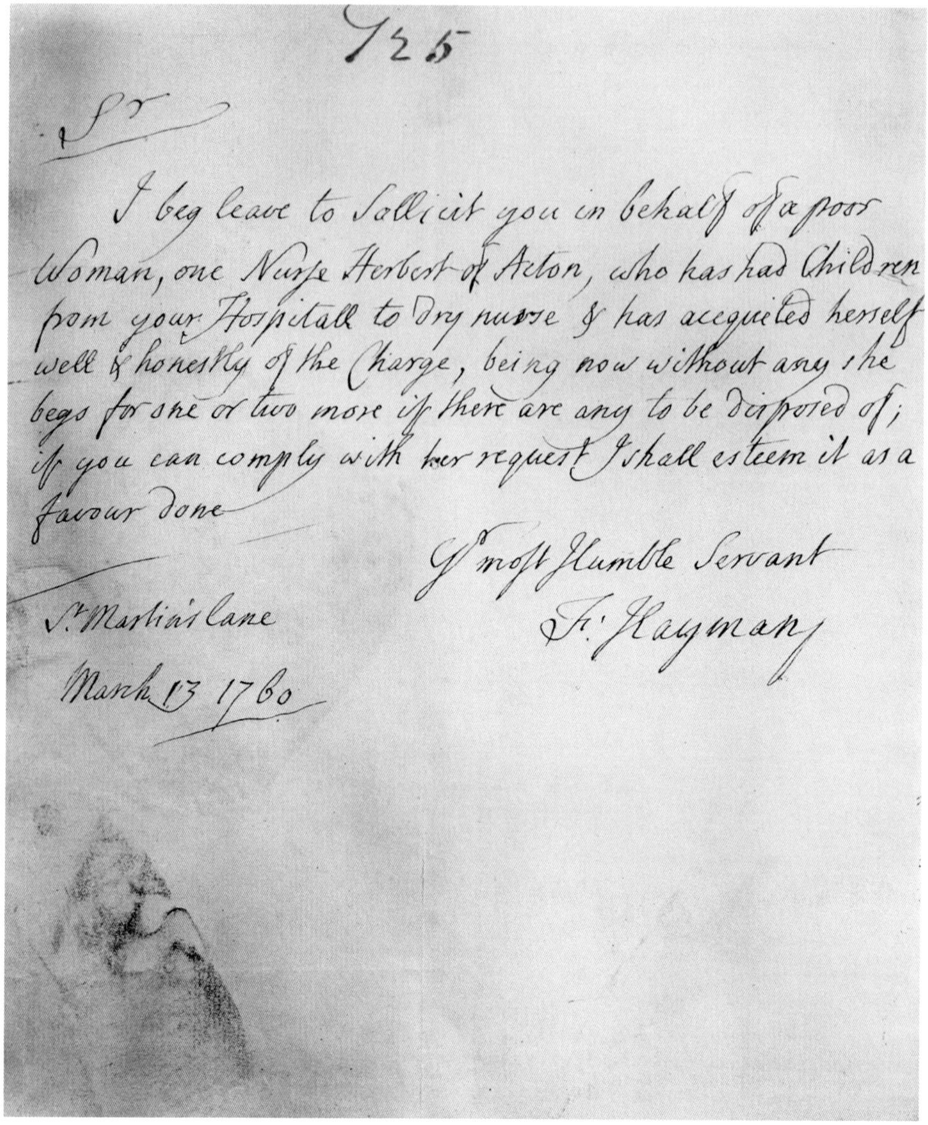
125

Sr

I beg leave to Sollicit you in behalf of a poor Woman, one Nurse Herbert of Acton, who has had Children from your Hospitall to Dry nurse & has acquited herself well & honestly of the Charge, being now without any she begs for one or two more if there are any to be disposed of; if you can comply with her request I shall esteem it as a favour done

Yr most Humble Servant

Fr. Hayman

St Martin's Lane

March 13 1760

37 Francis Hayman, letter addressed to Thomas Collingwood, secretary of the Foundling Hospital, 1760, London Metropolitan Archives

The summary descriptions of the cottage-door paintings given by early commentators and the Royal Academy catalogues (where they were simply called "Landscape") give little idea of how they were interpreted at the time. Natural child-rearing was, however, a live topic, especially among those who considered themselves forward-looking and fashionable members of society. The problem of abandoned babies was also one from which no one could escape – Sir Joshua Reynolds had a baby dumped on his doorstep, as did many other affluent city dwellers.[38] As indicated already, the literature associated with natural child-rearing dates back to the early years of the Foundling Hospital. Between 1741 and 1745, before its grand purpose-built Bloomsbury premises were completed, the Hospital occupied two houses in Hatton Garden. From 1743 or 1744 until 1749, Gainsborough himself lived in Hatton Garden, just a few yards from the temporary Foundling buildings, so he was well aware of the charity's activities even before he became personally involved by painting one of the roundels for the

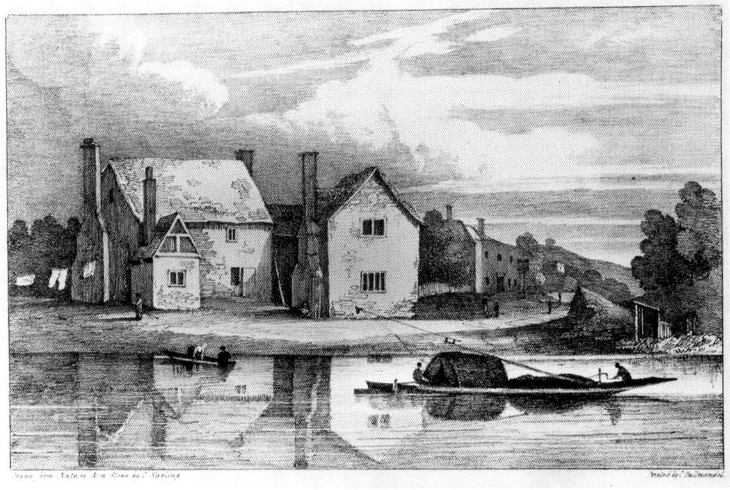

38 Charles Hullmandel after Charles Stirling, *Near Chertsey Bridge, Surrey*, c. 1840, lithograph, 13.6 × 21.5 cm ($5\frac{3}{8}$ × $8\frac{7}{16}$ in.), Guildhall Library, Corporation of London

council room of the new building.[39] The Hospital admitted children within two months of birth. They were sent out to be nursed and cared for in the countryside until the age of four or five, when they returned to the Hospital to be educated for a trade.[40] Children were placed as far afield as Yorkshire, Staffordshire, Derbyshire, and Lincolnshire but the majority were nearer London, in such areas as Chalfont, Epsom, Romford, and Staines.[41] The country foster-mothers were obliged to remain indistinguishable from their neighbours and the children not allowed to display any mark of the Hospital, rules that were designed to discourage public curiosity and the danger of abduction.[42] The nurses were monitored and their salaries paid by specially appointed inspectors, among whom were Gainsborough's banker Bertie Burgh and the painter William Hogarth, both of whom were governors of the Hospital.[43] Gainsborough's mentor Francis Hayman was also a governor. A letter from Hayman soliciting support for "Nurse Herbert of Acton" survives in the Foundling Hospital archive (fig. 37).[44] Another inspector well-known to Gainsborough was James Clutterbuck, the person for whom he painted as a gift a version of his portrait of the actor David Garrick.[45] Clutterbuck, a successful mercer in the Strand, oversaw children in the vicinity of his country retreat at Richmond.[46] Papers from this period of the Hospital's history provide startling evidence of the duties of the inspectors: one Mr Ward, reporting on a country wet-nursed child in January 1759, noted "the bottom bad with Clouts."[47] Hogarth was apparently a conscientious inspector in Chiswick and Clutterbuck in Richmond, but Burgh was ill-suited to the job. Already in personal financial difficulties by the late 1750s he managed, incredibly, to make himself responsible for more than four hundred children in the region of Chertsey in Surrey, only to abscond with the funds provided to pay the nurses (fig. 38).[48]

Despite setbacks of this kind, the Foundling Hospital was judged a success and one of its governors, Jonas Hanway, instigated a campaign to draw attention to the fate of children abandoned to parish care in London. A parliamentary committee examined parish records from between 1754 and 1762, although it was also noted that as early as 1715 a report had been written on the "Barbar-

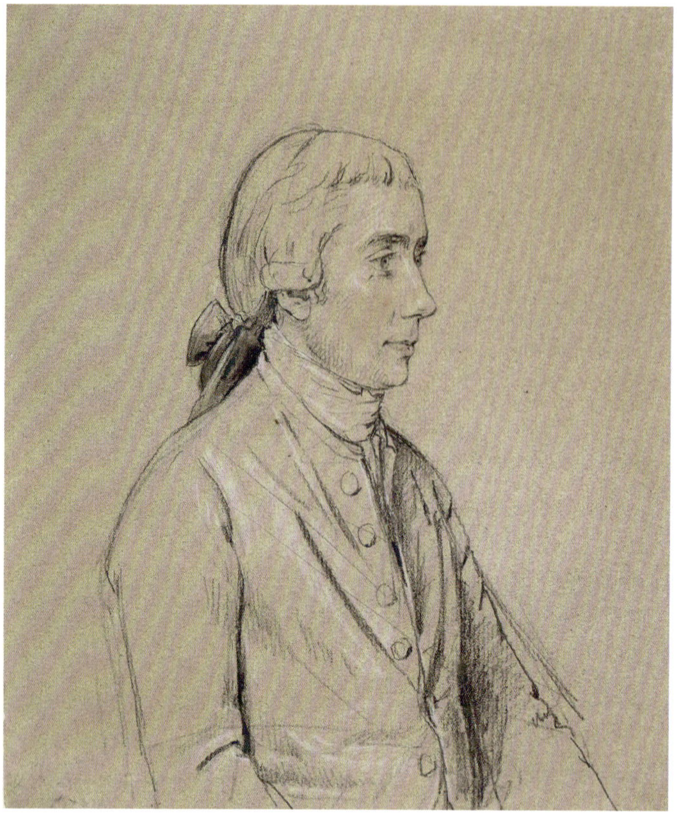

39 John Downman, *Dr Hugh Downman*, 1778, black, red, and white chalk on brown paper, 23 × 19.3 cm ($9\frac{1}{16} \times 7\frac{5}{8}$ in.), Fitzwilliam Museum, Cambridge

ity of Nurses" hired by churchwardens.[49] The 1760s enquiry found that certain parishes had already adopted the Foundling Hospital model – St James, Westminster, for example, boarded out its children with carefully selected cottagers on Wimbledon Common – but others left children to die in workhouses or in the care of unscrupulous nurses. It was concluded that parishes should participate in the Foundling Hospital scheme and send all children under the age of six out of London to be nursed, with those under two placed at least five miles from the Cities of London and Westminster, and those under six at least three miles. A reward of ten shillings was given to foster-mothers who successfully raised babies sent to them at under nine months, this being in addition to the standard two shillings and six pence weekly wage. The Parish Poor Act of 1767 was reviewed in 1778, when it was found to have produced "very salutary effects."[50]

Hand in hand with this new awareness of healthy child-rearing at an institutional level came a movement toward natural nursing among the middle and upper classes. Since the 1740s William Cadogan had strongly advocated breast-feeding by mothers, with wet-nursing by country foster-mothers as the most acceptable alternative. When the vogue for breast-feeding in fashionable society was at its height the Exeter doctor Hugh Downman published *Infancy, or the Management of Children*, a poem issued in three instalments between 1774 and 1776 (fig. 39). Downman, a relative of the artist John Downman, hails women who feed their own babies as "Ye real Mothers! Ye whose Hearts are full of Sensibility!," but concedes that not every woman might be able to fulfil this ideal.

For those who require nurses he advises:

> . . . Far from the Bounds
> Of the rank City, let some trusty Friend
> Explore the straw-built Cott; there, firm of Nerve
> Her Blood from every grosser Particle
> By hardy Labour and abstemious Fare
> Sublim'd; the honest Peasant's Mate shall ope
> Her Hospitable Arms, receive with Joy
> The infant Stranger.[51]

These words were published within a year of the completion of Gainsborough's first cottage-door painting. Suitable "straw-built Cotts" and peasant mothers were sought all over Britain. In Ireland, the city of Dublin boasted nearby green hills and mountains that made ideal nursery areas. The Irish playwright John O'Keeffe, an acquaintance of Gainsborough, remembered a young friend who "was nursed in the mountains of Wicklow, and when an infant his father and I took many a walk to see him." O'Keeffe himself was nursed "on the commons of Crumlin, near the Green Hills," and he placed his own daughter with Fanny Burke, a nurse who lived "In a straw-thatched cabin, at Rathfarnham, near Dublin, close to Lord Ely's Gate . . ."[52] An English writer, recording a visit to London in 1774, describes walking out to Richmond with his cousin "to See his child where its att nurse. Stay'd near 3 Hours there to see them Play Crickett on the green."[53]

The affection felt by good foster-parents for their charges is often remarked. John O'Keeffe's daughter was by 1786 a pupil at a school in Lincoln's Inn Fields. That year Patrick Burke, husband of the wet-nurse Fanny Burke, traveled all the way to London in order to see the little girl.[54] Following the death in 1783 of Prince Octavius, the second youngest of the royal children, his former wet-nurse Mrs Harris begged to be allowed into Westminster Abbey for the funeral. The king was apparently so moved by this gesture that he afterward sent a letter of appreciation to Mrs Harris.[55] The royal wet-nurses were, as might be expected, of a higher social standing than most. One, Mrs Muttlebury, was the wife of a customs official who in later life lived in a beautiful house on the West Cliff at Brighton; another, Mrs Williams, was married to an East India Company captain.[56]

London newspapers regularly carried advertisements placed by nurses and by families seeking nurses. These tell us much about the qualities of the ideal nurse. In addition to the obvious necessity of possessing "an exceedingly good Breast of Milk," nurses might live advantageously "in an open airy Part of the Town."[57] Some of those advertising as nurses had sufficient milk for two young babies, others had lost their own child soon after birth. All stress their own good health and character (fig. 40). Those wanting a nurse could afford to be choosy: one advertiser hoped to find a woman "from 25 to 30 years of Age, neither tall or lusty, of a clear Complexion."[58] A clear complexion was, among other things, a sign of freedom from venereal disease. Hogarth, in his paintings, had regularly used the presence of facial patches to identify prostitutes and other undesirables, knowing that such symbolism would have been immediately recognizable to his viewers. Facial features could also be read at a deeper level, as a means of interpreting character. A nursing manual of the early nineteenth century pays much attention to the outward signs of a suitable nurse. According to *The Good Nurse*,

> A woman who has a healthy complexion, with sound teeth and gums, and a moderate-sized breast, bears the exterior marks of a desirable foster-mother. We may judge of her natural and acquired character in a great measure from her countenance; her eye will discover to us whether she possesses a mild and affectionate disposition, and the form of her mouth will give a correct idea if her temper be amiable. Those who have studied physiognomy may ascertain the outline of character from observing the countenance: but those who are not so well skilled as Lavater may be deceived, however acute their discernment.[59]

Elsewhere the *Good Nurse* recommends the foster-mother who "breathes the fine morning air at sunrise, and labours through the day with the door of her cottage open," observing that the same woman could not sustain "that luxuriant and delightful state of health" if immured in hot carpeted rooms without access to pure air.[60] The words used call to mind Gainsborough's reported grumble that portraiture forced him to "stew" in "an elegant carpeted damn'd dungeon, with *two* windows shut, and *one half-open*, to paint *fools' heads*."[61]

There can be no doubt that Gainsborough would have been aware of the benefits of country child-rearing. It is likely he knew of Bertie Burgh's unfortunate connection with the Foundling Hospital through Burgh's partner James Unwin who continued an intimate friend. Apart from Hogarth, Giardini, and James Clutterbuck, many of Gainsborough's other associates were also governors of the Hospital, including the painters William Hoare (appointed in 1744) and Francis Hayman (1749), the sitters Welbore Ellis (1757), Robert Nugent (1759), Ralph Leycester (1767), Sir William St Quintin (1771), Ralph Bell (1771), and John Piggott (1786).[62] Gainsborough must also have been familiar with Hanway's well publicized efforts to improve the lot of parish workhouse children, and he painted a full-length portrait of one of Hanway's closest friends John Thornton (1720–90).[63] Gainsborough's friend and sitter the Reverend William Dodd was also a supporter of the first dispensary catering for childhood diseases, and preached a sermon, "Compassion to Infants Enforced," for the benefit of the dispensary in 1773.[64] Almost everyone, it seems, had a view on the merits of "natural" child-rearing as it affected their own families. Sir William Chambers, for example, took strong exception to the old-fashioned methods being used to nurse his grandchild, fearing "the worst consequences" as a result of the infant being "heavily Cloathed all day, Nursed in a Room with a constant large fire, put to bed Swaddled round with blankets and loaded with two or three more on the bed."[65] The Reverend Richard Graves, who was thankful to Cheyne for his own cure, ran a school just outside Bath and took a keen interest in all matters connected with the care of children. In December 1762 he reported that Rousseau's *Emile* was making "some noise" in Bath. It contained, he thought, "some good observations on nursing – & management of infants. But [Rousseau] is verbose pedantick & chimerical."[66]

40 Thomas Gainsborough, *The Cottage Door with Children Playing* (detail of pl. 11)

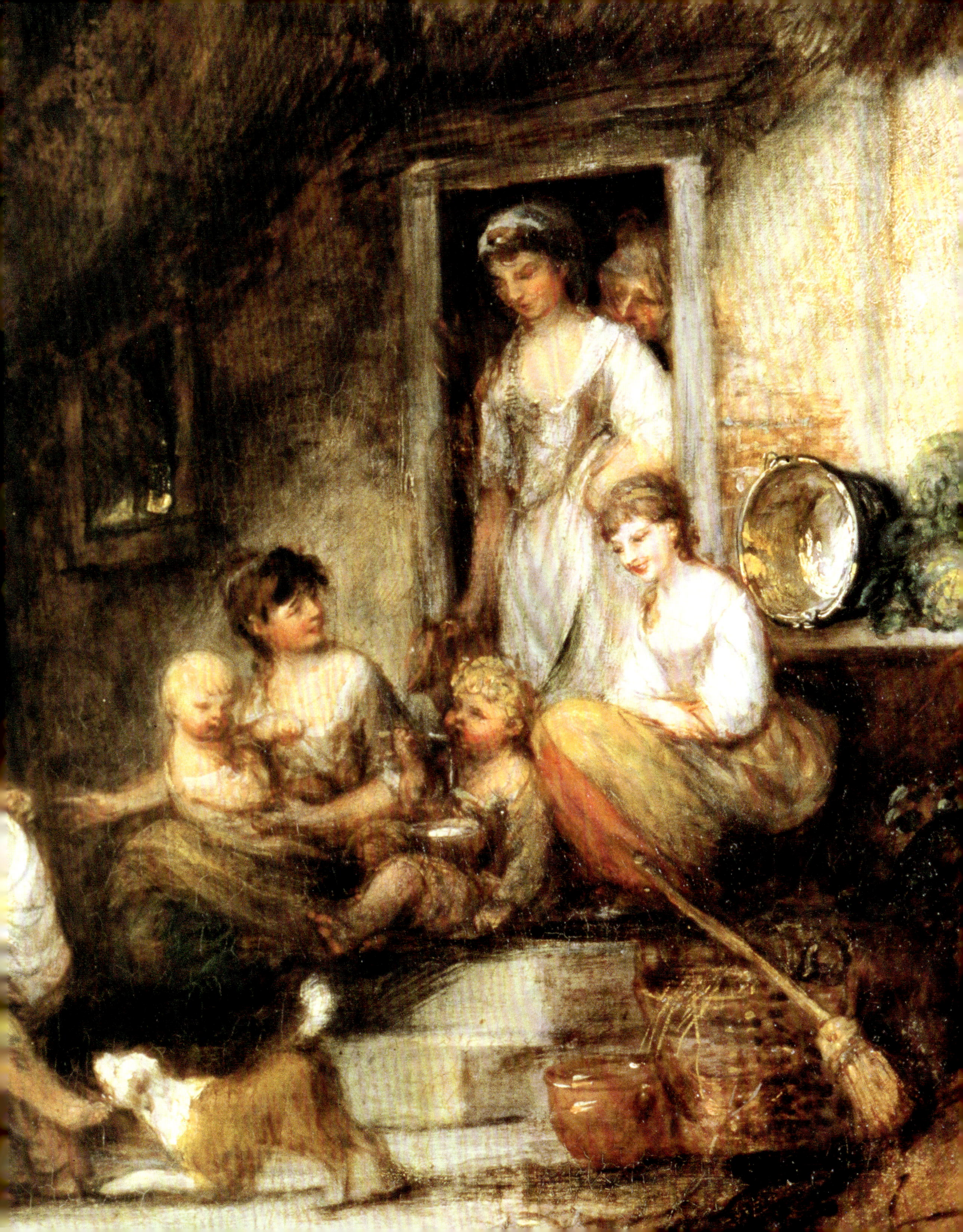

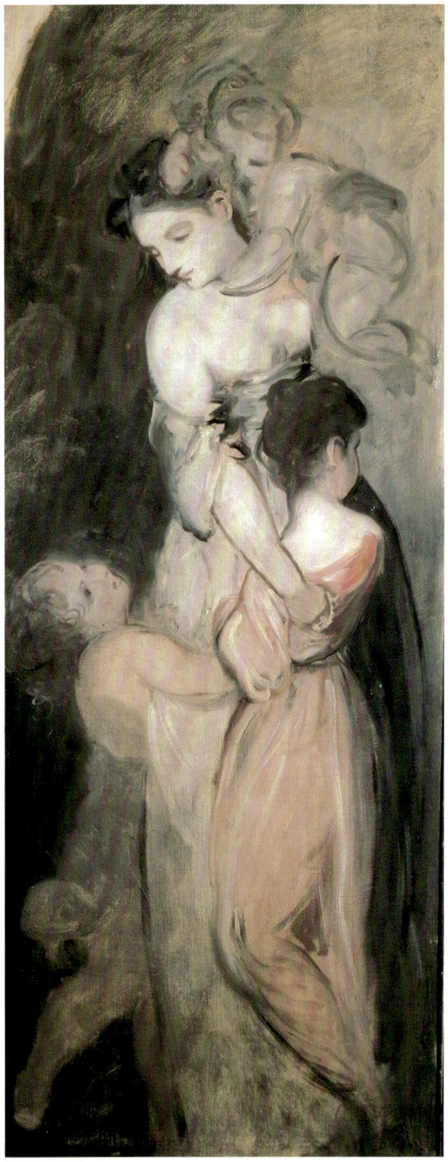

In broad art-historical terms Gainsborough's pyramidal groups of spot-lit figures in the *Cottage Door* reflect earlier representations of Charity and the Nativity (fig. 32 and pl. III).[67] These two themes are, of course, connected, and allusions of this kind make perfect sense if one associates the cottage-door pictures with the charitable care of infants. The emotion expressed through colour, light, and brushwork suggests that Gainsborough was not just painting landscapes with incidental figures, but a subject that held some deep personal meaning. It is interesting to learn that Reynolds's rejection of the infant left outside his house caused a writer in the *Morning Herald* to muse on Reynolds's painting of *Charity* for New College, Oxford and that artist's apparent lack of charity when faced with a practical problem on his own doorstep (fig. 41). The subject had evidently not proved "sufficiently inspiring" to the great man.[68] Gainsborough was sufficiently moved by his theme to return to it over and over again in a host of drawings and the four well-known paintings, not surprisingly, given his preoccupation with matters of health, his devotion to his own children, and his reputation for impulsive and generous acts of charity. The down-to-earth iconography of the cottage doors is all his own, but there is one earlier work of art that seems to have made a particular impression. Significantly, this is John Michael Rysbrack's *Allegory of Charity* designed as a chimney-piece for the Foundling Hospital in 1746 (fig. 42). The classically inspired infants depicted by Rysbrack are paralleled in the cottage pictures and there is even a curious echo between Rysbrack's child carrying a sheaf of corn and Gainsborough's woodmen who always seem too small in scale when compared with the main figure group.

Gainsborough's contemporaries would certainly have viewed the cottage-door canvases in the light of an approach to health and to childhood that is quite foreign to present-day experience. Those like Giardini, who were actively involved with the charitable care of infants, might have seen the ideal families Gainsborough depicted as models for the care they hoped to provide for the most needy in English society. By hanging his cottage-door picture in his lodg-

41 Sir Joshua Reynolds, *Charity* (sketch for part of a stained-glass window for New College, Oxford), 1777–9, oil on canvas, 213 × 83.8 cm ($83\frac{7}{8}$ × 33 in.), Ashmolean Museum, Oxford

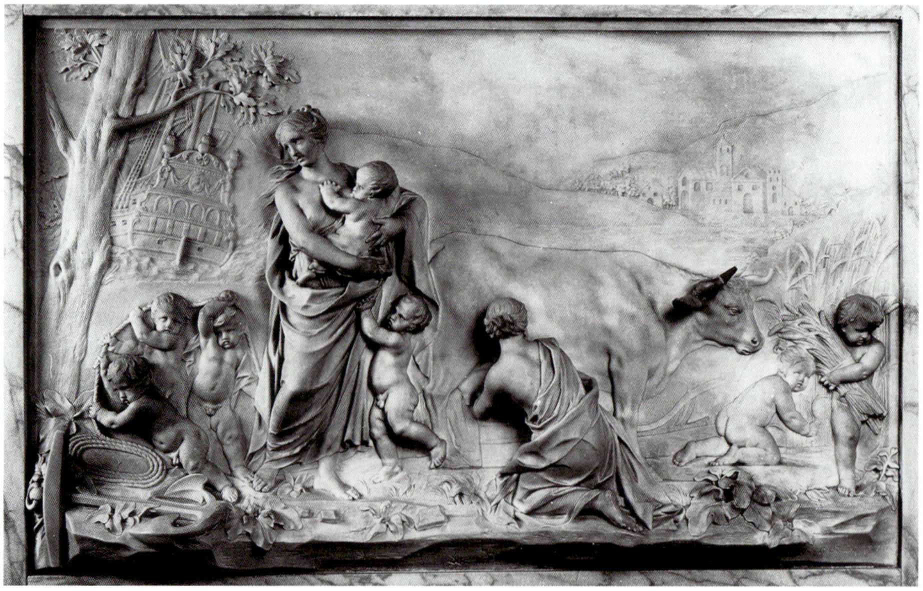

42 John Michael Rysbrack, *An Allegory of Charity*, c. 1746, detail of the marble chimney-piece in the Court Room, formerly in the Foundling Hospital, now in the Foundling Museum, London

ings, or perhaps in his public music rooms, Giardini may consciously have drawn attention to his personal involvement with the Foundling Hospital. At the very least he and his friends would have reflected on Gainsborough's remarkably *sensible* depiction of infancy and the English countryside.

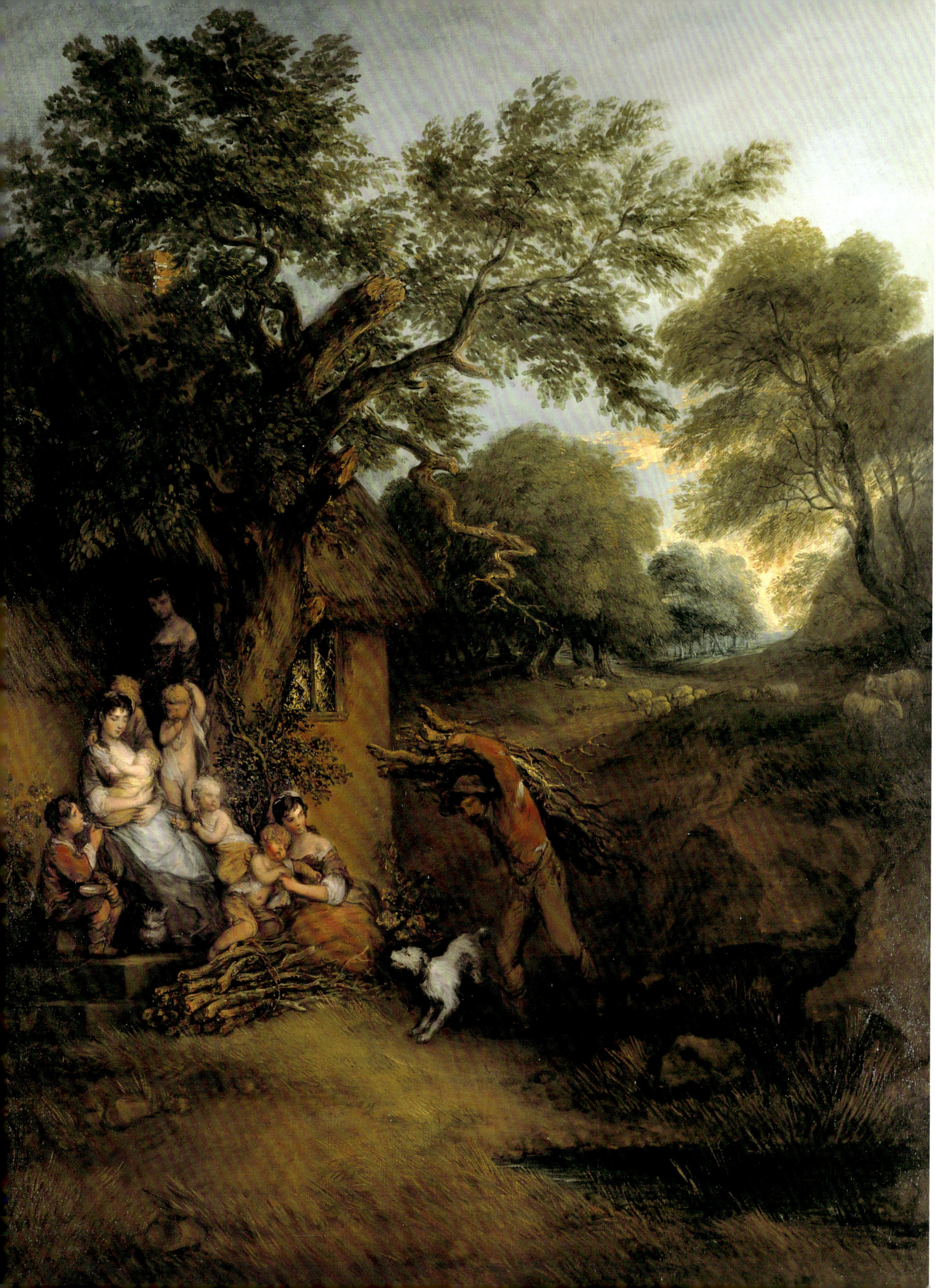

John Barrell

Spectacles for Republicans

In the 1770s and 1780s, at Bath and then in London, Thomas Gainsborough painted a series of landscapes in which rustic women and their children gathered in front of cottage doors.[1] The cottages were not situated in villages but isolated, usually in woodland glades. The children were cherubic and the women were well dressed, strikingly pretty, and apparently too young, one might think, to have borne so many children. These were evening scenes, and the family groups were usually waiting for the father of the household, seemingly imagined as the sole breadwinner, to return from work and complete the family circle (fig. 43 and pl. I). Often he is in view, bent and struggling toward the cottage under a burden of firewood, underwood perhaps collected from the forest floor. The light, however, falls not on him but on the women and children, so that his dark or dun-colored figure accentuates the contrast between his labor and their relative leisure – though sometimes a woman is shown holding a broom or a baby to mark her role in the family economy. Only in the last and largest of these scenes, *Peasant Smoking at a Cottage Door* (fig. 44 and pl. V), is the burden of labor lifted from the shoulders of the father: young, powerful, handsome, though notably less refined in appearance than his beautiful wife, he has joined the rest of the family before his cottage and shares some of the evening light, which falls less generously, however, on his face than on hers.

Since Gainsborough's landscape paintings were mostly painted for his own amusement and recreation, it seems appropriate to connect these cottage-door scenes with his famous remark in a letter to the musician William Jackson: "I'm sick of Portraits and wish very much to take my Viol de Gam and walk off to some sweet Village where I can paint Landskips and enjoy the fag End of Life in quietness & ease." They seem to speak of a desire to escape from business – a life spent "*in Harn*[*ess*]," as he put it, while others "ride in the Waggon" – and from the whims and importunities of his polite sitters, into an eroticized rustic idyll from which, however, except in *Peasant Smoking*, the burden of providing for his family stubbornly refuses to be wished away.[2] And among the admirers of these landscapes, few in the 1770s but steadily growing in the last years of his life, these "cottage doors" may have been enjoyed similarly as the expressions of a fantasy of retirement from the world, from the rituals and routines of public and social life, into an unattainable privacy, imagined not inconveniently therefore in the form of an impossible, and not finally very desirable, descent from gentility into rusticity.[3] The fantasy may be compared with the wish indulged by William Cowper in *The Task* (1785) of retiring to the remote cottage, perched on a hill and ringed with elms, that he passed in his rural walks and named "the

43 Thomas Gainsborough, *The Woodcutter's Return* (detail of fig. 2)

peasant's nest" – a wish that lasted only as long as it took him to recall the many inconveniences of cottage life.[4]

Yet though these "cottage doors" appear to speak of the pleasures of retirement from, among other things, the public and the political, the image they created of rural privacy was itself thoroughly embedded in a political notion of how the poor should behave. The fantasy they gave expression to had to be grounded in a degree of reality, if it was not to be dismissed too readily as mere fantasy, mere idyll; and this is achieved by the evidence of the labor by which these rustic families supported themselves, whether in the heavy bundles of firewood, the brooms, or simply, in *The Cottage Door* itself, the absence of a husband presumably out working whose return is eagerly awaited by the rest of the family. This image of retired domesticity required the cottagers to be represented as remote from society, as entirely focused on the family and having nothing to do with the more collective forms of leisure that characterized village life, in the alehouse or on the green. If their way of life was to be passed off as desirable, it had to be represented not as affluent, of course, but as decent and comfortable and consequently the women, at least, are strikingly well-dressed and neat, and are evidently far above what Adam Smith described as that "disgraceful degree of poverty which . . . no one can well fall into without extreme bad conduct."[5] In the process, therefore, of imagining the life of the rural poor as capable of supporting a polite fantasy of rustic retirement, the poor themselves were imagined just as the polite classes wished they were: too industrious to be poor, with too much self-respect to be ragged, and too contented with the privacy of domestic life to need or seek the company of others of their class, and without the quarrelling, the drunkenness, the gossip, the bawdy, the lechery that were widely supposed to characterize the poor who enjoyed their leisure collectively.[6]

The cottage-door scenes thus embody an idea of the "good" poor, "industrious, modest, quiet, neat" as Cowper described them, and in the process they define too, by their absence from the paintings, an account of the "bad" poor supposed to be none of those things.[7] Indeed, the more Gainsborough's admirers recognized these paintings as idylls, as "fancy-paintings," images of a fantasy, the more the reality of rural life may have been imagined as the opposite of the version they depicted. There is evidently, in short, a politics of class at work in the construction of these paintings; but no less evidently the paintings were not understood as political at all. The images of the poor they offered and excluded were too deeply grounded in the shared ideology of the polite classes even perhaps to be recognized as political, let alone to be open to controversy. If the paintings were political, they were not politicized: there seemed to be nothing in them to be for or against. The cottage door, however, or the cottage as the site of an idealized, private, domestic life, was far more widely invoked in the 1790s than in the 1770s or 1780s, and in that decade its meanings changed entirely.

* * *

44 Thomas Gainsborough, *Peasant Smoking at a Cottage Door* (detail of pl. v)

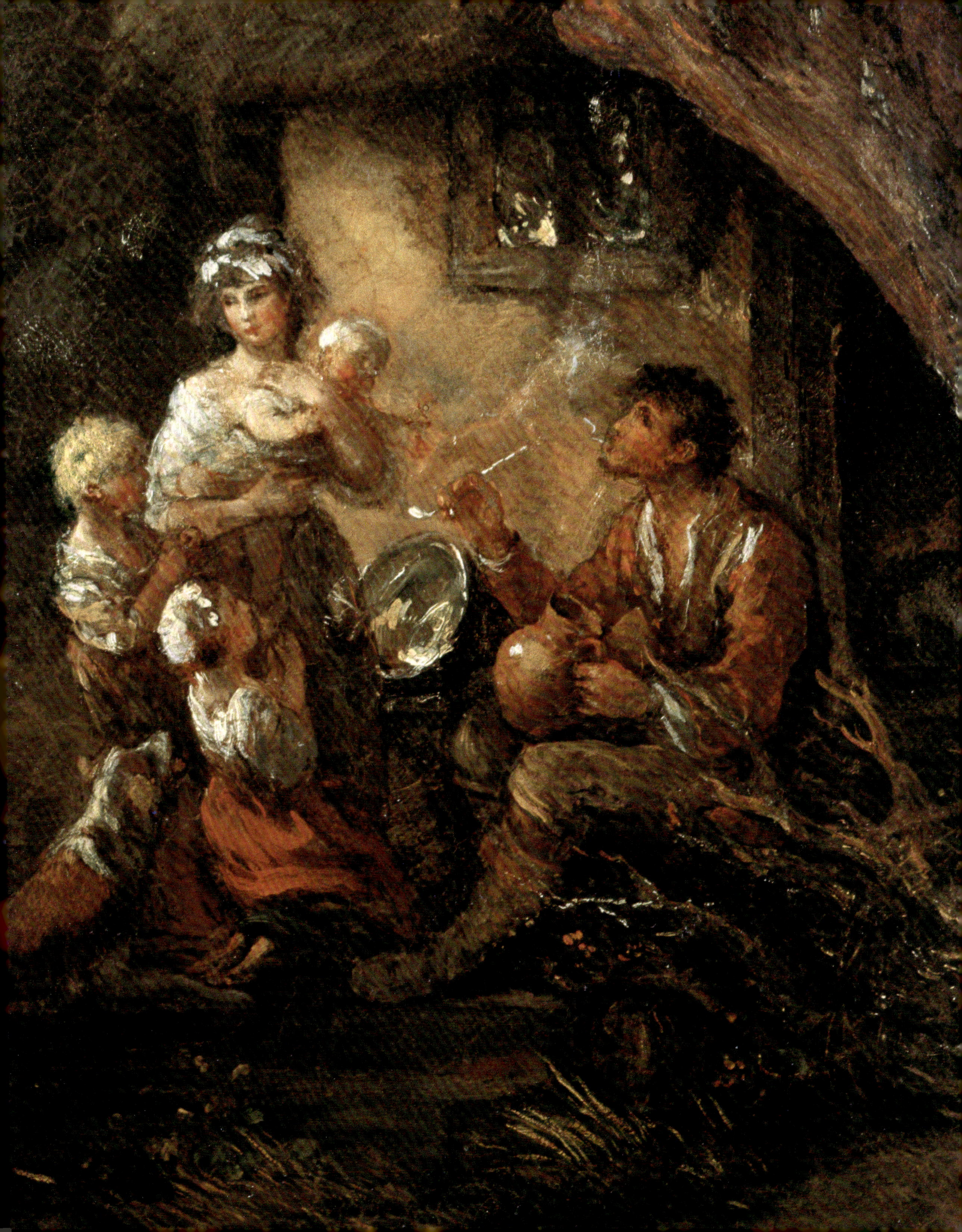

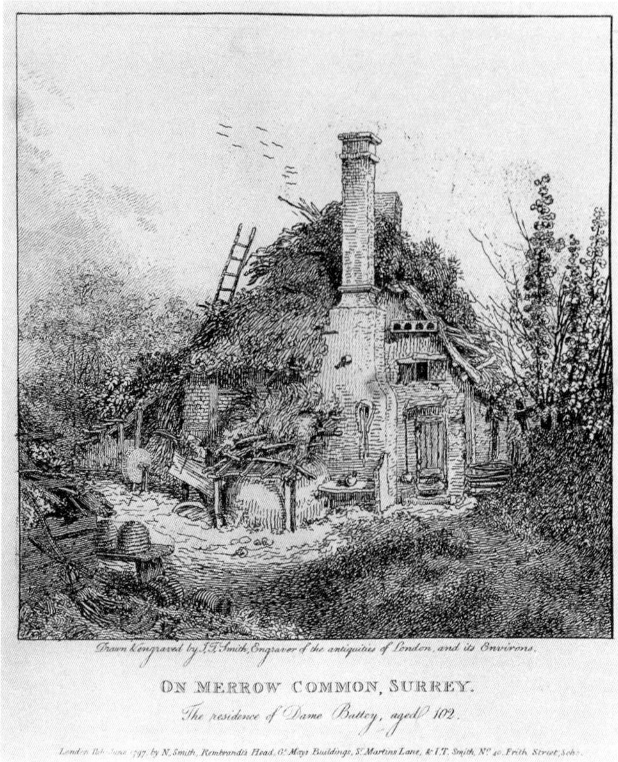

45 J. T. Smith, "On Merrow Common, Surrey. The Residence of Dame Battey, aged 102," from J. T. Smith, *Remarks on Rural Scenery; with Twenty Etchings of Cottages, from Nature*, London, 1797, etching, 12.7 × 12.6 cm ($5\frac{1}{2} \times 5\frac{1}{4}$ in.)

In the first part of her cautionary tale of *Black Giles the Poacher*, a "Cheap Repository Tract" published in December 1796, the evangelical poet and loyalist propagandist Hannah More described the "Mud Cottage with the broken windows, stuffed with dirty rags" that housed the poacher and his idle family. "You may know the house," she continued, "by the ragged tiles on the roof, and the loose stones which are ready to drop out from the chimney; though a short ladder, a hod of mortar, and an hour's leisure time would have prevented all this." Giles, she explained, had fallen "into that common mistake, that a beggarly looking cottage, and filthy ragged children raised most compassion, and of course drew the most charity." In fact, the reverse was the case: "for it is neatness, housewifery, and a decent appearance, which draw the kindness of the rich and charitable, while they turn away disgusted from filth and laziness."[8]

A few months later, the artist and antiquary John Thomas Smith published a small book of etchings of cottages (fig. 45), preceded by a brief essay in which he considered the sub-genre of landscape he called "*cottage scenery*." He did not claim that the sub-genre itself was new: it had been practiced by a number of Dutch painters and, in Britain, preeminently by Gainsborough, whose "profound and accurate observations of Nature" had enabled him "to give distinct characteristics and original varieties to his cottagery." Nor did he make great claims for it – he was content that "rural and cottage-scenery" should be "considered as no more than a sort of *low-comedy* landscape." His main concern was to distinguish between two "classes" of cottage scenery, "namely, the *neat*, and the *neglected*,"and he seems to have produced his definitions of these with *Black Giles* open on his desk.

Smith freely acknowledged that "in poverty, nothing will more easily, or more universally excite the attention of benevolence, than the appearance of neatness and cleanliness," and he went on to describe in great detail the ideal of cottage neatness, all straight lines and right angles, that "will be sure to call forth the praises of the good *housewife* and the thrifty *oeconomist*." But, he continued, all this "is nothing to the artist. *As* good *housewives*, or as thrifty *oeconomists*, we admit that it is all very well; but we then turn from this neatness and regularity, to what *we* must esteem a far more profitable subject – the neglected fast-ruinating cottage." The rest of a long paragraph describes his picturesque ideal in terms which seem to borrow and expand upon those by which Giles's cottage had been described: "here and there a wisp of straw stuffed through a broken pane," a "mutilated chimney-top," "the unrepaired accidents of wind and rain," "ragged children," and so on. All these "offer far greater allurements to the painter's eye, than more neat, regular or formal arrangements could possibly have done."[9]

The distinction Smith was making, between the rural imagery as seen in a moral and as in a picturesque light, was commonplace enough by the time he made it: it is a running theme in the writings of William Gilpin. There are, however, a number of novel features in Smith's version of the distinction. There is his interpellation of the "good housewife" alongside the economist, as if in conscious reference to the values which the Cheap Repository Tracts were attempting to impress upon the rural poor. There is the sheer length, which my summary cannot indicate, of his account of the disjunction, made visible in the two sorts of cottage, between on the one hand the discourses of political economy and of good housewifery, its domestic equivalent, and the discourse of the picturesque on the other. Most of all, there is his provocative borrowing of that figure from Hannah More whereby we "turn," we "turn away from," one kind of cottage in order to admire the other. If, according to More, "the rich and charitable" turn away from the neglected cottage in disgust, artists, according to Smith, do the very opposite: they turn from neatness in search of the visual stimulation that only neglect can offer.

There is no reason to believe that Smith was writing here in defence of the idle poor. He did not suggest they had a right to neglect their own property if they chose to do so, because their leisure time was their own; nor did it occur to him to point out that neglected cottages were as likely to be the sign of a parsimonious or irresponsible landlord as of an idle occupier. He may well have felt that the idle poor were every bit as much the authors of their own misfortune as More did, and that their idleness and neglect were not excused by the benefits they accidentally conferred upon the artist in the shape of picturesque ruins. His point was to defend the space of the artist, not of the undeserving poor, against the encroachment of More's increasingly pervasive and persuasive moral rhetoric, and to accomplish this he was perfectly willing to give that rhetoric its due. An artist, he may be taken as saying, can perfectly well inhabit two apparently contradictory discourses; just because he profits from the idleness of the poor he must not be presumed to condone it, or to approve all those vices which More connected with idleness: discontent, ingratitude, crime, and – worst of all – democracy.

A collection of etchings of neglected cottages needed such an elaborate and careful defence in the mid-1790s. Like everything else in those exciting, troubled years, the image of the cottage, which a decade before had evoked for the polite classes the idea of privacy and retirement, of a space and a life away from political conflict, had become thoroughly politicized in the intense propaganda war between loyalists and radicals. As I shall show, during the early years of the war with France the image of the cottage had become thoroughly involved with questions about the morality of the war with the French Republic, popular radicalism and the movement for parliamentary reform, and the declining standard of living of the poor under the burden of wartime taxation. For loyalists, the rural cottage became an image of the peaceful life Britain was fighting to protect and restore, or of the contentment the poor supposedly enjoyed or should be taught to believe they enjoyed even in times of great hardship. Writers hostile to the war with France or in favor of a reform of parliament also focused intently on the cottage, but on the cottage abandoned by poor peasants or laborers unable to resist the oppression of their landlords or to survive the rigors of a wartime economy, ruined and destroyed by invading armies, or deserted by families left unable to pay their way when a husband and father had enlisted and perhaps been killed. The figure of the ruined or deserted cottage was used sometimes to question the protection supposed to be offered to the poor by supposedly equal laws, sometimes it is evoked to take issue with the justice of a war which inflicts its greatest, most terrible costs on the most vulnerable members of the nation – a concentration on the domestic cost of the war which had the effect, Mary Favret has argued, of concealing the horrors of the fighting itself from a public which was unwilling to acknowledge them.[10] This is the context in which Smith was trying to preserve the cottage as a space which might still be thought of, if only for the purposes of art, as removed from politics, but he knew how controversial this aim might seem, and his awkward references to *Black Giles* show the strain he was under, unsure how much to concede to More's rhetoric and how far he should confront it.

One can get a clearer idea of the problems involved in the representation of the cottage from the poet and lecturer John Thelwall, who in 1794 was tried and acquitted on a charge of high treason for his activities in support of universal manhood suffrage, and who by the end of the following year came to be regarded by the government as the most dangerous radical in Britain. In 1793 Thelwall published a short essay on cottages as part of his long, brilliant, unclassifiable book called *The Peripatetic.* The eponymous central character of this work describes a range of cottages he and the companion on his walk came across in the fields just outside Bermondsey, an industrial suburb in southeast London, the last place in which the lovers of rural scenery would look for the pleasures of pastoral. However unpromising their situation, however overcrowded, and however uncomfortable they would be to those who are used to better, these cottages and their tiny gardens were, in Smith's terms, "neat," not at all neglected, and Thelwall represents them as in their own way idyllic, for they are places where laboring families, impoverished as they are, can escape from the labors of the day, breathe pure air, and enjoy the pleasures of domestic life. They are, however, as vulnerable as they are peaceful. The ground they occupy belongs to the owner of a modern villa, and sooner or later, Thelwall suggests, he will no longer be able to endure having his view spoiled by the sight of wretchedness and poverty. Whether in the name of taste or of ridding the neighborhood of a nuisance he will level the cottages to the ground, forcing their inhabitants to abandon the scenes they have lived in all their lives and to seek refuge in the unhealthy metropolis. Or else they will be driven away by poverty and famine.

The fate Thelwall foresees for these cottages and their inhabitants was familiar enough, most obviously from Goldsmith's *Deserted Village*. What was new, however, about these remarks on cottage scenery was the solution he proposed to the problem of rural poverty and the danger he apprehended in proposing it. "The slavish maxims of the age," he wrote, "have forbidden a tongue to the attachments or the necessities of the poor." But suppose, asks his companion, the laborers had a vote and voice; suppose elections to parliament were more frequent; suppose therefore members of parliament were dependent on their votes for re-election? would the workers in agriculture, the "*most important* part of the community" then be "neglected and despised?" "'Hush! Hush! my friend!'" exclaims Thelwall, "'suppress this freedom of speech, and remember THE ASSOCIATION! The fervors of patriotic humanity, and the confidence of friendship must no longer be indulged, since confederated placemen invite us to turn informers.'"[11]

The "Association" Thelwall refers to – its full name was the Association for the Preservation of Liberty and Property against Republicans and Levellers – held its inaugural meeting on November 20, 1792, a few months before the publication of *The Peripatetic*, and in the context of Britain's anticipated entry into the war with the newly declared French Republic, and of increasing loyalist alarm over the influence of Thomas Paine and the spread of popular societies seeking a reform of Parliament. It was dedicated to discouraging and suppressing seditious publications and, as Thelwall indicates, it also invited informers to report conversations that might disturb the peace of the kingdom, with the aim of prosecuting those who engaged in them. It rapidly gave birth to numerous local branches across Britain, and was certainly successful in restraining the freedom of speech in which Thelwall's companion so thoughtlessly or intrepidly indulged. The Association also published loyalist, anti-radical pamphlets and tracts, and one of its earliest publications was a tract by the philosopher and influential churchman William Paley, entitled *Reasons for Contentment, addressed to the Labouring Part of the British Public*.

This short essay was an admonition to the poor not to make themselves unhappy by comparing their situation with that of the rich. The poor, it insisted, were at least as fortunate, in many ways more fortunate than the rich: they did not suffer from the boredom, the enforced idleness of the rich, or the dissatisfaction that supposedly followed the easy satisfaction of desire. The point of Paley's tract, like the point of the Association itself or of More's Cheap Repository Tracts, was to persuade the poor not "to covet the stations and fortunes of the rich" or "to wish to seize them by force, or through the medium of public uproar and confusion"; in short, to dissuade them from enlisting in the popular reform movement and from seeking to replicate in Britain the events in France.

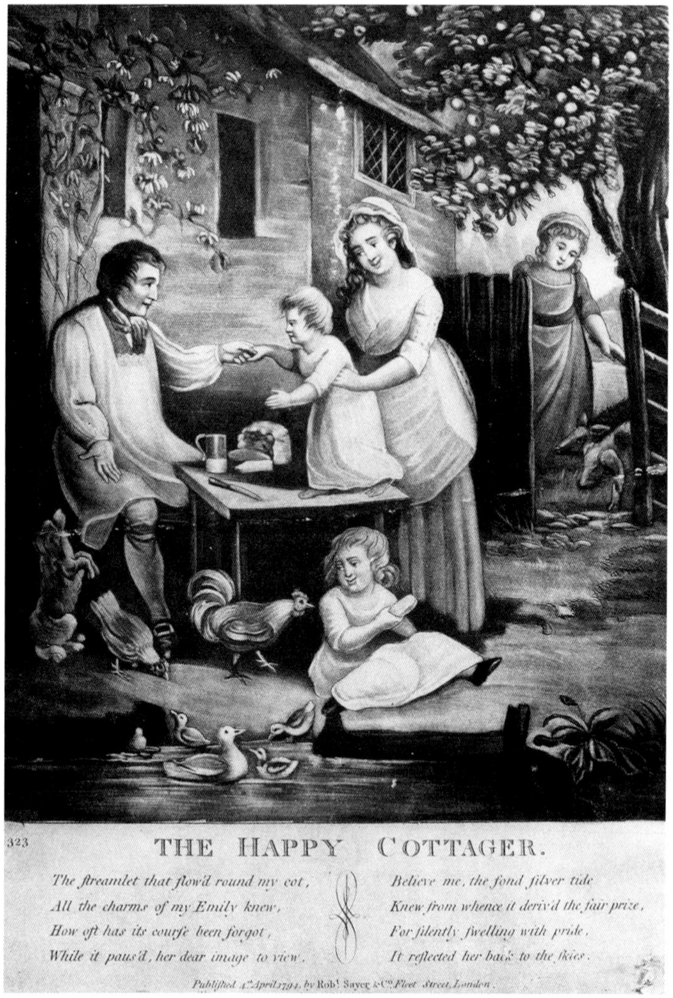

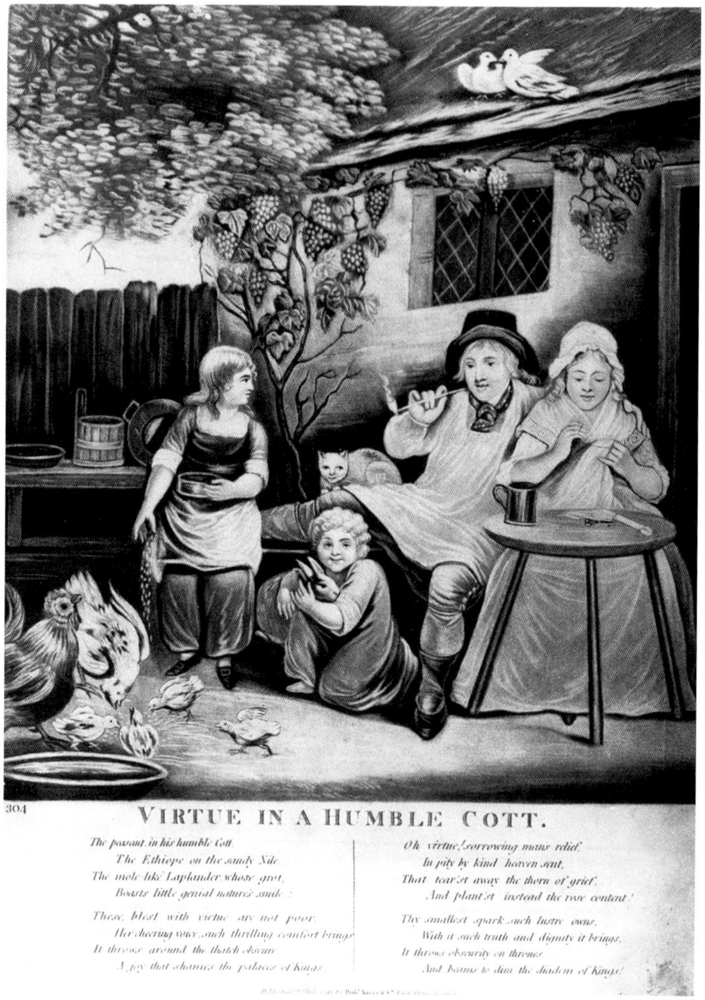

46 (*above left*) Artist unknown, *The Happy Cottager*, mezzotint, 33 × 25.4 cm ($13\frac{1}{2}$ × 10 in.), London 1794, private collection

47 (*above right*) Artist unknown, *Virtue in a Humble Cott*, mezzotint, 33 × 25.4 cm ($13\frac{3}{4}$ × 10 in.), London 1793, private collection

And against the specter of French discontent and anarchy it offered an image of peace and of the greatest happiness attainable on earth, in the form of a cottage-door scene in the manner of Gainsborough:

> the summer evening of a country village; where, after the hours of the day, each man at his door, with his children, amongst his neighbours, feels his frame and his heart at rest, every thing about him pleased and pleasing, and a delight and complacency in his sensations far beyond what either luxury or diversion can afford.

"The rich want this," Paley insisted, "and they want what they must never have";[12] and in saying so he revealed what was, as I shall show, the problematic double character of loyalist cottage-scenery, that it is at least as much concerned to provide the rich with "reasons for contentment" as the poor. On the face of it, it seems unlikely that Paley's tract could persuade many of the rural poor that they were happy; it was probably more successful in persuading the rich that the poor *ought* to be happy – happier indeed than they were themselves – and that there was no justification, therefore, for popular disaffection, "grumbling," and radicalism.

Paley's vision of cottage evenings is in many ways reminiscent of a development of Gainsborough's cottage-door imagery by the Fleet Street printseller Robert Sayer, who in the early years of the 1790s issued a number of anonymous mezzotint cottage-door scenes adapted for a vulgar urban audience, some in the very small and very cheap format known to printsellers as "cottage-prints." Sayer's images were pure rustic idyll, designed to evoke in the metropolitan artisan or shopkeeper a nostalgia for the simple, leisurely life of a countryside that they might barely have visited except on Sunday rambles in dingy semirural suburbs. *The Happy Cottager* (fig. 46), for example, is accompanied by verses that celebrate the romantic love that was the foundation of its family idyll; in *Virtue in a Humble Cott* (fig. 47), the doves on the roof symbolize both peace and conjugal fidelity, even the cat smiles, and the verses beneath speak of the lack of care that, as Paley had suggested, makes life in a cottage so much preferable to life in a palace.[13] There was nothing in these images for lovers of landscape: they depicted cottages and cottage gardens as private domestic spaces entirely cut off from the surrounding villages and fields by overhanging trees and fences of stout palings. But within those spaces all labor was forgotten, and happy young fathers smoked, drank, and relaxed with their pretty wives and pretty children – isolated from their neighbors, to be sure, but also out of reach of the surveillance of employers, landlords, or charitable polite visitors anxious to offer moral advice in exchange for deference. In short, these images, aimed directly at their vulgar audience, seem permissive; Paley's, which would reach the rural poor only through the hands of their superiors, were coercive.

From time to time the Association itself commissioned propaganda in the form of popular prints, designed to be sold in bulk to its supporters for distribution among their dependants, tenants, and employees. It is more than likely that it was responsible, early in 1793, for the appearance of a pair of caricatures by T. Ovenden, *John Bull in his Glory* (fig. 48) and *Citizen CoupeTête in his Misery* (fig. 49), which contrasted the English cottage with the squalid habitation of a Parisian *sans-culottes*.[14] John Bull is seated at a table by a roaring fire with his son (or son-in-law) and his daughter-in-law (or daughter) who is suckling a baby. Other children lounge in the foreground. The two men hold large mugs of ale, and, having torn big chunks from a substantial loaf, are about to turn their attention to the equally substantial joint of beef that Mrs Bull is bringing to the table. There will be enough beef, it seems, even for the expectant dog, but should John still be hungry when the beef is finished, he can fall back on the two hams that hang above the chimneypiece. As the image and the verses beneath it make clear, this abundance is the reward of piety, contentment, patriotism, loyalty, and domestic virtue: the cottage is an emblem of all that makes England the happiest land on earth. On the wall is a double portrait of George III and Queen Charlotte; next to it is the patriotic song, beloved of Associationists, "O the roast beef of old England," printed beneath a version of Hogarth's print of the same name.[15] The family, the verses tell us, is in the habit of singing songs "with merry glee," and the boy lolling on a chair in the foreground is about to lead them in a rendition of the national anthem. A large family bible sits, rather precariously, on a shelf; through the window appears the reassuring spire of a country church. The pendant to this image portrays the "sad Reverse" when religion and royalty

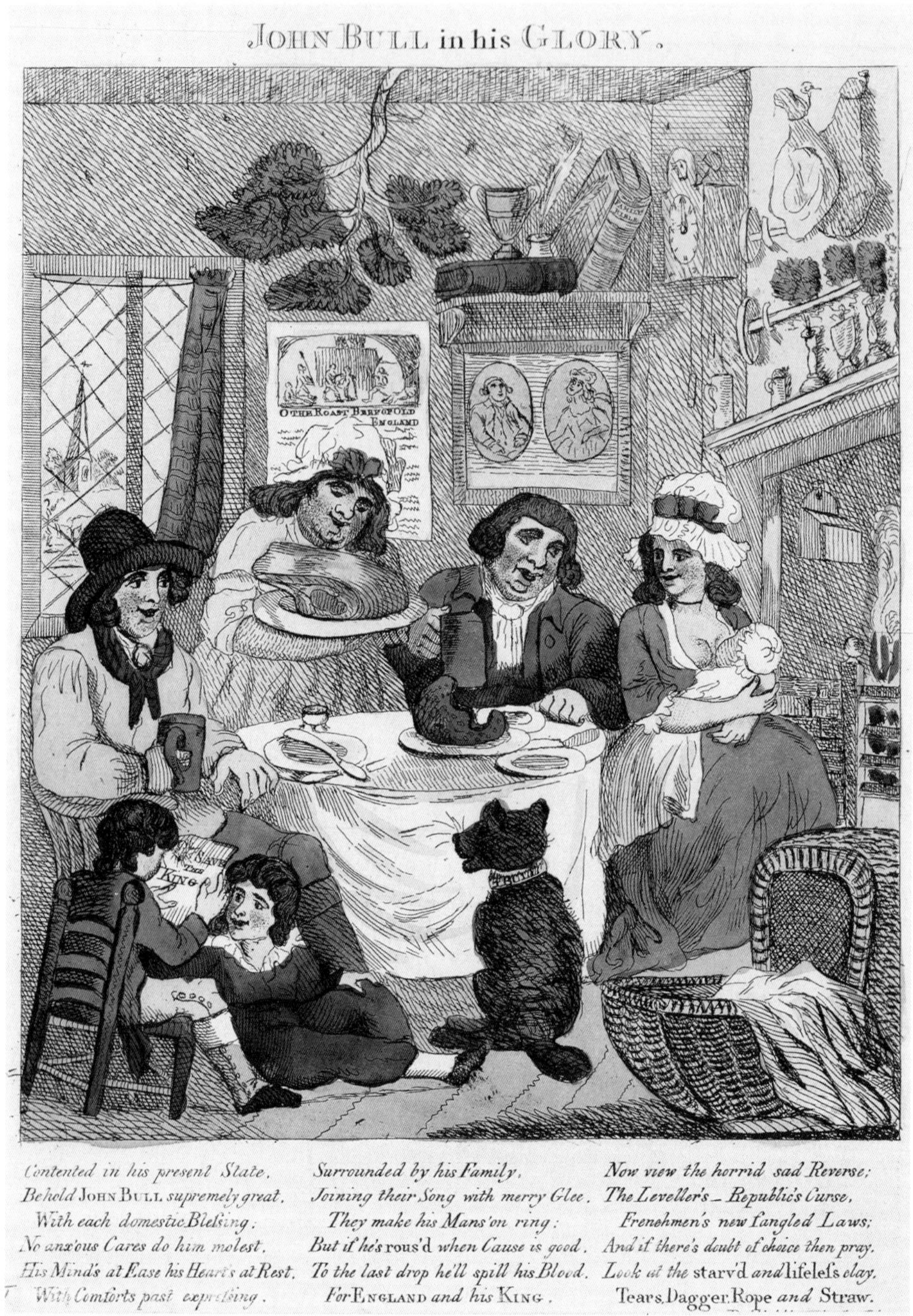

48 [T. Ovenden], *John Bull in his Glory*, engraving, 25.4 × 22.8 cm ($10\frac{7}{8}$ × 9 in.), London 1793, Library of Congress, Washington, D.C.

no longer secure the comforts and blessings of domesticity. The emaciated, near-naked, barefoot Citizen Coupe Tête sits despairing in a ruinous hovel decorated with images of the leaders of the Republic and with the skulls of royalist martyrs; outside the window another martyr is about to be guillotined, next to a gibbet hung with corpses. The citizen's distracted wife bewails the death of her eldest daughter; two younger children struggle over a bone; CoupeTête himself cannot decide whether to cut his own throat or to hang himself.

James Gillray borrowed from Ovenden's image of John Bull when, in 1794, he was commissioned by the Association to produce a print which was pub-

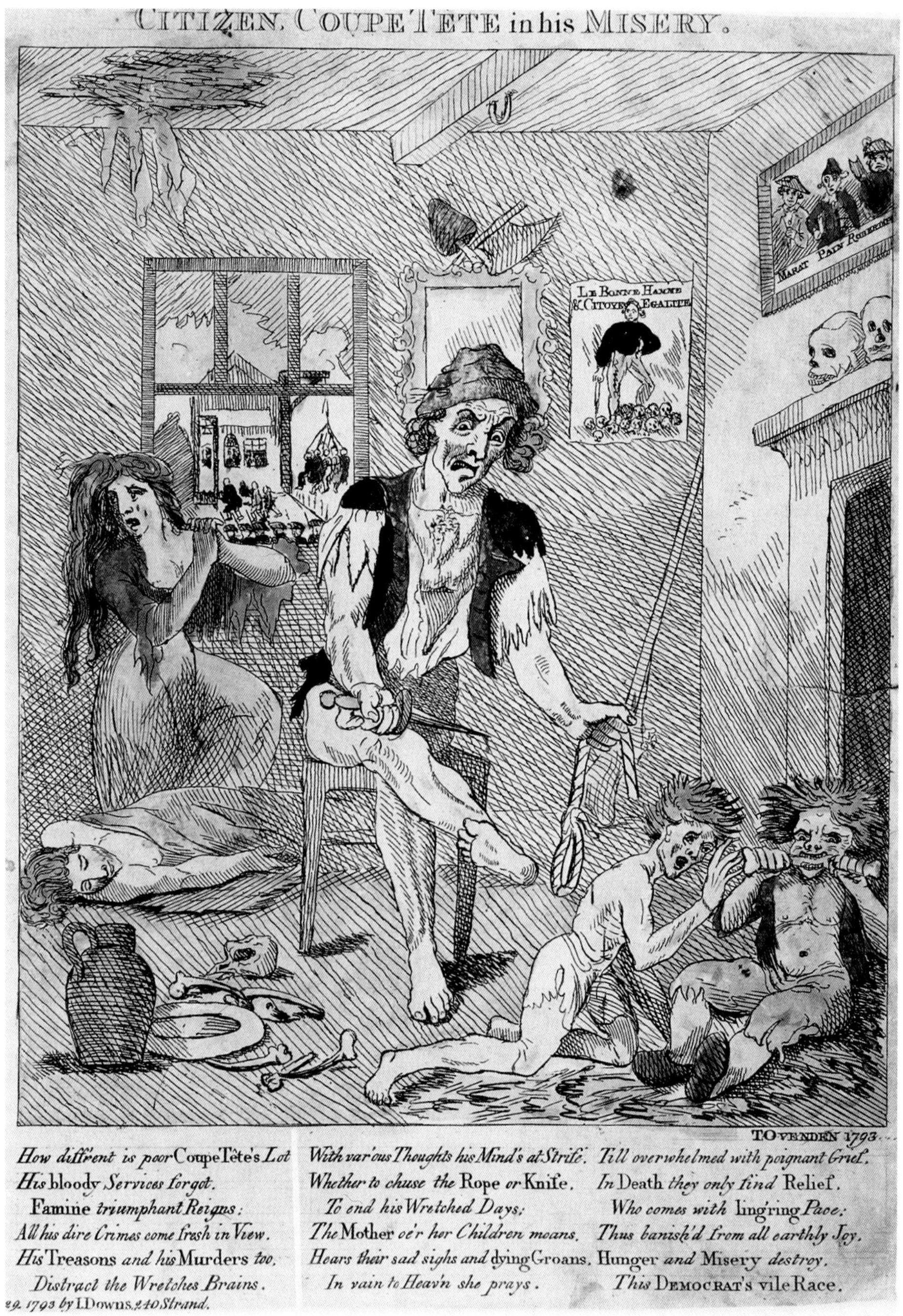

49 T. Ovenden, *Citizen Coupe Tête in his Misery*, engraving, 25.4 × 22.8 cm ($10\frac{7}{8}$ × 9 in.), London 1793, the Trustees of the British Museum, London, BM Sat 8293

lished in January the following year as *The Blessings of Peace . . . The Curses of War* (fig. 50). It consisted of a pair of cottage scenes, an interior and a cottage door, enclosed in roundels like the two sides of a medal; and the shocking contrast between them was clearly intended to establish that the war with France could reach out and destroy what had been represented, especially by Gainsborough, as the most privileged and protected haven of retirement and domestic peace. On the left, a countryman, perhaps a yeoman farmer, has returned home from the labors of the day to be greeted by his loving family and his dog. His wife and two youngest children cluster round him, while his

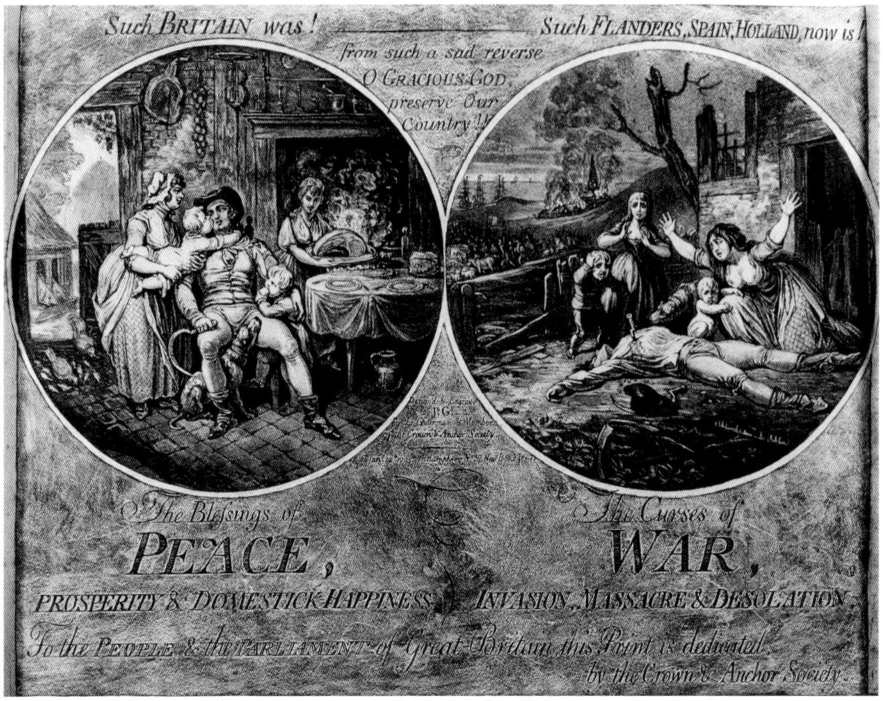

50 James Gillray, *The Blessings of Peace . . . The Curses of War*, etching and aquatint, 27.9 × 35.5 cm ($11\frac{3}{8} \times 14\frac{1}{4}$ in.), London 1795, the Trustees of the British Museum, London, BM Sat 8609

older daughter serves up another generous rib-joint of beef. Once again there is a loaf of bread, or perhaps it is a meat pie on the table, and another ham hangs by the door; pigs grunt in their styes, the promise of more ham to come; chickens peck about on the floor.

This too is an image of the peace and plenty that summed up the Georgian ideal of the good life, an image of the cottage as the heart of all that Britain is supposed to stand for by contrast with the rest of the world. This is the Britain that those who received this print as a gift from their landlord or employer, or who saw it hung up in their place of work or the local alehouse, were invited to identify with; the Britain they were fighting the French to preserve. It is of course "old" England, or an image of how Britain once was; but whatever awkward reflections might have been raised by that past tense, it may have been expected to suggest that Britain was like this only two years ago, before the war and the inevitable privations of a wartime economy began; and so it would be like this again when the French were finally defeated. And the right-hand roundel apparently made it clear that the war was, as the Prime Minister William Pitt repeatedly insisted, "just and necessary." If the French were not defeated, Britain would suffer as Flanders, Spain, and Holland had already suffered at their hands. Gainsborough's peaceful cottage door would become the scene of appalling atrocities occasioned by a French invasion: the cottage burned, the father bayoneted, the mother and eldest daughter raped (as their disheveled and disordered appearance makes clear); the survivors left to starve as their livestock is driven off to feed the army of the Republic.

Later in 1795 two London merchants or shopkeepers, one a goldsmith, one a cutler, issued another loyalist image of the cottage in the form of a "Constitu-

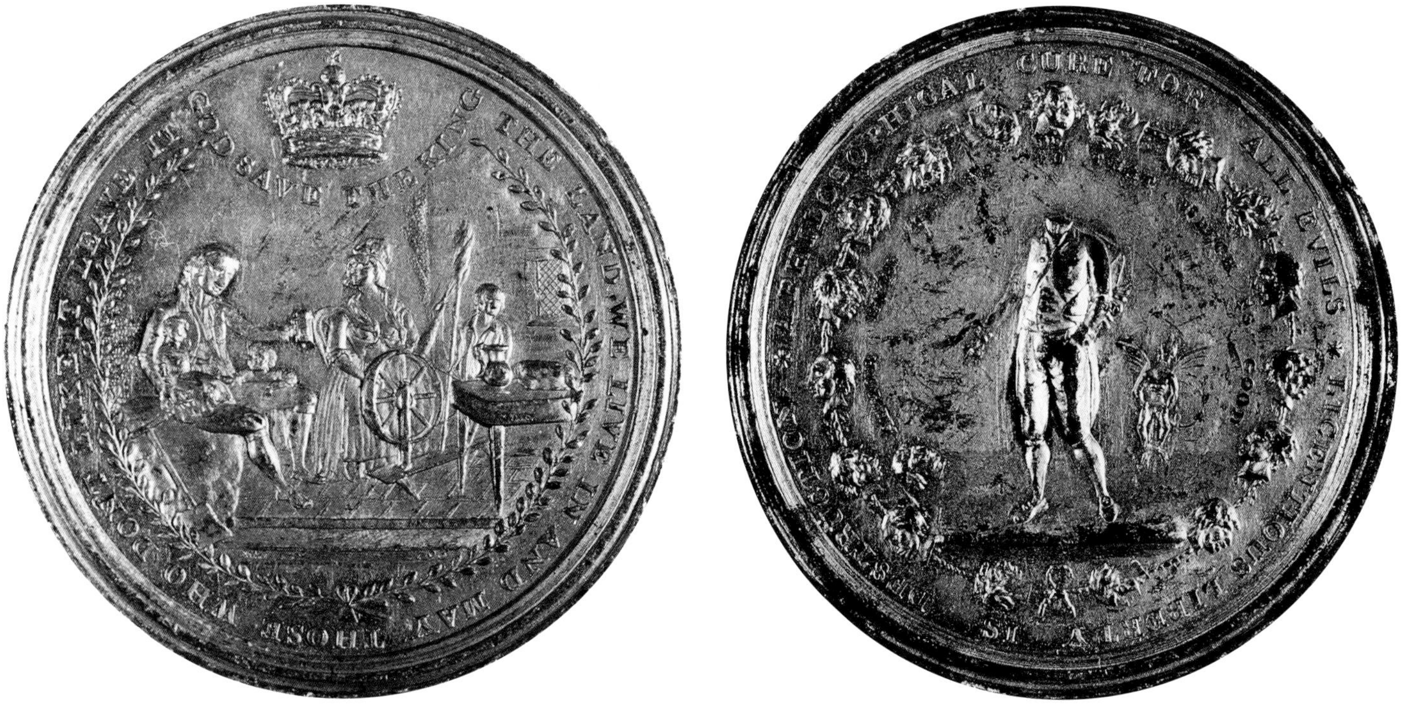

51 W. Whitley after Richard Newton, "The Constitutional Medal," white metal, 2.5 cm ($1\frac{7}{8}$ in.), London 1795, private collection

tional Medal" (fig. 51), struck in white metal (a cheap substitute for silver), and advertised to be sold at a discount to those, as they put it,

> whose Rank and Circumstances enable, and whose Zeal inclines them to prove their Affection to Government; as by distributing them amongst their Friends, Dependents and Neighbours, they may act as an Antidote to those pernicious Principles too successfully attempted to be instilled in the Minds of the Weak, and of the less informed Orders of the People.[16]

On the obverse of this medal, a family is seated on the paved terrace of a rural cottage, enjoying the best part of the day as Paley had imagined it: a laborer has returned from his work to relax in the bosom of his family and to enjoy a well-earned drink, poured out for him by the eldest and chubbiest of his well-fed children. In contrast with Gillray's image, it is here the housewife and mother who is the center of the family, as she is, for example, in Gainsborough's *Peasant Smoking at a Cottage Door* (1788; see pl. v), or in another of Sayer's cottage-doors for the popular urban market, the small cottage print *The Woodman Return'd to his Cott* (1793; fig. 52). To place her in the center is of course to emphasize that it is the virtues of domesticity that characterize the goodness and happiness of the laboring class, and to show her spinning, whether to clothe her family or to augment the family income, underlines the importance of industriousness among those virtues: it may be too dark for the laborer to go on with his work, but there is still light enough for his wife to do hers, and she will not stop spinning until she can no longer see to do so.

The main point of the scene, however, is of course that it too is an image not just of rural virtue but of Britain itself. On the advertisement for the medal,

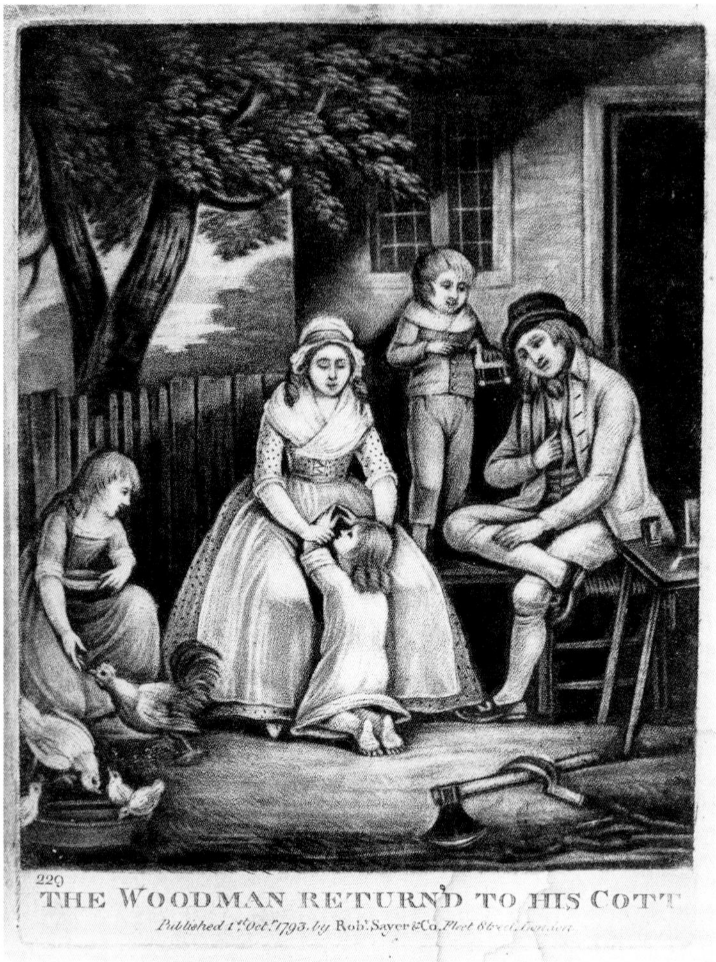

52 Artist unknown, *The Woodman Return'd to his Cott*, mezzotint, 12.7 × 10.1 cm ($5\frac{7}{8} \times 3\frac{1}{2}$ in.), London 1793, private collection

what is called its "constitutional side" – its obverse – is described in verses which announce that this picture of rustic happiness is the result of a benevolently monarchist constitution: the property of this family however small, the "plenty" they supposedly enjoy, the "freedom" of which they are actively "conscious" (for it is not a piece of unmeaning ideology) – all are secured by Britain's "equal laws" and by the crown that watches over this family and protects them. In the legend that encircles the image, this cottage scene is offered as an image of "the land we live in," and in the spirit of Merle Haggard's refrain ("if you don't love it leave it") republicans are warned that "those who don't like it" can "leave it."[17] What would happen to Britain if republicanism gained the ascendancy is shown on the reverse, in the contrasting image of anarchy, not explicitly represented or described as French anarchy, perhaps so that it can also function as a nightmare prediction of Britain's possible future, but obviously an evocation of the Terror that has been visited on Britain's "natural enemy."

In return, of course, the crown and the constitution are protected by the family. As the Shepherd of Salisbury Plain points out in Hannah More's tract of that name, also published in 1795, "a poor man like me is seldom called out to do great things, so it is not by a few great deeds his character can be judged by his neighbours, but by the little round of daily customs he allows himself in."[18]

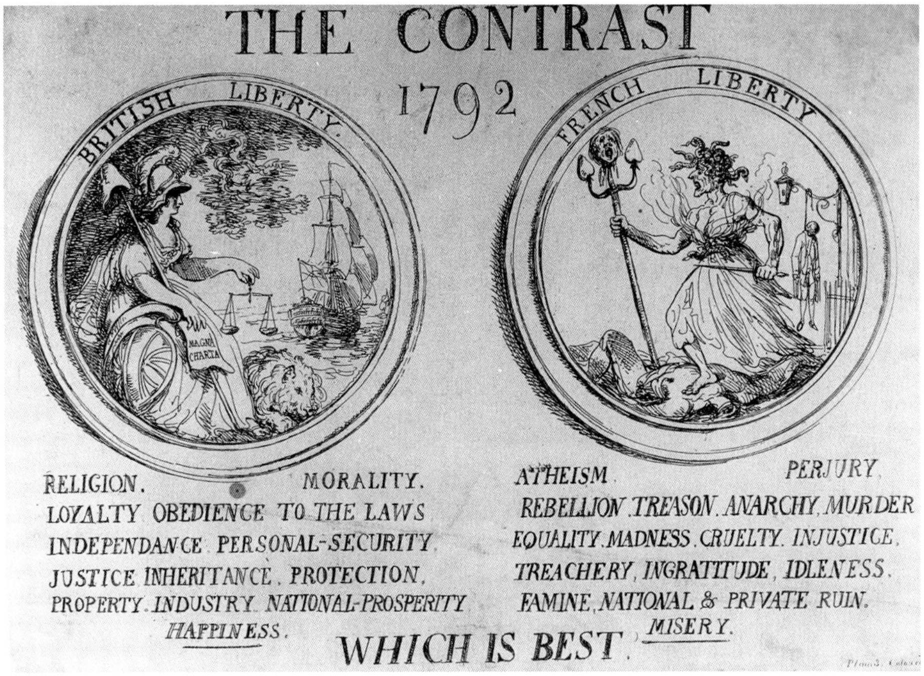

53 Thomas Rowlandson after Lord George Murray, *The Contrast 1792*, etching, 25.4 × 35.5 cm ($10\frac{1}{2} \times 14\frac{3}{4}$ in.), London 1792, the Trustees of the British Museum, London, BM Sat 8149

The parents of this family have no opportunity of displaying their patriotism by great deeds of public virtue; they display it instead by their neatness, their contentment, their industriousness, their gratitude for the blessings they enjoy, and by the sentimental affection which seems to guarantee that these private virtues are being handed down to their children. By their habitual perseverance in the daily practice of virtue, they support the constitution that supports them, and in doing so, the medal suggests, they become the embodiment of British freedom. Or at least the mother does: by a transparent but effective visual pun, we are invited to read her as an image of British Liberty herself – her spinning wheel as the shield bearing the union flag, her distaff with its bunch of carded wool or cotton as the staff and liberty cap. British Liberty had appeared on the very first propaganda caricature published with the encouragement and sponsorship of the Association, *The Contrast*, by Thomas Rowlandson after a design by Lord George Murray (fig. 53), which appeared in December 1792 in the month following the Association's foundation. Rowlandson's image, however, asks its audience to identify in their Britishness with an abstract allegorical figure; the visual punning on the medal invites one to see British Liberty herself as residing in the humble cottage, and to recognize her in every virtuous mother in the land. It is the visual equivalent of the trick Keats later played in his "Autumn: an Ode," in which Autumn does not appear, as expected, as an allegorical figure presiding over the harvest landscape but instead is glimpsed, fleetingly, as embodied in the harvest-workers themselves, a winnower, a dozing reaper, a careful gleaner, a cider-maker.

The formula employed by both Gillray's print and the "Constitutional Medal," as well as by Ovenden's paired images, the contrast between good and bad alternatives, was especially favoured by the Association, and appears in most if not all the visual propaganda it sponsored. The logic of such contrasts, the Association seems to have believed, was direct and inescapable: faced with the atrocities pictured on one side, who would not choose or identify with the wholesome images of Englishness or Britishness on the other? But as Diana Donald has pointed out, the formula may not have communicated its meanings quite so straightforwardly or univocally.[19] In this respect Gillray's image may have been more problematic than Ovenden's vision of plenty in John Bull's cottage, for *The Blessings of Peace* appeared at a most unpropitious time. Holland had just surrendered to the French, the Prussian and Austrian armies had been driven back across the Rhine, and the British army had been forced to abandon Northern Europe and return to England. The war had become increasingly unpopular in Britain, and the demand that Pitt should enter negotiations with the French to end the war was becoming more urgent, even in Parliament itself. Worse still, a burning summer had shriveled the harvest of autumn 1794 in the fields; and the coldest winter in living memory had similarly destroyed the winter wheat. By the time *The Blessings of Peace* appeared, serious shortages of food were already apparent in Britain; a famine was being forecast for later in the year; and Pitt's government, though in public it was denying that a food crisis was imminent, was desparately attempting to secure supplies of corn from overseas. For the poor to whom the print was addressed, the lavish plenty in the left-hand roundel may have seemed a cruel irony rather than an image of a life they could recognize as their own; at best it may have fueled the belief that farmers themselves were suffering no shortages, and that the scarcity was caused in part by their own greedy consumption of the food that should have been available to the poor.

There is an instructive comparison to be made here with More's *Shepherd of Salisbury Plain*, written later in 1795 when the food shortages had become extreme. More wisely chose not to pretend that the rewards of domestic virtue still included unlimited beef and pudding, if they ever had done. The shepherd is represented as feeding his invalid wife and eight children on bread and potatoes; his clothes are so old that they consist mainly of patches, though the patching is laudably neat; he can afford a fire only once a day, for only so long as it takes to boil the potatoes; in the freezing winter just passed the family had had only a thin blue rug to cover them all. For all this the shepherd enjoys a contentment which derives from his pious willingness to thank God for whatever he provided, however scanty. The plight of the shepherd's family is exaggerated, no doubt, to ensure that virtually all who read the tract will learn to be thankful for their own lot, however harsh; but More may have been right to calculate that the poor would be more likely to approve depictions of their life that acknowledged their hunger rather than pretending that each evening they tucked in to the roast beef of old England. Her example, however, was not one that Gillray could possibly have followed. The visual representation of abject poverty was regarded by loyalists as too disgusting to be capable of teaching a positive moral lesson; and whereas the woodcut on the title page of *Black Giles* (fig. 54) showed the poacher's idle children reprehensibly dressed in rags, the image that introduced *The Shepherd of Salisbury Plain* gave no indication of how often and how carefully the shepherd's clothes had been repaired (fig. 55). If Gillray's beef seems an insult to the poverty of the poor, he could not possibly have persuaded

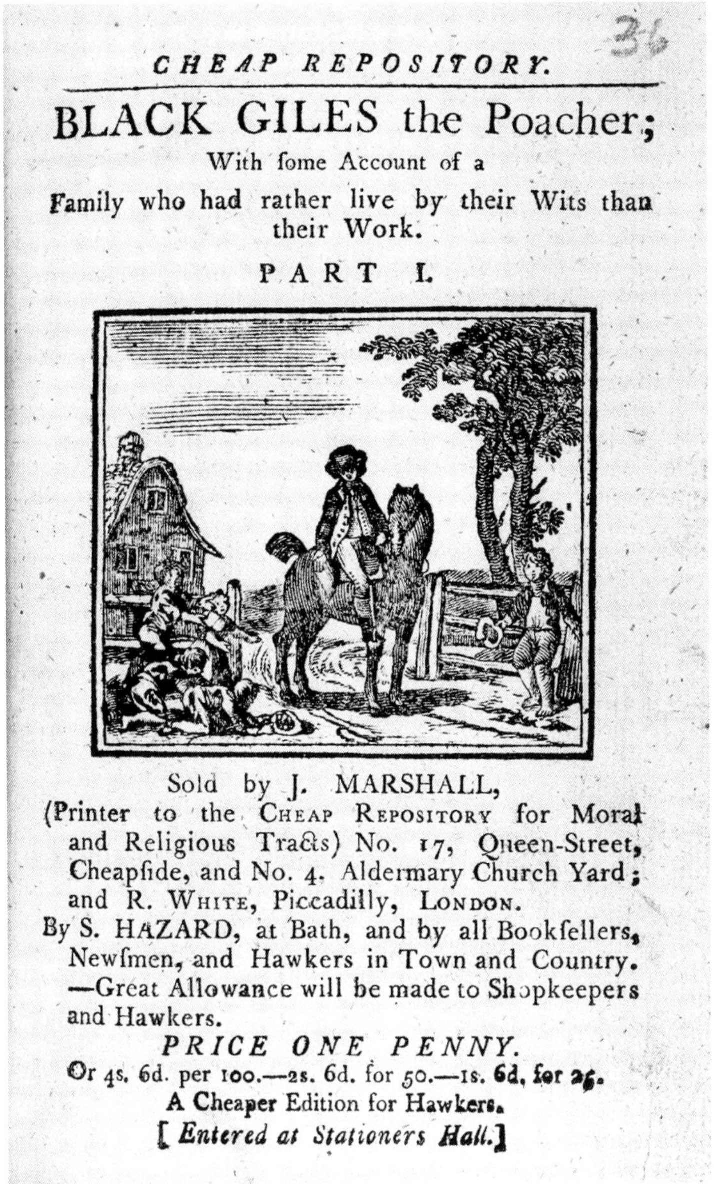

CHEAP REPOSITORY.

BLACK GILES the Poacher;
With ſome Account of a
Family who had rather live by their Wits than their Work.

PART I.

Sold by J. MARSHALL,
(Printer to the CHEAP REPOSITORY for Moral and Religious Tracts) No. 17, Queen-Street, Cheapſide, and No. 4. Aldermary Church Yard; and R. WHITE, Piccadilly, LONDON.
By S. HAZARD, at Bath, and by all Bookſellers, Newſmen, and Hawkers in Town and Country. —Great Allowance will be made to Shopkeepers and Hawkers.

PRICE ONE PENNY.
Or 4s. 6d. per 100.—2s. 6d. for 50.—1s. 6d. for 25.
A Cheaper Edition for Hawkers.
[Entered at Stationers Hall.]

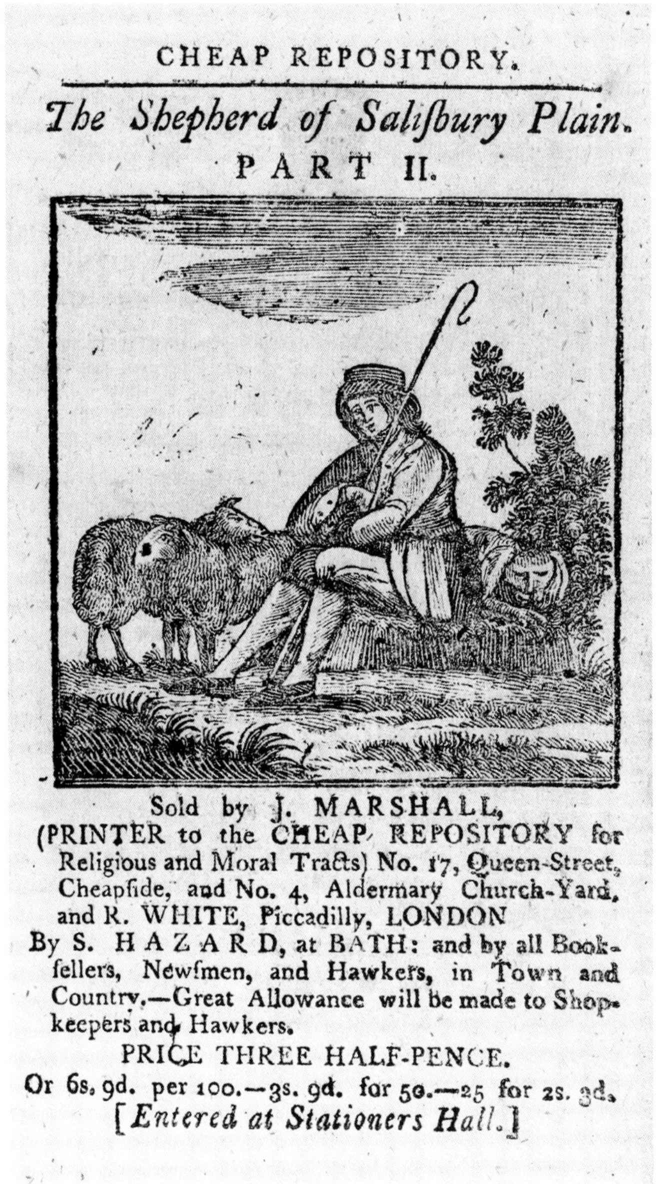

CHEAP REPOSITORY.

The Shepherd of Saliſbury Plain.
PART II.

Sold by J. MARSHALL,
(PRINTER to the CHEAP REPOSITORY for Religious and Moral Tracts) No. 17, Queen-Street, Cheapſide, and No. 4, Aldermary Church-Yard, and R. WHITE, Piccadilly, LONDON
By S. HAZARD, at BATH: and by all Bookſellers, Newſmen, and Hawkers, in Town and Country.—Great Allowance will be made to Shopkeepers and Hawkers.

PRICE THREE HALF-PENCE.
Or 6s. 9d. per 100.—3s. 9d. for 50.—25 for 2s. 3d.
[Entered at Stationers Hall.]

54 (*above left*) [?J. Lee], title page of Hannah More, *Black Giles the Poacher; with some Account of a Family who had rather live by their Wits than their Work. Part I*, woodcut, 5.08 × 5.09 cm ($2\frac{1}{2} \times 2\frac{7}{8}$ in.), London 1796, by permission of the British Library, 4420.i.2(2)

55 (*above right*) [?J. Lee], title page of Hannah More, *The Shepherd of Salisbury Plain. Part I*, woodcut, 7.6 × 7.6 cm ($3 \times 3\frac{1}{4}$ in.), London 1795, by permission of the British Library, 4418.f.3(9)

the Association to purchase from him an image which showed how frugal and deficient their diet had become.

As Donald also suggests, Gillray himself, who was too independent in his political attitudes to be comfortable in the role of "hired gun" for the Association, may himself have been unpersuaded by his own image of peace and plenty. On a proof impression of this print, he had written, "Of the truth of ye representation an appeal is made and submitted to the feelings of ye internal Enemies of Gt Britain." If this was taken to refer especially to the right-hand roundel, those internal enemies were presumably to be taken as the members of the reform societies, whose leaders, Thelwall among them, had just been acquitted of a charge of high treason which had alleged that they were conspiring to overthrow the government and constitute a republic on the model of France. If it was taken, however, to refer to the left-hand roundel, it might be read as sug-

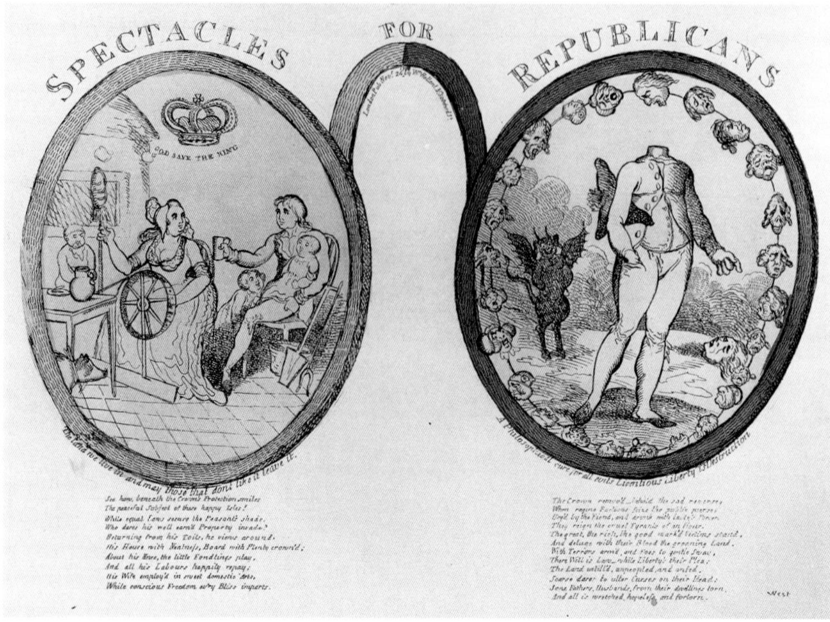

56 [Richard Newton], *Spectacles for Republicans*, etching, 25.4 × 35.5 cm ($10\frac{5}{8} \times 14\frac{3}{4}$ in.), London 1795, the Trustees of the British Museum, London, BM Sat 8695

gesting that the plenty enjoyed by the yeoman farmer was obviously a misrepresentation of the true state of Britain, and that, as many believed, the real "internal Enemies" were those who were attempting to pass it off as true, the members of the Association. In the final version of the print, and probably at the Association's insistence, these words were replaced by the anodyne dedication "To the People & the Parliament of Great-Britain."[20]

The "Constitutional Medal" raised its own awkward question about the contrast formula, especially when compared with the print on which it was based, *Spectacles for Republicans* by Richard Newton (fig. 56), presumably specifically commissioned as the design for the medal. Newton, who had been a brilliant teenage radical caricaturist until his publisher was prosecuted and imprisoned for selling Paine's *Letter Addressed to the Addressers*, appears to have been as uncomfortable as Gillray with his propaganda mission, or at any rate to have chosen to interpret it in his own way. Designing his left-hand roundel after many months of serious shortages, Newton leaves it to us to imagine the abundant food which had made his rural family so cheerfully plump: all that appears on the table, beside the jug of drink, is a provocatively empty plate. The housewife is provocative in a different way, offering to the spectator a full sight of her exposed and ample breast and even a glimpse of her nipple, as if to make visible the phrase "the bosom of the family." But if Newton found it difficult on the left-hand side of the print to discipline himself to the decencies of loyalist propaganda, he hardly seems to have tried on the right-hand, where a jolly devil looks much too good-natured to be dangerous, the body of the aristocratic Frenchman seems entirely unconcerned that his head has been removed, and the heads that surround him, as if in a daisy-chain, look too outraged or disappointed by their fate to look quite as dead as they should. All this, together with Newton's playful conversion of his two roundels into a pair of spectacles, may suggest that he was deliberately subverting the loyalist aims of his employers, but it is just as likely

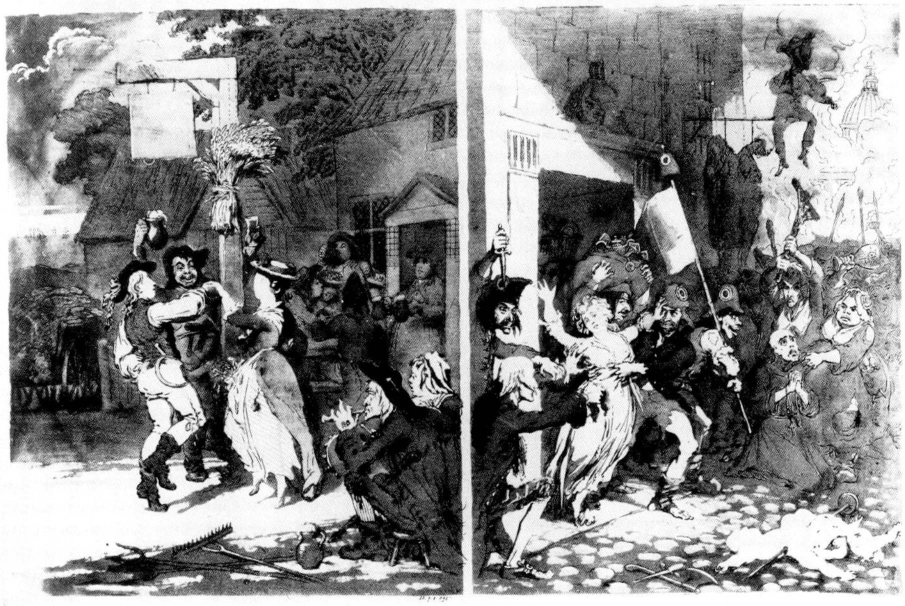

57 James Gillray, *Lawful Liberty/Liberty without Law*, unfinished, undated, unpublished aquatint, 22.8 × 30.4 cm ($9\frac{1}{4}$ × 12 in.), the Trustees of the British Museum, London, BM Sat 8301

that he was making the professional judgment that loyalist propaganda might need to be lighter if it were to reach beyond the poor who were already persuaded of their own contentment, and to engage those who might prefer to be amused than sermonized into loyalty.

The problem with such commissioned propaganda, intended to be bought by rich loyalists for distribution among the poor, is that if it were to sell it had to embody an image of the poor which corresponded with what the rich wished to believe about them; but if it were to persuade the poor it had embody an image in which they could recognize themselves, or which at least represented them in a light they did not find offensive. It is possible that the cottage scene as it appears in Newton's caricature – with its hints both of scarcity and cheerful sensuality – would have fulfilled those last criteria, but it was hardly calculated to appeal to its intended purchasers. Accordingly, when it was reproduced on the Constitutional Medal, the engraver, as well as clearing up the confusion in Newton's design as to whether the scene was set indoors or outside, also adjusted the housewife's clothing and put something chunky and appetizing on the plate, at the same time giving the laborer's legs a more classical tone and conformation. But short of rejecting Newton's design altogether, he could do nothing much to remove the element of caricature from the scene on the reverse, though he did his best by drastically reducing the size of the comic devil and adding some more admonitory text: "Abhor Evil Cleave To That Which Is Good." The result was an absurd mismatch between the two sides of the medal. The contrast formula, at least if it set out to sermonize rather than amuse, required its audience to be either strongly attracted to one side of the contrast or strongly repelled by the other, but there was nothing attractive or repellant about the Constitutional Medal, and it must have been difficult for those lucky enough to receive it at the hands of their superiors to identify very strongly with the family on the obverse, or to deplore with much conviction the scene on the "sad reverse."

In what may well have been his first attempt to fulfil the commission from the Association, the untitled, unfinished aquatint known as *Lawful Liberty/Liberty without Law* (fig. 57), Gillray also chose to represent the British poor in the cheerful mode of "low-comedy" that was the stock in trade of the caricaturist. The contrast here is between the liberty enjoyed by the rural poor in Britain at harvest home, as they dance and play outside a country pub, and an anarchic carnival of violence in France – a priest about to be beaten to death, others already hanged, babies bayoneted, an old aristocrat pleading with the *sans-culottes*, one of whom bears a teasing resemblance to Charles James Fox, who are dragging his daughter away to be raped. Had it been finished, it might well have been the most successful piece of visual propaganda issued by the Association, for it contrasted a genuinely horrific view of the new France with an image of old England, as a place of jolly alcoholic leisure; and Gillray as well as Newton may have been right in believing that there was a constituency among the poor who would prefer to recognize themselves in such an image than in a more sober and virtuous one. Festivals such as harvest home came rarely enough in the rural calendar, but they may well have been occasions when the laboring poor shared something of the "peace and plenty" of Georgian ideology, and became, briefly, "conscious" of the liberty they were continually told they enjoyed. But as Diana Donald has suggested, this image of the rural poor as, however briefly, released from labor and from the surveillance and discipline of their employers, and coming together in a community rather than divided into discrete families, was not calculated to win favor with the Association, and it seems likely that Gillray was required to substitute for it the relatively polite aquatint he eventually produced.[21]

The presumed rejection of *Lawful Liberty/Liberty without Law* by the Association indicates that the problem of using the cottage scene as a medium of loyalist propaganda may go further than I have so far suggested. For the Association clearly wanted cottage scenes to carry two different messages. On the one hand, it seems to have wanted such scenes to depict an idealized loyalist version of the rural poor as thoroughly domesticated and in full enjoyment of the rewards of domestic virtue and the protection of "equal laws." Thus imagined, they would share no grievances with other members of their class, and would have no interest in participating in collective political action – associating together for parliamentary reform, or engaging in Paley's "public uproar and confusion." On the other hand, the Association wanted the cottage scene to awaken the patriotism of the poor by representing the individual family as an image of a collective national identity. The logic of this doubling was clear enough in loyalist political theory, which represented the family as the nursery of patriotism, the place where we first learn that we share a collective identity with others that eventually reaches out to embrace the whole nation, and represented the nation, in turn, as a larger version of the family, with the king as father (so that the crown in *Spectacles for Republicans* fulfils precisely the same function as a portrait of the king might do). It was impossible, however, to represent this logic by means of the cottage-door motif, which so insistently valorized the domestic at the expense of, and in opposition to, any notion of the community or collective life. Once again it is instructive to contrast these cottage scenes with the

Cheap Repository Tracts, which were probably more successful as propaganda by being more narrowly concentrated in terms of ideology. They were much more concerned to teach industriousness, thrift, and piety than patriotism; they showed the good poor as myopically focused on their families, as if an essential part of domestic virtue was to be entirely unconcerned with any larger collective identity whether in terms of class or nation. The only sense of collectivity or community they permitted the poor was as members of the congregation of their parish church or of their Sunday school, where they were imagined as interacting not primarily with others in their own station in life but with the rich and charitable, supposed always to be on the lookout to reward or condemn them according to the degree of their domestic piety and their acquiescence in what they were told was the providential division of society into rich and poor.

One can read in various ways the relationship between More's tracts and the cottage paintings by Gainsborough with which this chapter began. On the one hand, More implicitly attacks the aesthetic of the picturesque which for John Smith, for example, and Uvedale Price,[22] had found its most complete expression in Gainsborough's landscapes and in "cottage scenery" where delapidation and unkempt nature were more highly prized than the neatness which for More was the sign of the good poor. This is precisely how Smith had read *Black Giles*. On the other hand, More can be seen as voicing the unspoken ideology of Gainsborough's paintings, his habit of imagining the "peasantry" as entirely defined by their domestic identity, each family inhabiting its own sequestered paradise, quarantined from contamination by any notion of collective life, even of collective labor. In the process of voicing that ideology, however, More made it much more overtly political; the adherence to the ideal of decollectivized domesticity became a test not only of the dutiful industriousness of the poor but of the deference that would keep them, and hopefully the nation itself, uninfected by the influenza of liberty disseminated by the *Rights of Man* or the popular reform societies. In the process, she was politicizing also the ideal of retirement from public life that the polite had been able to imagine through the lens of Gainsborough's cottage-paintings. If the Cheap Repository Tracts told the poor that their duty was to fear God, honor the king, work hard, and stay at home, the duty of the rich, as the tracts always implied and often demonstrated, was to be active in the surveillance of their inferiors, making sure the poor did just as they were told.

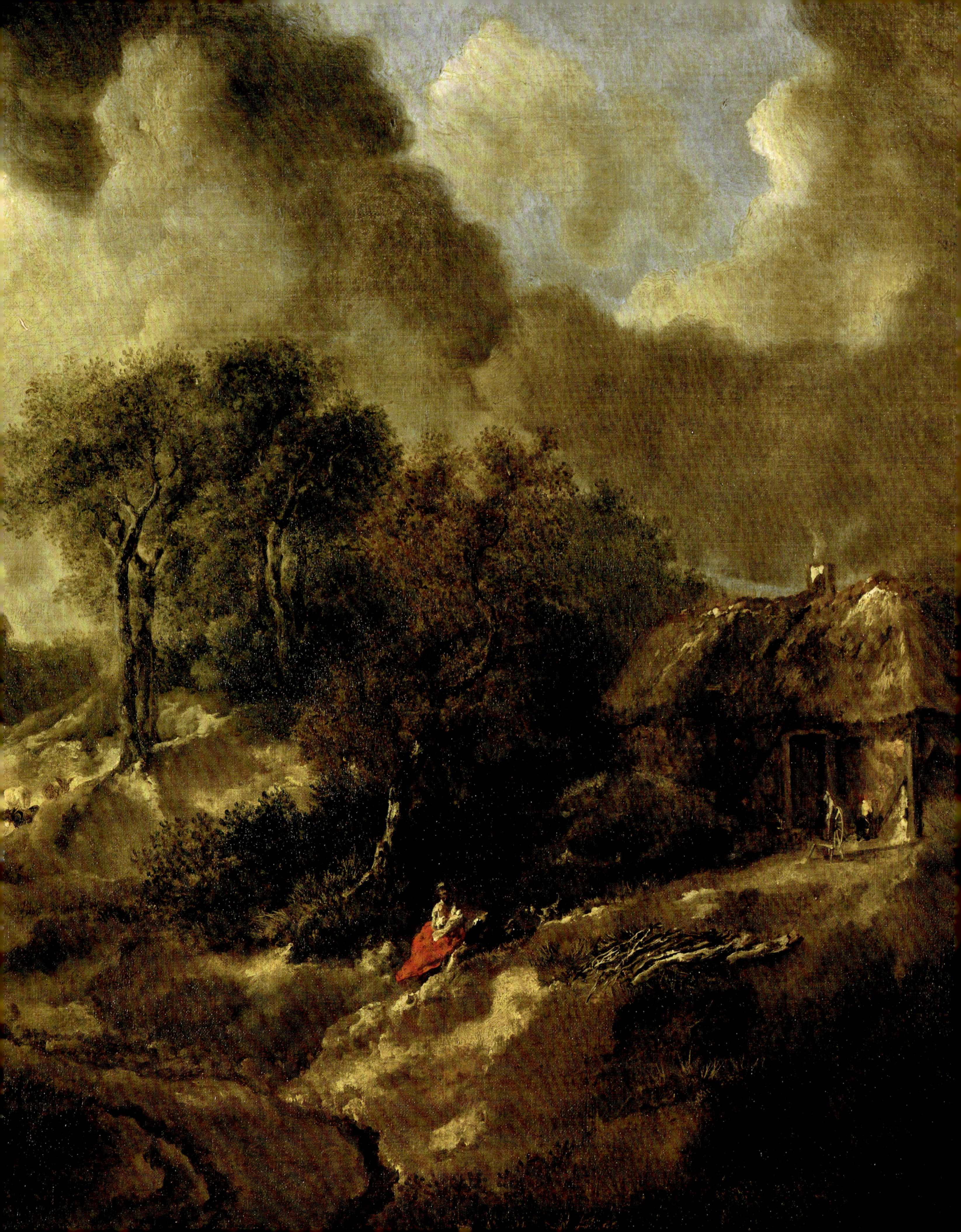

Part Two Gainsborough and the Theme of the "Cottage Door"

facing page Thomas Gainsborough, *Wooded Landscape with Figures, Donkeys, Pool and Cottage* (detail of fig. 60)

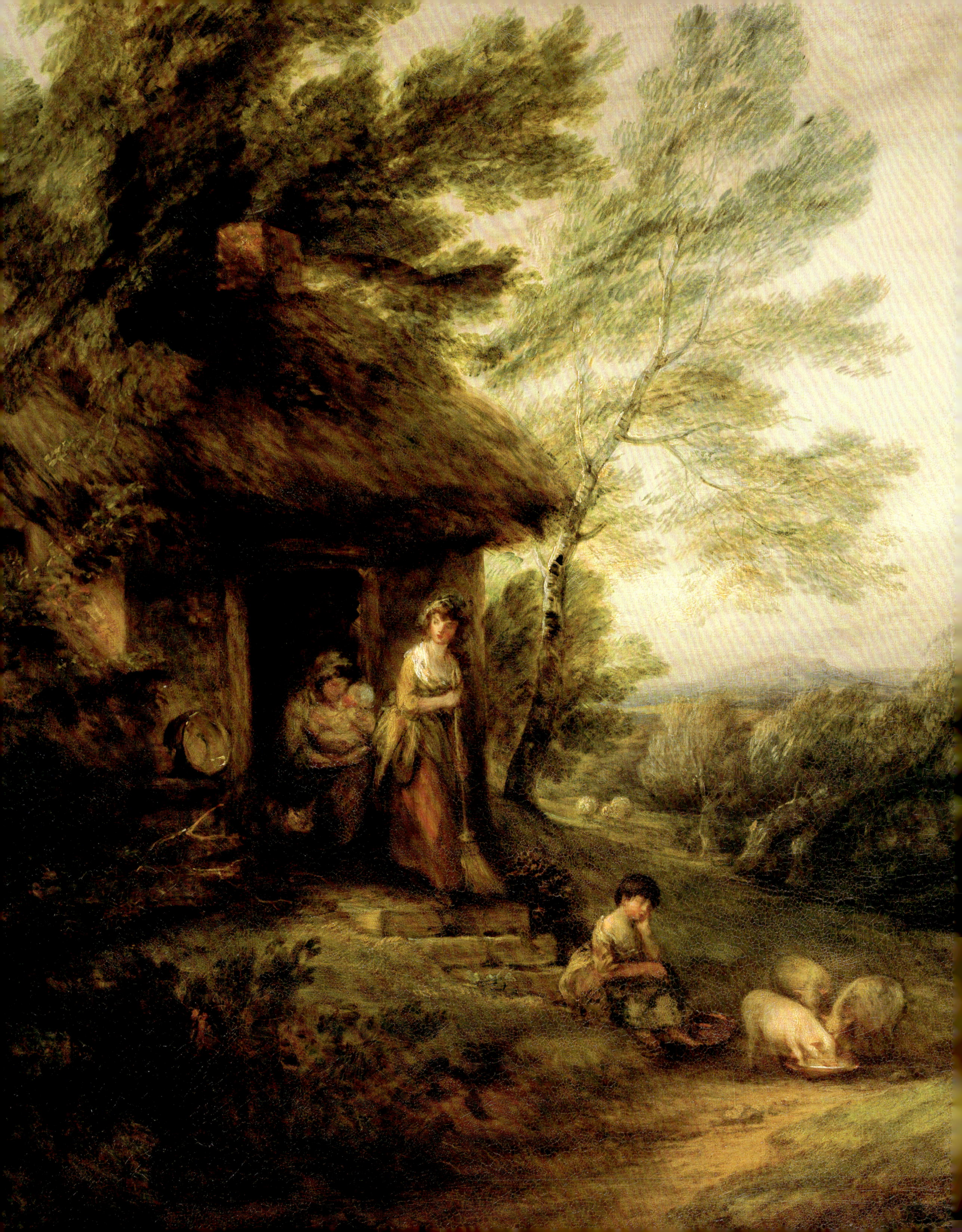

Michael Rosenthal

Gainsborough's Cottage Doors: A Matter of Modernity

In July 1788, well into his final illness, Gainsborough wrote to Sir Joshua Reynolds, "to beg a last favor, which is to come under my Roof and look at my things, my Woodman you never saw."[1] Reynolds reported of the visit he made that "the impression of it upon my mind was, that his regret at losing life, was principally the regret of leaving his art; and more especially as he now began, he said, to see what its deficiencies were; which, he said, he flattered himself in his last works were in some measure supplied."[2] These "last works" included not only *The Woodman*, now known only from Peter Simon's 1791 engraving (fig. 58), but also his *Peasant Smoking at a Cottage Door* which Henry Bate-Dudley had reported as having been completed that May of 1788, although it seems likely that the artist continued working on it until his death in August (see pl. v).[3] The former reprised a figure that had first appeared in a landscape of the mid-1750s (fig. 59) and the latter was the final working of a subject that had likewise been an early focus of Gainsborough's interest. Indeed, a landscape of about 1748 also pictured the relaxed family, the smoking chimney, and the pile of firewood (fig. 60).[4] So these two late works are linked radically to the earliest, and to themselves, for the figure of the man blowing smoke rings outside his cottage was developed from a study of the same model on which *The Woodman* had been based. This suggests that there are intimate connections between such "fancy pictures" as *The Woodman*, where an individual rustic serves as the subject, and landscapes or cottage scenes where such figures play a smaller part within a larger whole. The fact that the *Girl with Pigs* (Castle Howard) which had been exhibited at the Royal Academy in 1782 reappeared in a landscape of 1786 rather confirms that suggestion (see fig. 5 and pl. iv).

Before attempting a more detailed analysis of these late rural scenes, it is worth returning to Reynolds's appraisal of his erstwhile rival. His writing of "deficiencies" being "in some measure supplied" demands that one ask what those "deficiencies" were. Anyone who had been reading the *Discourses* so far would have known that an art which had developed, as had Gainsborough's, from the Netherlandish school, and which concerned itself with humble subjects, had to be considered inferior to the elevated fables realized in the abstracted linear manner of Florentine or Roman Renaissance art. But, Reynolds assured his readership, Gainsborough had learned a great deal of value from Rubens and Van Dyck, and that "whatever he attempted he carried to a high degree of excellence."[5] The meaning of this statement can be found in two earlier *Discourses* where Reynolds argued that "we have the sanction of all mankind in preferring

facing page Thomas Gainsborough, *Cottage Door with Girl and Pigs* (detail of pl. iv)

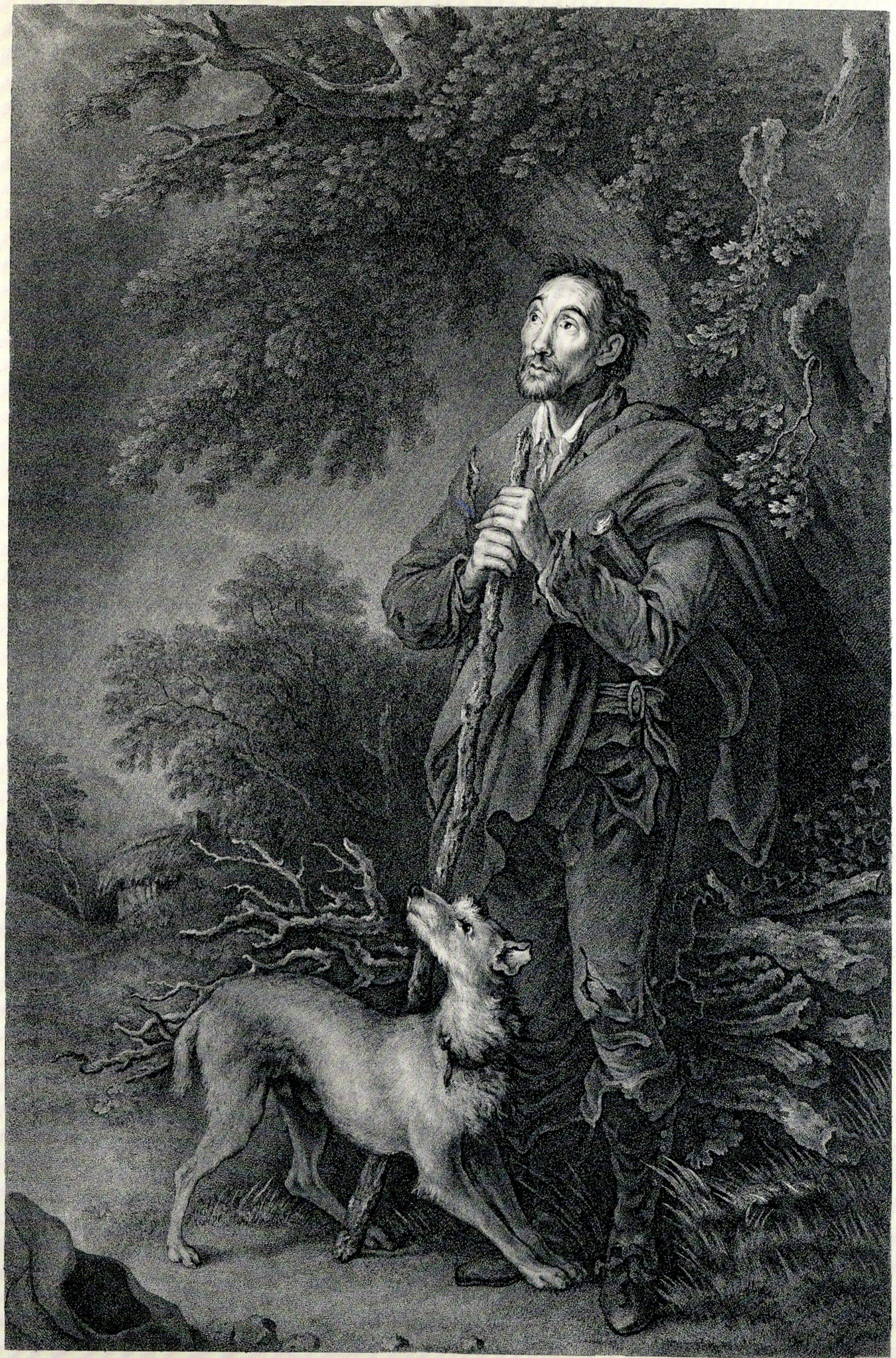

Painted by T. Gainsborough. Engrav'd by P. Simon.

THE WOODMAN.

Engraved from the original Picture, in the Collection of the Right Hon.[ble] the Earl of Gainsborough.

Publish'd. Apr. 1 1791 by John & Josiah Boydell, Cheapside, & at the Shakspeare Gallery Pall Mall London.

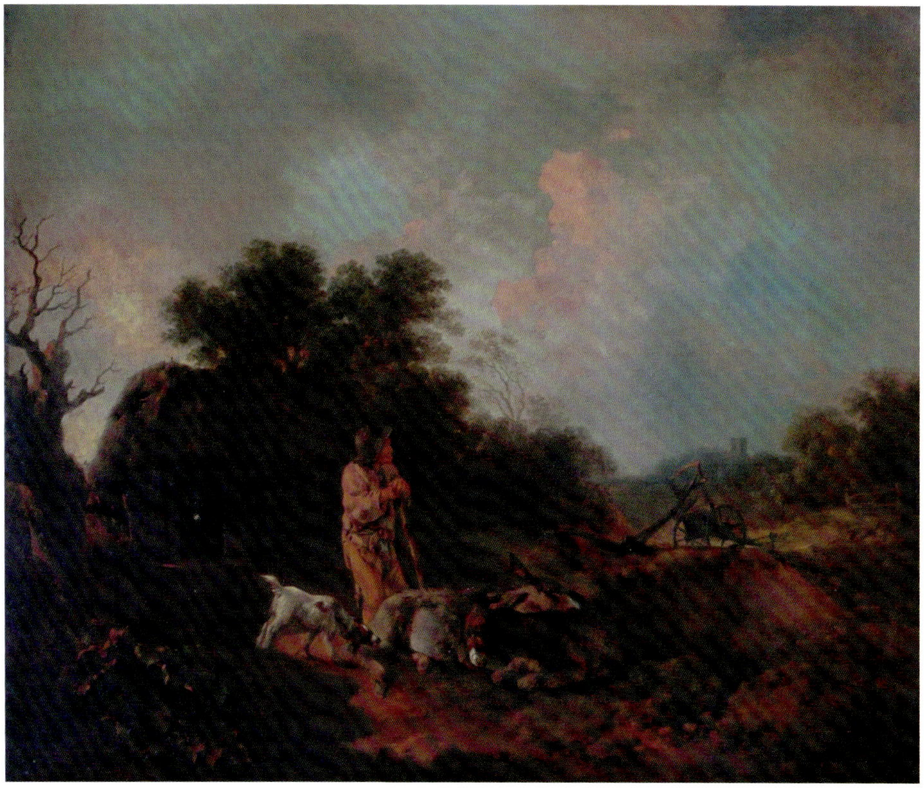

59 Thomas Gainsborough, *Wooded Landscape with Old Peasant and Donkeys outside a Barn*, c. 1755–7, oil on canvas, 49.5 × 59.7 cm ($19\frac{1}{2}$ × $23\frac{1}{2}$ in.), Michael Clarke-Jervoise, Harrogate (on loan to Temple Newsam House, Leeds)

genius in a lower rank of art, to feebleness and insipidity in the highest," and that:

> perfection in an inferior style may be reasonably preferred to mediocrity in the highest walks of art. A landskip of Claude Lorain may be preferred to a history by Luca Giordano; but hence appears the necessity of the connoisseur's knowing in what consists the excellency of each class; in order to judge how near it approaches to perfection.[6]

Reynolds's comments on Gainsborough's handling were consistent with this. His remark that "all those odd scratches and marks . . . this chaos, this uncouth and shapeless appearance, by a kind of magick, at a certain distance assumes form, and all the parts seem to drop into their proper places; so that we can hardly refuse acknowledging the full effect of diligence, under the appearance of chance and hasty negligence" closely alludes to what Vasari had written of Titian. William Aglionby's 1685 translation (reissued in 1719) claimed that Titian's works were "so full of strokes and spots, after a certain bold Manner, that they seem nothing near, but look very well at a distance" and, like Reynolds, stressed that this was the consequence of hard work: to achieve these effects "seems easie" but was actually "the most laborious of all."[7]

58 (*facing page*) Peter Simon after Thomas Gainsborough, *The Woodman*, 1790, stipple engraving, 64.3 × 43.2 cm ($25\frac{3}{8}$ × 17 in.), Gainsborough's House Museum, Sudbury, Suffolk

This allowed Reynolds to locate both Gainsborough and his works within a highly respectable painterly tradition, and equipped him with a rhetorical means of accommodating Gainsborough's handling within an academic environment from which the painter himself had withdrawn some time before. Others were

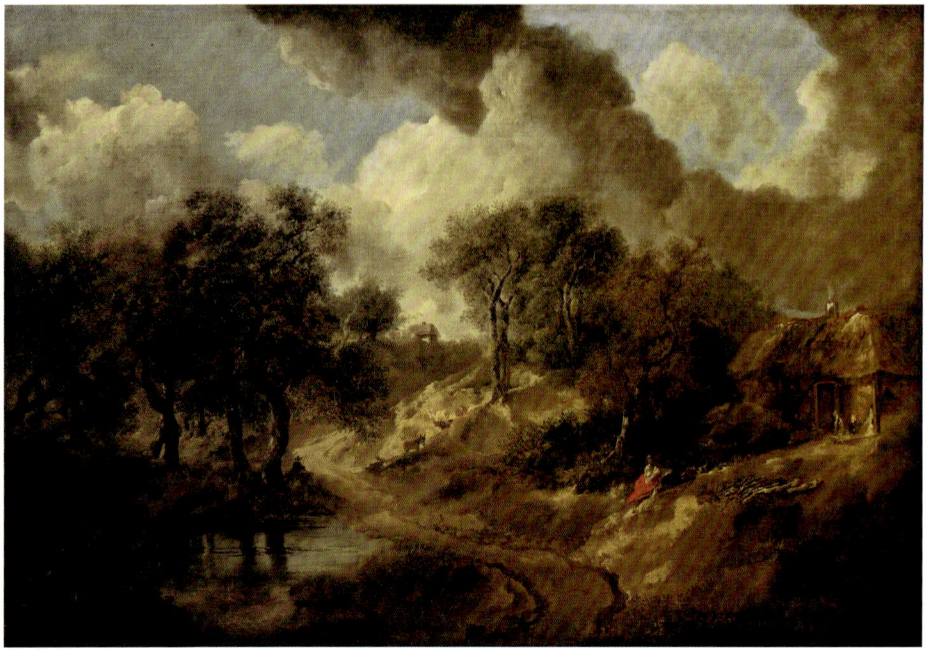

60 Thomas Gainsborough, *Wooded Landscape with Figures, Donkeys, Pool and Cottage*, c. 1748, oil on canvas, 66 × 95 cm (26 × 37$\frac{3}{8}$ in.), Kunsthistorisches Museum, Vienna

also aware of his paint surfaces. by 1782 Joseph Holden Pott had been writing that:

> Nothing can be more charming, forcible, and harmonious than his colouring now is, his pencilling is broad and masterly, the light and shade wonderfully well managed, and the effect of his pictures not to be equalled by any master, antient or modern. His figures are admirable, and being beautifully adapted to landscape, afford a strong proof of how much this propriety assists the good effect of the whole.[8]

William Jackson later identified three manners in Gainsborough's style. The "first was an imitation of Ruysdael, with more various colouring – the second was an extravagant looseness of pencilling; which, though reprehensible, none but a great master can possess" and his "third manner was a solid, firm style of brush." Consistent with this later style, Jackson found such subjects as the cottage door "so pleasing as to disarm criticism."[9] A critical vocabulary that includes such words as "reprehensible" or "propriety" signals that there was an ethical element to paint handling. "Extravagant looseness" would be as reprehensible in a person as in brushwork; whereas "solid and firm" (Jackson might almost have added "manly") implied virtue.

Thus it was probably the *facture*, among other things, of the later works that allowed Reynolds to speak of "deficiencies" being "in some measure supplied" and, for this reason, it behoves one to play close attention to the *matière* of these paintings. For instance, when it comes to the cottage-door series Gainsborough began around 1772–3, the paintings do not exhibit "odd scratches or marks" or present anything approximating a "chaos," or an "uncouth and shapeless appearance," although there are contemporary portraits from this same period that certainly do. By 1782, Joseph Holden Pott was recognizing in Gainsborough's work qualities that elevated it to parity with the most celebrated Old Masters, as John Hayes maintains that, from around the mid-1770s, Gainsborough became concerned "to deepen his expressive powers and to extend the range of his subject-matter and appeal."[10] This new seriousness coincides with the deliberate manner in which he orchestrated his return to exhibiting at the Royal Academy in 1777. At this moment Gainsborough took pains to appear as an artist with an expressive range and formal technique on a par with the Old Masters.[11]

This painterly self-consciousness had become evident around 1772–3 when Gainsborough painted the first of the cottage-door series, *The Woodcutter's Return* (pl. 1), which was purchased by the Duke of Rutland. *The Woodcutter's Return* was not painted onto a canvas of standard size. So if the support was tailored to the composition, the inference is that the latter was something about which Gainsborough had thought long and seriously. He painted an evening scene, with a woodman and dog returning to a cottage, its door festooned with women and children. The women holding children cannot but put the spectator in mind of images of the Madonna and Child; the woodcutter, conversely, appears a secularized version of Christ carrying the cross. Hayes succinctly notes that "the smaller children look like putti who have escaped from a Correggio altarpiece."[12] In keeping with these religious allusions (the significance of which will be discussed below) the paint has been laid on with great deliberation, richness, and technical variety. Figures are comparatively solid. Distant trees are rendered through fine, built-up brushwork. The cottage window picks up the creams and yellows of the sunset with extraordinary finesse, and the overwhelming impression communicated both by subject and handling is that Gainsborough was deliberately working in what contemporaries ought to recognize as an Old Master idiom (fig. 61).

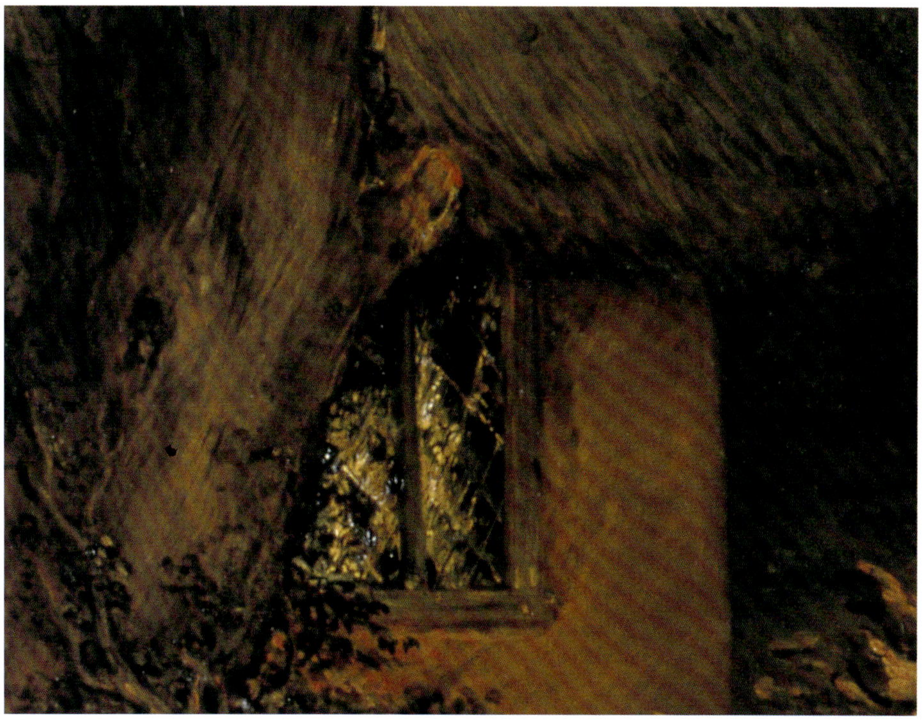

61 Thomas Gainsborough, *The Woodcutter's Return* (detail of fig. 2)

It may be significant here that, around the time of its creation, Gainsborough expressed his exasperation with Reynolds's views as to how something as culturally serious as history painting was to be achieved. This is known from a letter of 1773, wryly thanking his Bath neighbor, the pastel portraitist William Hoare, for sending him a copy of the fifth *Discourse*. Gainsborough complained that "betwixt Friends Sir Joshua either forgets, or does not chuse see that his Instruction is all calculated to form the History Painter, which he must know there is no call for in this country." He went on to contrast the "Ornamental Style" which appeared "form'd for Portraits," with a great style that "must consist in plainness & simplicity," and which could never serve for portraits.[13] Gainsborough consistently took care to appear unconcerned about such things as theorizing about art. This response shows that he was aware of the practicalities of making a living from painting. Moreover, his training at the St Martin's Lane Academy, presided over by William Hogarth, constantly stressed how modern life supplied endless subjects of the utmost seriousness. His training may well have impelled him to paint an alternative to what Reynolds wrote. *The Woodcutter's Return* contains formal references to the Old Master tradition, and in its style and subject matter posits a serious alternative to the kind of public art that Reynolds had been advocating.

Comparable points might be made about the *Cottage Door with Children Playing* that was sent to the Royal Academy exhibition of 1778 (pl. II). A preparatory drawing for the painting shows that the artist had more or less worked out his composition and grouping of the figures before starting on the canvas (fig. 62). This procedure is rare enough to demand notice. The academic tradition advocated by Reynolds stressed line over color; it held drawing to be central to any

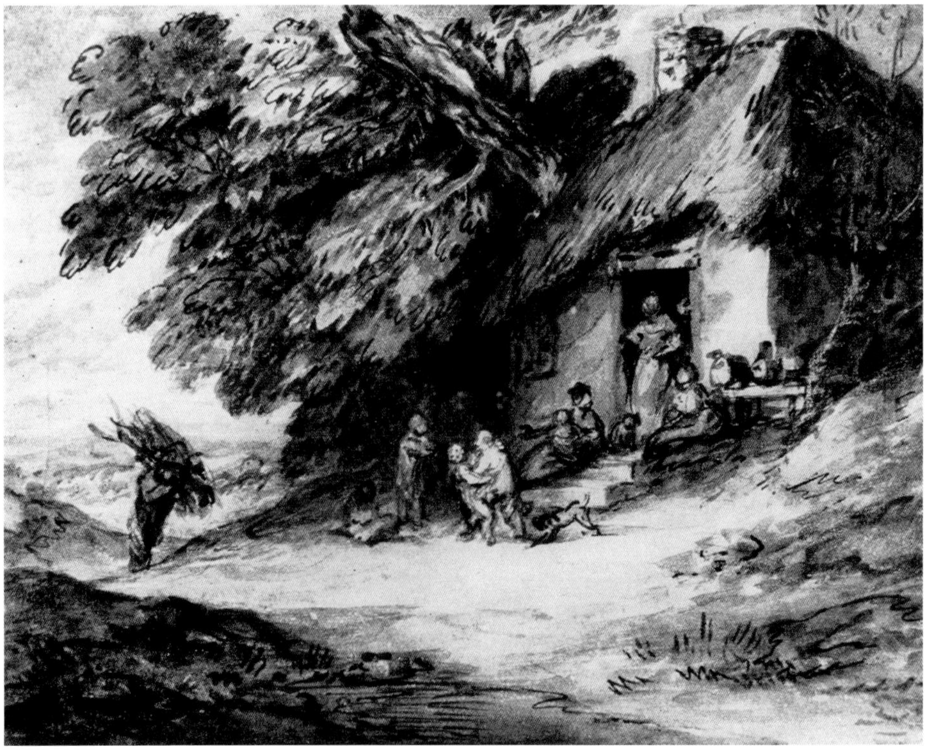

62 Thomas Gainsborough, *Wooded Landscape with Figures Outside a Cottage*, c. 1778, gray and black washes and white chalk, 27.1 × 34.6 cm ($10\frac{11}{16}$ × $13\frac{5}{8}$ in.), Collection of Sir Edwin Manton

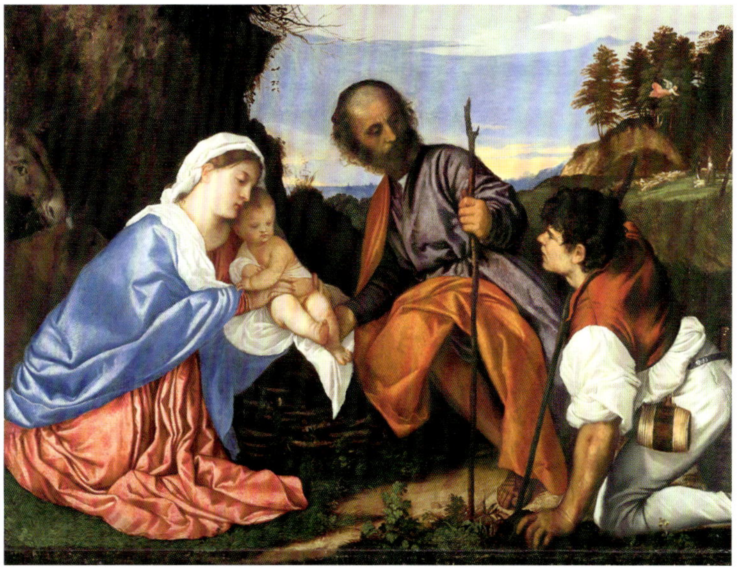

63 Titian, *Virgin, Child, and a Shepherd*, 1510, oil on canvas, 99.1 × 139 cm (39 × 54$\frac{7}{10}$ in.), National Gallery, London

serious art, for it was the indispensable armature of painting. Gainsborough, conversely, tended to work directly on the canvas, drawing (if at all) summarily, with the point of the brush, and making changes, painting figures in, painting figures out, as he went. Therefore, to try out this composition in a drawing (and there may have been more than one) signals something of the experimental nature, and seriousness, of the project.

In comparison with the earlier version there is a greater contrast between the woodcutter and what are presumed to be his family. Through the use of colour and the materiality of the paint handling, the woodman melts into his surrounds (fig. 63). By contrast, the women and children (with again an allusion to a Madonna and Child) are painted more firmly, with greater weight (see fig. 40). It is hard accurately to know what this contrast signifies, though one can evaluate its visual effect. The woodman appears worn into virtual dissolution by his toil: if echoing Christ carrying the cross then a theme of imminent death would be feasible. Gainsborough himself likened the necessity to earn his living to the drudgery of the carthorse, "confined *in Harn*[ess] to follow the track, whilst others ride in the Waggon, under cover, stretching their Legs in the Straw at Ease, and gazing at Green Trees & Blue Skies." Statements like this suggest that Gainsborough saw himself as much a beast of burden as the woodcutter.[14] The women and children are again reminiscent of Old Master religious painting in a general kind of way, as are some of the formal elements. The virtuosity of the yellow–purple contrast in the sky, for instance, realized in paint thin enough to lay bare the weave of the canvas, finds precedents in Titian's Holy Families (fig. 63). However, the way that the woodman's sleeve picks up the light so that it almost blends into the sky is Gainsborough's own.

The painting met with a good reception. The critic for *The General Advertiser*, mistakenly but forgiveably linking the subject to Shenstone's poem "The School Mistress," was particularly taken with the painting's light and color:

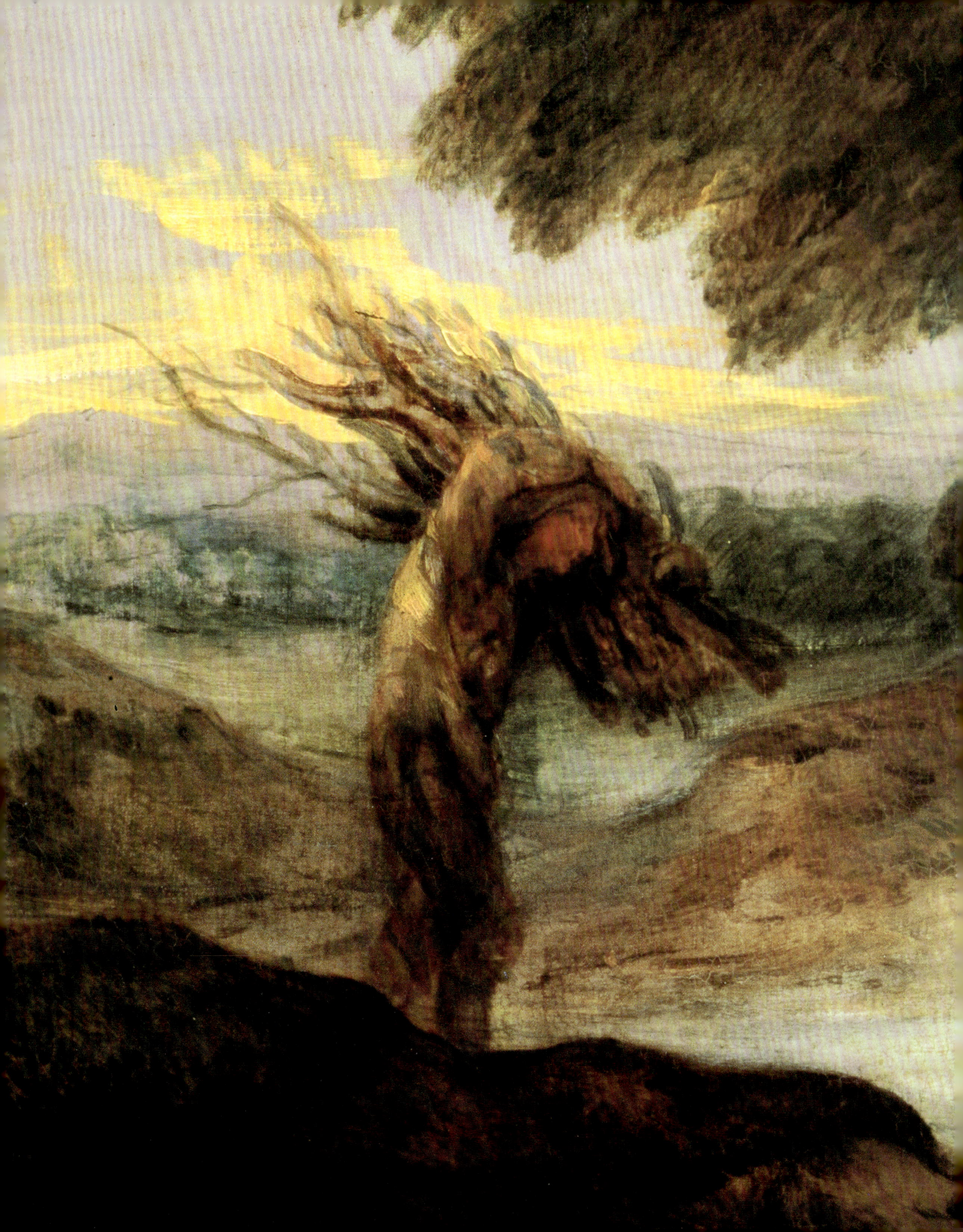

> The disposition is beautiful, and the keeping correct and masterly. It is in such performances as these, that the genius of Gainsborough is apparent. He gives his landscapes a warmth and beauty of colouring superior to most of his competitors; and we confess, we would forego the portion of pleasure we experience in viewing his portraits, for the ineffable delight we receive from his landscapes, and wish he would leave the one for the other.[15]

In praising the "keeping" so highly, this writer was recognizing the extraordinary technical skill manifest in harmonizing both tonal and coloristic values. As pigments cannot match the tonal range of nature, to create the illusion that they are doing so demands enormous skill in the harmonizing of tones through the use of color. To manage this was, in eighteenth-century Britain, to have achieved success in the "keeping" of a picture.[16] This critic, therefore, was well informed on the matter of painting. The management of the keeping was precisely one of those elements commonly admired in the Old Masters and that, in Reynolds's *Discourses* and elsewhere, was taken as the standard against which contemporary practice had to be measured. The same applied to "warmth and beauty of colouring." One needs, too, to take notice of the preference for Gainsborough's landscape over his portraits (though this may have been partisan). The same writer, for instance, went on to be critical of a Gainsborough portrait also on view for being "very faulty" in design, and "very bad" in drawing. While the keeping was "fine," the coloring was "cold," and the execution "hasty and harsh." In a way analogous to William Jackson he was identifying two manners in Gainsborough's painting, and far preferring one to the other.

The third variant on the theme of the cottage door was exhibited in the 1780 Royal Academy (pl. III). On a canvas of dimensions matching that of the *Woodcutter's Return*, Gainsborough painted a scene set deep in a forest where, in a cottage next to a busy stream, a nursing woman forms the apex of a roughly pyramidal group of figures. The composition was arrived at, to some degree, as Gainsborough went along. The "top branch of the main tree was originally placed slightly higher in the sky" and "the child at the far right was added after the completion of the rest of the group."[17] At some point Gainsborough extended the height of the canvas by adding strips at top and bottom – probably, as David Solkin has suggested, both to give the painting greater presence in the RA exhibition, and to signal the great seriousness he was attaching to these rural subjects.[18] The painting is a technical *tour de force* with built-up surfaces and bravura brushwork – the dry streak of creamy paint for the sky above the polled tree or the almost syncopated marks at the trunk of the principal tree. A brilliantly lit landscape stretches away to the left. The impression is that the shaded areas might have become a little too dark, although this manages to achieve what the painting's conservator Mark Leonard described as "an exceptional (and theatrical) sense of depth and atmosphere."[19]

Theatricality is the appropriate concept here, because, although it is consistent in direction, the strength of the illumination of the principal group is exaggerated, perhaps, in a properly academic way, to focus attention on it. The overarching tree contributes to this effect, too. The group focuses on a mother with fine, classical features which, as a comparison with his half-length portrait

64 Thomas Gainsborough (1727–1788), *Cottage Door with Children Playing* (detail of pl. II)

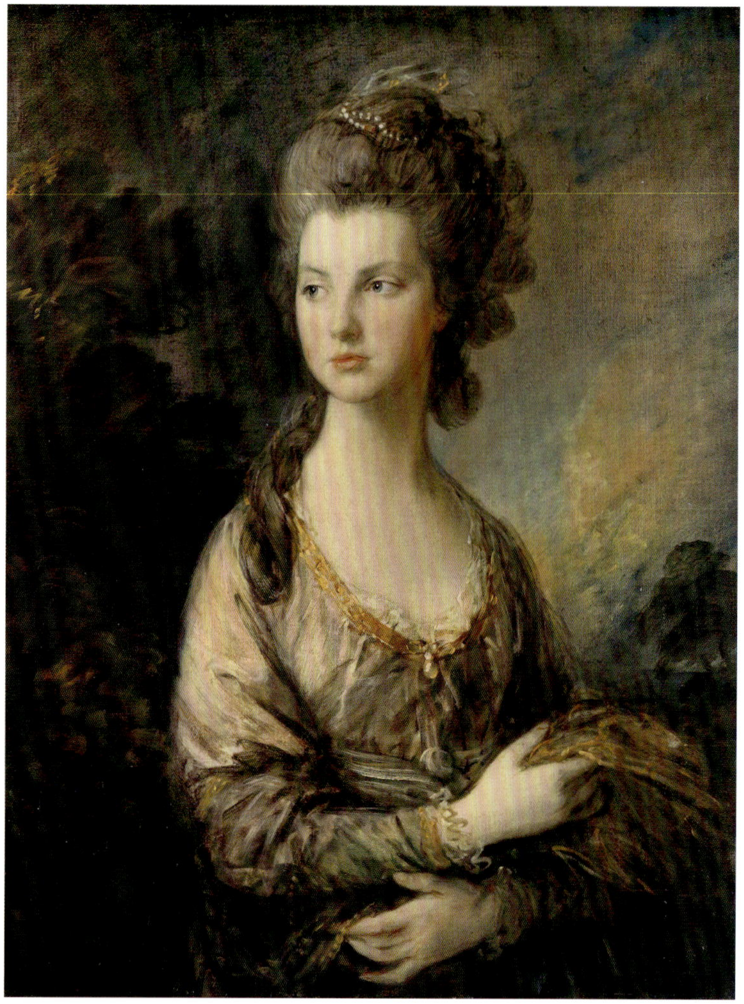

65 Thomas Gainsborough, *The Honourable Mrs. Thomas Graham*, c. 1775, oil on canvas, 89.5 × 69 cm ($35\frac{1}{4}$ × $27\frac{1}{8}$ in.), National Gallery of Art, Washington, D.C., Widener Collection

of *Mrs Graham* shows, rivaled those of any society beauty (fig. 65). And her hair is piled almost as high, which it is known from X-rays was deliberate, as though Gainsborough was encouraging the viewer to make this very association. It is impossible not to associate the woman and baby with a Madonna and Child, and it may be that her idealized beauty (for such is commonly also an attribute of the Virgin) is meant to reinforce that connection. At the same time, the host of non-biblical children attest to the secularity of the subject *per se.*

On inspecting these figures the spectator notices the extent to which the painting is concerned with describing, among the children, various manifestations of hunger. One child eats what may be a biscuit. Another spoons liquid from a bowl into the mouth of a third. The infant to the right stretches out a supplicatory bowl but is ignored, while the child in between gnaws on its knuckles. All is managed with restraint – this is no feeding frenzy – but it is an insistently repeated motif. Here it connects with actualities. In 1769 Gainsborough's Bath friend Philip Thicknesse published a harrowing *Account of the Four Persons found starved to Death at Duckworth in Hertfordshire*; and in *The Task* William Cowper later wrote of the "frugal housewife" who endures penury and who, once her children are grown and laboring, "shall not want/What, conscious of your virtue, we can spare."[20] The painting arguably is linked to the *topos* of frugality and virtuous stoicism, in that it shows the woman as behaving with fortitude and propriety. It is also the only cottage door without a male provider. This might be an invitation to the spectator to fill that role, or to feel virtue in knowing that he (and I am assuming that Gainsborough is appealing to men here), if confronted with such scenes in real life, would behave as charitably as Cowper, or indeed as any other person of sensibility.[21] The final painting of the series, the *Peasant Smoking at a Cottage Door*, is painted on a large canvas to emphasize its weightiness (pl. V). Here the link is, as it were, restored and the family is represented united in repose, with the woodcutter seated in front of the cottage, enjoying a pipe.

The artist continued to experiment as he worked this final variation on the theme. He painted out a standing woman to the left of the boy, and there was once another such behind the cottager.[22] He was evidently at pains to clarify this principal group. The dog, with its associations with fidelity, helps confirm that what one sees is exemplarily virtuous. The paint is worked to varying degrees – virtually minimalist in the landscape, scarcely less so in the indeterminate flock or herd with its ghostly mounted drover moving toward us along the track, in other passages, impasted. The effect of light through trees is appropriately dazzling, and recalls both Gainsborough's own work as well as Old Master painting in general.[23] Indeed, the rougher textures of the figure painting may allude to later Titian. The painting, formally aspiring to high artistic status, was meant as a pendant to *The Market Cart* (fig. 66).[24] To consider them in tandem will allow more accurate understanding of what kinds of contents Gainsborough had been painting into his surfaces.

Slightly smaller than the *Peasant Smoking*, *The Market Cart* is a spectacular demonstration of the craft of painting. Its technique varies. Impasted paint creates an illusion of clouds of grandeur and dense bulk, the illusion itself reinforced through their contrast with the thin, smooth, even wash of the pale blue sky. Foliage is hatched to allow for greater or lesser translucency and its refined glazes communicate what Henry Bate-Dudley described in December 1786 as a "a rich variation of the tints expressive of autumn – here the trees are verdant – a browner aspect there prevails – and all the varied greens and yellows temper the scene, and exhibit a pleasing harmony" (quite possibly repeating what Gainsborough had told him). The distance fades in glazes which Hayes sees as an acknowledgment of Claude, while the figures in the foreground are as subtly differentiated from the earth on which they rest.[25] Claude apart, both in subject and technique, *The Market Cart* would have been recognized as situated within that tradition of Netherlandish painting from which, as Reynolds observed, Gainsborough "learnt the harmony of colouring, the management and disposition of light and shadow, and every means which the masters of it practised to ornament and give splendour to their works."[26]

Flemish painting was associated with vulgar subjects and indiscriminate pictorial description. While Gainsborough might not scruple at the former, his handling was calculated to communicate generalities prized by the academic tradition; his trees are generic rather than individual species. Nor does he particularize his *staffage*. Gainsborough the ironist ("don't be in a hurry to deter-

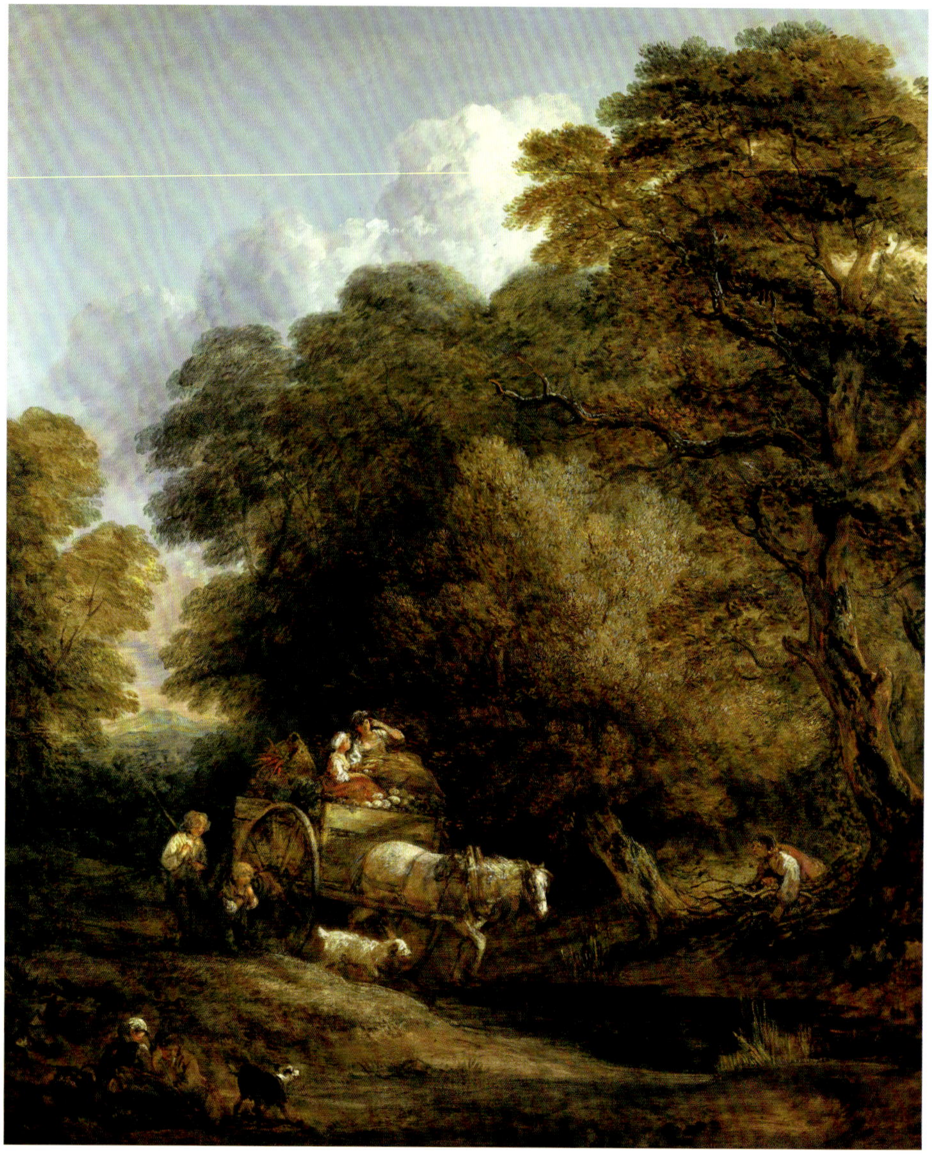

66 Thomas Gainsborough, *The Market Cart*, 1786, oil on canvas, 184.2 × 153 cm ($72\frac{1}{2} \times 60\frac{1}{4}$ in.), National Gallery, London

mine any thing about *me*, if you are, ten to one you are wrong," he wrote to William Jackson in 1770) turns Reynolds's strictures on their head.[27] To paint general nature, as he was, the painterly Flemish manner served as well as the linear Roman. Gainsborough was, with some irony, it seems, painting to a Reynoldsian brief while also proving Reynolds wrong. That is, he painted general subjects that engage with weighty themes and in so doing confirmed the peculiar qualities of contemporary British culture. The problem is that he did it in ways Reynolds could not have recommended or approved.

The Market Cart is itself laden with vegetables on which a girl and young woman repose while a boy and youth trudge alongside, as it is hauled through a hilly and wooded terrain. To one side a pair of figures, described by Bate-Dudley as "weary travellers," recline: their dog brindles at the cart, while the white dog padding along with the horse appears oblivious. To the right, a woodman handles his bundle so as to block access to the forest. There is no connectedness, such as one sees in the cottage doors, between these figures, and the contrast between the two paintings is striking. This imagery for this painting as well as the cottage doors had been established in the early 1770s in the exquisitely fine landscape painted for Viscount Bateman (Kenwood, London) which depicts peasants returning from market (figs. 1 and 67). Here, as Hayes points out, the motif of the cottage bathed in sunlight to the left when painted large served as the subject of the cottage door.[28] Further, the procession of mounted figures to the right relates to *The Market Cart*. Led on foot by a teenaged girl and red-headed boy, the procession's panniers are loaded with produce. In the gloom at the side of the road are slumped an old and a younger woman, begging. The boy draws the girl's attention to this, but she averts her gaze, spurns the opportunity to relieve the destitute. The formal rhyme of the beggars with the two figures reposing to the right of the cottage door amplifies the contrast between misfortune and fortune.

In the Bateman landscape, Gainsborough had been articulating in paint a response to the incursions of agrarian capitalism akin to that forcibly expressed in Oliver Goldsmith's 1770 poem *The Deserted Village*. Enclosure and engrossing, through which agricultural "improvement" was achieved, were perceived by their

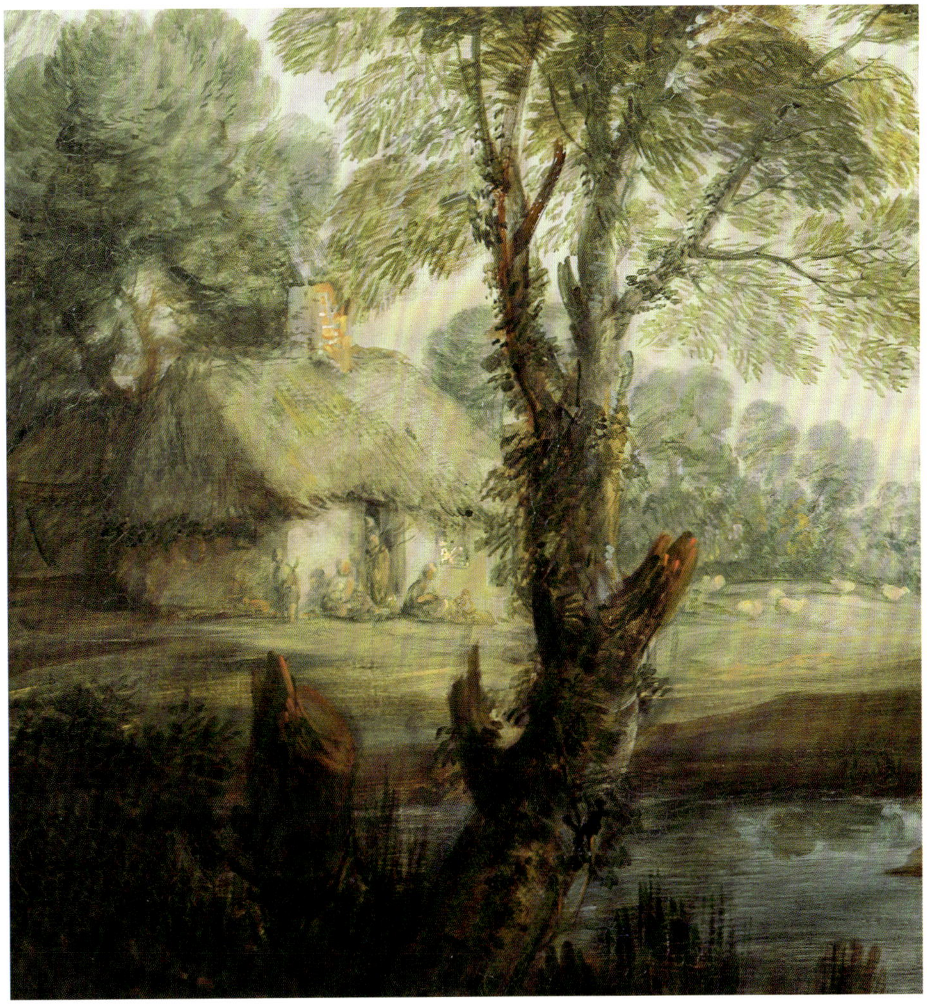

67 Thomas Gainsborough, *Peasants Returning from Market* (detail of fig. 1)

opponents as wrecking the moral economy of the countryside, most obviously manifested in migrations of the rural population. As Goldsmith put it, with these migrations the "rural virtues" left the land, along with "sweet Poetry . . . first to fly where sensual joys invade."[29] As Goldsmith wrote about rural depopulation, Gainsborough, persistently, painted and drew migrating peasants. In *The Market Cart* all save the woodman are on the move, from somewhere, to somewhere else. In the *Peasant Smoking* one discovers stability in stasis, the subject conforms to the *beatus ille* tradition of rural virtue and repose: "Unvex'd with quarrels, and undisturb'd with noise,/The country king his peaceful reign enjoys . . ." as Dryden had translated Virgil.[30]

The idea of the simple virtuous life played out in rural retirement, as against metropolitan racket, debauchery, and corruption, was persistent to the point of cliché in eighteenth-century Britain. Gainsborough invoked it when he wrote to William Jackson that he was "sick of Portraits and wish very much to take my Viol da Gam and walk off to some sweet Village where I can paint Landskips and enjoy the fag End of Life in quietness and ease," which words reinforce the possibility that there may have been some degree of personal identification with the fiction of the cottager.[31]

If rural retirement exemplified the moral life, Gainsborough's cottage doors had a serious ethical content, appropriate (as both Joseph Holden Pott and William Jackson had indicated in those comments quoted earlier) both to their recognizably masterly painting and their persistent paraphrasing of religious imagery. Likewise, the fancy pictures that developed out of the work of, among others, Murillo and presented, in the guise of semi-destitute children, secular variations of sacred originals, also taught the virtue of rural simplicity. I have already noted their close connection with landscapes in general and cottage scenes in particular, as though it were enough to isolate a figure from the latter to serve as the subject of one of the former. It bears remembering that Gainsborough, though dissolute in habits, was a believing and practising Christian. Beside the fancy pictures his later works more generally revealed a turn toward more serious subjects.

His *Country Churchyard*, now preserved in Maria Prestal's 1790 aquatint, went to the 1780 Royal Academy (fig. 68). It presented a homely reworking of the theme "Et in Arcadia Ego," which had been canonically realized by Poussin (fig. 69). In Gainsborough's painting a kneeling male and standing female rustic, both in the bloom of youth, puzzle out the inscription on the headstone of a grave. This reworking of a high art subject set now in an imagined arcadia of 1780s Britain would have put many in mind of Thomas Gray's *Elegy Written in a Country Church Yard*, the first sixteen lines of which, indeed, were inscribed on the print.[32] The ruinous church in Gainsborough's painting fits quite well what Gray memorializes (lines 21–4):

> For him no more the blazing hearth shall burn,
> Or busy housewife ply her evening care;
> No children run to lisp their sire's return,
> Or climb his knee the envied kiss to share.

and of which Gainsborough painted the living equivalent in his cottage doors.

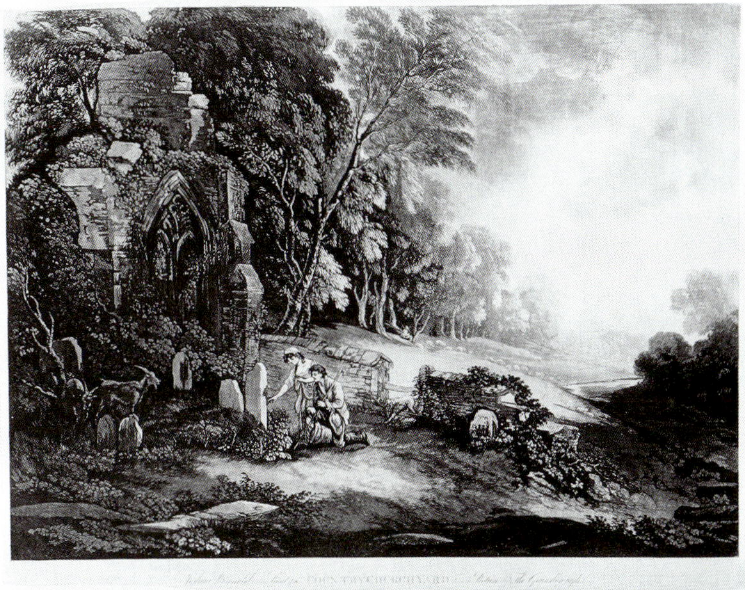

68 Maria Prestal after Thomas Gainsborough, *The Country Churchyard*, 1790, aquatint, 49.1 × 64.8 cm ($19\frac{5}{8} \times 25\frac{1}{2}$ in.), Gainsborough's House Museum, Sudbury, Suffolk

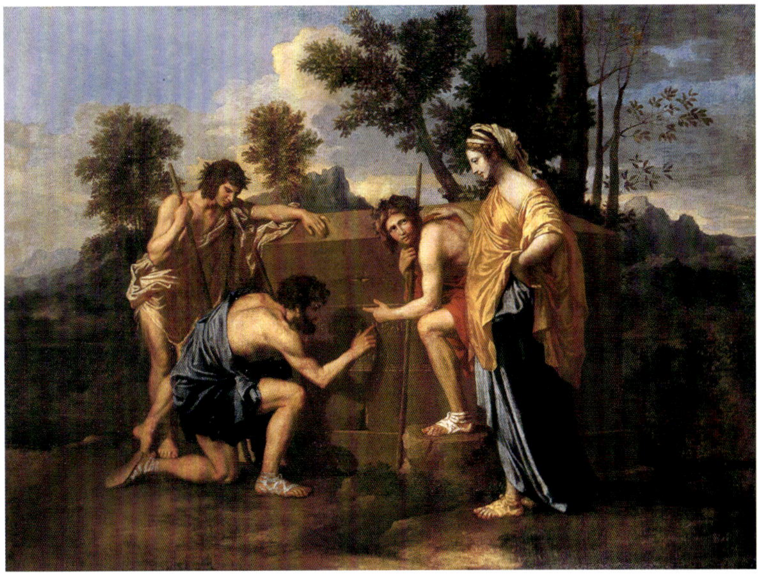

69 Nicholas Poussin, *Shepherds of Arcadia (Et in Arcadia Ego)*, 1650–55, oil on canvas, 85.5 × 121.5 cm ($33\frac{3}{4} \times 47\frac{5}{8}$ in.), Louvre, Paris

In 1783, in *Shepherd Boys with Dogs Fighting* (Kenwood, London) Gainsborough exhibited a composition adapted from Titian's *St Peter Martyr*, the coloring from Titian more generally, and the action from Hogarth's *Four Stages of Cruelty*. The work demonstrates how a "modern moral subject" might be realized in a painting of major artistic ambition.[33] As a corrective to the perverse scenario figured in *Shepherd Boys* he showed *Charity Relieving Distress* at Schomberg House the following year (fig. 70). The two women are as beautiful as any of the female cottagers, the iconography as explicitly Christian as the title is allegorical. The dove recalls the Holy Ghost, blessing the performance of a charitable act, while Martin Postle has brilliantly spotted that the beggar woman herself is a personification of charity, "loosely modelled" on the *Charity* Reynolds designed for New College Chapel, Oxford (see fig. 41).[34]

Contemporaries recognized part of what Gainsborough was attempting. When he exhibited *The Cottage Door* in 1780, one reviewer described it as a "beautiful scene, where serenity and pleasure dwell in every spot, and the lovely figures composed in the finest rural style, their situation worthy of them, forms a scene of happiness that may truly be called Adam's paradise."[35] The landscape of the cottage doors has conflated Eden with the Golden Age, perhaps in tacit recognition of the religious allusions in Gainsborough's subject. "Lovely" was an adjective deployed by others, as when Henry Bate-Dudley wrote of his "peasants" being in "that lovely class which his creative mind has formed to ornament his works: they exhibit grace, beauty, and elegance undadorned but by painter's hand."[36] According to the third Earl of Shaftesbury, ideal beauty was the image of ideal virtue. Indeed, Samuel Johnson had defined "lovely" when used adjectivally as "amiable; exciting love" to reinforce the message that quality was meant to convey.

This idea of virtue and beauty was being treated in subjects that by definition articulated a particular and critical stance toward the modern world. Gainsborough's reaction against the new agrarian capitalism manifested itself in a sympathy for its victims. Here it is signficant that one particular bugbear for the improvers, those for whom commons were simply potentially lucrative arable ground going to waste, was the fact that the poor, subsisting on their own terms, extended the notion of waste to their own time. The rural poor's preoccupation with the collection of firewood was a particular complaint, especially since, were these people working for a wage, they could buy coal.[37] In valorizing the woodcutter, as he eventually did, Gainsborough was demonstrating an ethical opposition both to the new market economy and, as will be seen, its effects on society.

To the innocence of the country it was traditional to oppose the corruption of the town; and both town and corruption were something the artist could not avoid. Gainsborough had to paint the wealthy, the very people who made the city appear a sink of corruption and iniquity, although he suffered few illusions about them. To William Jackson he wrote of "the fictitious Character of the Gentleman," and it is tempting to think that this might explain why he painted some of them so slightly as to attract critical disapprobation.[38] But the notion of the "fictitious character" fits with the well-known gripe about the "general tide of luxury which hath overspread the nation," as Smollett has Matthew Bramble pen in *Humphry Clinker*, and with general anxieties about the corruption of the great and the dissolution of social boundaries that reached a crisis in the 1780s.[39]

Gainsborough made a dispassionate critique of metropolitan life in *The Mall, St. James's Park* of about 1783 (fig. 71). Just before the 1784 RA exhibition from which he withdrew his exhibits, *The Mall* was advertised as a "magnificent picture of a park, with a variety of figures in the manner of Watteau."[40] To connect the painting to Watteau (Gainsborough, interestingly, later tried to deny the link) associated it with the exquisite *fêtes galantes* in which exaggeratedly precious aristocratic cyphers had been imagined as playing out their lives.[41] Watteau – represented as a satirist by the comte de Caylus – had painted what Reynolds tellingly referred to as "French Gallantries."[42] This was an effeminate inverse of masculine, beef-eating British society (remember the impact of Hogarth on the young Gainsborough here), and one that was, appropriately, painted in what had

70 (*facing page*) Thomas Gainsborough, *Charity Relieving Distress*, oil on canvas, cut down, 98 × 76.2 cm ($38\frac{1}{2}$ × 30 in.), private collection

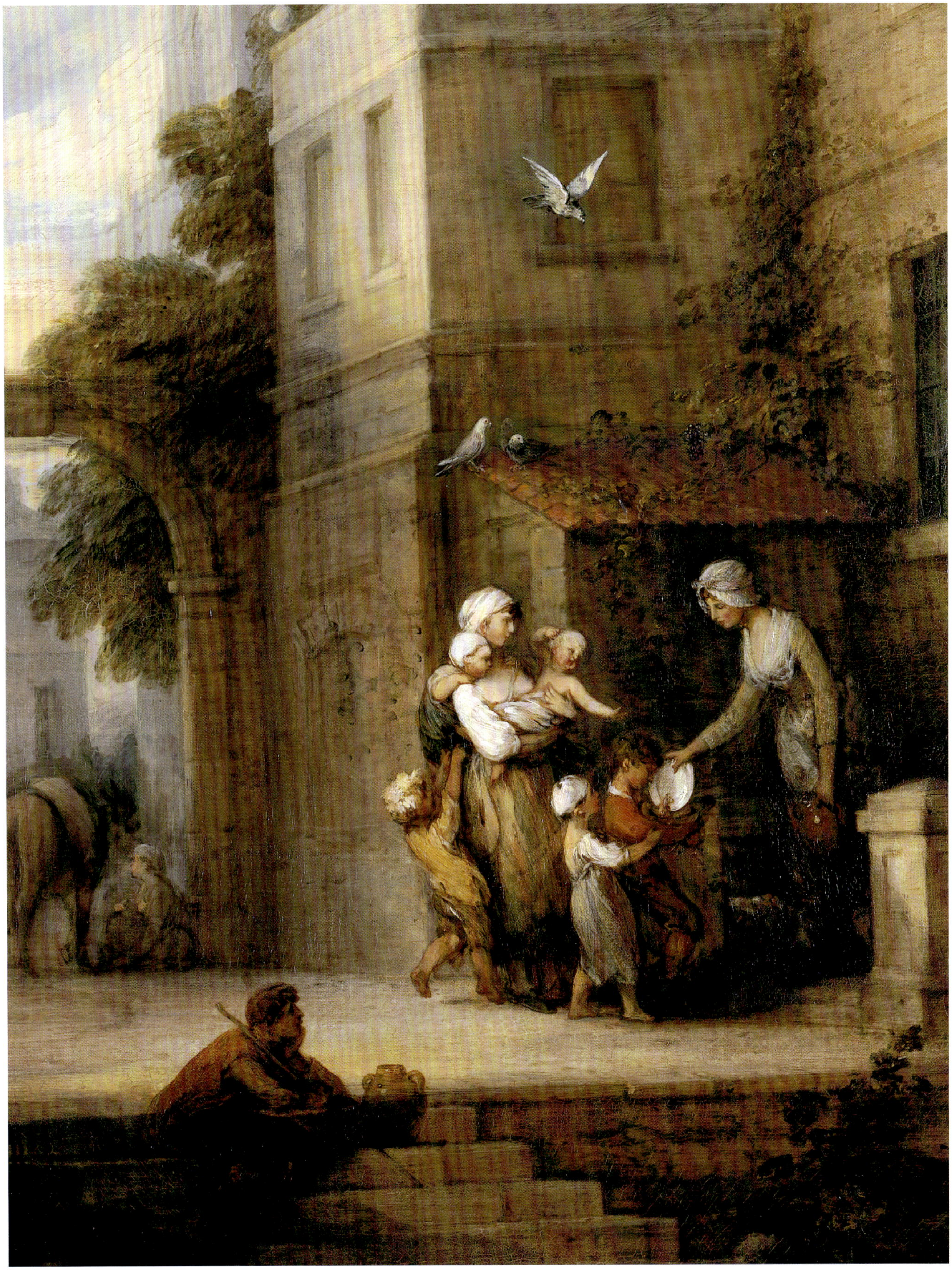

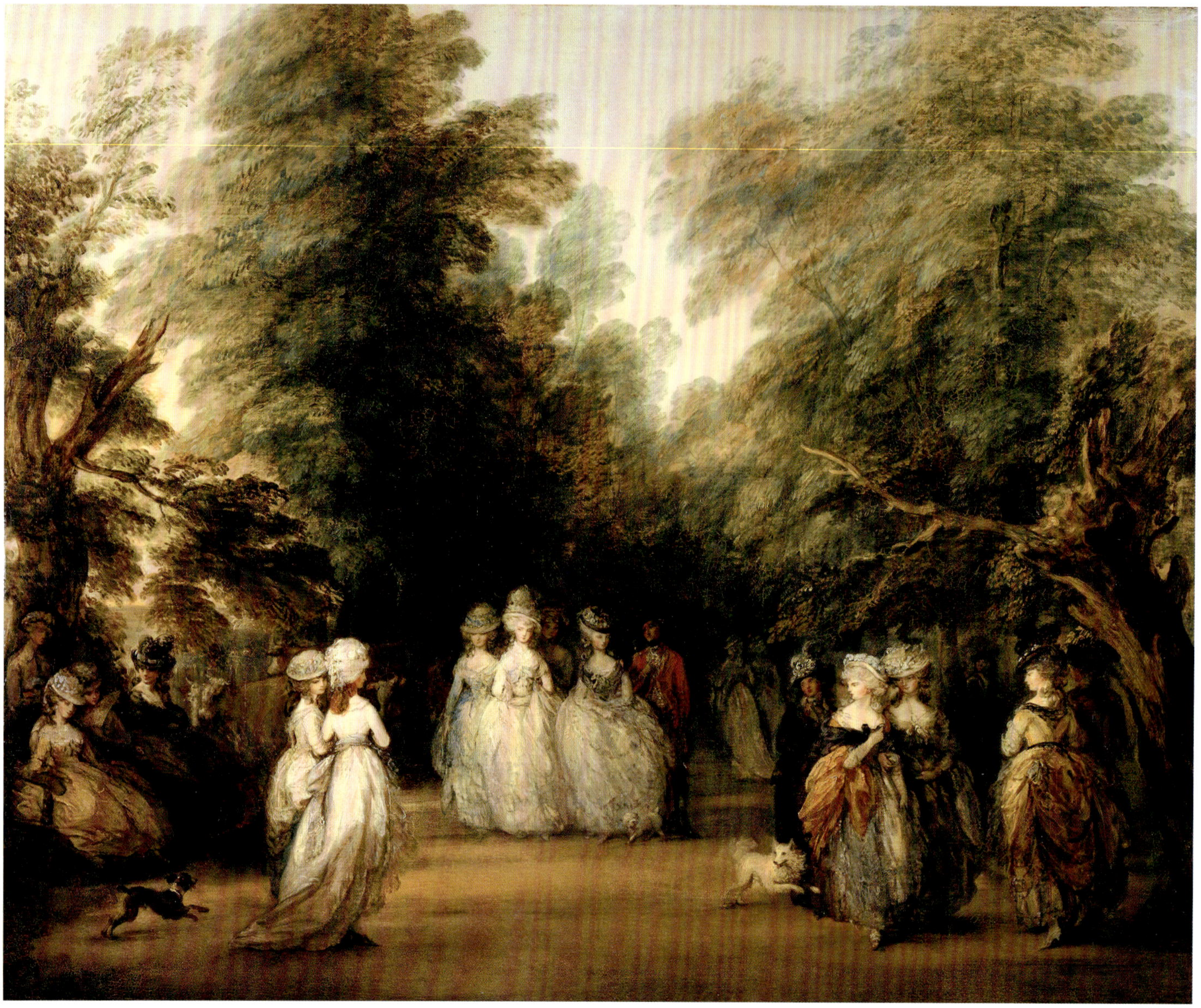

71 Thomas Gainsborough, *The Mall, St. James's Park*, c. 1783, oil on canvas 120.6 × 147 cm ($47\frac{1}{2}$ × $57\frac{1}{8}$ in.), Frick Collection, New York

been characterized by Reynolds as the "ornamental style."[43] Unlike the "solid, firm style of brush" that has been identified in the cottage-door pictures, *The Mall* exhibits an "extravagant looseness." The artificiality of *The Mall* presents an alternative not only to the style of the cottage doors but to their substance. It is tempting to see it as a comment on the new urban economy and its obliteration of the old countryside that Gainsborough loved. It may also explain why in painting the cottage doors as he did Gainsborough wished them to aspire to the status of the highest of high art.

If Gainsborough was challenging traditional history painting, it might imply a comment on some of the efforts of his contemporaries in that genre. It makes one reflect on the fact that some of Reynolds's histories such as *Venus Chiding Cupid* (Kenwood, London) were far from edifying, while those of Fuseli were obsessively private or obscure, and that James Barry's murals in the Society of

Arts were incomprehensible without his lengthy written guide to them. Moreover, it might have appeared, as Louise Lippincott has argued, that history painting, far from being the expression of disinterested public *mores*, was deeply implicated in the workings of commerce.[44] In addition, as the example of Jacques-Louis David, who exhibited *Les Horaces* in 1785, suggests, the kinds of subjects properly the province of history painting had become tainted with a dangerous republicanism. It makes an interesting contrast to see Boydell attempting to profit from paintings of scenes from Shakespeare, Britain's greatest writer.

If Boydell was relying on common cultural experience to make these paintings register with the public, so too was Gainsborough in the cottage doors. Painting what might loosely be classed Hogarthian modern moral subjects, he employed such familiar *topoi* as the notions of the virtuous life lived in rural retirement, or the strength of an independent peasantry as the foundation of national greatness. He then painted them in ways that were recognized by J. H. Pott and others as imbuing them with great cultural weight. It seems, however, that neither their modern content nor their challenge to history painting were fully grasped by his contemporaries, and instead his rural subjects were understood as pastoral fictions unrelated to contemporary experience. In this one may discern that Gainsborough's traditional moral universe, so powerfully and completely evoked in the cottage-door paintings, stood little chance against the values of the new economy.

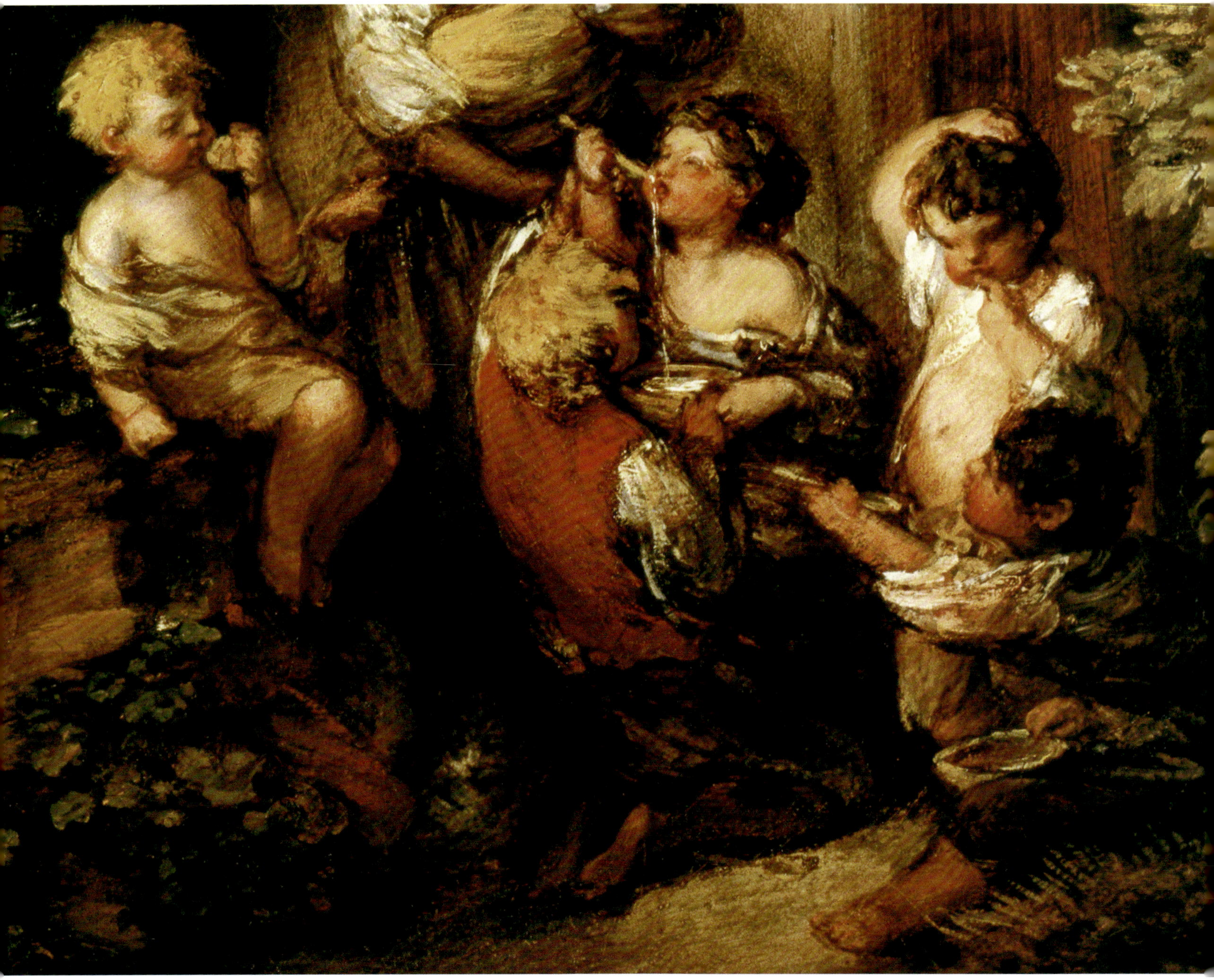

Amal Asfour
and Paul Williamson

Gainsborough's Cottage-door Scenes: Aesthetic Principles, Moral Values

A salient theme of Gainsborough's *Cottage Door* is nourishment (fig. 72 and pl. III). The idea carries physical, emotional, and even spiritual connotations that are explored in the grouping of the children and the maternal figure of the young woman nursing an infant. On the left of the group, perched on a tree stump, a cherubic boy holds a lump of food to his mouth as he gazes outward, perhaps at the shadowy urchin seated opposite on a low, grassy mound. The latter, holding a spoon in his extended hand and cradling a bowl in his lap, is also watched by the child standing to his right, hand on head, finger in mouth. The glances of these children connect with each other in a way that emphasizes the illuminated oval, completed by the woman, that their faces describe. This nest-like structure contains the youth kneeling beside the woman as he feeds a bare-shouldered toddler with an overflowing spoon. One might almost call it a blessed circle, in which food is plentiful, giving or sharing is a key motif, and the exposed, fleshy limbs of the young family suggest a celebration of physical wellbeing.

The theme is pursued in the depiction of the nursing woman standing tall above the cluster of youthful heads, her visual dominance stressed by the fact that the largest of the children is shown kneeling. With her bare chest and babe-in-arms, this figure might almost be interpreted as an emblem of fruitfulness. It is important to acknowledge her symbolic value, for the picture makes no attempt to account for the provisions that the children enjoy in any other terms. All signs of agricultural production are absent. The painting shows no animals, no farming implements, nothing to suggest that the family's food is the result of their own labor.

Similarly, where in comparable paintings Gainsborough might introduce a male provider – a woodman, for example, or a peasant enjoying a pipe of tobacco after the day's work – in this case there is no male figure to suggest an economic basis for this scene of domestic contentment (see fig. 79 and pl. V). Such traces of social realism are here eschewed in favor of a thematic focus that treats the matter-of-fact source of the children's food as unimportant. In this painting it seems as unnecessary to qualify the taking of physical nourishment as to explain the giving of maternal love. Food and love are analogues, equally natural components of the landscape.

72 Thomas Gainsborough, *The Cottage Door* (detail of pl. III)

That expanded sense of what is natural fosters a radical sense of unreality in *The Cottage Door* that seems to place it in a particular tradition of attitudes to landscape. In the spirit rather of an eclogue than a georgic, Gainsborough's image declares its affinities with soft rather than hard pastoral.[1] To invoke a biblical contrast, it is suggestive rather of a land of milk and honey than of eating bread in the sweat of thy face (Joshua 5:6; Genesis 3:19). Accordingly, the scene takes place in a state of partial isolation from the laws of nature, a point enforced pictorially by the way it is lit. The primary source of light is the bright highlight to the left, which one might provisionally take to be a setting sun. Bright patches picked out on the distant meadow and on the bridge, and the white water breaking around a boulder in the stream suggest that the light shines through the gap between the trees on the figures in the foreground. Yet this painterly realism is disrupted by the way Gainsborough selectively avoids depicting shadows that would interfere with the presentation of the grouped figures. Thus the shadow cast behind the seated boy on the right and the face of the boy perched on the tree stump opposite, modeled by shadows, would confirm the direction of the natural light. Yet the perching youngster casts no shadow on the figures in front of him, while the front of his upper arm, shoulder, and chest are brightly lit. Similarly, the face of the standing woman is partly modeled by shadow although her upper body remains radiantly illuminated. The strong light on the left shoulder of the child taking food from the kneeling boy fits into the same pattern of highlights that do not seem to emanate from the naturalistic source of light. The figures, that is, are spotlighted in a way that contradicts the indication of sunlight and opens up the idea, consonant with the unreal tenor of their depiction, that the light in which they are bathed comes not from in front or behind them, but from within (fig. 73).

One result of the compositional scheme in *The Cottage Door* is to discount realism in order to light the scene in a way that is pleasing to the eye, and the artifice underpinning Gainsborough's procedure here may be linked with his interest in transparencies. Viewed in his specially designed showbox, a landscape painted on glass has a light (or lights) placed behind it to create an impression of a picture illuminated from within itself. In the transparencies that quality is made sense of naturalistically by, for example, showing the bright reflection of a concealed sun or moon in a pool in the foreground or allowing the glow from the lights inside a cottage to shine through its windows and open door.[2]

No such rationale can be applied to the highlighted figures in *The Cottage Door* where the predominant artifice stresses the comfortable way in which the figures occupy the landscape. Large and prominent enough to be the subject of the painting, they are nevertheless contained by the natural scene, as infant-like in their setting as the child in its mother's arms. Is the painting's primary concern with the figures or with the landscape? The way the two are fused is indicated by the cottage itself, nestled in the surrounding woodland, its doorway as nearly natural as an architectural opening can be, its walls and thatched roof merging into the sylvan background as though to underline the continuity between the shelter afforded by the building and by the trees.

The idyllic unreality perceptible in this painting was not missed by its first viewers. When the picture was shown at the Royal Academy in 1780, an anonymous enthusiast referred to it as: "This beautiful scene where serenity and pleasure dwell in every spot, and the lovely figures composed in the finest rural style, their situation worthy of them, forms a scene of happiness that may truly be

73 Thomas Gainsborough, *The Cottage Door* (detail of pl. III)

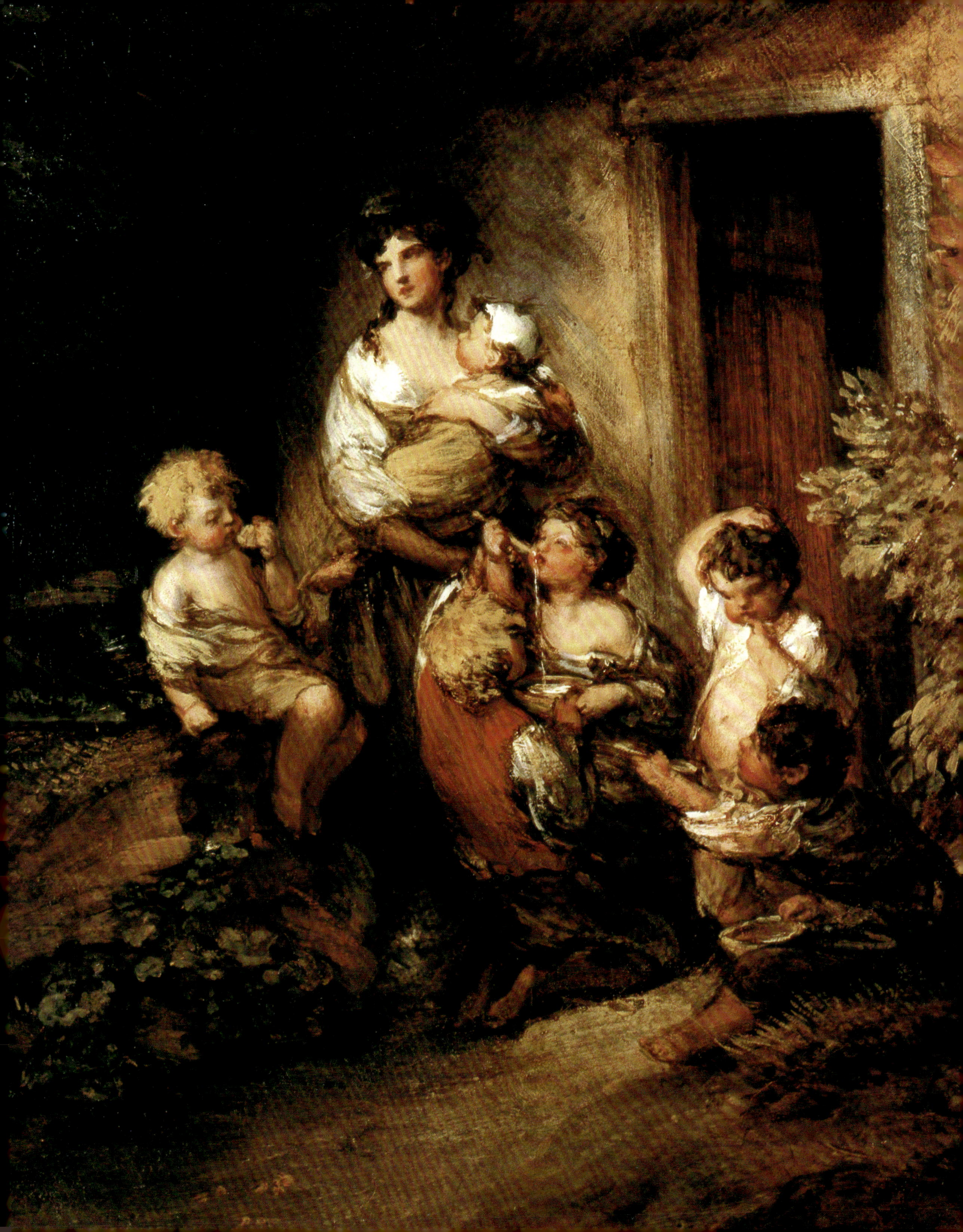

called Adam's paradise."[3] This is a world where physical laws are replaced by the appeal to a higher value, where the figures are endowed with an aura of sanctity, where the pictorial argument, one might conclude, is about the blessed and transforming nature of a mother's love.

Yet, while the description of the scene as "Adam's paradise" clearly sums up an important truth about the painting, there is a striking oddity about describing this particular picture in this way. If this is "Adam's paradise," it is so in the absence of Adam. With this in mind it is possible to look at the painting in a way that places less stress on the evident vision of harmony than on its darker elements. There is a hint of narrative in *The Cottage Door* that invokes multiple associations with the literature of the period. At an early date, James Thomson's *Seasons* was suggested as a poetic correlative for the mood of the painting.[4] Another comparison is provided by the episode of the "lost swain" from William Collins's "Ode on the Popular Superstitions of the Highlands of Scotland," and in particular the description of the waiting wife and children (lines 121–5):

> For him, in vain, his anxious wife shall wait,
> Or wander forth to meet him on his way;
> For him, in vain, at to-fall of the day,
> His bairns shall linger at the unclosing gate
> Ah, ne'er shall he return![5]

Thomas Gray was in Gainsborough's mind at this period, a fact attested to both by the mention in a letter probably written in 1783 and by *The Country Churchyard*, a painting exhibited at the Royal Academy in 1780, the same year as *The Cottage Door*, and now familiar from the aquatint made by Maria Prestal in 1790.[6] Gray's *Elegy Written in a Country Churchyard* has a particular resonance for *The Cottage Door*, notably in the stanzas containing the speaker's thoughts on the "rude forefathers of the hamlet" (16). Their demise is presented in terms of their lost domestic happiness (21–4):

> For them no more the blazing hearth shall burn,
> Or busy housewife ply her evening care:
> No children run to lisp their sire's return,
> Or climb his knees the envied kiss to share.[7]

In Gainsborough's painting, a comparable drama might be discerned in the contrast between the representation of children and the mother. While the children accept sustenance without question, the woman's gaze is "meditative and introspective."[8] Her face picked out by the light, this is the only presence in the painting that suggests an individual identity, a fact that goes some way to accounting for the rumor that Gainsborough inserted into the painting a portrait of an aristocratic lady in the guise of a "lovely cottager."[9] Irrespective of its accuracy, such a rumor serves to emphasize the sense of theater that pervades the scene, and so raises questions about its narrative possibilities. Does the way the woman looks out into the distance suggest an absence? If she is the mother of the children around her, where is their father? Do the dark clouds gathering over the roof of the cottage, and even the possible hint of evening (consonant with the passages from Collins and Gray just quoted), connote an atmosphere of impending disaster? The painting opens such questions, and the mood they evoke also finds expression in the contrast between the pensive mother and the untroubled children, a relationship that recalls the vision of childhood portrayed elsewhere in Gainsborough's work. Thus his *Painter's Daughters Chasing a Butterfly* (c. 1756, National Gallery, London), associated with a rhyme by John Bunyan, movingly depicts the children's blithe unawareness of the hidden dangers of the world as Margaret Gainsborough reaches out to take hold of the butterfly that has landed on the head of a thistle. Similarly, in a composition based on imagery found in Otto van Veen's *Amorum Emblemata*, his portrait of *Heneage Lloyd and His Sister* (1750–52, Fitzwilliam Museum, Cambridge) takes on thematic force as an examination of the fragility of youthful innocence.[10] As in these images, the Edenic unreality of *The Cottage Door* is infused with a sense of uncertainty. Adding to the dramatic overtones is the way the scene is given a temporal dimension. Indicators of the natural cycle range from the central image of mother and children to the time of day intimated by the sun placed low in the sky. The lush green of the trees mixed with golden browns opens a question about the time of year – late summer or autumn, one might speculate – while the fruitfulness of the scene is qualified by the dead tree arching in from the right foreground. The force of natural processes is also felt in the dark rain or even storm clouds overhead, the rushing water to the left, and of course the food that the children consume.

"Ay, ay, death is even in Arcadia." So runs George III's impromptu interpretation of the evocative Latin motto, *et in arcadia ego*.[11] The presence of the idea is felt repeatedly in Gainsborough's later landscapes. As E. K. Waterhouse remarked of the figures crouching before the tombstone in *The Country Churchyard*, "In spite of the Christian setting it would be surprising if they could read upon it any other words than *Et in Arcadia ego*."[12] In *The Cottage Door* the sense of harmony is counterpointed by darker elements in a manner that places the image in a pastoral tradition aptly summed up by King George's melancholy explication of the phrase. Here as elsewhere the full significance of Gainsborough's "familiar compositional prop of the dead tree-trunk"[13] should not be ignored. The forked branches at its top reach over toward the top of the tall tree to the left to form a curve that is extended by a living branch that merges visually with the dead trunk. The line inscribed by the upward thrust of the dead tree is answered by the lines formed by the brown and brownish-green leaves against the light sky opposite. This curving arrangement is developed and closed by the concave patch of light ground in the foreground below to create a framing ellipse that helps to reinforce the import of natural processes in the painting. In this composition the dead tree serves a symbolic function comparable to that which it serves in the Dutch paintings Gainsborough studied to add emblematic meaning to his landscapes at an early stage in his career.[14] The visual frame is a metaphorical barrier, a *memento mori* that both forms the entranceway into the idyll and emphasizes its fragility.

The occasion of King George's translation of *et in arcadia ego* was a visit to Sir Joshua Reynolds's studio where he saw Reynolds's portrait of *Mrs Crewe and Mrs Bouverie* (1767/69, private collection), showing the two women contemplating the inscription on a tombstone.[15] Characteristically dissimilar from

Reynolds in his use of the theme, Gainsborough's practice in *The Cottage Door* draws on the pastoral strategy of placing painful experience in the midst of rustic happiness that originates in the eclogues of Virgil, and found its most enduring eighteenth-century poetic voice in Gray's *Elegy*.[16] In the latter, the delightful vision of the *locus amoenus* is glimpsed through a frame composed of the most inexorable of negations (17–20):

> The breezy call of incense-breathing morn,
> The swallow twittering from the straw-built shed,
> The cock's shrill clarion or the echoing horn,
> No more shall rouse them from their lowly bed.

The tolling sound of "no more," heard again in the lines that follow (quoted earlier), remorselessly places the picture of happiness that the poet seems to see before his very eyes in an irretrievable dimension. Rescued by and yet entrapped within the poet's imagination, the joys and pains of this "pleasing anxious being" (86) are held together in a state of radical uncertainty and ambiguity that the elegist contemplates with calm fortitude and shapes into the "frail memorial" that is the poem.

Writing about the last in Gainsborough's series of cottage pictures, *Peasant Smoking at a Cottage Door* (see fig. 79 and pl. v), Henry Bate-Dudley describes "one of those sweet recesses, where the mind never fails to find a source of enjoyment," and goes on to say: "'Tis reading *Poetry*, and compressing all its enchantments to the glance of the eye."[17] *Ut pictura poesis* is the term one would use to characterize the way Bate conceives of this painting, and his view casts light on the evident qualities of *The Cottage Door*, replete with artifice and laden with many possible strands of meaning. Bate's reference to "the glance of the eye" is also important. The play of visual and poetic qualities that he discerns is characteristic of Gainsborough's mature landscape style and recalls the received notion of a gradual shift away from the overtly Dutch, observational approach to landscape typical of the period prior to Gainsborough's move from Ipswich to Bath in 1760.[18] Certain continuities between earlier and later styles should not be overlooked, and these are perhaps most marked in the cottage-door pictures where the imagery often carries an emblematic burden comparable to that found in several paintings produced during the early part of his career. The change in approach is important, however, and is particularly noticeable in a compositional procedure that cuts off the focus of the scene from the broader landscape, presenting an intimate, enclosed space defined by its curving structure, and in so doing privileges the play of formal qualities over any straightforward observation of nature.[19]

Thus in *The Cottage Door* the figures are placed in a clearing that is carefully isolated from any extensive vista into the larger panorama. Within the woodland glade numerous formal echoes strengthen the sense of a dominant aesthetic order. Its sylvan architecture, realized in an overarching, harmonizing play of line, color, and light that is picked up in the luminous foreground, suggests an almost tunnel-like approach from the viewer's space toward the cottage. This curving shape, naturally invoked and varied in the branches of the trees, also characterizes the other access to the cottage, the bridge, with its conspicuously concave appearance. Beneath the bridge the play of white water in the flowing stream provides one visual analogue for the cascading heads and faces of the woman and children; another might be the leaf clusters in the trees. The almost homomorphic way in which the scene is conceived thus reemphasizes the continuity between the figures and the landscape; it also creates a somewhat abstract sense of design that adds visual unity to the canvas.

In terms of stylistic models, the decisive reason offered to account for the developments in Gainsborough's approach to landscape that occurred most unmistakably during the later 1760s is the "intense excitement"[20] he felt in the presence of the works by Rubens that became accessible to him after his move to Bath. What should not be ignored is that any change in attitude signals an evolving understanding of the aims and limits of landscape art itself. Of fundamental importance in this respect is the fact that Gainsborough created his mature style at a time when theorists working within the broad empiricist parameters that characterized his intellectual milieu were becoming increasingly conscious of the problems posed for the artist by the nature of human vision. This was manifested as a growing awareness of the deep-seated discontinuity between visual reality and its graphic or painterly representations. In theoretical terms, discussion of the problem centered on perspective and, as far as the present argument is concerned, it came to a head in the work of Thomas Malton (1726–1801).

Simply stated, the world as it appears to the human eye is spherical in form, and that fact presents an insurmountable difficulty to the artist who wishes accurately to record the objects of sight on a flat canvas or piece of paper. This conclusion was announced by Malton in his *Compleat Treatise on Perspective in Theory and Practice* (1775), a popular book that advertised itself as the latest in a series of elaborations upon a celebrated but austere work on perspective by Brook Taylor (1685–1731) that had first appeared in 1715. Malton, a well-known figure in the close artistic world of eighteenth-century England, contributed to exhibitions organized by the Free Society of Artists and the Incorporated Society of Artists in the 1760s, exhibited his architectural drawings at the Royal Academy in the early 1770s, and during the mid-1770s gave lectures on perspective at his house in Soho.[21] Gainsborough owned a copy of the *Compleat Treatise* that was in his library at the time of his death.[22]

In the course of the work Malton feels compelled to address a question that had been a source of irritation to theorists since Brook Taylor. In certain situations, such as a wide-angle view of a row of columns, the strict application of the geometrical rules of perspective gives results that contradict a common-sense understanding of the appearance of the object.[23] In his *Dr. Brook Taylor's Method of Perspective Made Easy* (1754), Joshua Kirby (the friend of Gainsborough and Hogarth, both of whom contributed illustrations to his book) had argued that in such contentious cases rigid geometrical reasoning ought to be set aside in favor of an appeal, couched in language given precise definition by Locke and Berkeley, to "Custom and Experience."[24]

In a stout rejection of any such pragmatic softening of the rules, Malton launches into a consideration of the theoretical basis of his discipline. Rectilinear perspective, he declares, is strictly concerned with the application of geo-

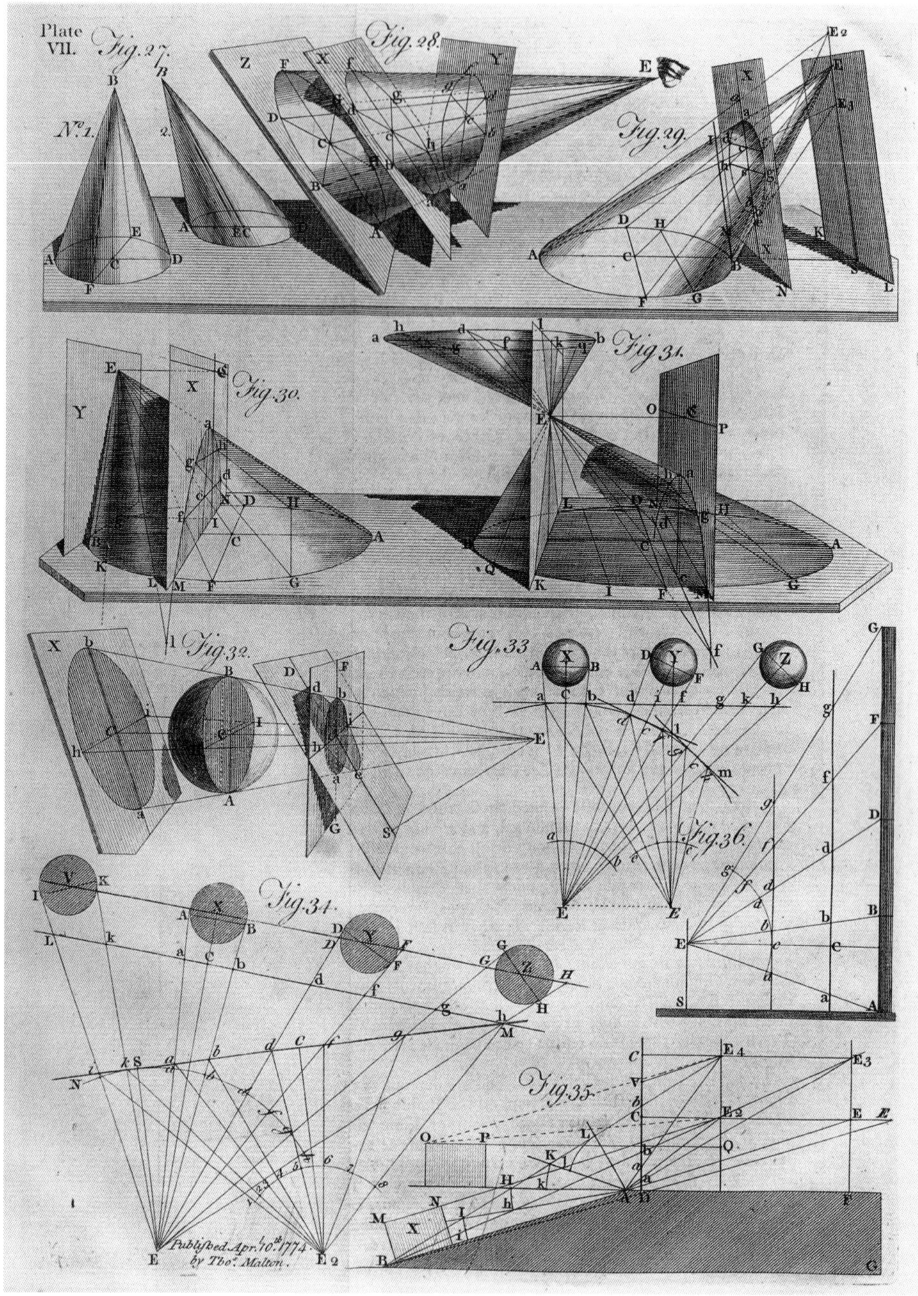

74 Thomas Malton, plate VII from *A Compleat Treatise on Perspective*, 2nd edition, London 1779

metrical principles. As such its aim is not to represent on a flat surface what we actually see, to depict objects "exactly as they appear to the eye."[25] The spherical nature of our visual experience makes that an impossible ambition. The two-dimensional representation of an object and its "true Appearance" are "two distinct things, which can never be united, on a Plane Surface or Picture."[26] The cause of this inescapable disunity lies in the "spherical Form, which the all-wise Creator has given" to the retina. It is "very reasonable to suppose, that, Objects appear, exactly, in proportion to the Angles under which they are seen."[27] Accordingly, the visual appearance of an object should be conceived of in terms of "an ark of a Circle" "cutting" the "Visual Rays" that pass between object and eye (fig. 74; see diagrams 33 and 34).[28]

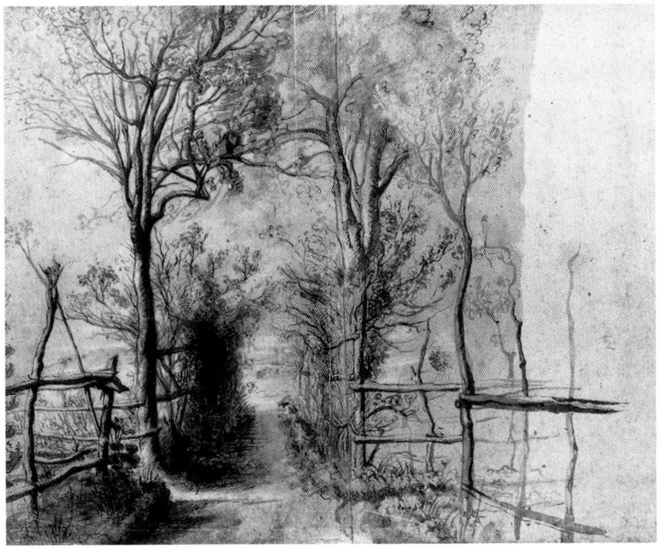

75 Peter Paul Rubens, *Path Through an Orchard*, 1615–18, pen over black chalk on paper, 31.3 × 40.3 cm ($12\frac{3}{8}$ × $15\frac{3}{4}$ in.), Fitzwilliam Museum, Cambridge

The conclusion has far-reaching ramifications for the representation of objects in two dimensions: "It is therefore manifest, that the true Representation, and, at the same time, the true Appearance, can only be represented on a spherical Surface, the Eye being in its Center; but that is not a perspective Representation."[29] What then is the purpose of perspective? Malton's is led to define it as a convention, a system of signs whose connection with the visible world is not ordained or natural but only customary. Concerned with developments in the theory of vision along with the philosophical positions with which these were linked, Malton's argument demonstrates the fundamental frailty of the idea that, in any straightforward sense, traditional graphic techniques could reproduce an artist's visual experience of reality.

Gainsborough's attitude to this problem can be inferred from what might be termed his curvilinear approach to landscape.[30] The curving structures characteristic of his later landscape style are deployed to suggest the effect of the scene on an observing eye situated inside the world of the image, at the centre, so to speak, of an optical sphere. Hence the placing of the illuminated group of figures in *The Cottage Door*, with arching trees overhead, arching forms to the left and right, and the curving ground in front. The light patch of sky to the left is similarly framed, inviting the eye to dwell on an alternative point of focus that confirms the painting's method. The strategic use of curving forms invokes the idea of an interaction between the landscape and a viewer placed inside its bounds. To respond to *The Cottage Door* on its own terms, therefore, is to respond to the picture's invitation to find a viewpoint within its self-contained visual universe. As that suggests, the painting works by making a deep-seated appeal to the viewer's imagination.

To clarify the aesthetic premises underpinning *The Cottage Door* it is instructive to contrast Gainsborough's procedure with that of Rubens. Where Gainsborough's curvacious views might call to mind the eighteenth-century popularity of the Claude glass, the straight perspectival view of Rubens's *Path Through an Orchard* recalls the use of the drawing frame (fig. 75).[31] This sketch, one of only

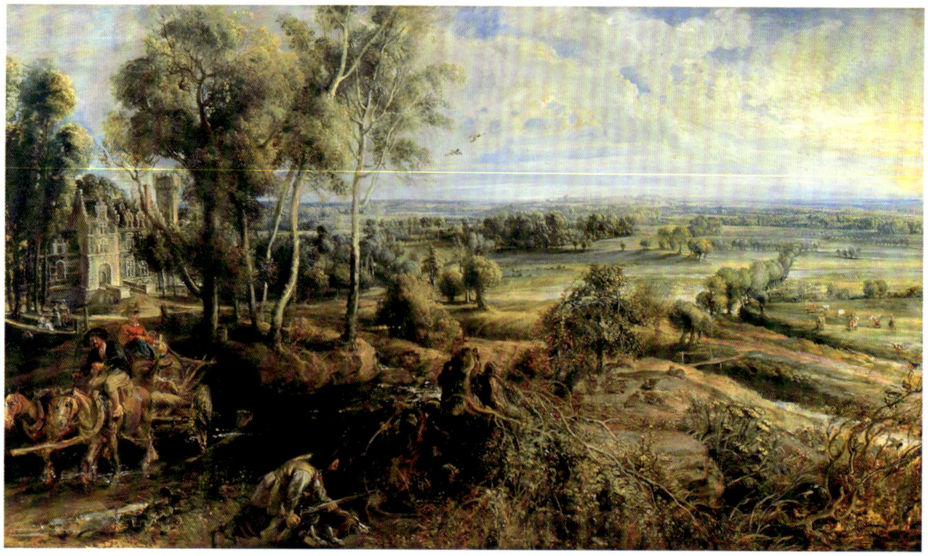

76 Peter Paul Rubens, *An Autumn Landscape With a View of Het Steen in the Early Morning*, probably 1636, oil on oak, 131.2 × 229.2 cm ($51\frac{3}{4}$ × $90\frac{1}{4}$ in.), National Gallery, London

twelve surviving drawings from nature by Rubens, apparently indicates four fenced-off areas demarcated by the meeting of two paths that form a slightly asymmetrical crossroads. The uprights and horizontals of the fencing, a combination of cut timber and saplings, incorporate the two larger trees that frame the entrance into a country lane or alleyway, hedged on either side, along which the viewer's eye is irresistibly led. The skeleton composed by the lines of trees and crossbeams suggests an interplay of human and natural elements that reveals a particular attitude to the landscape. If this is a study taken in nature of a particular motif, it is also a meditation on the shaping effect on the landscape of the human presence.

It has been noted that the inviting walkway overhung with leafy branches leading into the distance shown in this sketch recalls elements of the garden belonging to the house in Antwerp that Rubens bought in 1610 and depicted twenty years later in the background of his portrait of himself with his second wife and eldest son (c. 1631, Alte Pinakothek, Munich).[32] As the connection with the artist's Antwerp garden suggests, Rubens saw the view of the *Path Through an Orchard* with a "highly trained eye."[33] As in a formal garden the gridlike structure of fences and paths overlays and organizes natural forms, imposing on them a geometrical structure that is also the organizing principle in Rubens's sketch. The effect on the land of agriculture, perhaps more properly horticulture, guides the artist's perspectival representation of the scene, with its vanishing point at the end of the hedged lane. The same linear geometry underpins the mechanical or useful as well as the fine arts in a way that suggests that the relationship between the artist-viewer and nature as captured in this sketch is essentially unproblematic.

It is fruitful to apply the implications of the sketch's spatial organization to more substantial works by Rubens. His *Autumn Landscape With a View of Het Steen* and *Landscape With a Rainbow* are companion pieces celebrating the countryside surrounding Het Steen, the estate near the village of Elewijt that Rubens bought in May 1635 (figs. 76 and 77). One is able to locate precisely the view-

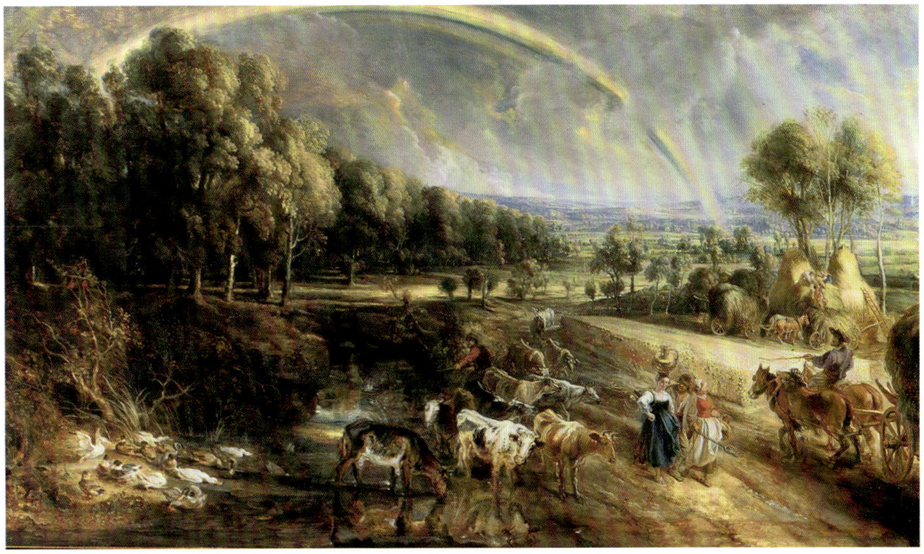

77 Peter Paul Rubens, *Landscape With a Rainbow*, c. 1636, oil on oak, 135.5 × 233.5 cm ($53\frac{3}{8}$ × 92 in.), Wallace Collection, London

point from which the estate is represented in these images. The painter's eye surveys the countryside from the tower, now demolished, that formerly adjoined the house. This elevation provided Rubens with the panoramic views over his land that he refashioned in these two paintings.[34] Both these works, it has been remarked, "capture something of the scale of the old world landscapes,"[35] and a consideration of the relationship between the two paintings and the Flemish world landscape tradition initiated by Joachim Patinir illuminates Rubens's artistic intentions in the scenes.

The *Landscape With a Rainbow*, for example, fuses the single vantage point gained from Rubens's tower with the idea of landscape as world view. Features of the scene combine to adumbrate perspectival lines that lead the eye into the picture. This can be seen most clearly on the left where the carter astride his leading horse points his whip in a direction that emphasizes the perspectival rendering of the edge of the harvested wheat field. The reflections of gray-blue sky in the river guide the viewer in the same direction, heading toward the transverse line of golden light that cuts across the composition in the middle distance. This elongated strip of sunshine leads from the thick woodland on the right of the picture out toward the open land, in particular toward the end of the rainbow, on the left. From that distant point the rainbow arches back, its form occasionally interrupted by clouds, to the bright light hovering over the dense woods on the right. Beyond the rainbow, aerial perspective carries the eye out into the "unfathomable distances" that recall the characteristic views depicted in the Flemish world landscapes.[36]

The sheltering arch of the rainbow, redolent with religious and moral significance, suggests the unifying power governing the fruitful lands of the estate. Framed by the arch, the foreground of the painting is punctuated with small scenes illustrating life in the country, tableaux in which the actors, unlike the artist, seem entirely unaware of the colored bow in the sky. As is clear by comparison with the *Autumn Landscape*, these vignettes are not intended to be viewed as chance elements in an unposed snapshot of life on the farm. The rural pursuits shown in the *Autumn Landscape* are not realistically arranged. In documentary terms, for example, it would make no sense to show a hunter and his dog, dependent on their silent cunning, right next to a noisy farm cart splashing through a ford. These details, inserted in the manner of the narrative episodes placed in a world landscape, serve an emblematic function, leading the mind into the realm of the image in a way analogous to that in which the geometrical structure encourages the eye to survey its geographical extent. In both paintings the view from the tower gives the artist a lordly overview, enabling the painter to transcend the limitations of the subjective eye and see instead what amounts to a *paysage cosmique*. The important implication is that, under the watchful eye of Rubens, Heer van Steen, the aspiration to harmony characteristic of the old world view might become a living reality.

Choosing an actual vantage point while invoking the *Weltlandschaft* brings a sense of objectivity to Rubens's two landscapes that is quite alien to Gainsborough. The changing basis of ideas discernible when turning from Rubens to Gainsborough's *Cottage Door* can be explained in terms of a shift from the lordly Rubensian eye to the subjective, sensible imagination. In the wake of the problem of depiction and vision stated by Malton, the curving, enclosing forms of *The Cottage Door* can be understood as describing the effect of the scene upon an eye taken to be within its confines. The essential presupposition of *The Cottage Door* is that what is seen is seen in the mind's eye, and if Gainsborough is responding to Rubens in this painting he is doing so by creating the effect of an immersion in a visual world charged with the sensual, painterly detail of Rubens from a radically changed intellectual starting point.

Contemporary contexts are readily available for the aesthetic principle that consists in an invitation to experience the painted landscape via an act of sympathetic imagination that bridges the gap between the viewer's real space and the image. It is present in the version of *ut pictura poesis* made use of by Bate-Dudley when he speaks of the "enchantments" of poetry being contained in the "glance of the eye," and an exact poetic analogy for the kind of imaginative self-projection solicited by *The Cottage Door* can again be found in Gray's *Elegy*. In the opening stanzas of the poem actual sight first becomes ineffectual in the gathering gloom and then gives way to the imagination of the poet contemplating the last traces of the nightscape from his vantage point among the rustic tombs. The pastoral world of the poem is then entered through an imaginative self-projection so complete that it ends with the speaker envisaging his own death and burial in the country churchyard, seeing the life he has led through the eyes of the inhabitants of this English Arcadia, and finally reading his own epitaph. As the situation in Gray's *Elegy* underlines, moreover, the very fact of approaching the rustic idyll by way of the imagination serves to stress its ineluctable remoteness.

Similar aesthetic assumptions find expression in Gainsborough's showbox, with its stimulating effects of light and its evocative demand that the viewer turn from real views to a private world of images in the mind.[37] The Eidophusikon of Philippe-Jacques de Loutherbourg also provides a point of comparison. This theatrical display, presented for the first time in 1781, displayed landscape scenes accompanied by music and sound effects designed to represent various moods and times of day.[38] The aim appears to have been to allow the spectator ("participant" might perhaps be a better word) to experience as fully as possible the imaginative and emotional force of the images and sounds incorporated in the show. With respect to *The Cottage Door* in particular, the radical appeal to the spectator's imagination finds a culminating instance in its exhibition in Sir John Leicester's Tent Room in London in 1818 where it hung alone, with mirrors "placed around to exhibit it to every advantage."[39] To enter the tent, it seems, was to enter the realm of the painting in a way that combined the subjective force of Gainsborough's showbox with the intimate luxury of total absorption in a private theatrical spectacle.

A conjunction of imagination and emotion that finds a natural frame of reference in the philosophical empiricism that prevailed in British intellectual life in the eighteenth century characterizes all these examples.[40] In this context, to rouse the viewer's imaginative involvement is to solicit an emotional response. In Gainsborough's mature art, form and content are both laden with an emotive charge. To say that Gainsborough's painterly rendering of forms is infused with feeling is to suggest that the aim of describing objects accurately is superseded by the manner in which they are rendered, that the concern with mimesis is overlaid with an exploration of the capacities of the medium to bring an emotional resonance to the image. The most convenient analogy for that play of form and feeling, one deeply rooted in eighteenth-century thinking about the arts, is with music.[41] In a painting these abstract formal effects work together with moving subject matter. The figures and motifs, the thematic content of an image, also provide an emotional focus, and to locate this focus in the cottage-door scenes is to clarify the central values to which the viewer of a particular painting is called upon to respond.

The dark qualities discernible in *The Cottage Door* are largely absent from the last in the series of cottage pictures, *Peasant Smoking at a Cottage Door*, which takes a more positive view of the values explored in the imagery (fig. 79 and pl. v). That is not to say that this happier rendering of cottage subject matter shows the way in which the narrative tensions of *The Cottage Door* might be definitively resolved. While the relationship between the two pictures helps to elucidate the context in which they should be viewed it does not undermine the special character and integrity of each of them.

The *Peasant Smoking* also shows a rustic family in front of their dwelling, which, as in *The Cottage Door*, forms part of a natural enclosure, with the deep thatch on the cottage roof emphasizing a continuity between the building and the surrounding foliage (fig. 78). The cottage itself is slightly more elaborate than in *The Cottage Door*, with its glazed window reflecting sunlight. Nor is there any hint of dilapidation, such as that which affects the daub meeting the right-hand doorjamb in the earlier picture. The *Peasant Smoking* again shows water to the left, in this instance a pool, and a sketchy view to some distant mountains. As in *The Cottage Door* the coloring of the foliage is variegated, the prognosis intimated by the sky is mixed, and the scene is framed by a prominent, overarching dead tree.

78 and 79 (*following pages*) Thomas Gainsborough, *Peasant Smoking at a Cottage Door* (details of pl. v)

A preparatory study for the *Peasant Smoking* shows a seated peasant alongside a standing mother carrying a baby (possibly two) in her arms, and an older child

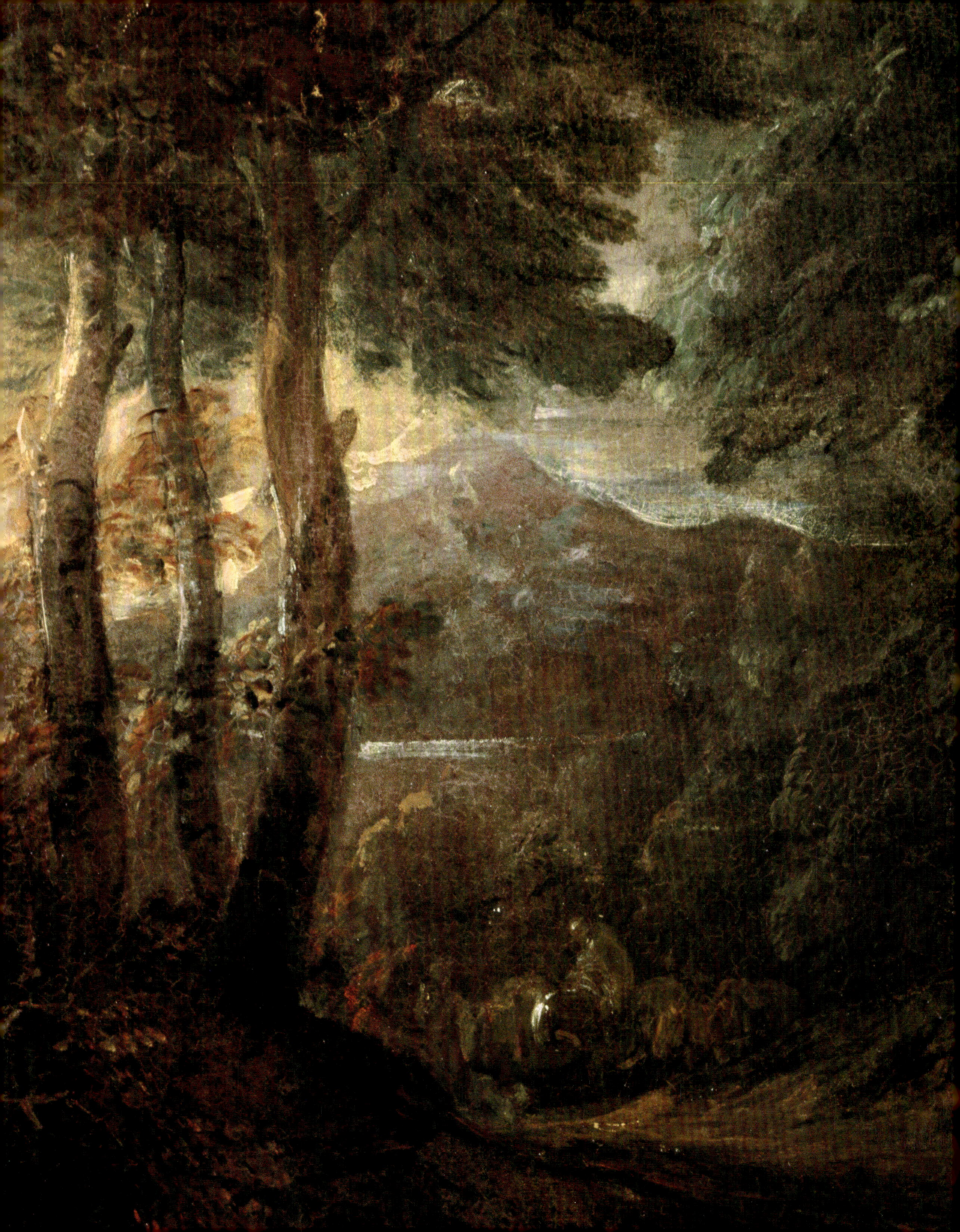

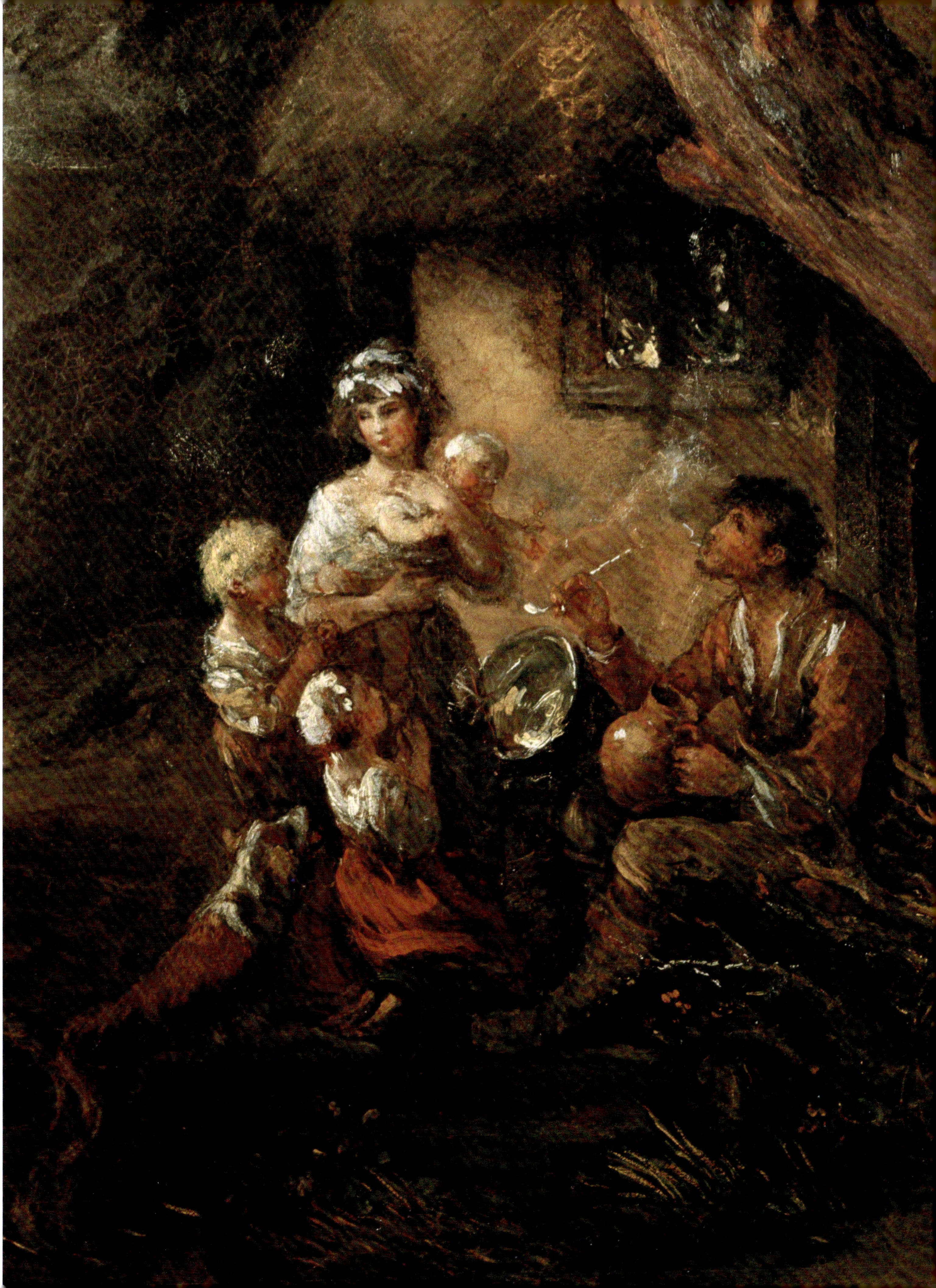

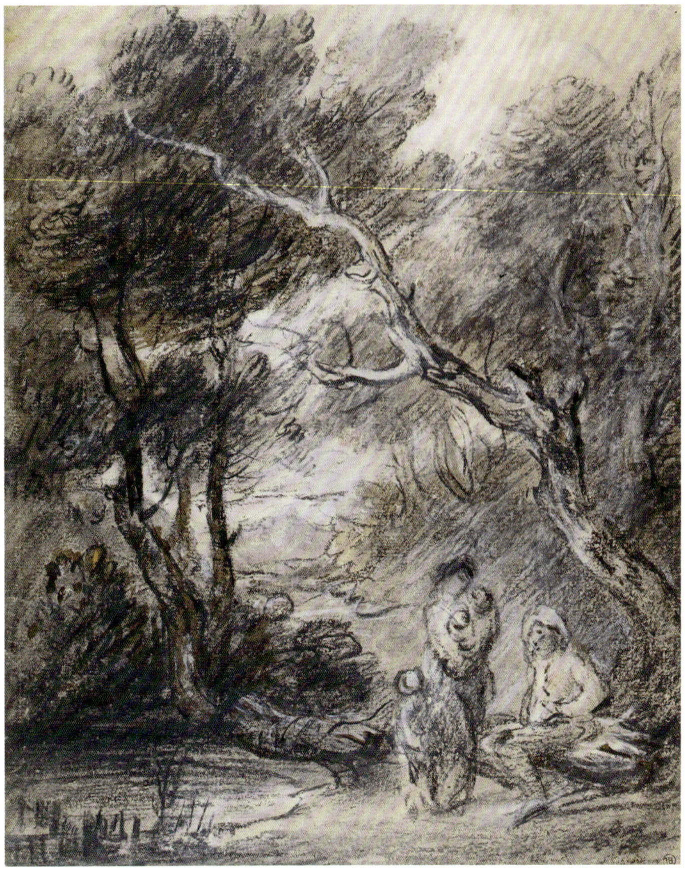

80 Thomas Gainsborough, *A Wooded Landscape with Figures by a Pool*, c. 1788, black chalk and stump with touches of red chalk, and gray and brown washes on buff paper, touched with body color, 39.4 × 31.7 cm ($15\frac{1}{2}$ × $12\frac{1}{2}$ in.), Yale Center for British Art, New Haven

standing beside her (fig. 80). The composition is similar to that of the finished painting, with the pool to the left, the dead tree arching overhead, and the view out to the distance framed by trees. The significant difference between sketch and painting is the absence of the cottage. Perhaps resting for a moment in a clearing beside a pool, the figures in the sketch are not at home. Depicted in a kind of no-man's-land, they convey an idea of travel, of motion, that is alien to the finished work. Also different is the portrayal of the male peasant. In the painting he is bareheaded, hale and hearty, with his pipe in one hand and a jug (presumably of ale) in the other. By contrast, the man in the sketch (as in another preparatory study)[42] bears some resemblance to the rather wizened figure Gainsborough used as the basis for his *Woodman*, associated with a passage from Book V of Cowper's *The Task*, and now familiar in the form of an engraving by Peter Simon (see fig. 58). On the strength of these differences, as indeed of the disposition of the figures, it would be perfectly possible to assume that the sketch shows nothing more than a chance meeting between the young mother with her children and the elderly peasant. In the painting, by contrast, the figures comprise a family group of integrity and contentment. The rather down-at-heel male of the sketch becomes the contented paterfamilias of the painting; any suggestion of distance between the figures in the sketch is transformed into the calm, close-knit domesticity of the painting; and perhaps most importantly the sense of journeying that can be detected in the sketch has disappeared from the painting. Here, with the day's work done, the family enjoys the restful peace of their arcadian home. Watched over by their mother and their dog (whose importance as a link in the chain connecting these people with the natural world should not be ignored), the two older children repeat their evening prayer to their musing father who looks heavenward in an attitude that reinforces the basic message of the scene. This is a time of harmony, peace, and contentment for which these simple rustic souls are properly thankful.

The *Peasant Smoking* was painted as a pendant to *The Market Cart*, a depiction of figures in transit (fig. 66).[43] The relationship between these companion paintings can perhaps best be broached via that central thematic contrast between motion and rest. In *The Market Cart* the sense of movement is developed and given some narrative interest by the presentation of the dark-haired woman, seated on the cart beside a young girl. Perched on a heap of vegetables, she leans backward at an angle conspicuously repeated in the basket of carrots lying precariously behind her (fig. 81). With her left hand perhaps adjusting her cap, she is watched (in an attitude that could conceivably express some anxiety) by the young girl next to her as well as by woodman to the right. The cart is neither driven nor led and the woman's posture places a certain note of vulnerability, of dramatic uncertainty, at the heart of this apparently calm scene.

That, of course, is not the way the image is usually viewed and it is not an opinion that can be insisted upon with any finality. It is, however, an argument that applies to Gainsborough's first treatment of the motif, *Crossing the Stream* or *Wooded Landscape With Peasants in a Country Cart Crossing a Ford*, a painting that exists in two autograph versions (fig. 82).[44] These show a driver seated beside a woman on a covered wagon that is being pulled through flowing water by a horse. There are two peasants to the left, a dog in the foreground, and a hollowed-out dead tree to the right that contributes to a framing effect completed by an inward leaning tree (on the left) and the near bank of the stream. The posture of the woman, which bears comparison with that of the woman in *The Market Cart*, can here be more clearly interpreted. With her left hand reaching to cover her exposed chest and a partly overturned basket on her right arm, she creates a slightly louche impression. Her body is angled away from the coachman who leans invasively toward her as he points to something on his left, while the butt of his whip, pressed against his body with his right arm, almost touches her. The defensive slant of the woman's body is contradicted by that of her head, which inclines toward the man, as though she is listening to what he has to say despite her better judgment. The little drama played out between the sexes is most clearly expressed in the smaller version of the painting (shown here), in which the figures in their respective attitudes are more distinctly portrayed.

It seems likely that the idea for this composition was adapted from an emblem by the Dutch artist Jacob Cats (1577–1660), knighted by Charles I in 1627, from whose work Gainsborough took inspiration for another painting dating from the same period, *Girl with Pitcher* (1782, National Gallery of Ireland, Dublin).[45] Cats's emblem shows a masked woman leaning out of a coach drawn by two horses, one upright and strong as though walking on firm ground, the other bent and tired as though struggling through mud (fig. 83). With his whip in his left hand,

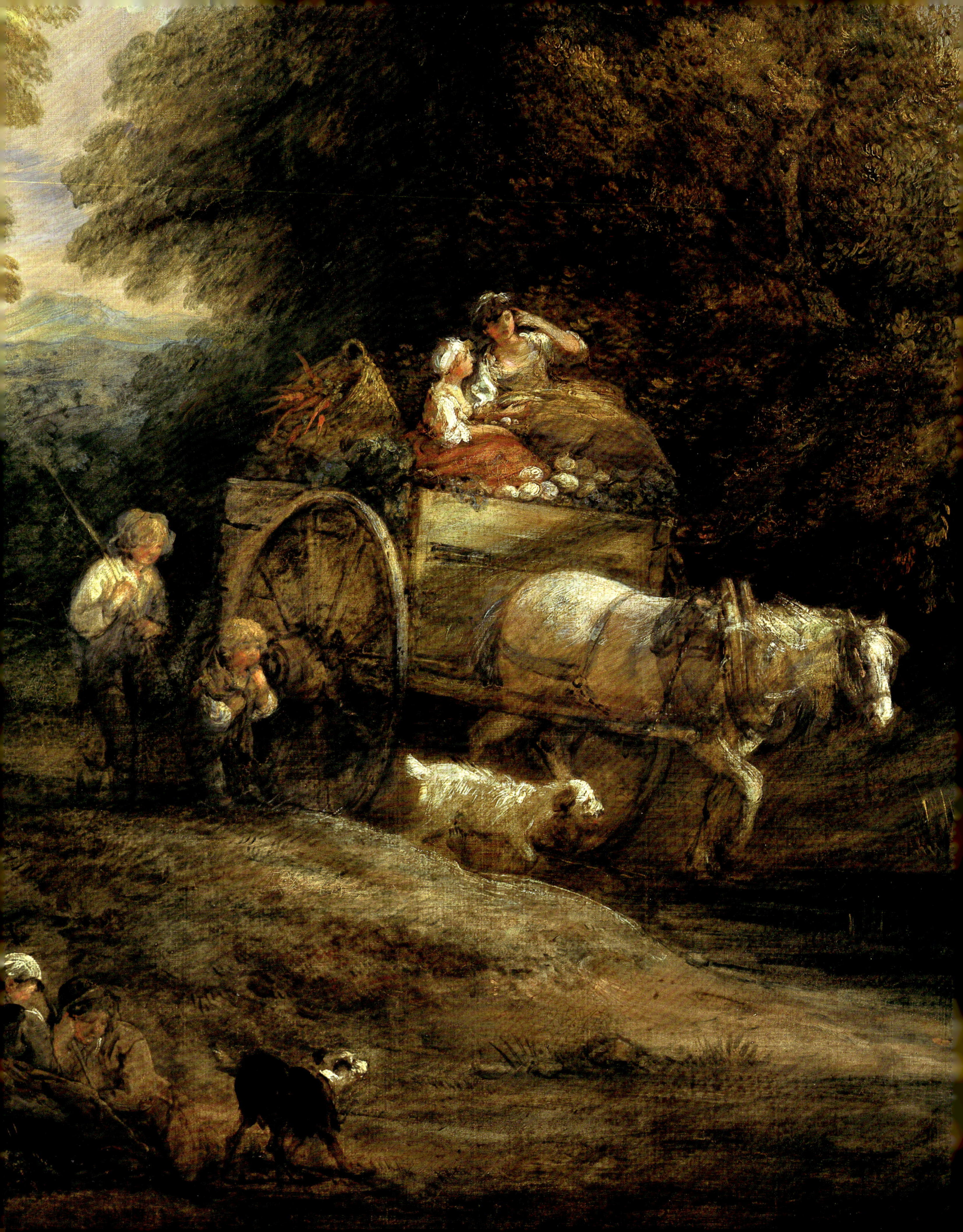

82 Thomas Gainsborough, *Crossing the Stream*, 1782–4, oil on canvas, 69.9 × 90.2 cm ($25\frac{1}{2}$ × $35\frac{1}{2}$ in.), Lehigh University Art Galleries/Museum Operations, Bethlehem, Pennsylvania. Gift of Marion Brown Grace

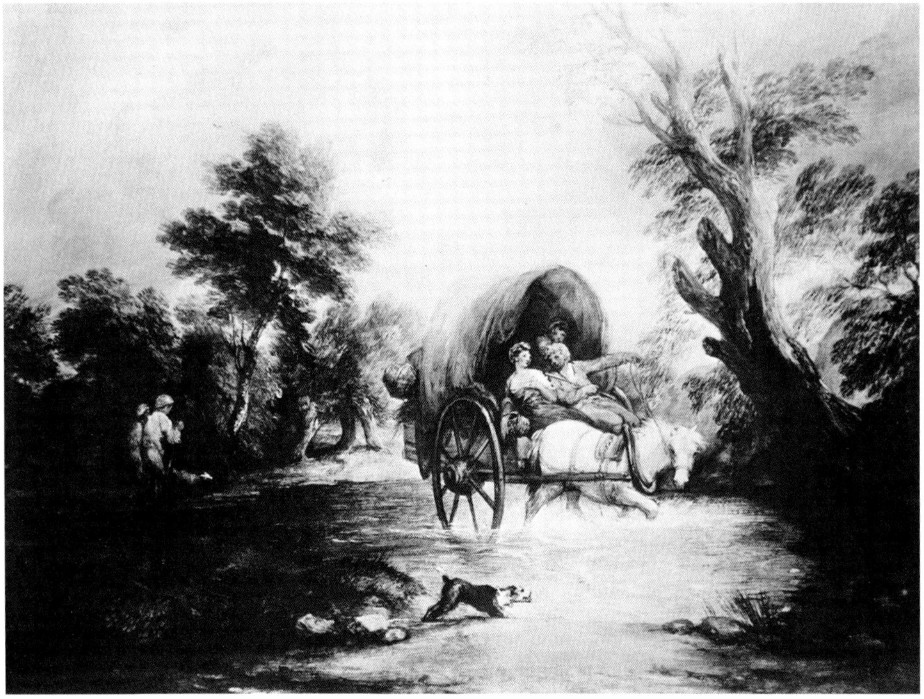

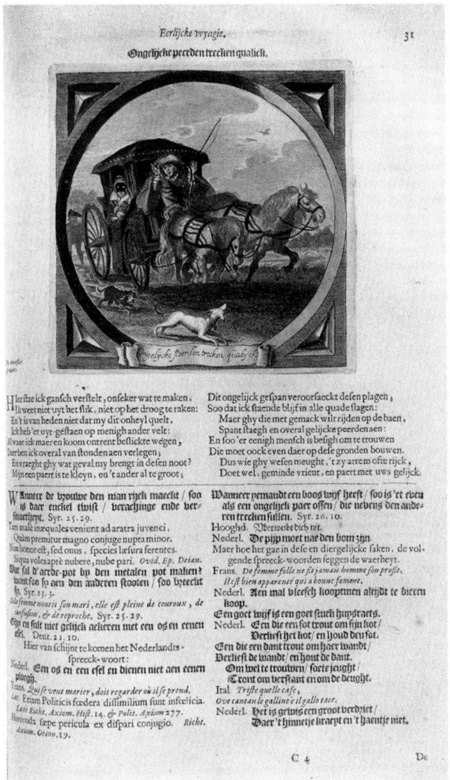

Eerlijcke vryagie. 31

Ongelijcke peerden trecken qualick.

Hier staε ick gansch verstelt, onseker wat te maken,
Ik weet niet uyt het slik, niet op het droog te raken:
En't is van heden niet dat my dit onheyl quelt,
Ick heb 'et uyt-gestaen op menigh ander velt:
Als waer ick maer en koom ontrent beslickte wegen,
Daer ben ick overal van stonden aen verlegen;
En vraeght ghy wat geval my brengt in desen noot?
Mijn een paert is te kleyn, en 't ander al te groot;
Dit ongelijck gespan veroorsaeckt desen plagen,
Soo dat ick staende blijf in alle quade slagen:
Maer ghy die met gemack wilt rijden op de baen,
Spant staegh en overal gelijcke peerden aen:
En soo 'er eenigh mensch is besigh om te trouwen
Die moet oock even daer op dese gronden bouwen.
Dus wie ghy wesen meught, 't zy arrem ofte rijck,
Doet wel, geminde vrient, en paert met uws gelijck.

Wanneer de vrouwe den man rijck maeckt / soo is daer enckel twist / verachtinge ende versmaetheyt. Syr. 25. 29.
Tam male inæquales veniunt ad aratra juvenci,
Quàm premitur magno conjuge nupta minor.
Non honor est, sed onus, species læsura ferentes.
Si qua voles aptè nubere, nube pari. *Ovid. Ep. Deian.*
Wat sal d'aerde-pot by den metalen pot maken? want soo sy aen den anderen stooten / soo breeckt sy. Syr. 13. 3.
Si la femme nourit son mari, elle est pleine de couroux, de confusion, & de reproche. Syr. 25. 29.
Ghy en sult niet gelijck ackeren met een os en eenen esel. Deut. 22. 10.
Hier van schijnt te komen het Nederlandts spreeck-woort:
Nederl. Een os en een esel en dienen niet aen eenen ploegh.
Frans. *Qui se veut marier, doit regarder où il se prend.*
Lat. Etiam Politicis fœdera dissimilium sunt infœlicia. *Lat. Richt. Axiom. Hist. 14. & Polit. Axiom 277.*
Horrenda sæpe pericula ex dispari conjugio. *Richt. Axiom. Œcon. 19.*

Wanneer yemandt een boos wijf heeft / soo is 't even als een ongelijck paer ossen / die nevens den anderen trecken sullen. Syr. 26. 10.
Hooghd. Uberweibe dich nit.
Nederl. De pijp moet nae den bom zijn.
Maer hoe het gae in dese en diergelijcke saken, de volgende spreeck-woorden seggen de waerheyt.
Frans. *De femme folle ne fit jamais homme son profit.*
Il est bien apparent qui a bonne femme.
Nederl. Aen mal vleesch kooptmen altijdt te dieren koop.
Een goet wijf is een goet stuck huysraets.
Nederl. Een die een sot trout om sijn kot /
Verliest het kot / en houd den sot.
Een die een dant trout om haer wandt /
Verliest de wandt / en hout de dant.
Om wel te trouwen / soecte jeught /
Trout om verstant en om de deught.
Ital. *Triste quelle case,*
Ove cantan le galline e il gallo tace.
Nederl. Het is gewis een groot verdriet /
Daer 't hinnetje kraeyt en 't haentje niet.

C 4 De

83 Jacob Cats, "Ongelijke peerden trecken qualick," from vol. 1, of *Alle de Wercken*, Amsterdam and Utrecht 1700

the driver uses his right to draw his passenger's attention to something outside the picture. Following the coach is a walking figure, while in the foreground are two dogs whose dispositions mirror those of the horses: one is sprightly and alert, the other is cringing and suspicious. The title of the emblem is *Ongelijcke peerden trecken qualijk*, which can be translated as "unequal horses draw amiss." The nature of their inequality is explained by a series of mottos attached to the emblem. Taken from biblical and classical sources, these clarify that the message concerns domestic discord caused by marital misalliance and their tone may be summed up in the following examples: "A woman, if she maintain her husband, is full of anger, impudence, and much reproach." "Blessed is the man that hath a virtuous wife, for the number of his days shall be double." "An evil wife is a yoke shaken to and fro: he that hath hold of her is as though he held a scorpion."[46]

Seen against the background suggested by *Crossing the Stream* and the emblem by Cats with which it can be linked, the relationship between the sexes plays an increasingly prominent part in the thematic contrast between *The Market Cart* and its pendant, *Peasant Smoking*. Where the earlier painting shows a moment of activity, a moment *en route*, the latter shows a conclusion, an arrival, a time of restful peace, and that opposition is emphasized through the use of the father figure. His presence in the *Peasant Smoking* completes the ideal family group; his absence in *The Market Cart* stresses not only the provisional nature of the moment depicted but also the responsibility and authority conferred on the women placed in charge of the cart. To conceive of that charge in terms of the kinds of imbalance between husbands and wives that interested Cats is to find the idyll of *The Market Cart* becoming tinged with tones more usually associated with eighteenth-century domestic comedy.[47]

81 Thomas Gainsborough, *The Market Cart* (detail of fig. 66)

Without insisting upon a facile correspondence between the artist's biography and the artwork, it is worth pointing out that Gainsborough's own home life was sometimes almost worthy of comic treatment. His wife was indeed referred to as "his Xantippe."[48] Married to a proud and characterful woman who styled herself "a prince's daughter" (she was in fact an illegitimate child of the 3rd Duke of Beaufort),[49] and father to two troublesome daughters of his own, Gainsborough oscillated between trying to assert his masculine authority and making amends for his own loose ways and spendthrift behavior by allowing his wife to run his affairs. As he wrote to his sister in 1775: "If I tell you my wife is weak but good, and never much formed to humour my Happiness, what can you do to alter her? If I complain that Peggy [his younger daughter] is a sensible good Girl, but Insolent and proud in her behaviour to me at times, can you make your arm long enough to box her ears for me whilst you live at Bath?"[50] He goes on to relate how he has uncovered a clandestine romance between his elder daughter, Mary, and the musician Johann Christian Fischer (1733–1800) that resulted in a short-lived mismatch consecrated at St Anne's Church, Soho, in February 1780. In 1776, again writing to his sister, Gainsborough describes how he has attempted to assuage his wife's "disobedience Pride and insolence, and eternal Obraidings & reflections" by giving her sole charge of his finances: "I . . . very soon found th[at] (as a punishment for so unmanly a condesention) instead of convincing, it was a further incouragment to Govern me, and invert the order of Nature in making the Head the foot and the foot the Head."[51] The situation as Gainsborough describes it is neatly encapsulated in the Italian motto accompanying Cats's *Ongelijcke peerden trecken qualijk*: "Triste quelle case, | Ove cantan le galline e il gallo tace." Those are sad households where the hens sing and the cock is silent.

These scenes of strife are, to adapt Gainsborough's expression, "unnatural" and as such they provide a stark contrast with the orderly world of the *Peasant Smoking*. As Gainsborough well knew, the perfect microcosm depicted in that painting, with each family member fulfilling his or her allotted role, could be a far cry from reality. The dreamlike nature of the ideals portrayed in such images of country life as the *Peasant Smoking* was reflected upon in a passage from a work particularly connected with Gainsborough, Cowper's *The Task*.[52] In Book I of the poem Cowper conceives of the proper roles of men and women in terms of a hygrometer or weather house. This device, built in the shape of a miniature house, signals meteorological changes by the emergence from inside the model building of a man in rainy weather and a woman when it is fine. In 1803 the weather house was shown in an illustration by William Blake included in the edition of Cowper's works edited by William Hayley (fig. 84).[53] Contemplating the mechanical figures leaving or entering the shelter of their house according to the clemency of the weather, the poet first imagines himself as the "Fearless" male adventurer walking out in the rain while his "More delicate" womenfolk are confined indoors. He then recalls a real peasant dwelling (shown in Blake's illustration in the medallion that has Cowper's pet hares in the foreground) chanced upon on one of his rambles (1. 210–36):

> Peace to the artist, whose ingenious thought
> Devised the weather-house, that useful toy!

84 William Blake, *The Weather-house*, engraving for William Cowper, *The Task*, from *The Life, and Posthumous Writings, of William Cowper, Esqr.*, ed. William Hayley, vol. III, London 1803–4

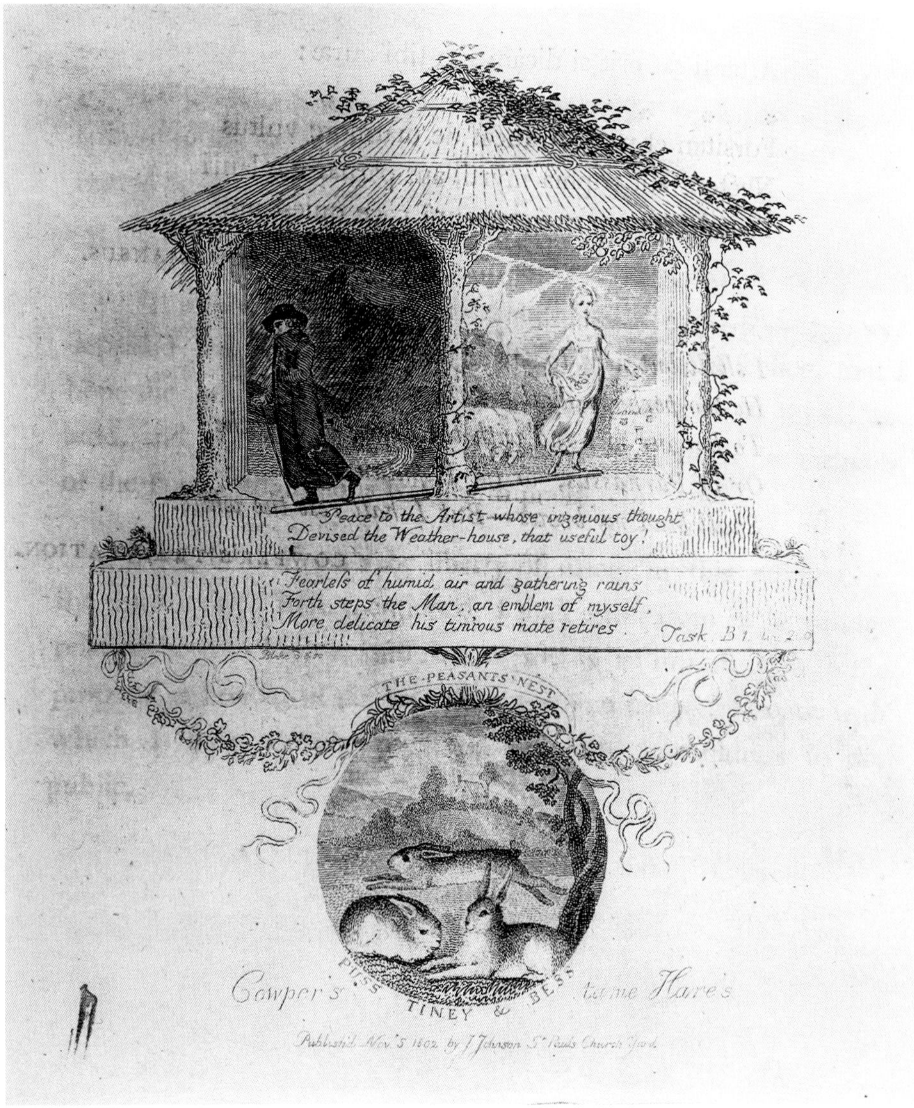

Fearless of humid air and gathering rains
Forth steps the man, an emblem of myself,
More delicate, his tim'rous mate retires.
When Winter soaks the fields, and female feet
Too weak to struggle with tenacious clay,
Or ford the rivulets, are best at home,
The task of new discov'ries falls on me.
At such a season, and with such a charge
Once went I forth, and found, till then unknown,
A cottage, whither oft we since repair:
"Tis perch'd upon the green-hill top, but close
Inviron'd with a ring of branching elms
That overhang the thatch, itself unseen,
Peeps at the vale below; so thick beset
With foliage of such dark redundant growth,

I call'd the low-roof'd lodge the *peasant's nest*.
And hidden as it is, and far remote
From such unpleasing sounds as haunt the ear
In village or in town, the bay of curs
Incessant, clinking hammers, grinding wheels,
And infants clam'rous whether pleas'd or pain'd,
Oft have I wish'd the peaceful covert mine.
Here, I have said, at least I should possess
The poet's treasure, silence, and indulge
The dreams of fancy, tranquil and secure.[54]

Cowper uses the image of the hygrometer to shed an artificial light on the reality of peasant life. Like the cottages in Gainsborough's paintings, the actual cottage, "itself unseen," is all but absorbed into its natural setting, its thatched roof lost among the "ring of branching elms." In the poet's eye the real building is transformed into the "*peasant's nest*," a place he covets as a peaceful hideaway, far from the sights and sounds of social and industrial life (urban as well as rural) that disturb the "dreams of fancy." The poet's train of thought leads from the weather house to the idea of the properly contrasting roles and occupations of men and women, and then to the rustic cottage. In pursuing those associations the poet treats the weather house as a metaphor for the sense of natural order that he finds in country life. Underlying this vision of the "*peasant's nest*" is the precept from the Sermon on the Mount (Matthew 6:26): "Behold the fowls of the air: for they sow not, neither do they reap, nor gather into barns; yet your heavenly Father feedeth them."

In the passage that follows, however, the poet contrasts this idyll with the disagreeable realities of rural life. The easy optimism that emerged when the Christian sentiment was fused with the image of the mechanism powered by nature is now exploded (I. 237–51):

Vain thought! the dweller in that still retreat
Dearly obtains the refuge it affords.
Its elevated scite forbids the wretch
To drink sweet waters of the chrystal well;
He dips his bowl into the weedy ditch,
And, heavy-laden brings his beverage home
Far-fetch'd and little worth; nor seldom waits,
Dependent on the baker's punctual call,
To hear his creaking panniers at the door,
Angry and sad and his last crust consumed.
So farewell envy of the *peasant's nest*.
If solitude make scant the means of life,
Society for me! thou seeming sweet,
Be still a pleasing object in my view,
My visit still, but never mine abode.

The poet beats a hasty retreat from the realities of rural solitude back to society. And yet, as the conclusion to this passage demonstrates, the positive images used to characterize country life in this text have an enduring metaphorical value. The poet's illusions about the "*peasant's nest*" may be shattered but the "pleasing object" remains, not as a real "abode" but as an ideal, a pleasure of the imagination, to adopt a resonant phrase, that is the vehicle for a moral vision. The imagery is not there to be taken literally because, like the Gospel, it carries a message of hope, a Christian dream of happiness that is independent of its postlapsarian reality.

Placed beside *The Market Cart*, the elements comprising the idyllic holism of the *Peasant Smoking* come into sharper focus: the restful peace of home contrasting with the uncertainty of the journey; respect for the roles assigned to men and women; and due thanks given to the "Great Giver of All" (to use Gainsborough's phrase)[55] for blessings received. Gainsborough's cottage scenes are overtly artificial in character. Like the weather house, the painted image is a delightful luxury, a "toy" as Cowper calls it. As in *The Task*, however, the artifice of the imagery is embraced for its ability to convey values. Its very unreality, enhancing its imaginative force, infuses the image with the quiet urgency of an aspiration. The capacity of the artefact to affirm and at the same time to make provisional a dream of contentment by recreating reality in the fugitive realm of the imagination is precisely what distinguishes Gainsborough's cottage scenes. It is that quality that links Cowper and Gainsborough with Gray, and all three eighteenth-century artists with the pastoral tradition stemming back to Virgil.[56] Gainsborough's late landscapes employ connections between sight and imagination to convey values that are also discernible in the disposition of figures and motifs. Although those values are essentially elusive, the pictures evoke many contexts that help to clarify their purpose. To tease out those contexts is to show the way form and content work together to express ideas and emotions characteristic of the time in which the images were made and of the artist who made them. It is to engage in a process of discovering and describing the parameters that define the relations between life and art in a particular work and at a particular moment in time that transforms the simple appreciation of artworks into a history of art.

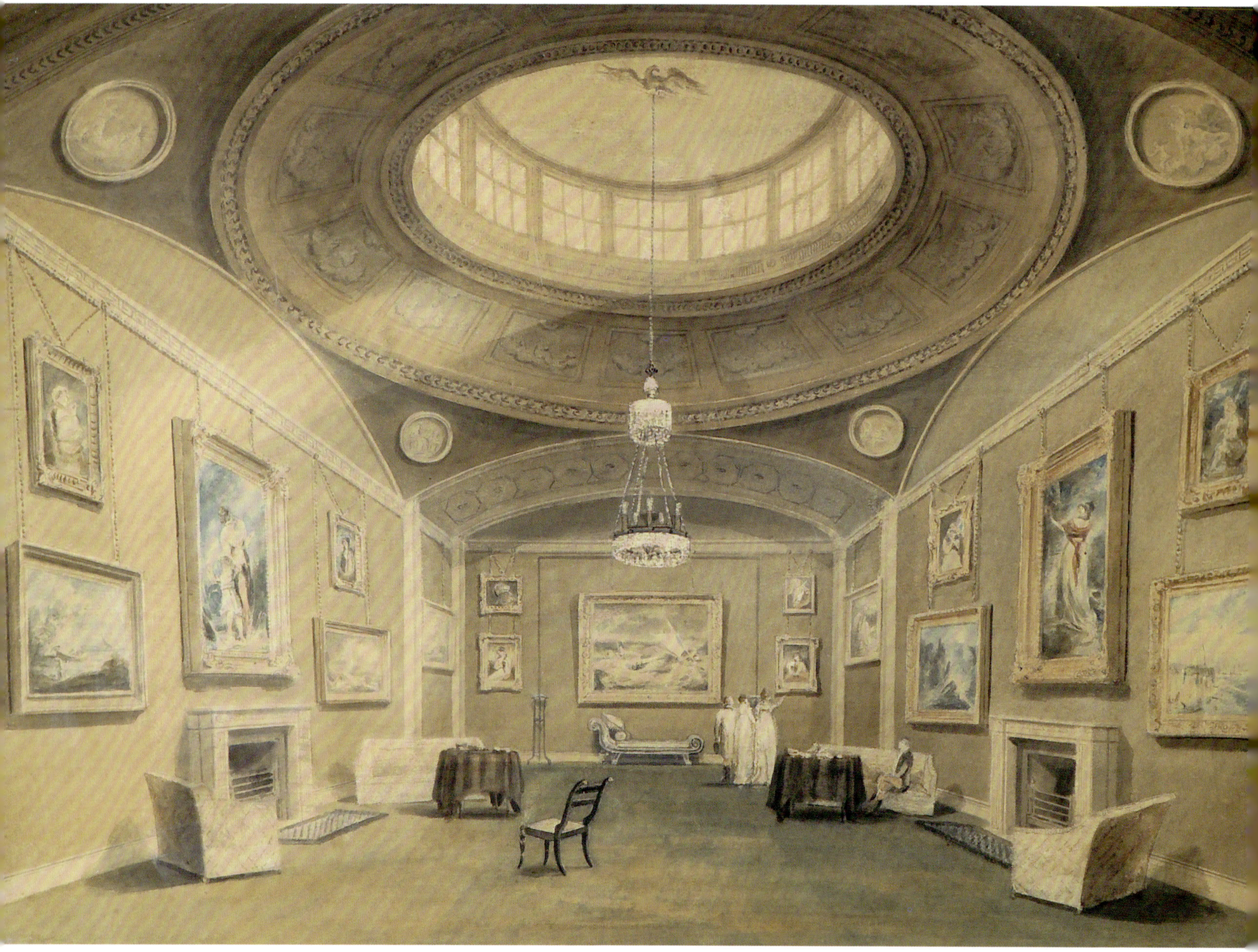

Part Three Collectors and *The Cottage Door*

85 John Buckler, *Picture Gallery of Sir John Fleming Leicester, Bart.*, at 24 Hill Street, London, 1806, pencil and wash, 43.2 × 71 cm (17 × 28 in.), University of Manchester (Tabley House Collection)

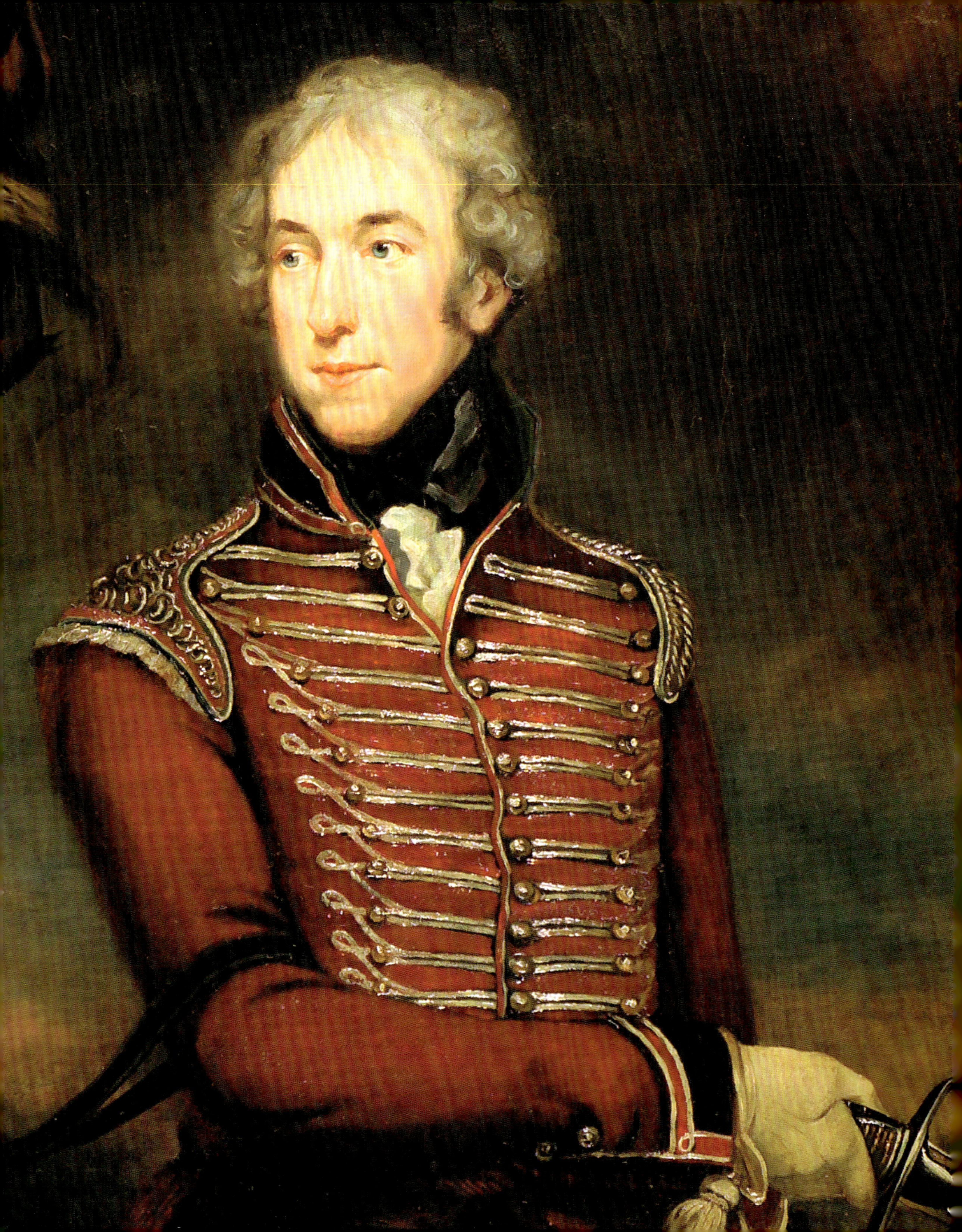

Dongho Chun

The Early Collectors of The Cottage Door

"This is news of the Arts," announced John Constable in a letter to his friend John Fisher and went on to say, "the lights are more to be seen in the late sale at *Lord De Tabley's* – all *new* pictures. They sold there for £8000 – *£2000 more than he paid for them*."[1] The so-called De Tabley sale, an auction of Sir John Leicester's celebrated collection of British painting, took place on 7 July 1827 at his mansion in London.[2] According to the daily *Morning Chronicle*, no other picture sales had excited so much interest for many years. "The grand Picture Saloon was crowded to excess with Noblemen, Amateurs and Artists . . . on each of the principal pictures being produced, the company testified their admiration of them by the clapping of hands."[3] Among the fifty-seven pictures on sale the highest bid was offered by the Earl of Grosvenor for Thomas Gainsborough's *The Cottage Door* (pl. III) at 500 guineas after heated competition, and sold to him "amidst the applause of the whole company."[4] Now considered to be the "most majestic of Gainsborough's 'Cottage Door' compositions,"[5] it constituted a group of pictures Gainsborough produced in the 1770–80s, in which idealized rural peasants and children are depicted in front of humble cottages set in wooded landscapes. The purpose of this essay is to trace the early history of *The Cottage Door* within the framework of the vibrant collecting and display culture in the early nineteenth century and to examine the role its collectors played in making and unmaking the reputation and aura of the painting. The essay does not examine the intrinsic aesthetic values of the painting but rather explores what Ellis Waterhouse dismissed as the "fashionable collecting and the satellite manoeuvres of the art trade and public exhibitions,"[6] and seeks to locate the trajectory of the painting in just such a "vulgar" context.

When *The Cottage Door* was first exhibited at the Royal Academy in 1780, it did not attract much public attention. Although it received some favorable comments in the press and Horace Walpole found it "charming,"[7] the painting remained unsold until 1786 when Thomas Harvey purchased it from Gainsborough for an unknown price.[8] Harvey was a prosperous master weaver based in Norwich, a major provincial city in the eighteenth century. A cultured man, he was fond of the arts and a close friend of the actress Mrs. Siddons, the actor Kemble, and the painters Beechey and Opie. He is now best remembered as a patron of the Norwich painter John Crome, but he was an important collector on his own. His passion for collecting started in the 1780s and it was during this period that he assembled a significant collection of contemporary English and continental Old Master paintings. More than anything else Harvey's acquisition of Gainsborough's *The Cottage Door* was likely to be a product of his fever for collecting in this period. Although Harvey encouraged Crome to copy the

facing page James Northcote, *Sir John Fleming Leicester, Bart.* (detail of fig. 86)

painting, there is no evidence to suggest that Harvey held it in higher esteem than other pictures in his collection or tried to promote it in public.[9] This does not necessarily mean that Harvey purchased it out of vanity. According to Daniel Coppin, who bought the painting from Harvey, he regarded it as a "study picture,"[10] meaning perhaps a model picture to be appreciated and copied closely. While it is not clear if Harvey had possessed any other paintings by Gainsborough before the purchase of *The Cottage Door* in 1786, he definitely developed a genuine preference for Gainsborough's landscape afterward, for a letter of 22 May 1788 from Gainsborough to Harvey shows that Harvey purchased a landscape (now unidentified) from Gainsborough and that Gainsborough even instructed Harvey, who was a competent amateur painter, how to clean his pictures in the damp English weather: "if ever you should find anything of a Chill come upon the Varnish of my Pictures, owing to its being a Spirit of Wine Varnish, take a rag, or little bit of sponge with Nut oil, and rub it 'til the mist clears away, and then wipe as much of it off as a few Strokes with a clean Cloth."[11]

Unfortunately Harvey disposed of a considerable number of pictures between 1807 and 1815 to cover his business failures and *The Cottage Door* was among the earliest departures. It was sold in 1807 to Coppin for an unknown price. Coppin was a tradesman in Norwich and his main business was gilding, but as was common in this period especially in the provinces, he was a jack of all relevant trades, working as a housepainter, glazier, and plumber as well. He was a kind of artist too, being a member of the Norwich Society of Artists and its president in 1816. Like many a minor artist, he also acted as a dealer.[12] It was probably in this capacity that he acquired *The Cottage Door*, given that just two years later in 1809 it became the property of Sir John Leicester, who was instrumental in promoting its visibility and status in public eyes and minds.

By the time Sir John acquired the painting, he was widely known and recognized as a leading patron and collector of contemporary British art (fig. 86). Head of one of the most ancient landed families in Cheshire, Sir John began to display a serious interest in collecting art after his return from the Grand Tour in 1786. One of his first acquisitions included Gainsborough's *Greyhounds Coursing a Fox*, purchased from the studio sale in 1789 of Gainsborough's works after his death, and Sir John purchased another Gainsborough, known as *Mountain Landscape*, at a Christie's auction in 1797.[13] Thus Sir John had been somewhat familiar with Gainsborough's art when he acquired *The Cottage Door* in 1809. The news that Coppin intended to sell the painting was first brought to Sir John's attention in 1808 by John Britton, a writer of antiquarian and architectural subjects. Describing it as "perfect," Britton strongly recommended its purchase to Sir John. After some negotiation over the price (Coppin initially asked for 500 guineas), Sir John bought it the following year from Coppin at 400 guineas (he paid 200 guineas in cash and and to make up the difference gave Coppin two paintings valued at 100 guineas each, one by Richard Wilson, the other by Francis Bourgeois).[14] Having compiled the now untracked 1808 catalogue of Sir John's collection, Britton was obviously acting as Sir John's artistic adviser and agent at the time, and it is not surprising to find that Britton reintroduced the painting to public discourse by publishing an engraving and

85 James Northcote, *Sir John Fleming Leicester, Bart.*, c. 1802, oil on canvas, 124.3 × 100.8 cm (49 × 39 in.), University of Manchester (Tabley House Collection)

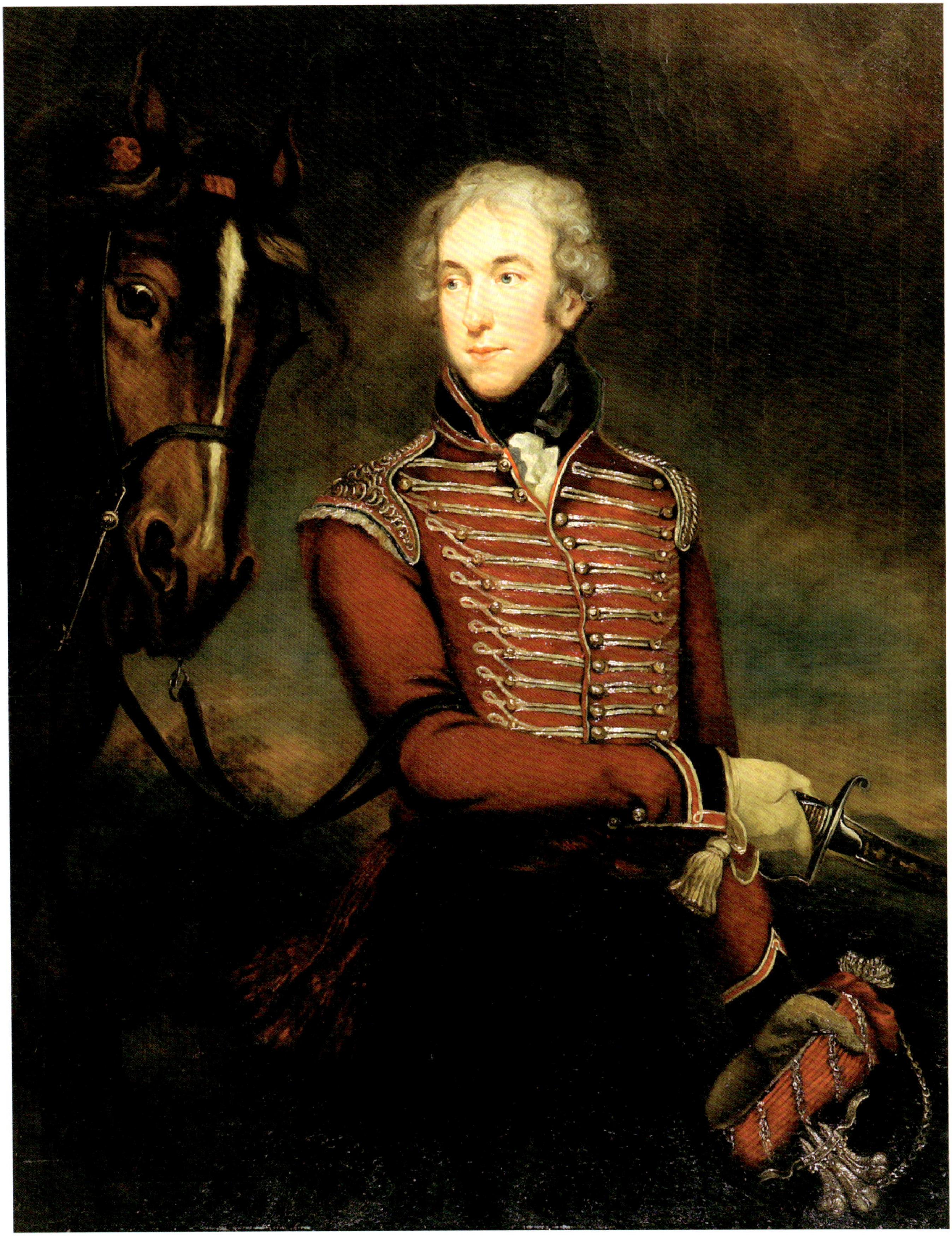

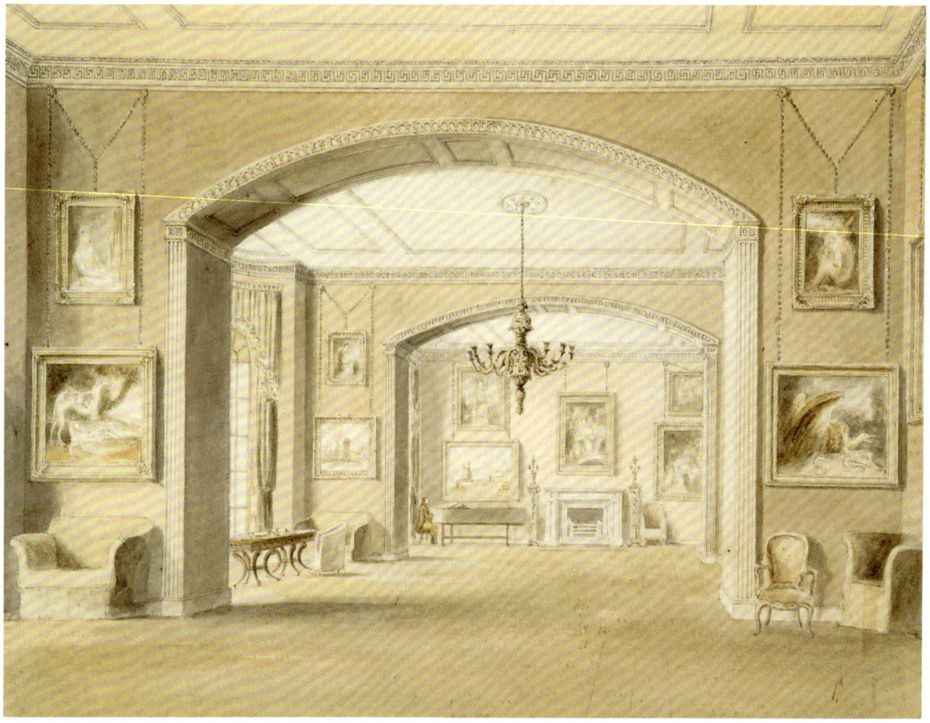

87 John Buckler, *Picture Gallery at Tabley House*, 1809, watercolor, 29.2 × 40.7 cm (11 × 16 in.), University of Manchester (Tabley House Collection)

enthusiastic account of it in his *Fine Arts of the English School*, a lavish volume published in 1812 to promote British art.

Sir John's purchase of *The Cottage Door* at such a high price (it was the most expensive painting in his collection) does not necessarily imply his unbound admiration for Gainsborough's art. Although he possessed two pictures by Gainsborough before the acquisition of *The Cottage Door* in 1809, it turned out to be the last Gainsborough he bought while Gainsborough's work was not in short supply on the art market. How, then, is the purchase to be understood? Instead of attempting simply to explain Sir John's acquisition of the painting as a sign of his love of Gainsborough's art (this is not to say that Sir John did not like it), I construe it as part of Sir John's programmatic campaign to patronize and collect contemporary British art. Needless to say, there were many other collectors and patrons who possessed some works by contemporary British artists mingled with continental Old Masters, but what distinguished Sir John from the others was his uncompromising devotion to obtaining specimens of British art only.[15] This deliberate act of cultural patriotism or nationalism was extremely unusual and pioneering indeed, as Sir John and his cronies persistently stressed. It was also a risky and controversial venture for a landed grandee like Sir John, given that aristocratic taste in England at the time was dominated by the well established and by now ineluctable canon that championed sixteenth and seventeenth-century continental Old Master paintings.

In the letter to Sir John recommending *The Cottage Door*, Britton said, "I really wish to see it in your British Gallery: I am confident that it will form a leading feature in it."[16] This gallery refers to a large, lantern ceilinged room in Sir John's mansion in Mayfair, the most modish living quarter in London (fig. 85). In addi-

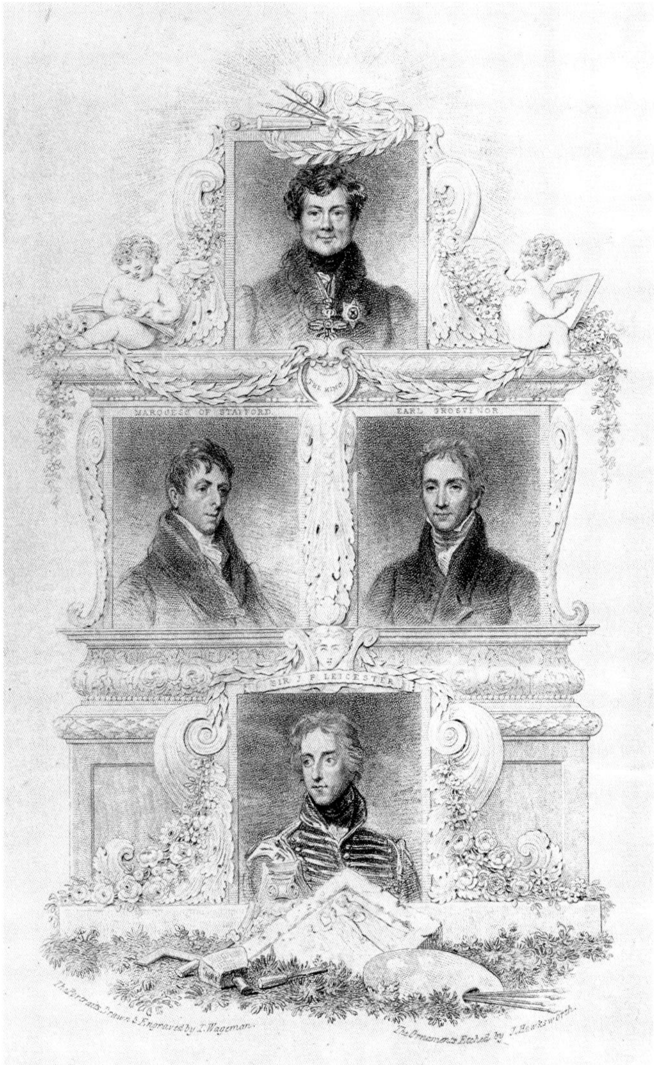

88 Thomas Wageman, *Portrait of Four Major Collectors*, engraving from C. M. Westmacott, *British Galleries of Painting and Sculpture*, London 1824

tion to his London gallery, Sir John built another gallery in 1809 at Tabley House, his country seat in Cheshire (fig. 87). These two galleries were designed to display Sir John's collection of British art, and that in London in particular attracted much attention from the art world and the press, especially when it was opened in 1818 to the general public, though on a selective basis, for free.[17] Nonetheless, display of works of art and the setting up of special galleries in patrician residences in London, not to mention in their country houses, was a well-established practise among rich aristocrats, and London mansions of major aristocratic families in the eighteenth century were full of continental Old Masters as well as family portraits. The unprecedented availability of Old Master paintings in England in the 1790s as a result of the French Revolution and its aftermath included the dispersal of many prominent continental European collections and transformed some aristocratic houses in London into sumptuous galleries of art – in particular, the Marquis of Stafford's Cleveland House and Lord Grosvenor's Grosvenor House.[18] As Thomas Wageman's quadruple portrait engraving of 1824 intimates (fig. 88), Sir John came to be regarded by some contemporaries as a collector on a par with George IV, the Marquis of Stafford, and Lord Grosvenor. Published in a book entitled *British Galleries of Painting and Sculpture*,[19] this portrait engraving purports to show who the most important collectors were at the time in hierarchical order: at the top is the king who was a well-known, if spendthrift, lover of the arts, in the middle were two noblemen famous for their spectacular collections of Old Masters, and at the bottom was Sir John, a baronet but, technically speaking, not a member of the nobility. The juxtaposition of Sir John with the other three is both revealing and misleading – revealing because of the implicit acknowledgment that collecting British art was as worthy a project as collecting Old Masters, misleading because the image generates the false impression that Sir John's collection was as magnificent as those of the others in terms of quantity and monetary value.

In spite of the meagerness of Sir John's collection in size and value compared with some patrician collections of Old Masters, it still stood out from the crowd of art collections at the time by the fact that it was exclusively composed of works by British artists – that is, pictures by those who were living and working in Britain. The centerpiece of the collection was *The Cottage Door*. As Britton predicted, it became the key feature in Sir John's collection and as such received special treatment. Reporting on 12 May 1818 of Sir John's gallery of British art in London, the fashionable daily *Morning Herald*, for example, mentions that "among some most admirable pictures of Gainsborough here, is that Cottage Piece, which, of all his works, has had the greatest and most deserved reputation. A room is allotted entirely to it, and mirrors are placed round to exhibit it to every advantage."[20] It is not clear what motivated Sir John to pay such unusual attention to the display of the painting, and no documents survive to indicate his real intentions. At any rate, the idea of exhibiting a single picture surrounded by mirrors was not entirely new, having been successfully experimented by Jacques-Louis David with his *Sabine Women*, which was exhibited between 1799 and 1805 in a room reserved for that picture only at the Louvre in Paris.[21] This is not the place to delve into the ambiguous and often contradictory responses of the English to the reception of French culture even during the Napoleonic wars, but there was undoubtedly an air of francophilia especially among the English aristocracy, and in all likelihood Sir John, no philistine of French language and culture,[22] must have known David's famous and innovative exhibition. If that was the case, the installation of *The Cottage Door* owed its origin to the French model, which suggests the ambivalence or inconsistency in Sir John's attitudes toward the French influence even in the middle of his exclusive gallery of British art.

Ironically, the collection of Sir John (by then Baron de Tabley), whom the obituary writer for the *Gentleman's Magazine* described as "the greatest patron of the native school of painting",[23] was broken up immediately after his death on 18 June 1827 and the speed at which the procedure leading to the De Tabley sale on 7 July 1827 was processed was extraordinary. Already on 30 June the *Morning Chronicle* carried Christie's advertisement announcing the sales of Sir John's collection as well as his London house.[24] Following the advertisement, private viewing of the collection at the venue continued until 4 July; for the last two days before the sale the collection was opened to the general public for viewing.[25] The De Tabley sale, held at Sir John's London house, was, in retrospect, an epoch-marking event in the history of British art, not merely because it was the dispersal of the finest collection to date of British art but also because it turned out to be highly successful, contrary to the fears of many artists whose works were included in the sale that sale prices would be low and that its subsequent impact on their reputation and future prices would be detrimental. The unexpected success was interpreted by the daily *Morning Post* as "one of the greatest triumphs to English art, which has occurred since Sir Joshua's. The prejudice against English genius is now for ever dissipated, because, there can be no personal favour in an open sale".[26] The writer goes on to insist that "[t]he English Nobility seem at last to be convinced, that a fine picture by a living Artist of the originality of which there can be no doubt, is more valuable than a trumped up, stippled up, doctored up LEONARDO or TITIAN!" This statement precisely applied to the Earl of Grosvenor, renowned for his collection of Old Masters, who bought *The Cottage Door* at 500 guineas, the highest price realized at the sale.

There was, however, a hitherto unknown, though transitory, owner of *The Cottage Door* between Sir John and Lord Grosvenor – Thomas Lister Parker, the executor of Sir John's will. Originally Sir John appointed two executors, Parker and George Leycester, in his will drawn up on 11 December 1826.[27] However, George Leycester from Toft in Cheshire, a fellow of King's College, Cambridge, died in London on 5 July 1827, [28] just seventeen days after the death of Sir John himself and two days before the De Tabley sale. Although Christie's advertisement in the *Morning Chronicle* of 30 June 1827 for the sale reads, "directions from the *Executors* [my italics] of the Right Hon. Lord DE TABLEY, deceased, to sell by auction," if one considers the timing of the death of Leycester, there is little doubt that Parker was chiefly responsible for the decision to auction the collection in such a hurry. Understandably, the sale of the collection was the easiest and quickest way to procure hard cash in order to discharge Sir John's debts, a fairly common practice at the time to release pressing debts of the recently deceased.

Interestingly, however, the sale was also in the best interest of Parker himself, as is disclosed from Sir John's second codicil:

> Whereas my Messuage or Mansion House situate in Hill Street London stands charged with the principal sum of two thousand Pounds and Interest unto Thomas Lister Parker Esquire by way of Mortgage Now I do hereby charge and make chargeable upon the said Messuage the sum of one thousand Pounds and I give and bequeath the same unto the said Thomas Lister Parker absolutely And I also give to him the Picture in my Gallery therein of the Cottage Door by Gainsborough.[29]

To put it simply, the sales of the London house and the collection meant for Parker a handsome gain of £1,000 as well as the money arising out of selling the most valued picture in the collection, in addition to recovering the loan of £2,000 lent to Sir John. This prospect perhaps accounts mainly for the swift arrangement for the De Tabley sale. Indeed, the sale had taken place eleven days before Sir John's will and eight codicils were officially proved on 18 July 1827.

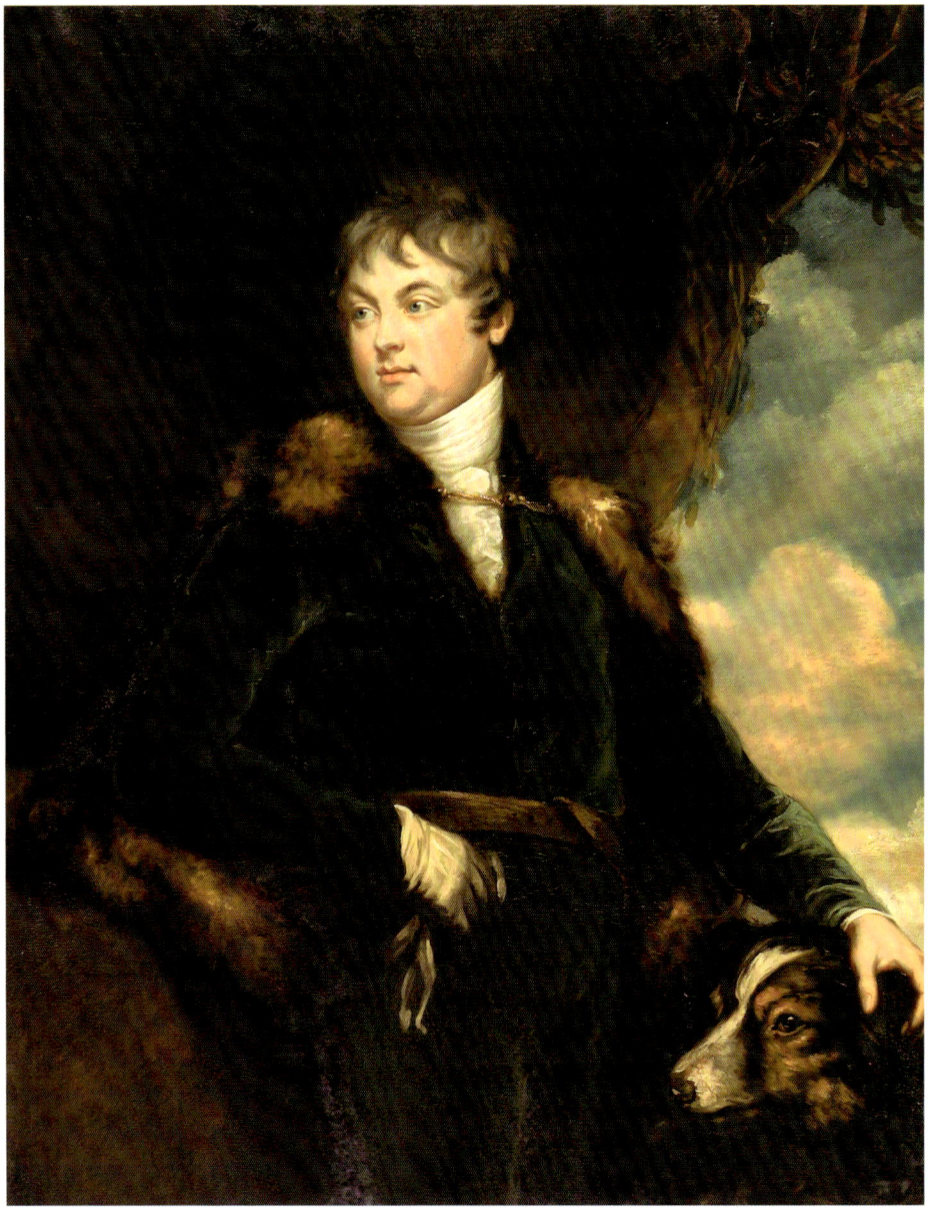

89 James Northcote, *Thomas Lister Parker*, c. 1802, oil on canvas, 124.8 × 101.5 cm (50 × 40 in.), University of Manchester (Tabley House Collection)

Parker (fig. 89) came from a long-established landed gentry background and was a relative of Sir John: Parker's paternal grandmother was a sister of Sir John's mother. Fellow of both the Society of Antiquaries and the Royal Society, Parker was also an important patron of contemporary British artists (fig. 90).[30] Judging from surviving evidence, Parker's taste for British art was heavily influenced by that of Sir John: Turner and James Northcote were their favorites and they sometimes exchanged paintings with each other. Unfortunately, however, Parker was not good at keeping a watchful eye on his purse and was prone to spending beyond his means. His lavish expenditure – altering his sixteenth-century house, laying out a landscape garden, collecting antiquarian objects and paintings – eventually forced him to sell his estate and mansion in Browsholme, Lancashire, and from 1824 he lived at Tabley as a kind of personal assistant to Sir John.

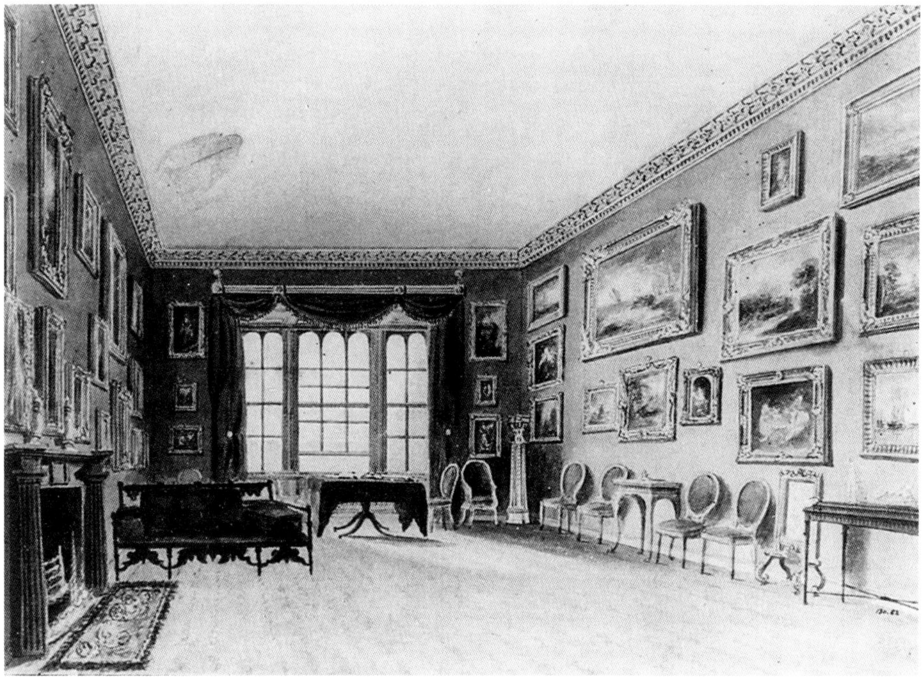

90 John Buckler, *Drawing Room at Browsholme Hall, Yorkshire*, 1809, medium and dimensions unknown, location unknown

To put all the blame on Parker for the De Tabley sale is not fair, however, because Sir John was deeply in debt and in his will explicitly endorsed disposal of his pictures and authorized his executors to sell them to settle his personal debts in an attempt to prevent the venerable Leicester estate from dissipating. Nevertheless, judging from a careful reading of Sir John's will and the eight codicils, one thing is certain: neither Sir John nor Parker cherished *The Cottage Door* enough to designate it as a family heirloom while many other pictures from Sir John's collection remained unsold as family heirlooms. This is somewhat ironic if one remembers the extraordinary care taken of the picture in Sir John's gallery.

The next owner of *The Cottage Door*, Robert Grosvenor, later first Marquis of Westminster, was Sir John's neighboring landowner in Cheshire. Also coming from an old landed family in Cheshire, Grosvenor became one of the most prominent English collectors in the early nineteenth century, turning his London mansion Grosvenor House into an internationally renowned palace of art (fig. 91). When he succeeded to the earldom in 1802, aged thirty-five, his family fortune was on a rapid rise. His lead mines in North Wales were generating £50,000 a year and the Grosvenor estate in London began to produce an ever-increasing rent. With this large amount of disposable income in hand, Grosvenor embarked on a series of ambitious projects to visualize his wealth and status – rebuilding his country house Eaton Hall, near Chester, acquiring a grand London house, and ceaselessly purchasing magnificent Old Masters to adorn his residences. It all started in 1803 with the rebuilding of Eaton Hall to the designs of the architect William Porden. As Porden insisted that "your Lordship should be superior to everyone else, and that you should be followed, not follow any man in matters of taste,"[31] Eaton Hall, constructed in two stages, 1803–12 and 1820–25, at the total cost of more than £100,000, became the most extravagant

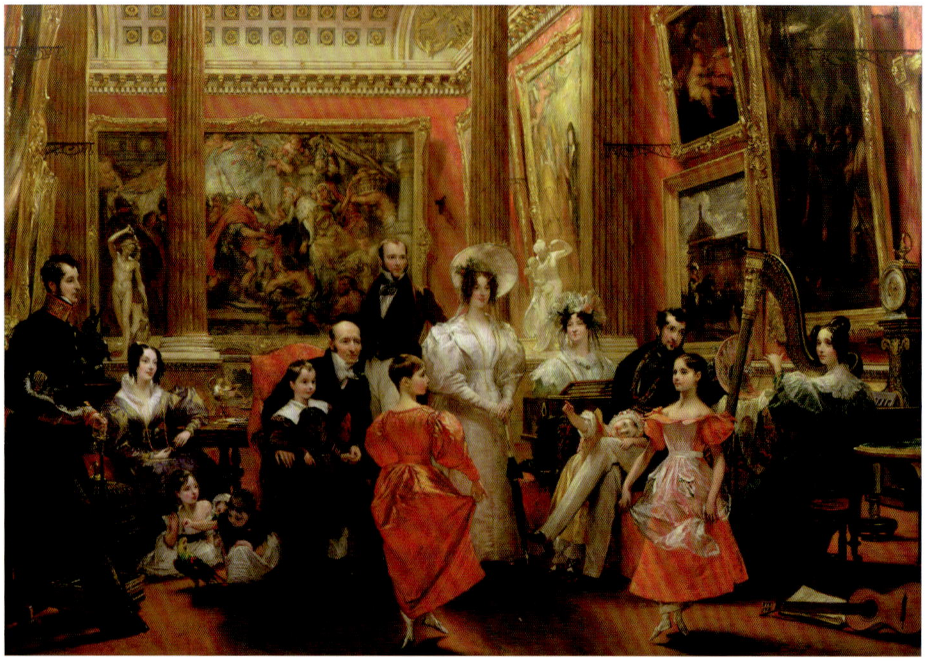

91 Charles Robert Leslie, *The Grosvenor Family*, 1831, oil on canvas, 101.6 × 144.7 cm (40 × 57 in.), private collection

Gothic Revival country house in early nineteenth-century England.[32] Soon after work on Eaton Hall commenced, Grosvenor began to look for a grander town house in London than Millbank House in Pimlico that he had inherited from his father. Negotiations were entered in 1805 to buy what was known then as Gloucester House in Mayfair, named after its recently deceased owner, the royal Duke of Gloucester. In February 1806 Grosvenor bought the lease of the house at £20,000 and renamed it Grosvenor House.[33] Extensive alterations and redecoration followed under the supervision of William Porden.

Not surprisingly, as soon as he secured the town house, Grosvenor began to look for paintings to adorn the empty walls and in early 1806 he managed to buy the entire collection of Welbore Agar Ellis. Although not from a patrician background, Ellis had amassed an impressive collection of Old Masters, with particular emphasis on French and Dutch seventeenth-century paintings. After he died in 1805, his collection of sixty-five pictures was due to be auctioned at Christie's in May 1806, but it was bought *en bloc* by Grosvenor a month or two before the projected sale.[34] News of the purchase spread quickly within the contemporary art world and became a subject of much gossip. The influential connoisseur Sir George Beaumont privately disapproved of the purchase, as he thought it better to bid for the best pictures and to leave the inferior ones at a public auction.[35] The acquisition itself was negotiated by the picture cleaner William Seguier on behalf of Grosvenor while the painter Francis Bourgeois and the dealer Noel Desenfans acted for Ellis's executors. After some wrangling over the price, it was finally settled at 30,000 guineas. Naturally, Seguier believed that he had struck a good bargain for Grosvenor, whereas, according to Joseph Farington, "many good judges differ from him in opinion".[36]

While forming a collection of Old Master works, Lord Grosvenor also planned to collect English paintings and to create a room for them in Grosvenor House. In 1806 he told Benjamin West, then president of the Royal Academy, of his plan "to have a room furnished with English pictures only" in Grosvenor House.[37] Yet the scheme did not materialize. Grosvenor's decision to drop the plan and his loss of interest in contemporary English art were solely due, according to William Porden, to the influence of "a Picture Cleaning tribe & dealers in old pictures" – Farington recorded in his diary on 15 July 1807 that "Porden said a Picture Cleaning tribe & dealers in old pictures have at present prejudiced Lord Grosvenor's mind so far against the merit of modern art as to interrupt his design of making a Collection of Modern pictures".[38]

The picture cleaning tribe and dealers referred to are William Seguier, and his father and brother, who ran a picture restoration business. Born into a Huguenot family long settled in London, Seguier became a valued artistic agent and adviser to major collectors in the early nineteenth century, such as Sir Charles Long, Sir Robert Peel, the Duke of Wellington, and George IV as well as Lord Grosvenor.[39] As the Superintendent of the British Institution in London for many years, Seguier's connection with these powerful and influential men of the age was undoubtedly a key to his success, culminating in securing the post of Keeper of the National Gallery when it was first established in 1824. As shown earlier, Seguier was responsible for negotiating Grosvenor's purchase of Ellis's collection and he was in fact in charge of looking after Grosvenor's collection in London. After the acquisition of the Ellis collection, Seguier was busy with arranging pictures in Grosvenor House, a duty he seems to have undertaken with dedication and enthusiasm. He regularly wrote to Grosvenor at Eaton to report the progress in London and was even working on New Year's Day in 1808:

> Your Lordship will perceive by the enclosed arrangements that I have introduced the whole of the Flemish Pictures (intended for Town) excepting three – viz. the inferior Hobbema the Landscape of Koninck and the large Van Goyen. . . . I shall strictly attend to your Lordships order which was communicated to me by Mr. Porden and your Lordship may be assured that I shall not let any person see either the rooms or the Pictures.[40]

As the letter unmistakably demonstrates, it was Seguier who was basically responsible for the hanging and, curiously, Grosvenor was adamant that nobody should be allowed to see the arrangements before it was ready for public inspection. This instruction is particularly noteworthy because it shows that Grosvenor was acutely aware of, and intended to emulate, the enormous public attention paid to the opening in 1806 of the Marquis of Stafford's superb collection of Old Masters in Cleveland House, the first nobleman's house in London opened to a selected public on a regular basis.[41] After much work and preparation, Grosvenor House was eventually open in June 1808 to fashionable London society. Conservative presses such as *The Times* and the *Morning Post* highly praised the magnificence and elegance of the residence and its interior decoration.[42] Yet not everyone was impressed. The Earl of Lonsdale, for example, who was a distinguished collector of seventeenth-century Dutch paintings, told Farington that he thought it "most expensively furnished, but in a bad taste".[43] Farington himself was not much enticed either, for he postponed visiting the house until the last day of its opening on July 1, and did not bother to record his impression at all in his diary. Instead he noted what Constable told him of Benjamin West's response. West, the only living artist whose two paintings – the *Death of General Wolfe* and the *Battle of La Hogue*, both of which were inherited from Grosvenor's father – were represented in the house at the time, bitterly complained of their being ill hung, insisting that "it was a national concern".[44]

Meanwhile, Grosvenor kept augmenting his collection by continuing to acquire Old Masters, the most splendid of which were the four large religious paintings by Rubens purchased in 1818 at the cost of £9,205. Also during 1817–19 a picture gallery was added in Grosvenor House to accommodate his growing collection.[45] Moreover, in 1821 Grosvenor engaged the engraver John Young to produce an illustrated catalogue of his collection in Grosvenor House. Reproducing all the 143 paintings in the London residence room by room, this catalogue is the first of a series of illustrated catalogues Young produced for the collections of Sir John Leicester, Philip Miles, Lord Stafford, and John Julius Angerstein. The immediate inspiration for the idea of such a catalogue appears to have stemmed from the publication in 1818 of W. Y. Ottley's scholarly four-volume illustrated catalogue of Lord Stafford's splendid collection in London.[46] In fact, Lord Grosvenor and Lord Stafford became related by marriage: Grosvenor's eldest son Richard married Stafford's daughter Elizabeth Levenson-Gower in 1819. A classic case of aristocratic endogamy of wealth and status nourishing each other, the marriage was a fitting match: both families held to Whig politics, and both Lord Grosvenor and Lord Stafford were among the four richest men in England, named by the Chancellor of the Exchequer in 1819.[47]

By the 1820s Grosvenor's collection in London, along with that of Lord Stafford, was widely regarded as one of the most glorious in the country,[48] and the distinguished German art historian Gustav Waagen, on his visit to England in 1835, found Grosvenor's collection "truly princely."[49] In assembling such an outstanding collection Grosvenor had a remarkable sense of concentration and single-mindedness, a disposition his daughter-in-law Lady Elizabeth noted. "When Lord Grosvenor is possessed of an idea," she wrote to her mother, "one might just as well talk to the winds".[50] This character is discernible also in Grosvenor's tenacious pursuit of *The Cottage Door*: although he was no great lover of English art and *The Cottage Door* was the only picture he bought at the De Tabley sale, he was reported to have been "determined to possess it (we have been told that his Lordship said) had it cost him One Thousand Pounds."[51] Upon the purchase, it was immediately hung in the new picture gallery in Grosvenor House, and competed for public and press attention amid impressive Old Masters.[52] This entire anecdote suggests that Lord Grosvenor was concerned far more with adding another famous painting to his pantheon of masterpieces than with advancing the cause of British art. By the time Grosvenor died in 1845, however, *The Cottage Door* seems to have lost its appeal, judging from the fact that it was relegated to hang in the ante-drawing room, a relatively insignificant space in the house, along with other smaller paintings by Gaspar Dughet, Pietro da Cortona, and Francesco Zuccherilli.[53] Although the painting remained in the house until Grosvenor's great-grandson, the second Duke of Westminster, sold it to the dealer Joseph Duveen in 1921, who in turn sold it to Henry Huntington in 1922, it never regained the glory and attention it once commanded in Sir John Leicester's gallery of British art. Perhaps it was unable to outshine the Old Masters in Grosvenor House, a destiny Gainsborough would have well anticipated.

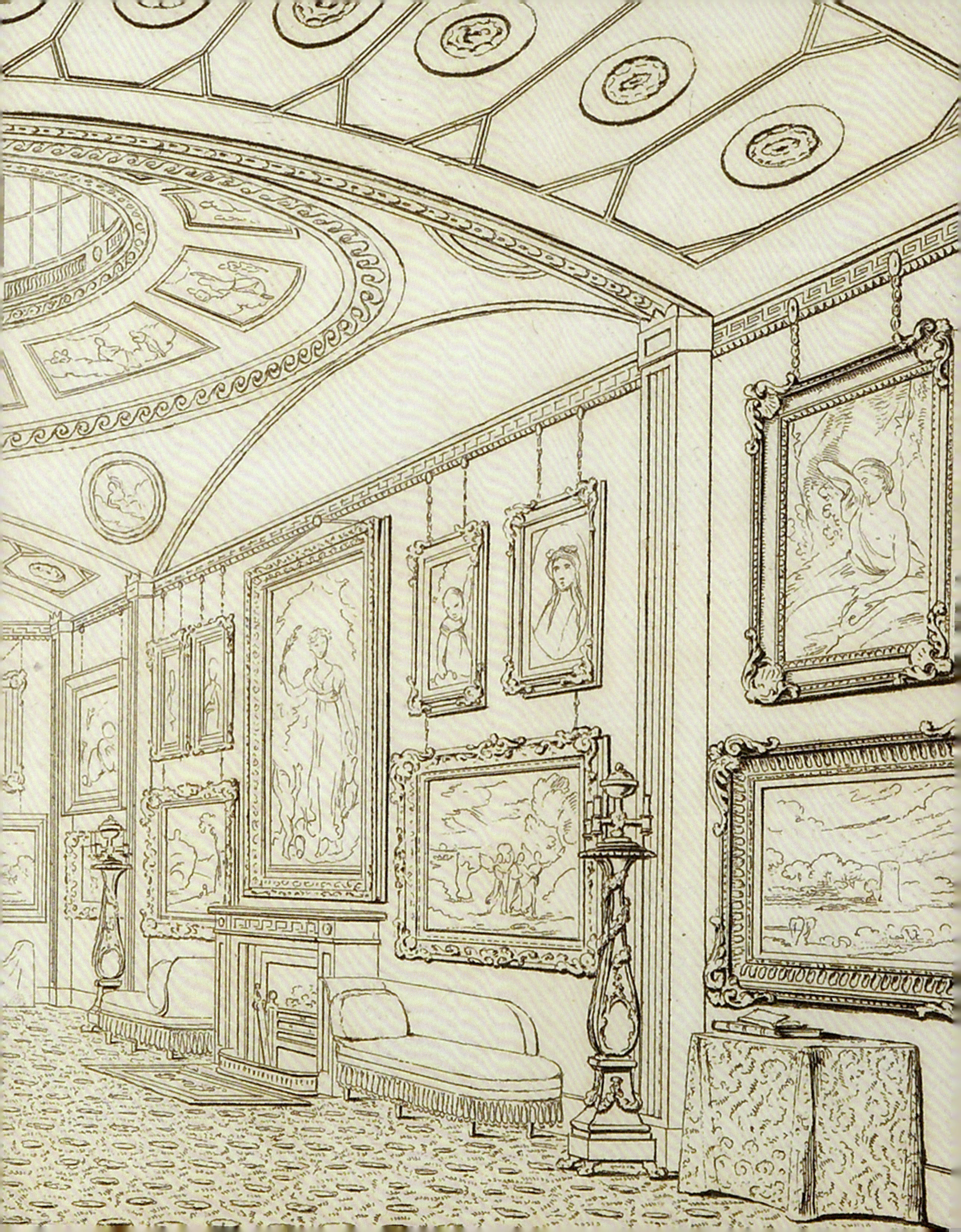

Ann Bermingham

Gainsborough's Cottage Door *in Sir John Leicester's "Tent Room"*

When Sir John Leicester opened his collection of modern British paintings to the London public in the spring of 1818, *The Morning Herald* reported that Thomas Gainsborough's painting, *The Cottage Door*, had been allotted a room "entirely to it, and mirrors are placed around it to exhibit it to every advantage" (pl. III). In his 1819 descriptive catalogue of the collection William Carey noted that the painting hung in a "tent room", and in his 1821 illustrated catalogue John Young added that by this time the *Cottage Door* had been joined in the tent room by James Ward's *Fall of Phaeton* and by William Behnes's cast "from the right hand of the late B. West, Esq."[1]

My essay examines the possible rationale for this dramatic installation of Gainsborough's *Cottage Door* and for the 1821 addition of Ward's painting and the cast of West's hand. Given that *The Cottage Door* was singled out in this way from all the other works by British artists in the collection, it seems important to explore this fact in the context of both Gainsborough's evolving reputation as an artist and, ultimately, his place in the nascent British School. Moreover, as I hope to demonstrate, the installation not only reflects on Gainsborough's status but, as a viewing experience, it suggests a new understanding and appreciation of his art. I wish to begin the discussion by briefly setting out what is known of Sir John and the physical arrangement of his gallery at 24 Hill Street, in particular the details of the "tent room", before moving on to these larger issues.

Sir John Leicester and His Collection

Sir John Fleming Leicester (1762–1827), created Baron de Tabley in 1826, was in his day if not the only then at least the most renowned patron and collector of modern British art, and the first private collector of British art to open his collection to the public (fig. 92). At his death, the *Monthly Magazine and British Review* lamented that, "the English school of painting has lost one of its best friends. In his encouragement of painting, sculpture, and engraving, he was at once liberal, generous, and indefatigable. . . . His superb collection, formed at immense cost, was frequently opened for public inspection".[2] Sir John insisted that the works of British artists were equal in quality to those of continental Old Masters. In opening his collection, he followed the example of collectors of Old Masters such as the Marquis of Stafford and the Earl of Grosvenor who allowed public access to their collections in the first decade of the new century.

facing page Artist unknown, Lord de Tabley's British Gallery at Hill Street in 1818 (detail of fig. 95)

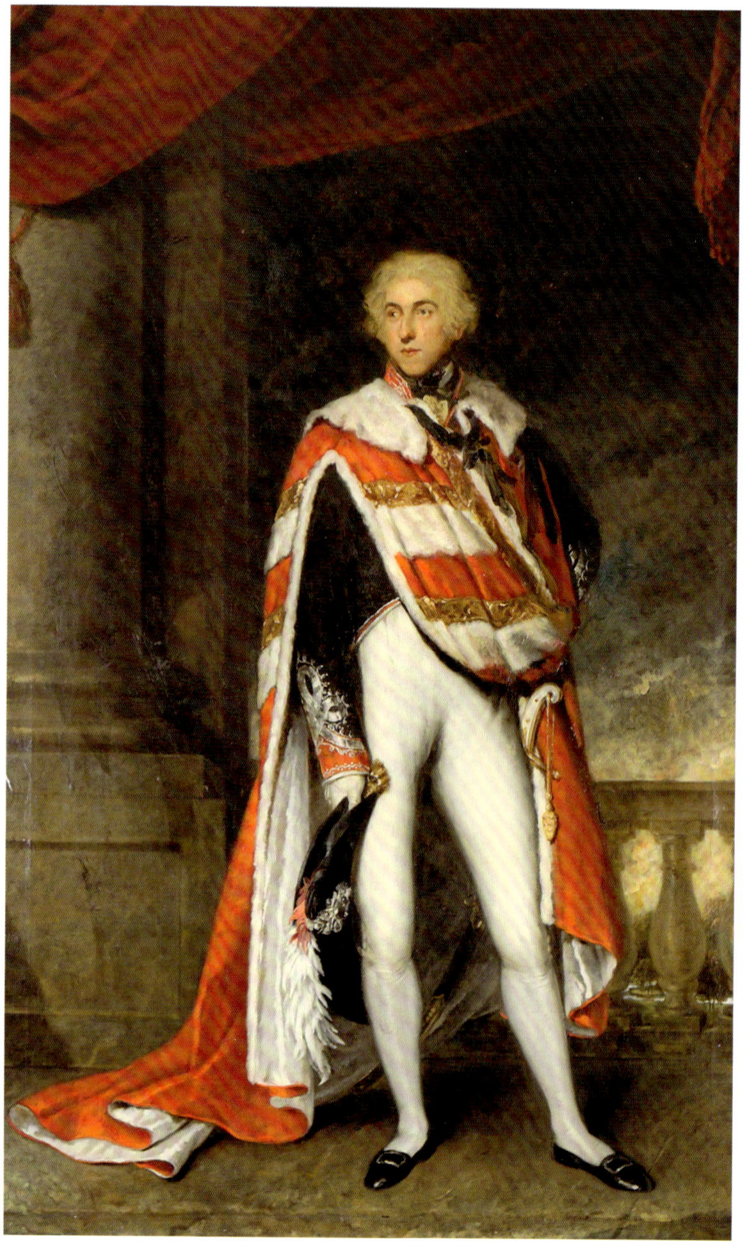

92 Joshua Reynolds, Giuseppe Marchi, Jame Northcote, and John Simpson, *Sir John Fleming Leicester, Bart., 1st Lord De Tabley, in Peer's Robes*, 1789–1828, oil on canvas, 233.7 × 144.8 cm (91 × $56\frac{1}{2}$ in.), repainted by John Simpson in 1826. University of Manchester (Tabley House Collection)

Such actions were motivated by a number of reasons: requests by artists for greater access; aristocratic *noblesse oblige*; a desire to display taste and to make a statement that the collections were of such a quality as to demand public attention and approbation. In opening his gallery in this way, Sir John, like these other men, positioned his collection of British paintings as one of public significance and, more pointedly, himself as a patron, if not *the* patron, of the British School.

Starting in 1818 the gallery was open to the public two days a week between 6 April and 25 May. The following year visiting was allowed on Mondays only from one to four o'clock but the period allocated was changed from the first day of March to 17 May.[3] Admission followed the procedure used by the Marquis of Stafford at Cleveland House, that is to say one applied for a ticket to Sir John "to whom, or some Friends, the Party must be known."[4] The public therefore was not the general public but rather, as *The Repository of the Arts* noted, "persons distinguished for talents and rank, the most exalted of our amateurs, and the most celebrated of our artists."[5] Nonetheless, the gallery was heavily visited. The *Morning Herald* reported that on opening day 1818 carriages thronged the street cutting it off completely from other traffic. The *Morning Post* set the number of visitors on opening day in 1819 at 500, while James Northcote reported that as late as 1823 the gallery was still attracting "great attention," claiming that it saw 700 visitors a day.[6]

Sir John had not always been a collector of British art exclusively. As a young man he started collecting in the late 1780s after his return from the Grand Tour, and at that time his tastes included works by Teniers, Carracci, Guercino, Claude, and other Continental artists favored by the British aristocracy. His interest in British art, Gainsborough in particular, also dates from this early period. One of his first English purchases was Gainsborough's *Greyhounds Coursing a Fox*, which he made in 1789 at the sale of works from Gainsborough's studio in Schomberg House after the artist's death in August 1788.

By 1801 Sir John was well enough established as a patron of British artists to be invited to the annual Royal Academy dinner, and by 1806 his growing collection of British art merited a notice in the *Morning Post*, which reported that "Sir John Leicester has fitted up his superb gallery in Hill Street . . . with the choicest specimens of British Artists only."[7] He was not alone in his passion for British art, in which he was joined by several distinguished men of title and fortune such as Turner's friend and patron Walter Fawkes of Farnley Hall; Alexander Davidson; Charles James Hoare; George O'Brien Wyndham, the third Earl of Egremont; George Granville Leveson-Gower, the second Marquis of Stafford; Sir George Beaumont; Sir Francis Baring; Henry Phipps, the first Earl of Mulgrave and Viscount Normandy; and by Sir John's near relation, Thomas Lister Parker. While none of them exceeded Sir John in the number of British works they owned, all were active in collecting British art in the first two decades of the nineteenth century, and several were founding members of the British Institution. Nevertheless, Sir John's collection was the most substantial and well rounded. Art historians have attributed his devotion to British art to his desire to acquire a peerage from George IV, and while this seems probable it does not diminish his importance as a collector and patron of British art.[8] Sir John played the role early in the century that Robert Vernon, whose collection of British art now forms portions of the Tate and National Gallery, played at mid-century.

Hill Street House

The London townhouse that served as Sir John's picture gallery at 24 Hill Street was leased from Robert Heathcote in 1805 for 12,000 guineas.[9] The house was let with most of its contents except for some moveables such as paintings, plate, and china. Located just off Berkeley Square, the address was reasonably fashionable, fashionable enough to serve as Great Gaunt Street in William Makepeace Thackeray's *Vanity Fair*.[10] Sir John was fortunate in that number 24 was located

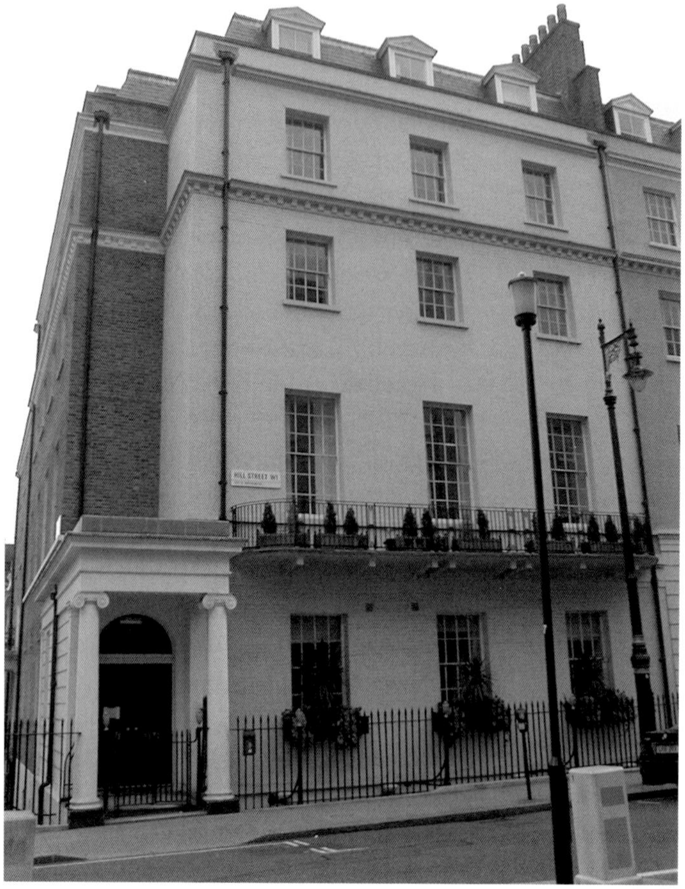

93 Exterior of 29 Hill Street (previously 24 Hill Street), London

on the south corner of Hill Street and John Street and thus had side as well as front and back windows (fig. 93). In addition, the back of the house, which faces southeast, had a conservatory, which opened the main floor of the house to views, light, and air. Although Hill Street does not appear in John Rocque's famous 1746 map of London, it is almost certain that it was under development by 1745.[11] Many of its residences were built by Thomas Cundy, senior (1765–1825).[12]

From the 1805 estate agent's report drawn up by Mr. Phillips of Bond Street there is a description of the house at the time that Sir John bought it.[13] One learns from it much about the first floor rooms of the house that served as his picture gallery. The report describes their disposition, decoration, and furnishings in this way:

> THE LIBRARY: Which is a Noble and capacious Apartment OF EXQUISITE DESIGN, has been created within the last Twelve Months, is Forty-eight Feet in Length, and Thirty Feet in Width, with a vaulted Roof, decorated in the Grecian Style, with a Dome Twenty-eight Feet high; the Ceiling Spherical and painted a warm Sky; the Base of the Dome and hemispherical Ceiling are enriched by appropriate allegorical Devices in Chiaro Oscura; the Cornices, and every ornamental Finishing, chaste and correspondent; Two expensive and elegant

> STATUARY MARBLE CHIMNEY PIECES, of Grecian Design, enriched by Busts of Homer, Demosthenes, Cicero, and Virgil; with handsome polished Steel Register Stoves, fenders, &c. The Doors are imitative of Massy Bronze, with Devices in alto-relievo, emblematic of the History of Minerva and Attributes. At the Southern Extremity is a large and handsome CONSERVATORY or GREEN HOUSE, (partly glazed with Stained Glass) opening onto the Library, from whence, when filled with Flowers and Plants are diffused the [illegible] the Room, [illegible] and comprises Four brilliant French Plate Glasses, of singular Magnitude, Beauty and Perfection; draped Curtains of Broad Cloth, trimmed with Black Velvet; Sophas; Chaise Lounges and Chairs, expensively covered and elegantly formed; Library and Sopha Tables, and Bookcases; Carpets &c. The whole en-suite and of a superior Description.
>
> THE BOUDOIR: Is fitted with Taste a la Turque, of Circular Form, and Canopy Ceiling, richly hung with Silks, and Pannels of brilliant Plate Glass, warmed by an elegant Parisian Stove, and encircled by Turkish Squabs.
>
> THE WITH-DRAWING ROOMS: Are spacious, of excellent Proportions, fitted with beautiful Statuary Marble Chimney Pieces, and finished with enriched gilt Cornices; SPLENDEDLY FURNISHED with rich Crimson, Blue and White Silk Hangings, draped and disposed with peculiar Taste. The Sophas and Chairs are elegantly designed, and formed of massy gilt Frames, covered with rich Silk – The tables, Cheffoniers, and Commodes, are formed of Rose Wood, enriched by ORMOLU Busts and antique Devices, of the most exquisite Workmanship – NOBLE PIER and CHIMNEY GLASSES, and particularly a lofty and brilliant GLASS, secreted within the Wainscotting of Front Room, producing when drawn out, (by reflecting the Suite of Rooms on this Floor), the most beautiful and happy Effect. The whole of the Floor is covered with handsome Carpeting, corresponding in Pattern with the general Taste and Design of this Suite of Magnificent Apartments.

From this one sees that the rooms that eventually made up the gallery spaces were the library, withdrawing rooms, and the boudoir *à la turque*. An inventory of the contents of the house from June 1805 gives a spare but helpful idea of the rooms on the first floor. It lists a front-room, two drawing rooms, a chamber, dressing room, the Library, and greenhouse.[14]

No doubt it was the spacious library with its lantern ceiling that attracted Sir John to the property.[15] A watercolor by John Buckler (c. 1806) shows the library after it had been converted into the main picture gallery (fig. 94). The room is viewed from an entrance door located in the center of the north wall looking toward the south wall: paintings are suspended from gold chains attached to the cornice below the ceiling (a novel feature commented upon in contemporary accounts); gilt lions' heads are used to cover the place where the chains attach to the cornice. The room was heated by two fireplaces located on the east and west walls. Buckler's watercolor depicts the gallery as a windowless room lit only by the lantern ceiling. The drawing's depiction of the south wall does not conform to the 1805 sale report, which described the library as opening on this side to the conservatory. Whether the drawing represents an actual change made

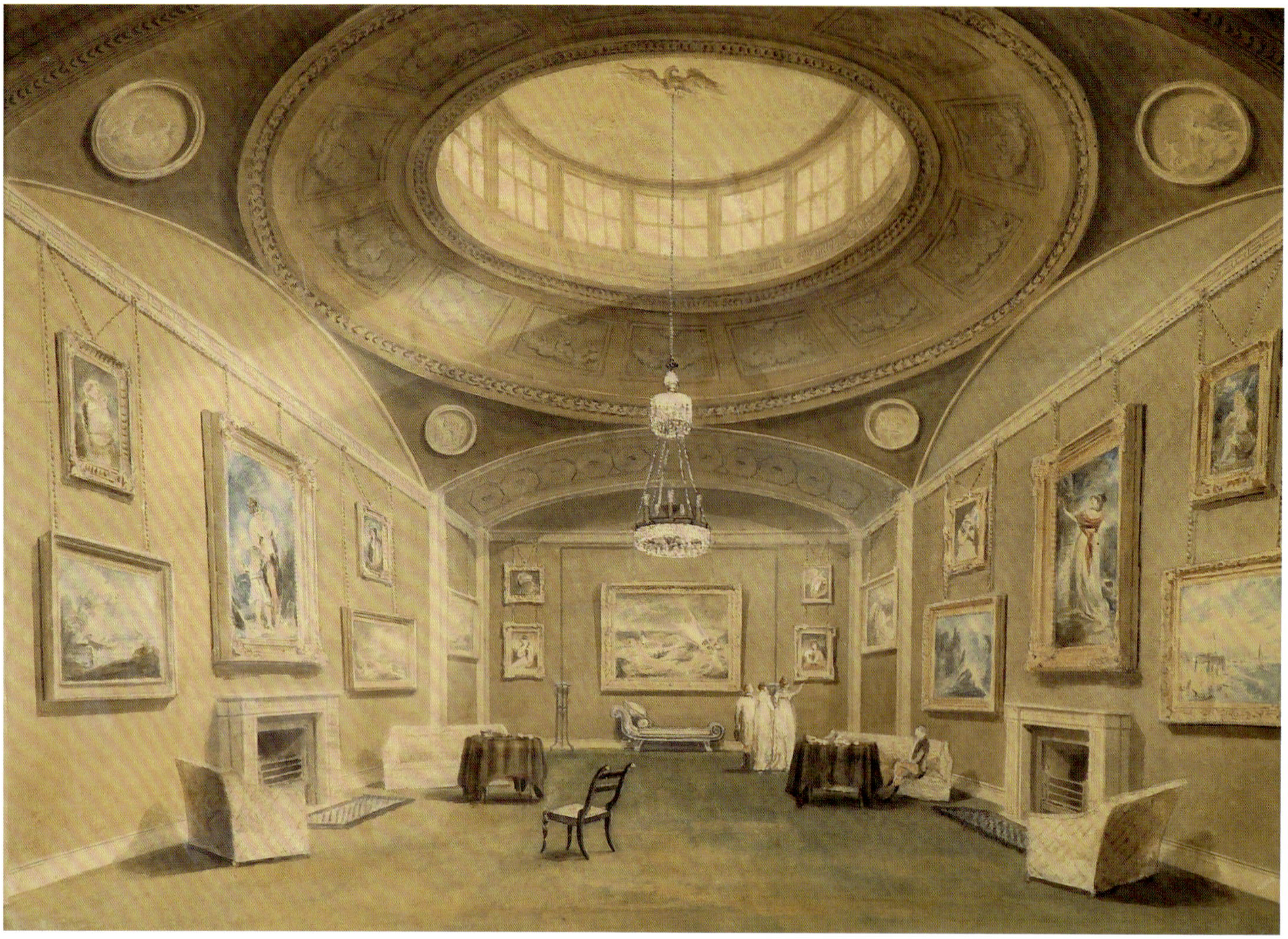

94 John Buckler, *Picture Gallery of Sir John Fleming Leicester, Bart.*, at 24 Hill Street, London, 1806, pencil and wash, 43.2 × 71 cm (17 × 28 in.), University of Manchester (Tabley House Collection)

to the space or an imaginary view showing what the gallery would look like if a wall were constructed separating it from the conservatory, is impossible to say. All subsequent views of the main gallery, starting with the illustration that accompanied William Carey's 1819 catalogue of the collection, show it opening to the conservatory, which appears as a heavily draped alcove at the south end (fig. 95).[16]

Both Carey and Young in their catalogues of the collection list the rooms of the first floor and their contents. According to Carey (1819) they comprised a gallery with thirty-one pictures, an ante-room with eight pictures, a tent room with one picture, a drawing room with three pictures, and a second drawing room with five pictures. Two years later Young lists a gallery with thirty-one pictures, an ante-room with eight pictures, a tent room with two pictures and a cast, a drawing room with eight pictures, an entrance to the gallery with a bust, and a gallery with four pictures. When the house was sold after Sir John's death, an advertisement in the *Morning Chronicle* described the first floor as having a "capital suite of drawing rooms, the front apartment with folding sashes glazed with plate glass, and opening into a spacious balcony; second drawing room, tent

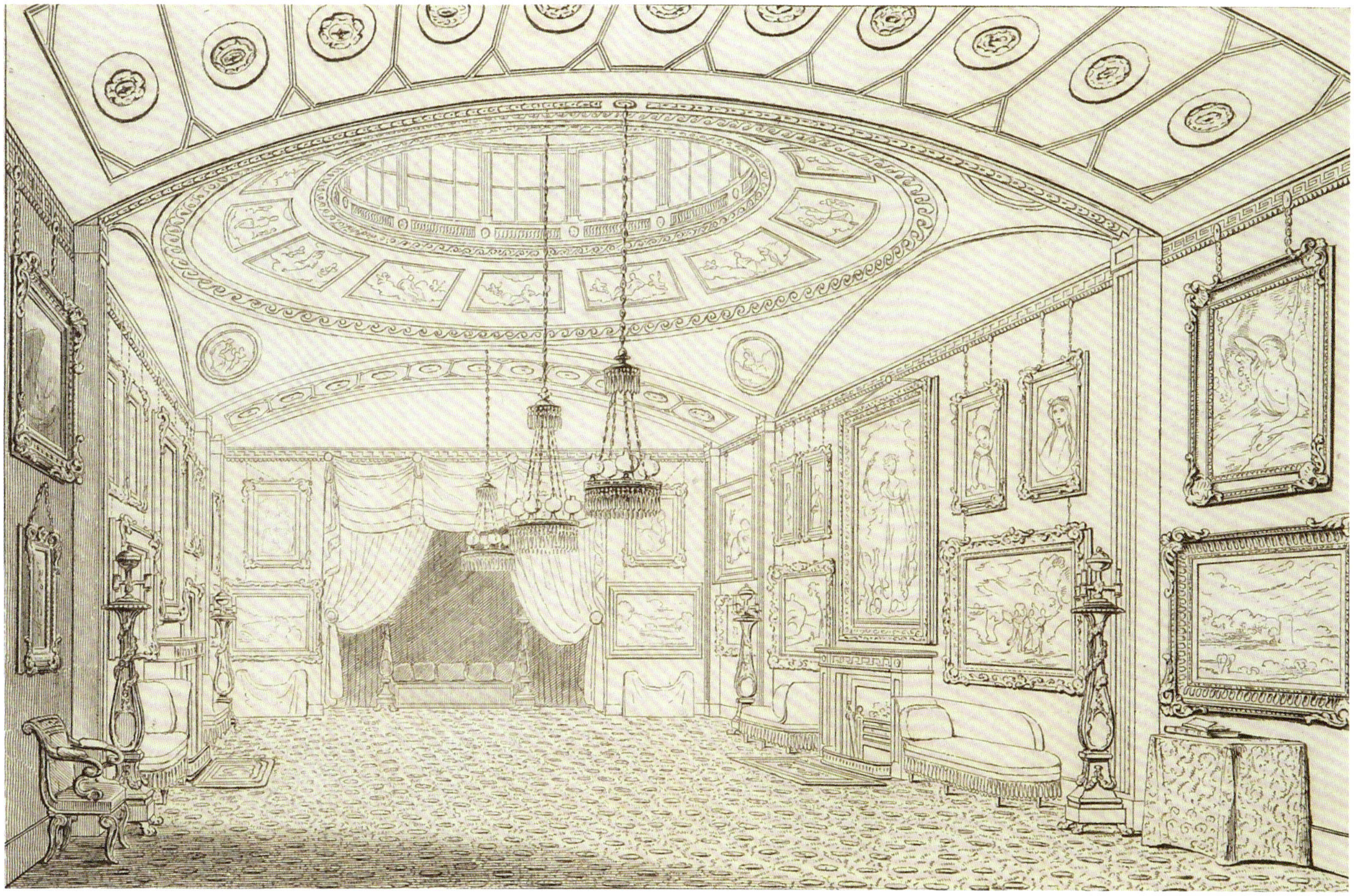

95 Artist unknown, Lord de Tabley's British Gallery at Hill Street in 1818, engraving from William Carey, *A Descriptive Catalogue of a Collection of Paintings by British Artists, in the Possession of Sir John Fleming Leicester, Bart*, 1819, University of Manchester (Tabley House Collection)

room and vestibule, noble picture salon with carved ceiling and circular lantern sky-light, with spacious conservatory beyond it."[17] From these accounts one can conclude that there were five rooms on the first floor, including the large gallery and tent room, that were hung with pictures.

After purchasing the lease on the Hill Street house Sir John set about redecorating and reconfiguring the rooms in order to accommodate himself, his mistress Emily St. Clare (with whom he lived openly; fig. 96), and his growing collection of British paintings. A plasterer's bill from 1805 suggests that carpentry and repairs were done throughout the house.[18] It appears that Sir John wished to reserve the first floor as a picture gallery, and as the collection grew new rooms were converted to display paintings. Eventually this meant that the ground floor had to be renovated and made into living quarters. For this he hired Thomas Cundy senior, the architect who may have built the house and who had certainly done a major renovation of it the year before Sir John bought it and was therefore familiar with the property. In June 1809 Sir John asked him for an estimate of what it would cost to convert the "Egyptian Hall" on the ground floor into an eating room, corridor, ante-room, and to create a "room to receive pictures."[19]

It is the "tent room," or the room that the 1805 estate agent's report describes as the "boudoir a la Turque," that is of most interest here. As the report makes

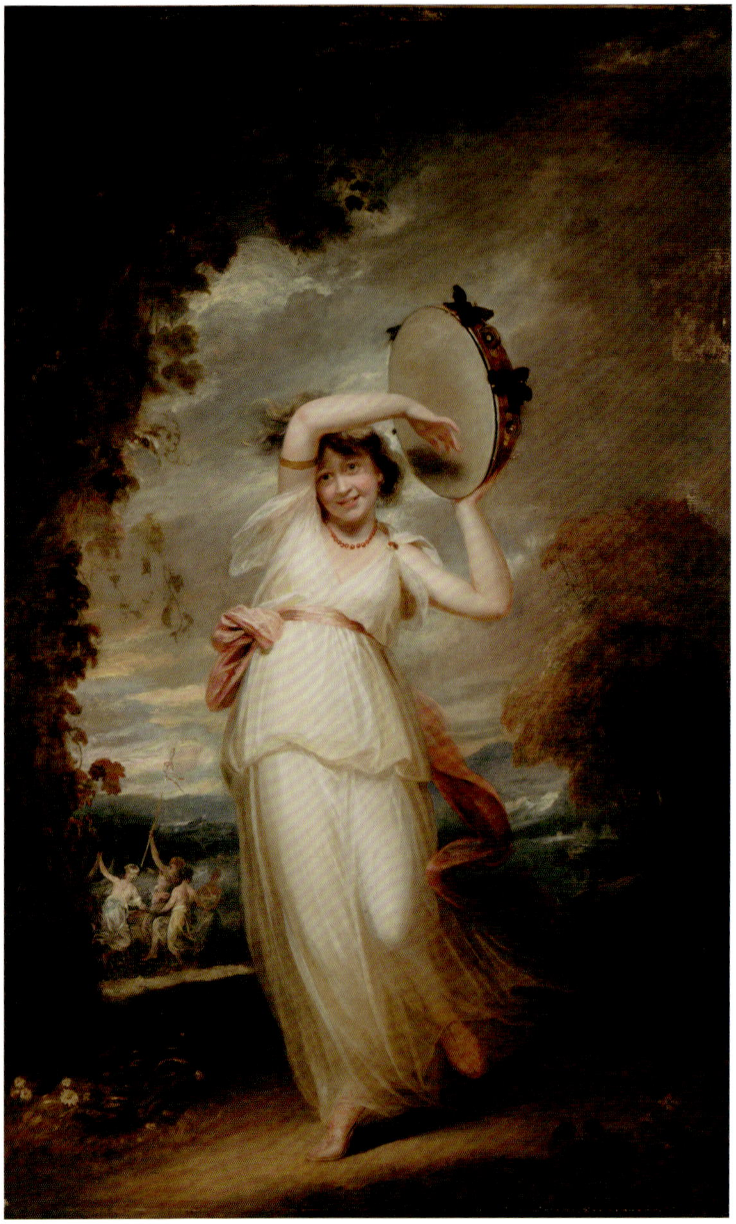

96 John Hoppner, *Emily St. Clare as a Bacchante*, c. 1806, oil on canvas, 239.7 × 148.6 cm (94⅜ × 58½ in.), Nelson Atkins Museum, Kansas City, Missouri. Gift of Robert Lehman

plain, the boudoir was located on the first floor and was already tented and installed with mirrors. Most probably it was on the east side of the house, for it appears to have had windows. Tent rooms came into vogue at the end of the eighteenth century and were popular during the Regency when a taste developed for heavily draped rooms. The taste was promoted by the Prince Regent who in 1787 had a draped bed-chamber built in the Marine Pavilion at Brighton.[20] In about 1805 he hired Walsh Porter to refurbish the rooms of Carlton House, which had been designed by the architect Henry Holland in a severe French classical style. Porter festooned the walls and windows with swagged curtains, heavy flounces, and furbelows.[21] Joseph Farington noted disapprovingly in his *Diary* in May 1806 that "Although Carlton House as finished by Holland was in a complete & new state, He [the Prince Regent] has ordered

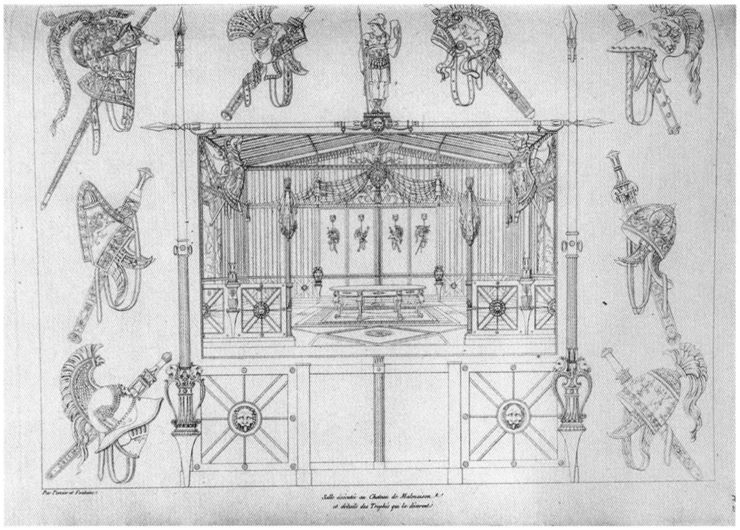

97 C. Percier and P. F. L. Fontaine, *Tent Room at Malmaison*, c. 1801, engraving from *Recueil de Décorations Intérieures, Comprenant tout ce qui a Rapport à l'Ameublement . . . etc.*, Paris 1801

the whole to be done again under the direction of Walsh Porter who has destroyed all that Holland has done & is substituting a finishing in a most expensive and motley taste."[22]

Tent rooms are thought to be French in origin; they appear in Charles Percier and Pierre Fontaine's *Recueil de Décorations Intérieures* (1801) as Napoleon's Salle de Conseil at Malmaison and as a design suitable for a bedroom (fig. 97). These French examples *à l'antique* have a decided military air. This antique style of tent room was gradually replaced by a more sumptuous and exotic mode. Thomas Hope had a boudoir draped *à la turque* as a tent room in his Duchess Street house to hold "Egyptian, Hindoo, and Chinese idols and curiosities."[23] Tented rooms like these were meant to evoke a fantasy of the sensuous Orient, and were often decorated with sofas, ottomans, lambrequins and crescents, recalling more a pasha's seraglio than a Roman warrior's tent.

The room described in the inflated language of the estate agent's report as "boudoir a la Turque" is designated in the inventory of the house's contents as simply a "chamber." It contained, the inventory notes, a Bath stove and fender, a Wilton carpet, two Holland blinds, and "an elegant 6 feet wide mahogany couch bed of antique design on platform and casters with tulliage Cotton Hangings lined and bordered and tastefully draped in to Curtains boarded & fringed complete with rings, etc." An anonymous watercolor drawing from this period, now at Tabley House, of just such a bed on a raised platform seems to illustrate the inventory's description of the chamber (fig. 98).[24] It suggests that the "boudoir a la Turque" was more antique than it was Turkish, and this leads one to suspect that any heavily draped room at this time was described in common parlance as "a la Turque."

A boudoir can be, but is not always, a bedroom. The term also describes a "small elegantly furnished room, where a lady may retire to be alone, or to receive her intimate friends."[25] The term came into use in the 1780s to describe small, comfortable rooms where one might be private; by the early nineteenth century such rooms were associated almost exclusively with women.[26] This fem-

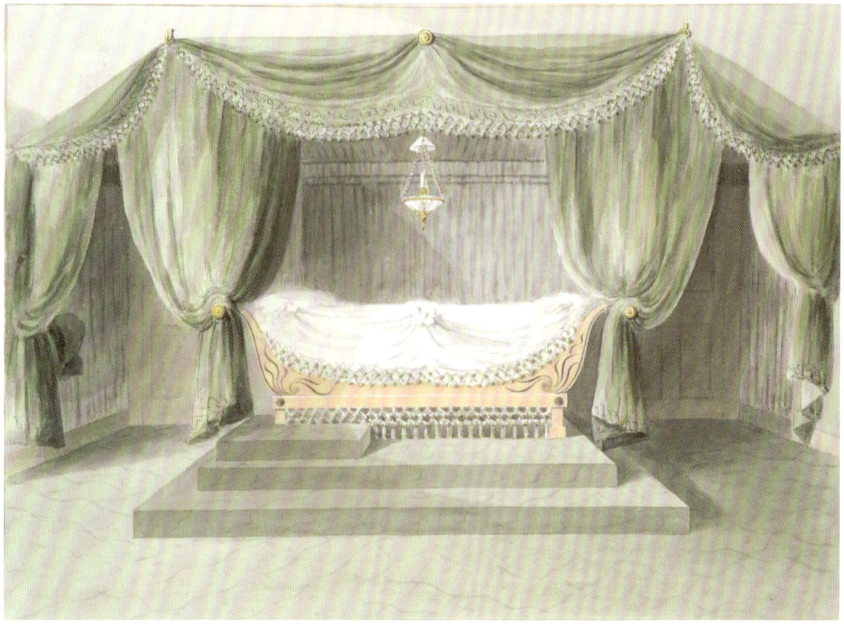

98 Artist unknown, *Tented Room*, c. 1806, pencil and watercolor, 35 × 48.7 cm ($13\frac{1}{2}$ × 19 in.), University of Manchester (Tabley House Collection)

inization of the boudoir may account for the decline of the military or antique style of tent room and the introduction of the more sumptuous Turkish style. Boudoirs are often found in plans of Mayfair town houses on the first floor tucked between the larger drawing rooms; they were often not only small but also of unusual shape.[27] They contained bookcases, comfortable seating, musical instruments, and instead of a sleeping bed something more like a day bed or couch bed for reclining.

It is unclear from the estate agent's report or the inventory if the draped room on the first floor that they describe, and which appears to be depicted in the watercolor, was used as a sleeping room or as a private retreat. There were three bedrooms in the garret and workmen's bills suggest that there was more than one dressing room in the house.[28] In any case, from all accounts it appears likely that this tented room continued to be used after 1805 as either the main bedroom or as a boudoir for its decoration and contents appear to have remained unchanged till 1818.

Sundry decorators', painters', plumbers', and carpenters' bills give a vivid picture of the seasonal rhythms of the house and its occupants. Heavy cleaning was done in late winter to ready the house for the arrival of Sir John who served in Parliament and thus spent the season in London. During the years when he lived with Emily St. Clare a piano forte was rented for the spring months – after he parted from her the annual rental of a piano forte ceased. Even before 1818 when the galleries were officially opened to the public, they had been opened to artists and friends, and this meant that they were continually being maintained in good repair. Just before opening day pictures were rearranged, revarnished, and their frames were cleaned. They were hung and rehung, as new paintings were added or to accommodate the fact that some pictures might be taken away to be exhibited at the Royal Academy or the British Institution. After the galleries closed in May there was repair work to be done to the furniture and

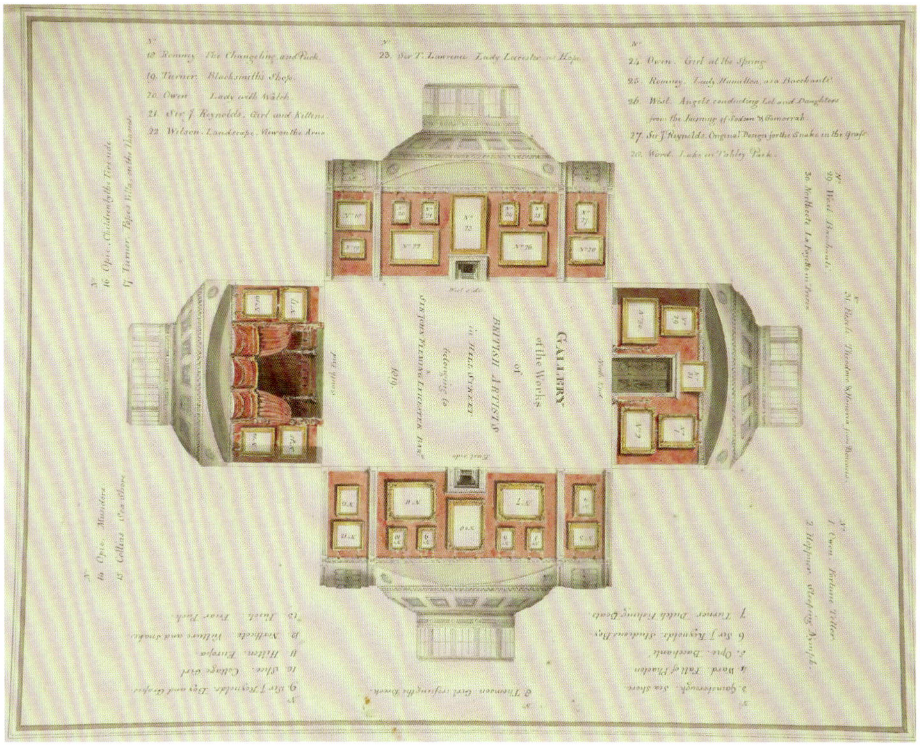

99 (?)William Carey, *Plan of the Main Gallery in Hill Street belonging to Sir John Fleming Leicester*, 1819, pencil, pen, and watercolor, 35 × 48.7 cm ($13\frac{1}{2}$ × 19 in.), University of Manchester (Tabley House Collection)

carpets. Every summer after Sir John quitted London and through the fall and winter months, carpets and drapes were taken up, cleaned, and put back, rooms were painted and plastered, heating stoves were cleaned, bricks and roof tiles were replaced, gutters emptied and patched, windows caulked and washed, chandeliers and lamps were polished and regilded, and paintings were reframed.

A major refurbishment of the first-floor gallery spaces including the boudoir appears to have taken place in 1818, perhaps in response to the public opening of the galleries. From Sir John's framer, gilder, and general handyman, Henry Tijou, we read of extensive reframing and of how the main galleries were rearranged numerous times to arrive at a satisfactory hang before the publication of William Carey's 1819 catalogue, which numbered all the pictures and listed them room by room (fig. 99). At this point Sir John consulted Jeffrey Wyatt for an estimate of the cost of enlarging the main gallery by extending it south into the greenhouse and pushing out the east wall, or alternatively building a whole new gallery over the stables.[29] More important for my purposes are the bills from the London upholsterers and cabinetmakers Thomas and Henry Turner that show that all the gallery rooms were redecorated with new hangings, drapes, carpets, and furniture. In December 1818 it appears that the "boudoir" was transformed into the "tent room."

In July 1809, a few months after Sir John purchased *The Cottage Door*, the painting was seen by Henry Eldridge at Hill Street mounted on an easel, and in November of the same year Mr. Tijou reframed the painting.[30] The frame he made matched the frame he had made earlier that year for Benjamin West's painting of a *Bacchante with Symbols*, which was close in size to *The Cottage Door.* West's painting hung in the library or main gallery. This suggests that Sir John

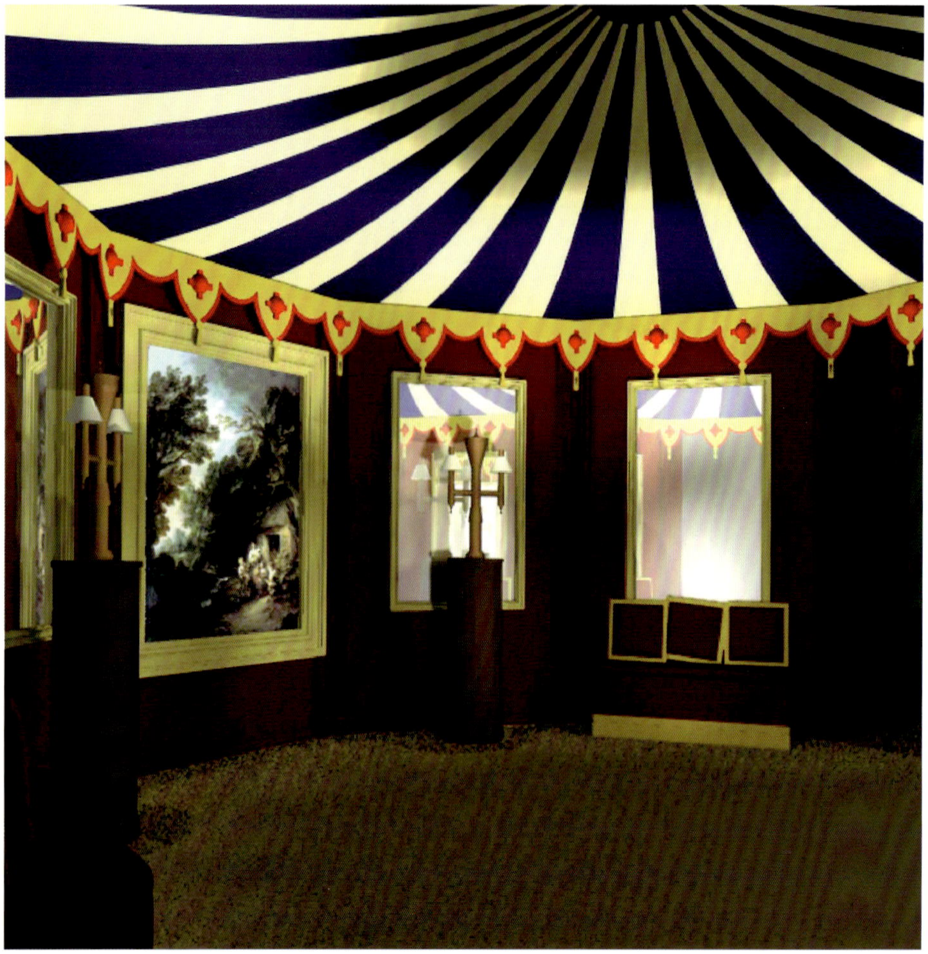

100 Clare Brown, working design for a reconstruction of Sir John Leicester's tent room at Hill Street House, c. 1818. Stephen Saitas Designs

had Gainsborough's painting reframed so that it would harmonize with that room's impressive ensemble of paintings, and only after the construction of the tent room in 1818 was *The Cottage Door* moved to this new location.[31]

The Turners' invoice for the construction of the tent room describes the purchase of "55 yrds $\frac{3}{4}$ fine white calico," the "dying 86 yrds $\frac{3}{4}$ calico blue," and the "making up of the calico into roof for the tent room."[32] It goes on to itemize the covering of two windows, the purchase of fifty-five yards of crimson moreen to drape the walls in "fluted" folds, the creation of a yellow cloth "pelmet valance" bound with crimson rosettes and crosses, finished with gold-colored tassels, which extended round the whole of the tent room. Finally the room was to be furnished with five "long ottomans" with feather cushions for their backs, all covered with crimson moreen and trimmed with gold cord. As this suggests, the refurbished boudoir – now tent room – was in a more pronounced Turkish style than anything previously (fig. 100). Certainly it was colorful: a blue and white tented ceiling with crimson walls and furnishings trimmed with gold, yellow, and red accents. The natural light from two windows was sealed off and in this darkened interior visitors could lounge comfortably on ottomans to view the works on display. Presumably, the mirrors not only reflected *The Cottage Door* so that it could be seen from the ottomans but also helped to disperse the light

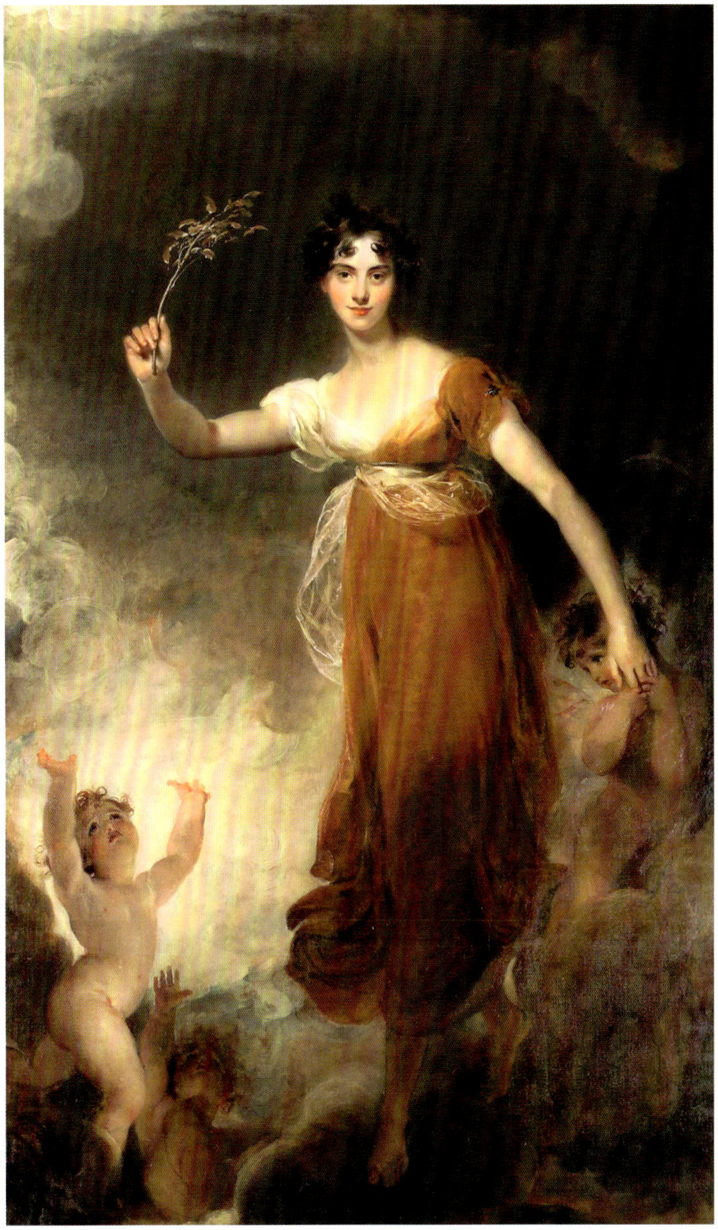

101 Thomas Lawrence, *Georgina Maria Leicester, as Hope*, R.A. 1814, oil on canvas, 237.5 × 145.5 cm (93 × 57 in.), University of Manchester (Tabley House Collection)

in the room. The total cost of refurbishing the tent room was £135. 15s or a little more than a quarter of the price Sir John paid for *The Cottage Door.*[33]

If it is correct to assume that Sir John placed Gainsborough's *Cottage Door* in the refurbished boudoir *à la turque*, then that room must have originally been fitted up for quite another purpose. It appears that in 1809, the same year Sir John purchased Gainsborough's painting, he parted from Emily St. Clare, settling on her £700 per annum. The following year, he married Georgina Maria Cotton, aged sixteen, who was about thirty years his junior (fig. 101).[34] It is likely, therefore, that before Sir John bought and installed Gainsborough's painting, the Turkish boudoir served either as the main bedroom or as Miss St. Clare's private sanctuary.

* * *

The British School and the "Anti-British Prejudice"

In *Some Memoirs of the Patronage and Progress of the Fine Arts, in England and Ireland, During the Reigns of George the Second and George the Third* (1826), William Carey noted that in the eighteenth century, "an Englishman of rank in London, would have considered his character as a Connoisseur irretrievably forfeited, by having a landscape, or an historical picture, by an English Painter, hung up in his apartments."[35] As a result of this "Anti-British Prejudice" in matters of art, Carey noted that "Lord de Tabley's early patronage of his countrymen was derided as a proof of bad taste, and his liberality in remunerating their labours, censured as an ignorant profusion."[36] Nevertheless, by "combining zeal with amenity, and good sense with good taste, he [Leicester] maintained his ground with firmness. . . . His selection of pictures in the contest for and against their merits, became the talk of the day, and the subject slowly acquired something like a public interest."[37] As a result of Leicester's stoic perseverance "A sounder taste was slowly diffused to a certain extent: an English Gentleman might commend an English painting, without being put to the blush for his bad taste in doing so."[38]

By the time he published his *Memoirs*, Carey was a seasoned polemicist and apologist for the British School. As early as 1807 he had given an account of the Hill Street gallery in the short-lived periodical *The Artist* in which his praise for Sir John's generous and foresighted patronage barely masked a pointed criticism of other less courageous collectors. "Sir John Leicester is the first patron, who, in a country abounding in artists and teeming with excellence, has dared to set the example of an English Gallery. . . . the collection forms one of the most gratifying spectacles, which even London can boast."[39]

Underlying Carey's defense of modern British art was a fervent nationalism forged during the Napoleonic wars. His characterization of collecting patterns that excluded work by British artists as an "Anti-British Prejudice" underscores this, and it was shared by other critics and commentators such as Prince Hoare whose important yet short-lived *Magazine of the Fine Arts and Monthly Review of Painting, Sculpture, Architecture and Engraving* (1821) was devoted to reviewing the state of art in Britain and contained illustrations of Benjamin West's gallery and Leicester's gallery along with essays praising their collections, their modes of display, and their taste.

The cry for patronage heard in publications like Carey's and Hoare's was hardly new; its history reached back into the eighteenth century and underpinned the justification for the founding of the Royal Academy. As Reynolds explained in his first *Discourse* (1769), "elegance and refinement" are the last effects "of opulence and power."[40] Morris Eaves has noted that such an argument imagines patronage as something that goes hand in hand with an expanding commercial empire.[41] In the context of English constitutional liberty, the government and public-spirited institutions rather than kings were felt to be the proper sources of artistic patronage. In opposition to French royal absolutism, the image of Periclean Athens was held up as the model of what art patronage should look like in Britain.[42] Such a vision of collective public-spirited patronage appeared to be realized at the turn of the century with the establishment of commercial galleries such as Boydell's Shakespeare Gallery and the founding of the British Institution. By the 1820s, however, the situation had changed. The failure of Boydell's, Maklin's, and Bower's galleries introduced an anti-commercial strain into the discussion of patronage, and turned the conversation to the need for governmental support or for individual acts of patronage by great men.[43] It is in this context that Sir John's patronage of modern British art and Carey's fulsome praise of it must be seen.

In his preface to his catalogue of Leicester's collection Carey recalled the day the previous May when Leicester first opened his gallery:

> Who that witnessed it can ever forget the feelings which it excited? The crowd of beauty and fashion, the chief nobility and gentry, the distinguished members of the legislature and of the learned professions, the taste and educated mind of England, assembled there in the triumph of their countrymen. . . . They carried with them a conviction, that when people so gifted by nature have begun to treasure the fame of their artists, as a portion of the public glory, they must, by perseverance, and affording a liberal patronage, like Greece and Italy, attain to the highest excellence in the Fine Arts.[44]

Most notable in this description is the implicit appeal it makes to public welfare and to a larger national purpose. However much Sir John may have privately intended to use the collection to secure a peerage, the public discourse is one of patriotic duty to support British artists and educate the nation in the glories of the national school. In the presence of national artistic genius, the crowd gathered at Hill Street discovers its true identity, Carey suggests, as citizens of a new Athens or Florence. In short, Sir John's collection of British art enables its viewers to transcend private local attachments and petty interests of class, wealth, and power. Through the cultural munificence of a private individual, the elegant yet diverse crowd, representative of commercial Britain, forges a new collective identity as a cultured, artistic nation.

One cannot but imagine that in this period when there was growing agitation for reform and expansion of the franchise that such a vision of the nation and the public was problematic. As Linda Colley has remarked, "To most of Britain's governors in this period, then, nationalism was like a Pandora's box: something which was best left alone."[45] On the one hand Carey's description presents a comforting vision of national and cultural unity; on the other it implies that a group capable of appreciating the brilliant cultural artifacts of the nation deserves to be called "England." It envisioned, if not actually forged, a republic of taste from a shared national artistic culture. In some minds it may well have been but a short terrifying step from a cultural republic of shared taste to a political republic of shared power. Thus art which had always been used to distinguish the nobility and aristocracy and to secure favor for them (just as Sir John intended his collection should do for him) could also function as a weapon against privilege. The fact that it was a "great man," the "English Maecenas" as Young called him, and not the government or commercial interests effecting this metamorphosis of the crowd at Hill Street may indeed have caused resentment.[46]

In the case of Leicester this resentment took the form of an unwillingness on the part of the government to buy his collection for the nation and a reluctance to elevate him to the peerage. In 1823 when Sir John offered his collection, the

Prime Minister, the 2nd Earl of Liverpool, declined it, explaining that Parliament would not sanction the expense.[47] Lord Liverpool went on to say that he had visited Sir John's collection and that while he thought that "works of Modern Artists ought to form the essential part of such a National Collection . . . I do think however that in such case the old Masters must find a Place in it, and more particularly the larger pictures, which are not adapted to private Collections."[48] One year later Parliament approved the purchase of John Julius Angerstein's collection of Old Masters for £57,000. Liverpool was a Tory and Sir John a Whig as well as a longstanding friend and supporter of the Prince Regent, now George IV. In addition to declining Sir John's offer, the Prime Minister also appears to have stood in the way of Sir John's efforts to be elevated to the peerage.[49]

In the case of Sir John's collection there was the added irritation that the collection was not only too modern but too national in scope and reputation, too much the sign of a new, potentially inclusive culture. As such it could be viewed as a rebuke to the Tory government, and this was precisely the way in which it was viewed by the *Examiner* in 1818, which called it a "satire on the government . . . which unconscientiously creates sinecures of thousands a-year for lazy, worthless courtiers and constitution killers, but never expends a guinea in furtherance of British genius in Painting."[50] A collection of British art for a national gallery was problematic when the definition of who precisely was the nation remained unresolved.

Viewing The Cottage Door

Sir John's unusual installation of *The Cottage Door* may have had to do with the fact that the painting was widely considered to be the jewel of the collection.[51] *The Morning Herald* claimed that while the collection "displays the genius of British Art to the highest advantage . . . [a]mong some of the most admirable pictures of Gainsborough here, is that Cottage Piece, which, of all his works, has had the greatest and most deserved reputation."[52] The artist and antiquarian, John Britton, described it to Sir John as "the *very first* picture by this Artist I ever saw," and William Carey remarked that "the subject is treated in the best taste of the pictures of this class."[53] At the sale of the collection at Christie's after Sir John's death, the sale catalogue called *The Cottage Door* the "chief d'oeuvre of this delightful painter."[54] Artists too were struck by the painting's quality. After viewing it in the gallery Turner called it an image of "pure and artless innocence," and Farington reports that after visiting Hill Street, Henry Edridge felt "the superiority of Gainsborough over the other Landscape Painters, Turner, Calcott &tc whose works are in that collection."[55] In her account of the painting, Anna Jameson took Reynolds to task for his assertion that Gainsborough did not paint landscape with a "poet's eye," insisting that it was "superfluous" to point out *The Cottage Door*'s "soft tranquility of sentiment, the shady retirement and the warmth that seems to penetrate through the rich summer foliage, and the rustic grace of the figures."[56]

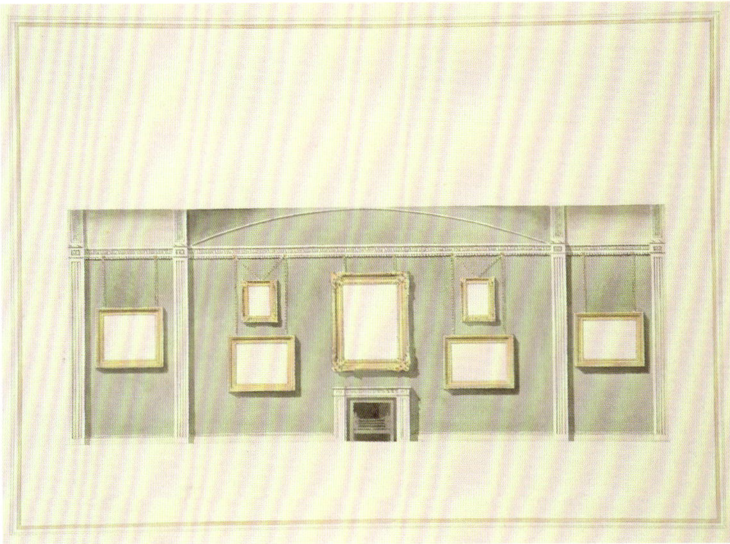

102 Artist unknown, *View of a Long Wall of the Main Gallery at Hill Street belonging to Sir John Fleming Leicester*, c. 1806, pencil and watercolor, 35 × 48.7 cm ($13\frac{1}{2}$ × 19 in.), University of Manchester (Tabley House Collection)

The isolation of *The Cottage Door* in the tent room not only made the close examination of the painting's merits possible but also provided a mode of aesthetic encounter that points ahead to exhibition spaces like the Grosvenor gallery where individual paintings were hung so that they could be studied in near isolation from other works in the room.[57] At a time when the Royal Academy hung paintings from floor to ceiling in their annual exhibition, artists struggled to create works that could stand up to this kind of viewing experience. They resorted to bright colors, large canvases, and dazzling painting techniques to draw attention to their works in exhibition.[58] Gainsborough had refused to exhibit at the Royal Academy after his portrait of the daughters of George III was hung too high. In place of the visual cacophony of the Great Room at Somerset House, Gainsborough preferred his works to be seen in the controlled light of his studio. He also created a showbox which is a box in which an image painted on a glass slide is illuminated by candlelight.[59] The image can be viewed by only one person at a time. The experience of viewing is solitary and meditative. Such an experience points ahead to Sir John's tent room as well as to the role of the photograph in art history, which illustrates single works of art in such a way as to allow their formal properties to be closely examined. Like the photograph or the colored slide of the art historian, or even Gainsborough's showbox, the tent room announces and facilitates an appreciation of the work of art that is wholly aesthetic and a visual pleasure that is derived from a formalist understanding of issues of style and technique.

This kind of close looking was less easy to accomplish in the main gallery where paintings were hung in what Giles Waterfield has dubbed the "picturesque style" (fig. 102).[60] This decorative hang was popular in private domestic galleries throughout the nineteenth century. The look was uncluttered and contrasted strongly with the *cap-à-pié* hangs used in the Royal Academy exhibitions and in other public venues. The picturesque hang was dictated by the size of the works rather than their style, genre, or date. It created a graceful ensemble of paintings

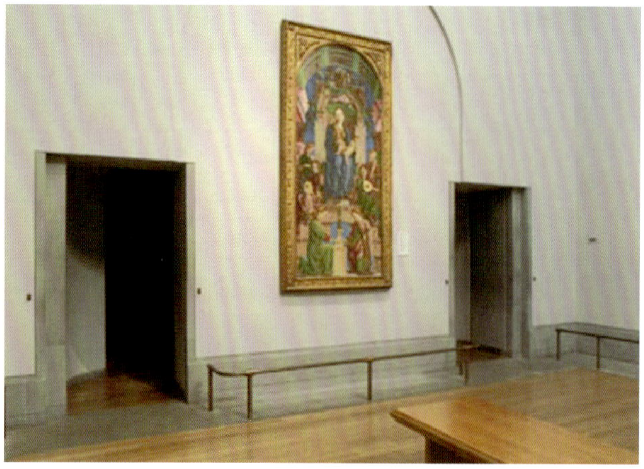

103 Entrance to the installation of Leonardo da Vinci's cartoon of the *Virgin and St. Anne with the Christ Child and St. John* in the National Gallery, London, 2005

that harmonized with the architectural features of the room. In this respect, the paintings functioned as furniture, as part of the overall design of the interior. By contrast, the tent room's darkened, hushed, meditative interior created an intimate encounter with the *Cottage Door.* The room was something like a sacred space with an effect, one imagines, not unlike that produced today in the room set aside for the exhibition of Leonardo's cartoon of the Virgin and Saint Anne in the National Gallery, London (fig. 103).

This kind of intimate and informed aesthetic encounter is not something one immediately associates with viewing practices of the early nineteenth century. Yet once it is sought, a desire for it can be found in the writings of William Hazlitt, John Britton, Anna Jameson, Gustave Waagen, Prince Hoare, William Carey, and others who made a point of visiting art galleries and describing what they saw. In lamenting the poorly developed viewing habits of her contemporaries and the need to reform them through the knowledge of objective aesthetic criteria, Mrs. Jameson proclaimed:

> Let us ever keep in mind that there must be some criterion to appeal to, higher and more fixed, than the power of feeling and association, which varies in every individual. . . . There is an immeasurable difference between the mere liking for pretty pictures, the love of novelty and variety, and the feeling and comprehension of the fine arts."[61]

If *The Cottage Door* was understood to be one of Gainsborough's greatest works, if not his greatest, which rewarded close, informed viewing then the tent room provided the perfect setting where this kind of viewing could take place.

For many of these writers and critics, Gainsborough was the one British artist who provided the viewer with the most to grapple with technically. In large part this had to do with his method of "penciling" or paint handling, what Reynolds had called his "odd scratches and marks" (figs. 104 and 105). Gainsborough's calligraphic method of applying paint in long feathery brushstrokes, which were often comprised of pure hues and which when viewed from a distance coalesced into a luminous and atmospheric image, was an aspect of his art that dazzled contemporaries like Reynolds and is referred to again and again in nineteenth-century discussions of his work. Turner, speaking again of *The Cottage*

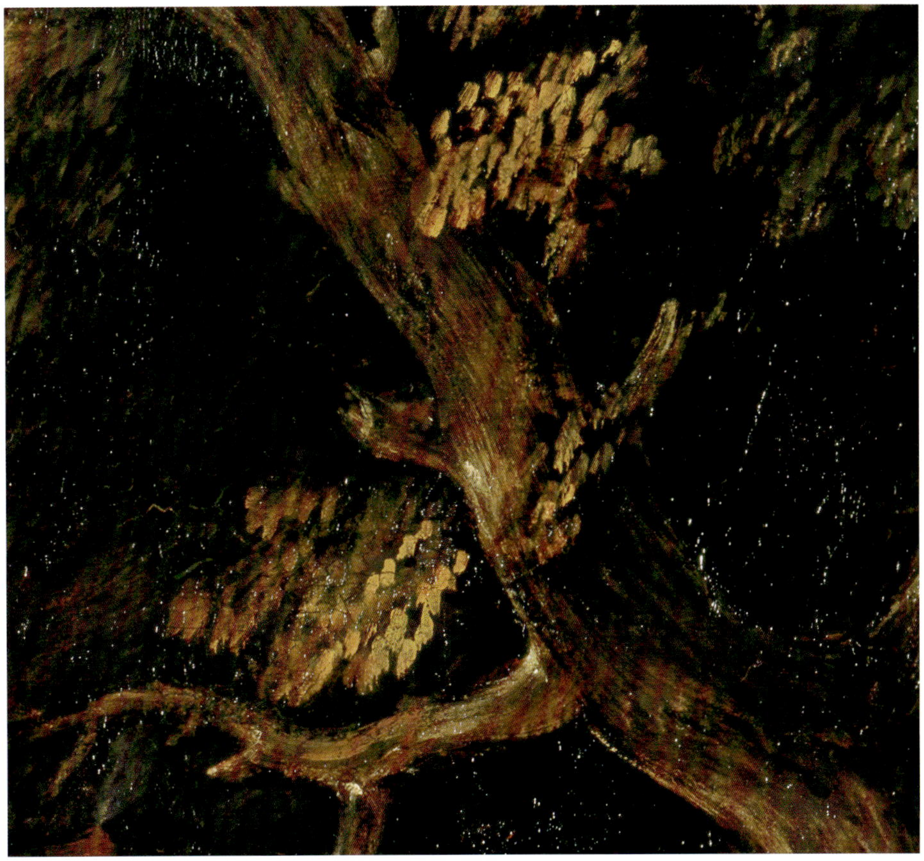

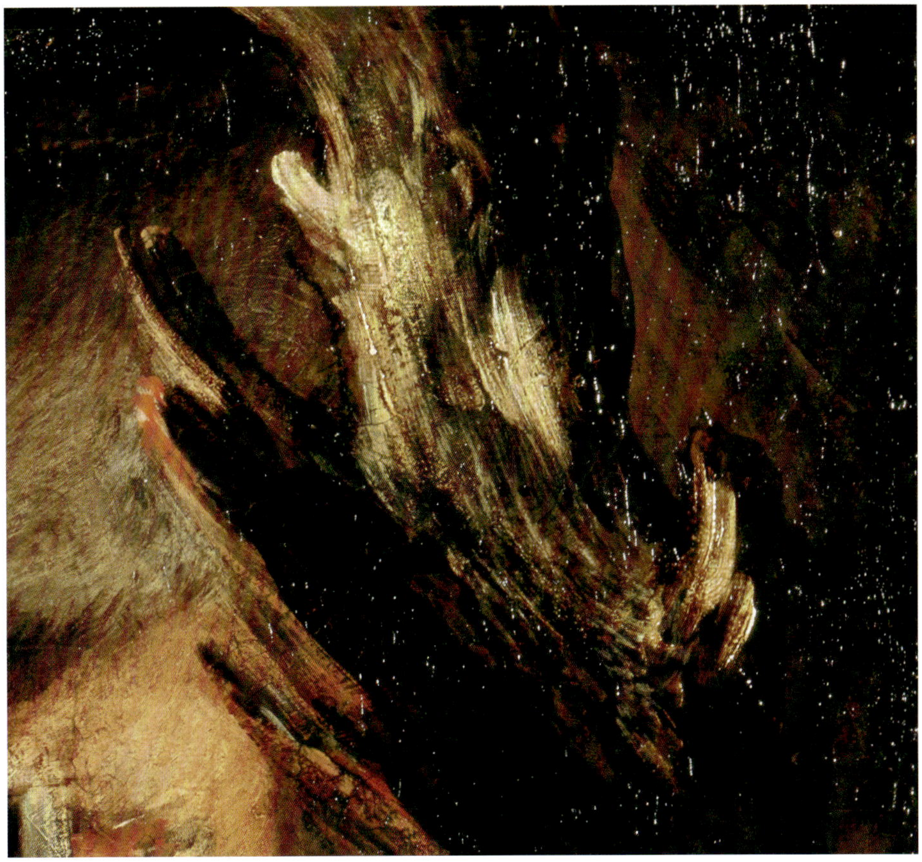

104 and 105 Thomas Gainsborough, *The Cottage Door* (details of pl. III)

Door, remarked on its "truth of forms, expression, full-toned depth of colour; and expertness of touch."[62] The sureness of Gainsborough's touch was such a commonplace that one finds it in popular discussions of his style, as in Ackermann's *Repository of the Arts:*

> touched here, touched there – the touches oblong, square, oval, round, rugged, and of all manner of shapes, which even the artist himself is not aware of till produced by the momentary impulse. This produces what is called taste, fire, genius – but it is management. It refers to rules. The mind, at the time of executing this fiery manner, is resolving a whole together.[63]

Gainsborough's mastery of the medium of paint lead later commentators, like Sir Walter Armstrong, to see him as a pure painter. In Armstrong's account Gainsborough emerges as a trailblazing modernist and the one British artist who "felt no temptation to be literary, to be anecdotic, to be didactic, to be anything but artistic within the limits of his own emotions and the materials he was using."[64]

This formalist appreciation of Gainsborough seems of a piece with the instalation of *The Cottage Door* in the tent room. Not only did the instalation permit a leisurely and critically focused appreciation of the painting's formal excellencies but also its subdued light echoed the conditions of Gainsborough's studio and presumably the ideal light under which his works were meant to be seen. John Williams (Anthony Pasquin), a critic and contemporary of Gainsborough, complained that the light level in Gainsborough's studio was so low that objects were barely visible.[65] Reports of this and other unusual studio practises circulated in the art historical literature of the time, and recent scholars like John Hayes have even speculated that *The Cottage Door* was painted by candle light.[66] The addition of mirrors meant that not only could the work be seen from any part of the room but, more importantly, their reflections would disperse the lamp light, creating a softer, more even, ambient illumination.

As Kay Dian Kriz has explained, landscape in the early nineteenth century came to be prized as an essentially British genre.[67] Second in national importance to landscape was genre painting with the examples of Hogarth and David Wilkie defining the uniquely British characteristics of the genre. The British Institution's exhibitions in 1813 and 1814 of Hogarth and then Reynolds, Gainsborough, Zoffany, and Wilson enshrined them as great British masters who represented genres in which British artists excelled. While admired, history painting could not in all truth be called truly British, and portraiture, while popular, had always held an ambiguous place in the hierarchy of British art.[68] Gainsborough's rural subjects like the cottage doors, which depicted landscape and the peasantry, had the advantage of combining aspects of two major British genres in one image.[69]

It was Gainsborough's landscapes and fancy pictures (a term used to distinguish figural subjects from Gainsborough's portraits of real people) that dominated the British Institution's retrospective exhibition of his work in 1814, and garnered the most attention. Thirty-four landscapes and fifteen of Gainsborough's fancy pictures were exhibited, including three cottage-door subjects, Sir John's painting, the painting known as *Cottage Door With Children Playing* (pl. II), and the small cottage-door scene now at Ipswich (pl. IV).[70] Remarking on the exhi-

facing page Thomas Gainsborough, *Cottage Door with Girl and Pigs* (detail of pl. IV)

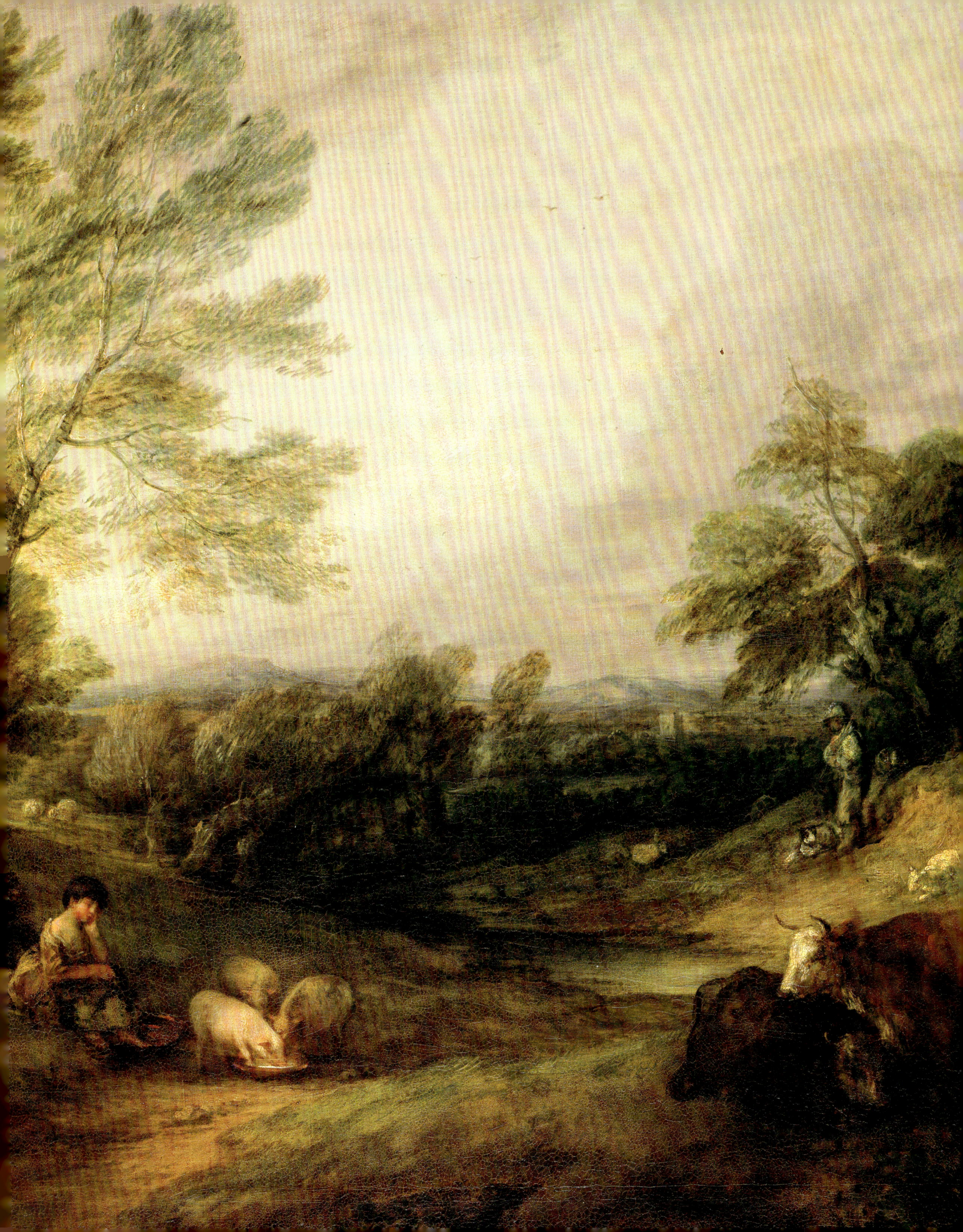

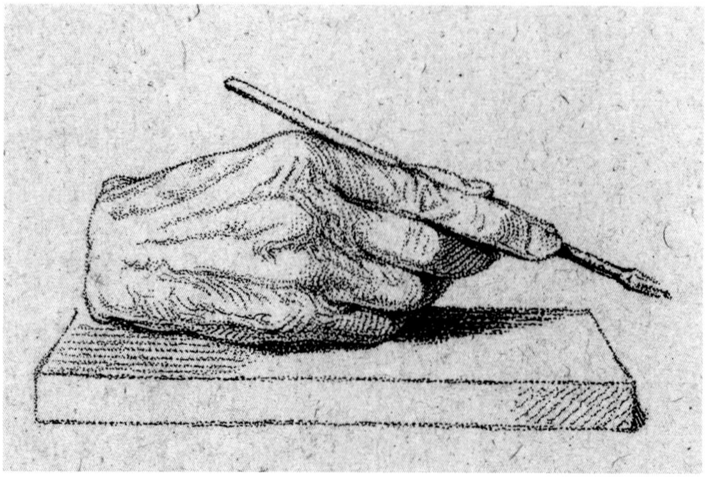

106 Artist unknown after William Behnes, *Cast from the right hand of the late B. West, Esq*, engraving from John Young, *A Catalogue of Pictures by British Artists, in the Possession of Sir John Fleming Leicester, Bart. With Engravings from the Whole Collection*, London 1821

bition, Hazlitt called the fancy pictures the works upon which "Gainsborough's fame chiefly rests," and Wilkie, the leading genre painter of the day, declared that Gainsborough "looks admirably, and seems to rise above himself."[71] Significantly, it is as a fancy painting that Carey described *The Cottage Door* in his catalogue. Remarking on the fact that in rustic poverty men find happiness living within their means, Carey asked the viewer to note Gainsborough's "feeling for unsophisticated life" and described the beauty and grace of the figures at length. With respect to the painting's landscape features, Carey briefly noted that the setting "has never resounded to any other sound but the axe of the woodman," that the trees are "lofty and venerable," the sky is "not bright," and the whole is in Gainsborough's "latter manner."[72] The painter Thomas Hearne also focused on the genre-like qualities of Gainsborough's cottage scenes, noting that his "representations of the simple life are given with such taste as to delight and never offend. He is never coarse; His Peasant in rags has no filth; no idea of dirt or wretchedness is ever excited."[73] As John Barrell has observed, it is easy to see how such idealized images of the peasantry and rural life might become metaphors for the nation itself.[74]

As if to underscore its particular relevance to the British School and its leadership in landscape and genre painting, *The Cottage Door* was first exhibited alone in the tent room, and then later with Ward's *Fall of Phaeton* and the cast of West's hand (figs. 107 and 106). I believe these later additions are comments on the death of West in 1820, and perhaps too the fall of history painting in Britain with him. The presence of the cast suggests this commemorative intention, for as Young writes, "This Cast was taken from the hand of Mr. West by Mr. Behnes, a few hours after the President's decease. Whatever may have been his thoughts at the awful moment of dissolution, it is evident, from the obvious action of the hand, that the disposition to express those thoughts by the pencil was his ruling passion."[75] In addition to the cast of West's hand, Sir John had also by this time added a bust of West by Behnes to the collection, displayed at the entrance to one of the galleries. (Behnes went on to become "sculptor in ordinary" to Queen Victoria.) Unlike these later sculptural purchases, Ward's *Fall of Phaeton* is listed as early as 1817 in an anonymous catalogue of the collection. It appears in Carey's

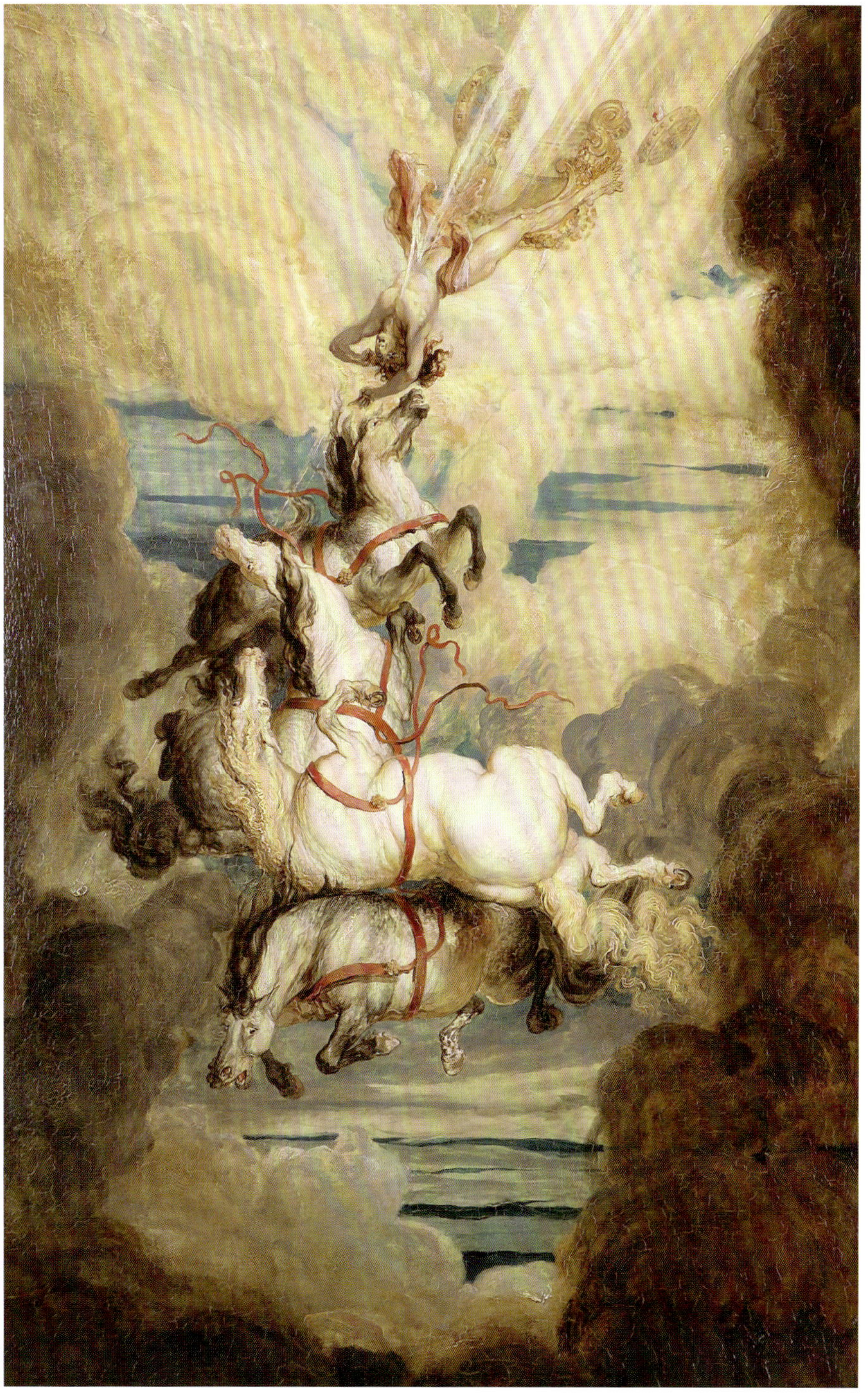

107 James Ward, *The Fall of Phaeton*, 1808, oil on canvas, 112.7 × 74.5 cm ($44\frac{3}{8} \times 29\frac{3}{8}$ in.), University of Manchester (Tabley House Collection)

catalogue and then Young's, who describes it as a "finished sketch" and accompanied its entry with the verse:

> But Phaeton,
> His yellow hair seized by the flames,
> Falls headlong, and shoots thro' a long tract
> Of air, as in a serene sky a star falls.[76]

Positioned elegiacally in Young's catalogue, Ward's painting along with Behnes cast would have appeared as an homage to the late president. When combined in the tent room with *The Cottage Door* such an homage would have extended to the British School itself and the central places that Gainsborough and West played in its establishment.

Such a tribute is understandable coming from a collector devoted to the British School, but even more understandable given the fact that West, in his capacity as president of the Royal Academy, had been an outspoken supporter of Sir John. In his catalogue of the collection, Carey quotes a letter from West praising Sir John and defending what West called his "patriotic example and love for the Fine Arts of your country."[77] West's support of Sir John also appeared in the *European Magazine* where he was quoted as saying, "no English gentleman ever did so much for modern art as Sir John Leicester."[78] At his death, Sir John owned three works by West: *Bacchante with Cymbals, The Angel of Revelation* (bought from Carey), and *Angels Conducting Lot and His Daughters from Sodom and Gomorrah*. At one point he owned West's *White Horse of the Apocalypse* but exchanged it in 1818 for the painting of Lot and his daughters.[79] A room devoted to what Sir John saw as the greatest exemplar of the British School and to an Academy president devoted to the cause of modern British art and to Sir John's efforts to promote it was, I believe, the artistic and emotional heart of the Hill Street collection.

Conclusion

To sum up, the tent room emerges as a statement about the British School, about its major patron, genres, artists, and characteristics and its national, and perhaps even political, importance. In pointing out the public significance of the tent room, however, I do not want to underemphasize the private experience it offered viewers and the even more private and personal significance it may have held for Sir John.

For all its power as a signifier of the British School, the tent room itself remains something of an incongruous setting for a rural genre piece such as Gainsborough's *Cottage Door*. Its sumptuous and exotic trappings, redolent of the Orient, do not fit the homespun simplicity of native peasant life celebrated in the painting. Perhaps it is less the style of the room than the effect created by it that explains the odd choice of décor. Its small size and heavily draped and darkened space set the tent room apart from the rest of the galleries and made it a private retreat where one could be intimate with art. Like the cottage itself, it partook of a fantasy of retirement, comfort, and interiority.[80] The cottage emerges in the discourse of the later eighteenth century as the place of domestic love and intimacy, underscored in Gainsborough's painting by the nursing mother at the doorstep surrounded by children. In this same spirit of physical closeness and nurture the tent room offered viewers a womb-like space for viewing.

The tent room encouraged close looking and formal appreciation. This was the kind of viewing that Gainsborough's richness of touch rewarded. Isolated from the other works in the collection, the tent room made *The Cottage Door* a talismanic object. To enter the room was to experience an intimate and sacred encounter with Gainsborough's unique genius. Multiplied in the room's mirrors the painting's reflection fused the viewer with the viewed, linking the viewer to an ideal image of rural England and by extension to the mythic nation.[81] But, perhaps more immediately, the mirrors allowed the attentive viewer, who closely examined Gainsborough's touch, to see in their reflections the miraculous fusion of these singular marks into a systematic compositional whole in the way described by commentators from Reynolds to Armstrong. The mirrors enabled a double vision, an optical shuttling back and forth between close examination of detail and a longer view of the whole, between the lively touches and their magical resolution into a pictorial illusion. It was in keeping with what Gainsborough, according to Reynolds, always desired: that his pictures "should be seen near, as well as at a distance".[82]

The conversion of the boudoir into a room intended to hold *The Cottage Door* involved the substitution of one talismanic object for another. In place of a mistress, a work of art. It was Anna Jameson who best understood how this substitution could come about. Remarking on how those who possess fine pictures "and really love them" are familiar with their minute beauties, she observed that "every good picture . . . is not mere surface and colour; it has a countenance, like the countenance of a friend or a lover, of which certain expressions are revealed only to certain eyes, at certain moments."[83] As she suggests, the eye of the lover and the connoisseur are one and the same. The tent room as a replacement for the boudoir seems an incomplete erasure, the result of an attempt to replace one beloved countenance with another, and the evidence of a failure finally to do so. In this way one might understand the incongruity of the setting as the result perhaps of Sir John's unconscious fusing of the past and present.

Gazing into the tent room's mirrors at *The Cottage Door*, Sir John could see at once the image and its setting. While the intimacy and seclusion of the tent room might encourage other viewers to experience the painting in isolation, as an object of pure painting, it is doubtful that such an experience was available to Sir John. For him the painting had a history and a context, and they both, the tent room declared, were part of his most intimate self.

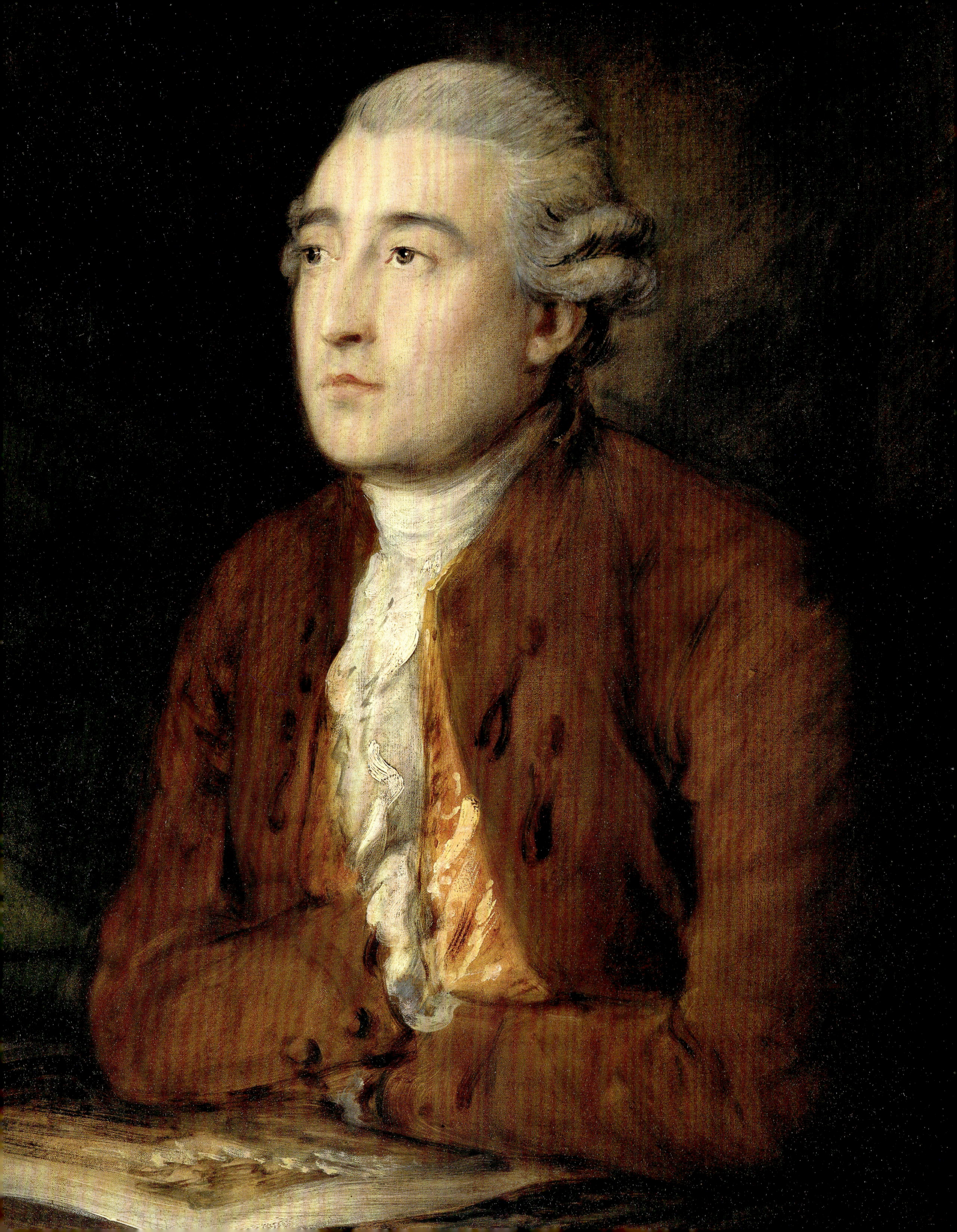

Part Four Gainsborough and de Loutherbourg: Sensation and the Landscape of Special Effects

facing page Thomas Gainsborough, *Philip James de Loutherbourg* (detail of fig. 119)

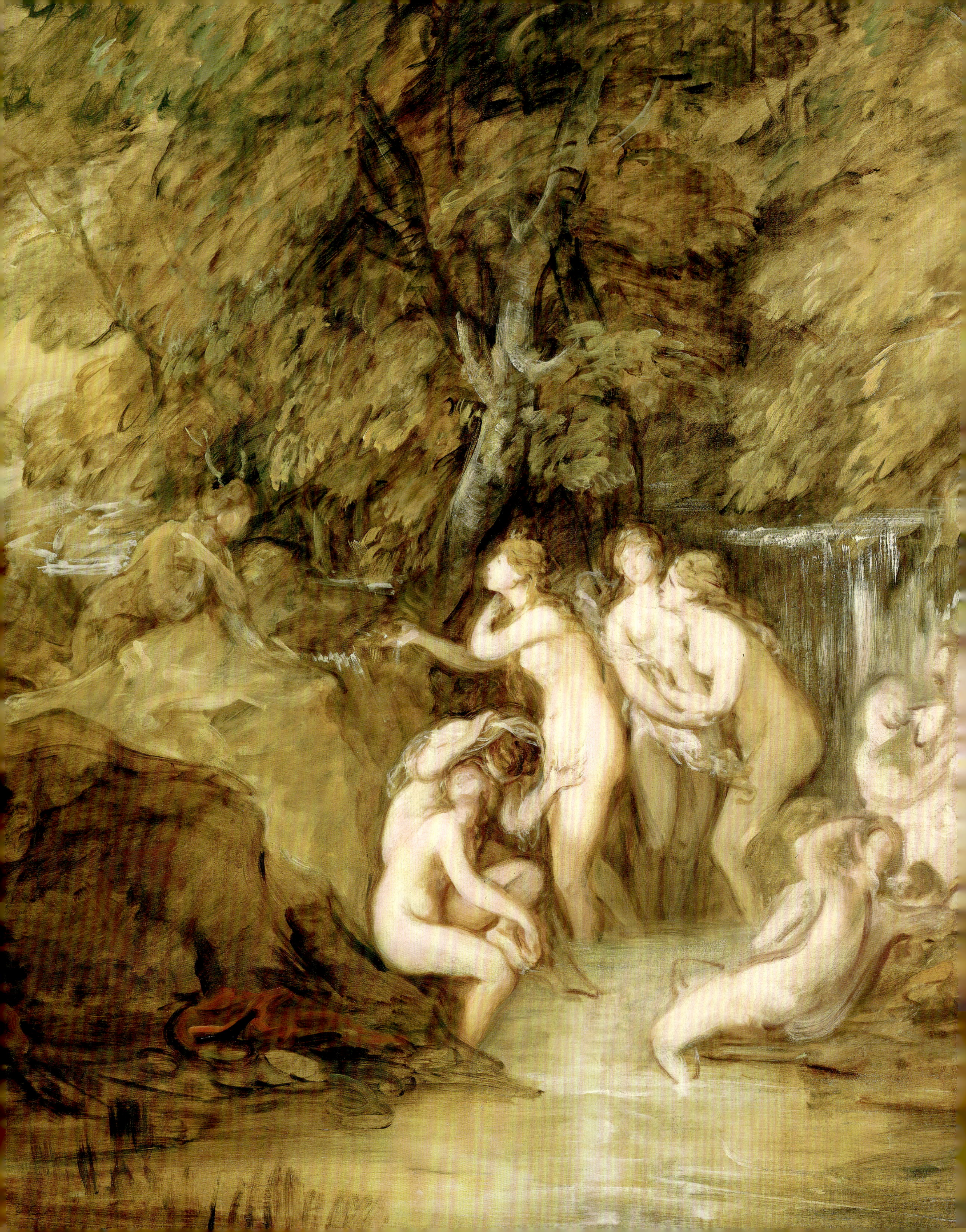

William Vaughan

Magic in the Studio

When Sir Joshua Reynolds referred to a particular optical effect achieved by Thomas Gainsborough in his pictures as "a kind of magick"[1] he might seem to have been doing no more than engaging in a conventional form of praise for artistic virtuosity. However, his comment came at a time when the issue of magic and aesthetic culture had become a matter of public interest. Typically, what seemed to be a compliment was in fact an act of containment.

The recognition of the significance of the debate about magic in the late Enlightenment has been growing in recent years, countering the more dismissive attitude of an earlier generation of scholars. After the publication of Keith Thomas's monumental *Religion and the Decline of Magic* in 1971[2] it was generally assumed that magic played little part in western high culture once it had been ousted from scientific enquiry and organized religion during the rationalist revolution of the seventeenth century. It was thought to have subsisted only in murkier backwaters and certain minor cults, or in parodic form as a type of popular entertainment.

Recently, however, the issue has been re-explored and a rather different scenario has emerged. Magic, it is now claimed, did not so much disappear from polite culture during the Enlightenment as relocate. This is essentially the argument made by Roy Porter in *Witchcraft and Magic in the Enlightenment* (1999). Porter claims that this relocation was principally to the newly fashioned area of autonomous aesthetic experience. Art became magical as science ceased to be so. This was the moment at which "supernaturalism," as Porter put it, "entered the studio and the garret."[3] Such arguments have been followed up more recently with explorations of artists of the period in connection with overtly magical practices. Iain McCalman in his book *The Seven Ordeals of Count Cagliostro*[4] has studied the relationship between the landscape painter Philip Jacques de Loutherbourg and the magician and faith healer Count Cagliostro.

McCalman, like Walter Benjamin before him, has shown how the particular instance of Cagliostro's career had deep implications for the unsettled social and political conditions in the period surrounding the French Revolution of 1789. Porter, however, makes a broader claim; he asserts that from the eighteenth century to the present the magical has been a critical feature in aesthetic evaluation in western society, thus marking it out for a particular kind of status. It is within the context of such claims that I wish to explore allusions to magic in the discussions that intersected with art practice in later eighteenth-century London, focusing particularly on the period's discussions of the work of Gainsborough, and further considering the extent to which these discussions

facing page Thomas Gainsborough, *Diana and Actaeon* (detail of fig. 117)

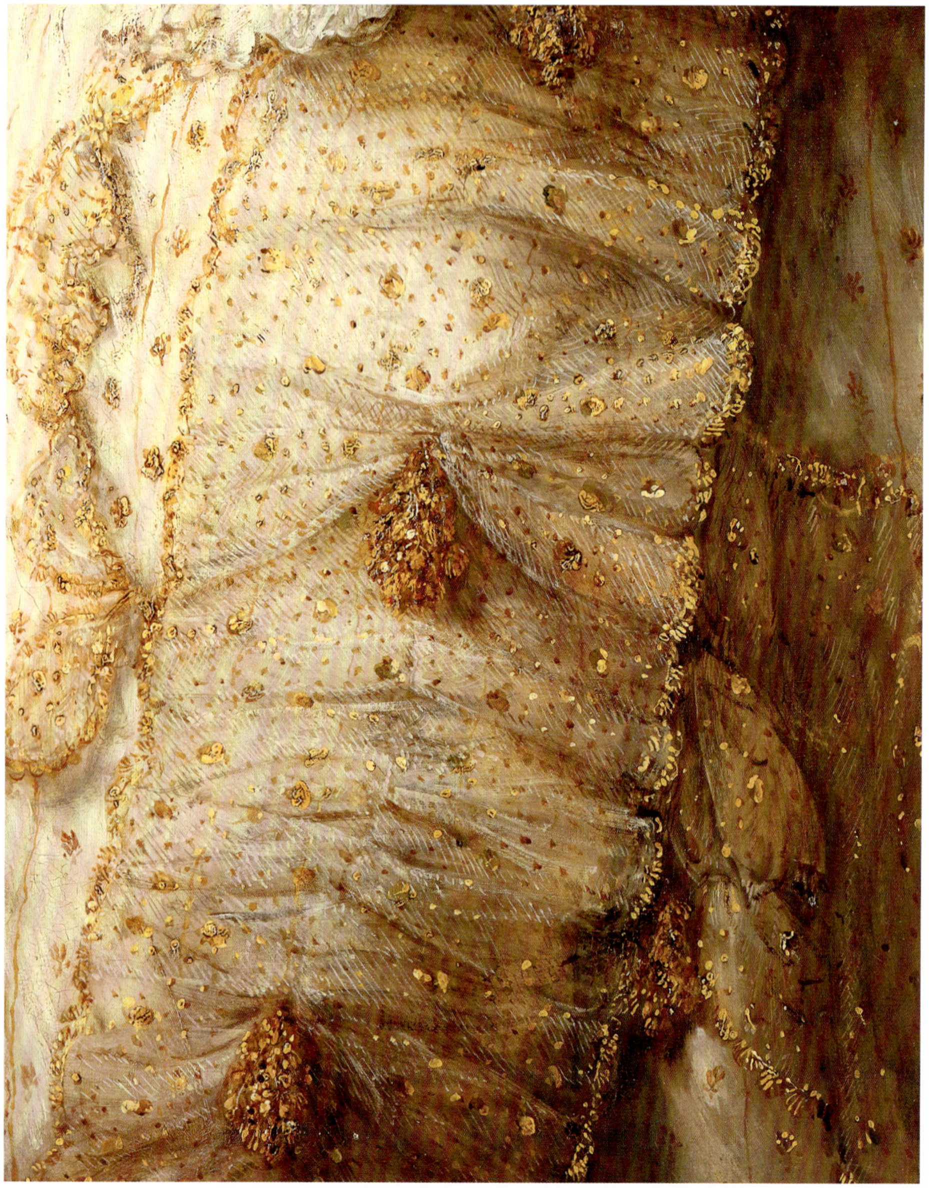

108 Thomas Gainsborough, *Queen Charlotte* (detail of fig. 109)

might signal a change in the expectations surrounding the art object and the viewing experience that have remained an active part of the artistic landscape.

⋆ ⋆ ⋆

Gainsborough himself did not give many leads in the matter. As is well known, he was notoriously obtuse where artistic theory was involved. Scholars wishing to explore his engagement with it have had to rely largely on circumstantial evidence, as when Michael Rosenthal reconstructed the artist's attitudes to academic practice in relationship to his major painting *Diana and Actaeon*.[5] Yet, as I hope to show here, circumstantial evidence suggests that Gainsborough was keen to promote the sense of the magical in his art, while being equally keen to distinguish between his kind of magic and that of the popular showman.

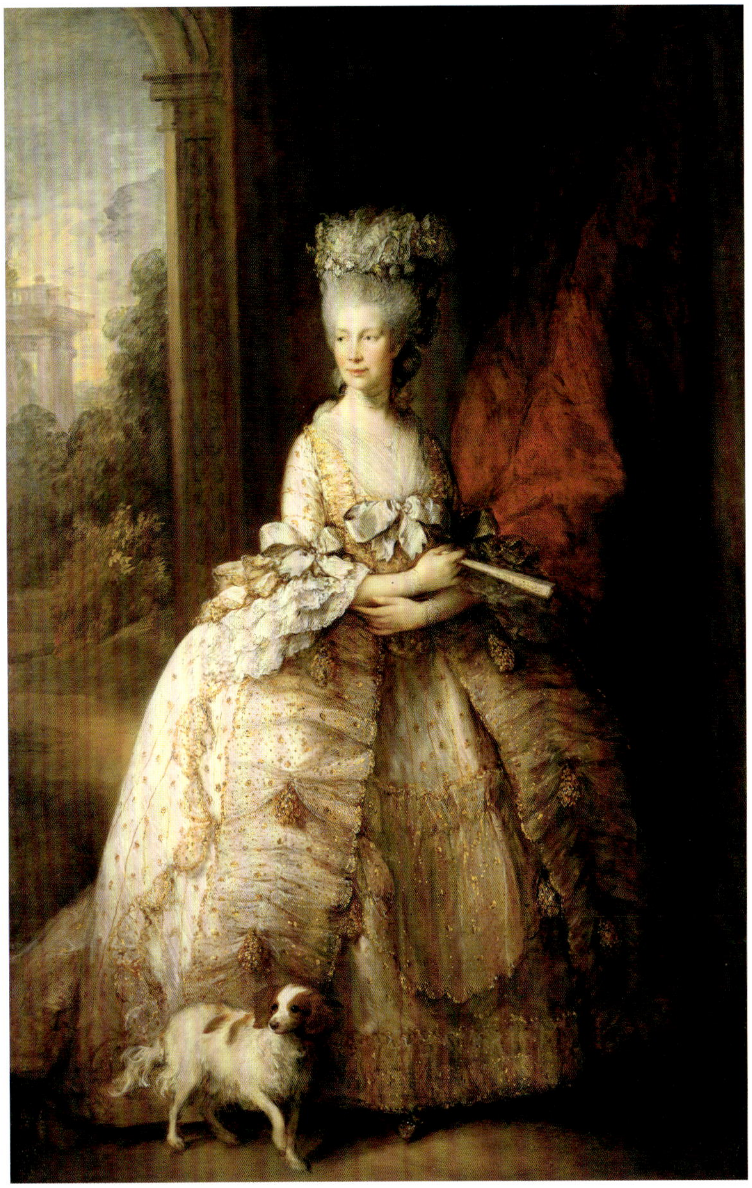

109 Thomas Gainsborough, *Queen Charlotte*, 1781, oil on canvas, 238.8 × 157.8 cm (94 × 62 in.), The Royal Collection, London

The complexities this posed can be found in Reynolds's eulogistic discourse on his old rival delivered a few month's after the latter's death. When mentioning Gainsborough's achievements as a "kind of magick," Reynolds dwelt on the remarkable way in which the seeming "chaos" of his paint surface resolved itself at a certain distance into recognizable forms. In particular, he referred to "those odd scratches and marks, which, on a close examination, are so observable in Gainsborough's pictures, and which even to experienced painters appear rather the effect of accident than design."[6] Such an effect can be seen, for example, when looking closely at the drapery of Gainsborough's major picture, the portrait of Queen Charlotte, exhibited at the Royal Academy in 1780 (fig. 108). When one stands back from the portrait one sees with Reynolds how "this chaos, this uncouth and shapeless appearance by a kind of magick, at a certain distance assumes form" (fig. 109).[7]

Reynolds was referring to the well-known but still puzzling experience whereby separately perceived brushstrokes suddenly combine in the mind to form an image when one stands at a certain distance from a canvas. The phenomenon is caused by a fundamental condition of vision, the result of a complex and still largely unexplained process of interaction between brain and optical stimulus without which we would literally not be able to discern images.[8] What is particular about the process in relation to Gainsborough is that the artist in his later years painted with such breadth – or even abandon – that the point at which brushstrokes blended sufficiently to indicate form became perceptible at a normal viewing distance, rather than becoming evident only when a spectator went up unusually close to a work – as was the case with more conventional paintings in the period.

Equally important is the point, referred to by Reynolds, that Gainsborough himself wished this effect to form a part of the viewing experience of his work. Reynolds knew this particularly well since it had been the Academy's refusal to hang Gainsborough's *Three Eldest Daughters of George III* sufficiently low in the exhibition of 1784 for the phenomenon to be perceivable that had caused the artist to withdraw from exhibiting at the Academy altogether.[9] In his letter to the Academy withdrawing the painting, Gainsborough explained that it had been hung too high for what he termed the "work of the picture" to be visible.[10]

This "work" was the result of unusual studio practices of which Gainsborough's contemporaries were well aware. Artists' studios in those days formed an intriguing threshold between public and private worlds, both socially and professionally. On the one hand they were the private places where artists constructed their remarkable works. On the other hand they were places to purchase works, to sit for portraits, or simply to visit in order to satisfy one's curiosity. From the accounts of contemporaries, most notably Osias Humphry's,[11] one learns of the extraordinary practices that Gainsborough adopted when making portraits. These included the use of a darkened room to start the work, the close scrutiny of the sitter alongside the canvas, and later in the process the truly bizarre use of brushes on six-foot poles to carry out bravura painting. It is perhaps hard how to assess how much of this special practice was a necessity and how much a show. But it is certainly clear that it was unusual. And if Gainsborough never made overt claims to the possession of magical powers, he certainly made it clear that the exotic rituals of his studio were essential for the achievement of his unique works.

Reynolds's reference to the "magick" effect in Gainsborough's art, while conveying wonder, also stresses a technical sleight of hand at the expense of higher intellectual values. It was a convention to praise the illusionist skills of painters of "lesser" genres, as for example when Diderot referred to Chardin as a "grand magicien" in his *Salon* of 1765.[12] Diderot was able to celebrate the "magic" of Chardin's painting technique, its ability to transform everyday objects into sites for contemplation and wonder, while calling at the same time for the French school to rise to the higher challenge of morally guided history painting. Chardin was, after all, not attempting to subvert existing hierarchies and seemed content to manifest his "magical" powers within the strict confines of his genre.

Reynolds, writing within the more fluid and ill-defined context of British art practice, felt the need to be more censorious.

"Magick" was no word of praise in his vocabulary, as we can gauge from the sixth discourse of 1774 in which he treated the topic of imitation. As a prelude to his defense of his own practice of borrowing poses from the Old Masters, something recently demonstrated spectacularly in his *Three Ladies Adorning a Term of Hymen* (fig. 110),[13] Reynolds set out to stress that artistic achievement was the result of laborious study (in particular copying) and not the consequence of some mysterious innate gift. "It is very natural," he observed, "for those who are unacquainted with the cause of anything extraordinary to be astonished at the effect, and to consider it as a kind of magick."[14] After attacking the ignorance that led some to suppose pictorial prowess was a "kind of magick," Reynolds further told the tale of how people in the Near East were so unable to account for the ruins that remained from the buildings of earlier and superior civilizations that they claimed they were "built by magicians." Reynolds observed that "the untaught mind finds a vast gulph between its own powers, and those works of complicated art, which it is utterly unable to fathom; and it supposes that such a void can be passed only by supernatural powers."[15]

Having thus characterized the belief in the "magical" nature of art as the province of the ignorant and non-European, Reynolds went on to take his fellow artists to task for encouraging such beliefs among their spectators. "And, as for artists themselves," he said, "it is by no means [in] their interest to undeceive such judges, however conscious they may be of the very natural means by which their extraordinary powers were acquired; though our art, being intrinsically imitative, rejects this idea of inspiration, more perhaps than any other."[16]

Reynolds mentions no names but it is tempting to think that he might have had Gainsborough in mind as one of his targets. He must surely by that date have heard of Gainsborough's extraordinary studio practices and also witnessed that broad form of painting that stressed the effect he was later to describe as being like magic. Indeed, it was already a common conceit to refer to the "magic" of Gainsborough's method in press reports of the time.[17] Furthermore, 1774 was the year in which Gainsborough had moved from Bath to London, where he might seem to be making a direct challenge to the President's portrait business.

It was not from Gainsborough, however, that the riposte to Reynolds's remarks on imitation came. It came, as is well known, in the form of the painting sent by the Irish artist Nathaniel Hone to the Royal Academy for exhibition in 1775, with the title *The Pictorial Conjuror, Displaying the Whole Art of Optical Deception* (fig. 111). With Reynolds's favourite model, James White, posing as the conjuror, Hone alludes to Reynolds's process of transforming Old Master compositions into his own pictures. Particularly prominent is the reference to the derivation of the *Three Ladies Adorning a Term of Hymen* (see fig. 110) from two prints of seventeenth-century paintings. Reynolds accuses his fellow artists of deception, Hone seems to be saying, but is he not up to some trickery of his own?

Much attention has been paid to how Hone satirized Reynolds's pictorial plagiarism.[18] Less attention has been paid, however, to the way in which Reynolds's

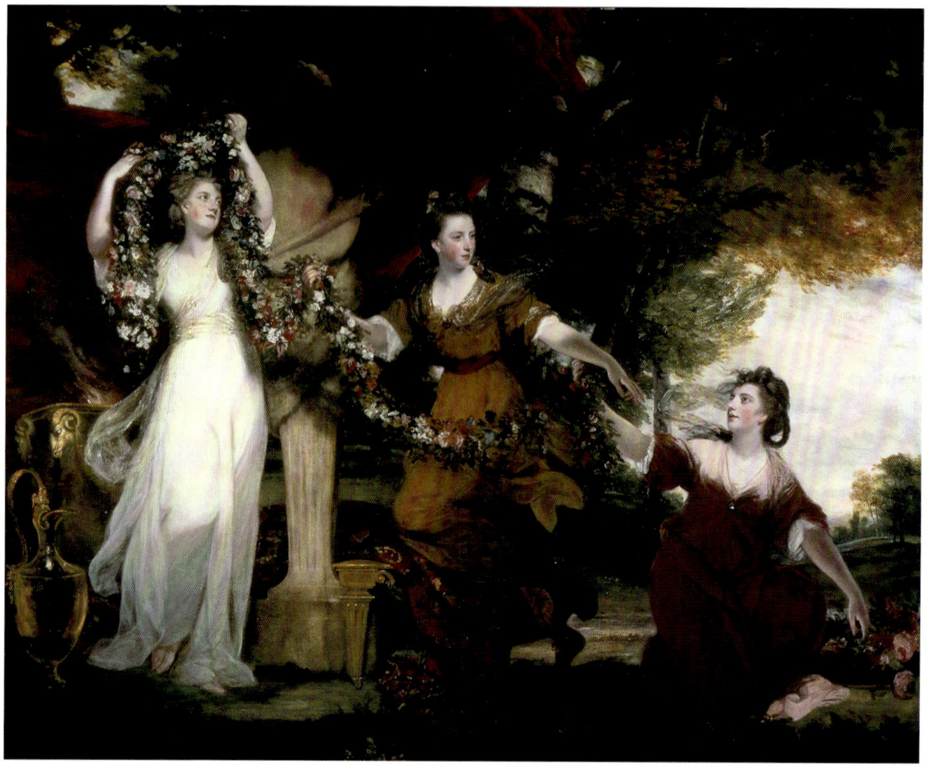

110 Joshua Reynolds, *Three Ladies Adorning a Term of Hymen*, 1774, oil on canvas, 234 × 295 cm (92 × 116 in.), Tate, London

remarks about magic, and his attack in the sixth discourse on his fellow practitioners for encouraging such beliefs, creates the whole topic of Hone's picture, and is the reason why Reynolds is portrayed in it as a mountebank magician. The painting touches on the growing debate about the inate and unaccountable powers of original genius during the period.[19]

Reynolds's claim to promote and practice an art that dispensed with the appeal to pictorial magic in pursuit of higher claims of truth appears to have been well recognized among his admirers. While Gainsborough may have been praised in the press for the magical effects he achieved, Reynolds was praised for dispelling such tricks. The point is made by Thomas Warton Jr. in 1782 in verses he published in praise of Reynolds's painted window in New College Chapel, Oxford. Contrasting the "gothic" and superstition-laden building with the enlightening window that Reynolds had placed in it, Warton exclaimed:

> Thy powerful hand has broke the Gothic chain,
> And brought my bosom back to truth again;
> To truth, by no peculiar taste confin'd,
> Whose universal pattern strikes mankind;
> To truth, whose bold and unresisted aim
> Checks frail caprice, and fashion's fickle claim;
> To truth, whose charms deception's magic quell,
> And bind coy Fancy in a stronger spell.[20]

Reynolds's wish to counter "deception's magic" in the painting process may have been spurred by a knowledge of the increasing use of such phrases

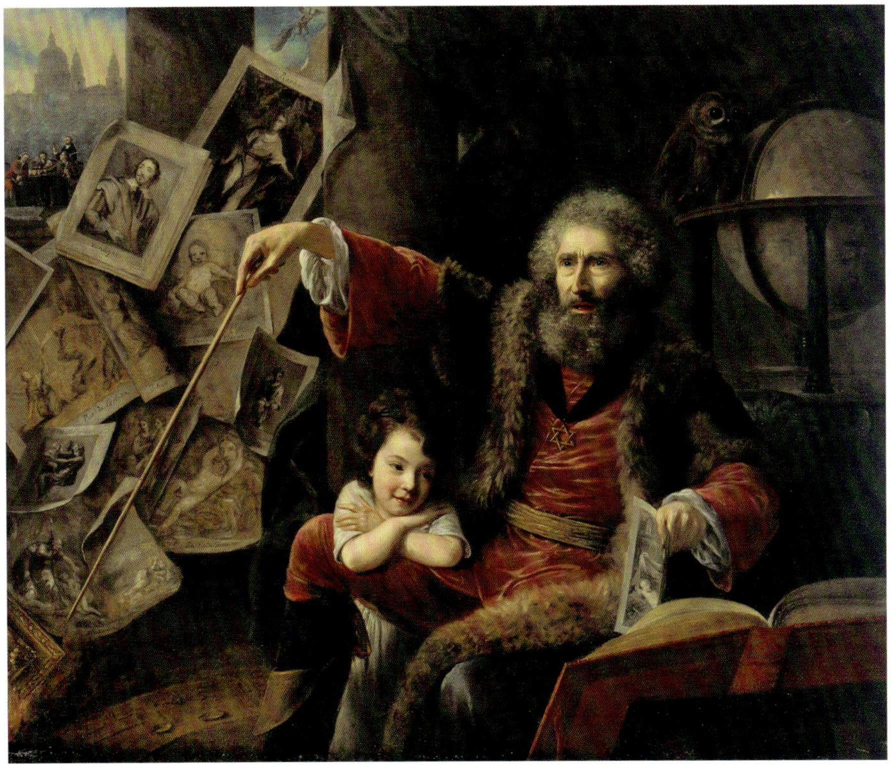

111 Nathaniel Hone, *The Pictorial Conjuror, Displaying the Whole Art of Optical Deception*, 1775, oil on canvas, 145 × 173 cm (57 × 68 in.), National Gallery of Ireland, Dublin

among aestheticians and connoisseurs in a manner that went beyond the simple praising of the magic of illusion. For instance, while providing an essentially physiological account of aesthetic experience in his celebrated treatise on the sublime, even Reynolds's friend Edmund Burke maintained a space for the irrational in what he called the "magic of grace."[21] At the popular level, too, the magical nature of painting as a process of inexplicable allure and transformation was becoming a common trope.

I do not imagine that Sir Joshua Reynolds was much of a frequenter of shops selling popular games and pastimes. If he had been, however, he would have found his worst suspicions confirmed. At the same time that he was condemning the vulgar perception of artistic prowess as "magical," there were toys enough on the market that played with the idea of the artist as a magician (fig. 112). One of the most popular of these, called the *Magic Painter*,[22] was introduced in France in about 1769 and on sale in London shortly after. The example here, made in France around 1770, shows a fashionable couple visiting a painter's studio – a common occurrence at the time, as is known. But this was not the main focus of the trick. The trick was the way in which the painter could make, as if by magic, a picture appear on his easel. Players were handed a card, and whatever was on the card would "magically" materialize on the painter's easel. The trick was accomplished by the use of a magnet, which could be used by the skillful operator to swivel a wheel of images to move to the point where the picture in question would appear on the easel. The properties of magnets, it should be remembered, were not common knowledge at the time and showmen were still able to employ them to dupe an unsuspecting public. One such

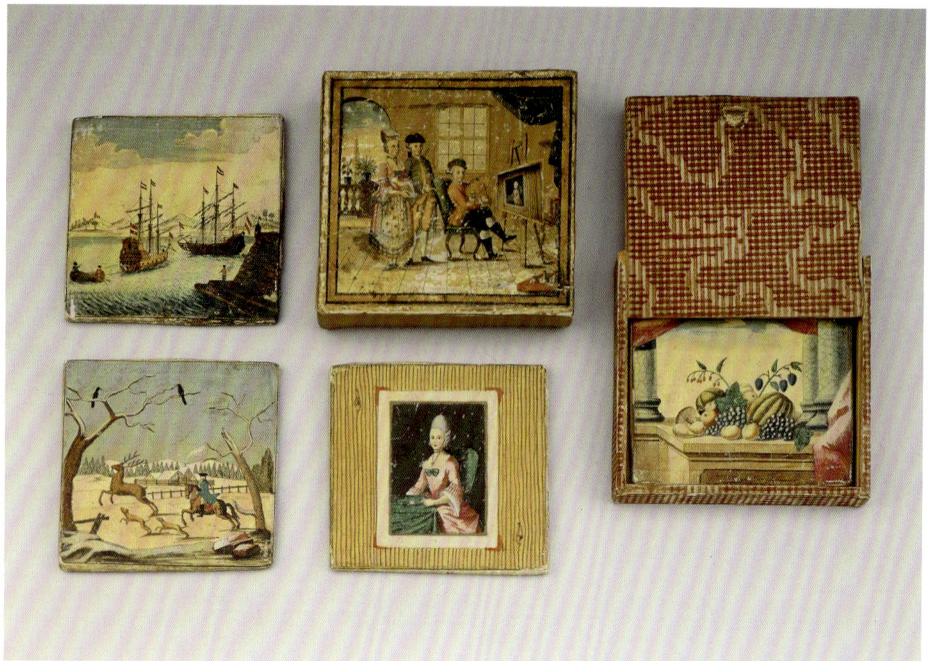

112 Magic Painter Game, France, c. 1770, wood panels, colored and varnished engravings, and magnets, 2.5 × 11.4 × 12.8 cm (1 × 4½ × 5 in.), Getty Research Institute, Los Angeles

showman momentarily duped the young Emile in Rousseau's book of that name.[23] It was also the time when the Austrian Mesmer claimed to be able to use the powers of the magnet for the purposes of faith healing.

The vogue for "magic painters" may also have been stimulated by the growing prominence of another device that played on the connection between imagery and magic. The "Laterna Magica," as it was first called, was one of a whole range of optical devices that had emerged out of the scientific revolution of the seventeenth century. As such it takes its place beside the telescope and the microscope. Yet whereas these instruments extended the scope of investigation to the distant and the minute, the magic lantern was more a matter of display. The very application of the term "magic" to it, something that occurred early in its history, implied a segregation of it from the apparatuses of enquiry. In the age of rational discourse it was considered to be nothing more than an engine of illusion, suitable only for popular entertainment. When Paul Sandby wished to denigrate Hogarth's *Analysis of Beauty* he included in one of his satires of the artist a figure spewing imagery out of his mouth in simulation of a magic lantern projection. The satire implied that Hogarth's concept of beauty was no more than a delusion (fig. 113).[24] In theoretical writings, indeed, the magic lantern was commonly used to refer to chimera. In his *Critique of Practical Reason*, for example, Immanuel Kant warned against the danger of making theology "merely a magic lantern of phantoms."[25]

Yet during the later eighteenth century the magic lantern began to be employed – both literally and metaphorically – for weightier purposes. Its powers of magnification and projection enabled it to change radically the use of the image in public presentations. Be that as it may, it is clear that the growing popularity of projected optical displays in the late eighteenth century began to

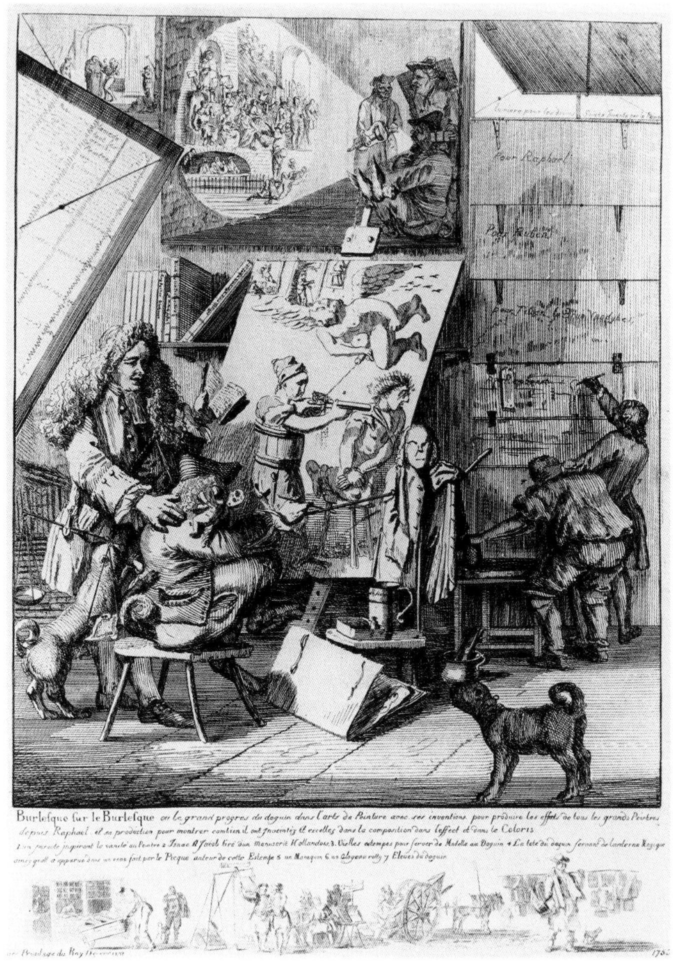

113 Paul Sandby, *Burlesque sur le Burlesque*, 1754, engraving, 26 × 35 cm ($10\frac{1}{4}$ × 14 in.), The Trustees of the British Museum, London, 1868-8-8-3946

attract the attention of fine artists, many of whom began to appropriate the process for their own use.

We are perhaps most aware of the Eidophusikon, devised by the French landscape painter Philippe-Jacques de Loutherbourg and exhibited to the public in the 1780s.[26] An experienced scene painter, de Loutherbourg created a small-scale mechanical theater that used dramatic lighting to simulate the changing effects of the times of day and spectacles like fire and storm. As *entre actes* he used projected images painted on thin paper. Like Gainsborough, de Loutherbourg was an artist sometimes praised for the magical effects that he achieved. In a review of one of his Derbyshire scenes the *Morning Post* in 1784 declared, "wherever the master throws his pencil, we are enchanted by his magic" (fig. 114).[27]

It seems that the fascinating effects achieved by the Eidophusikon were a stimulus to Gainsborough to construct his own "showbox," for displaying illuminated landscapes.[28] Yet although there are some points of comparison between the showbox and de Loutherbourg's spectacle, there are also differences. Gainsborough's images were painted on glass slides and were probably inspired by the work of the glass painter Thomas Jervais (fig. 115). Gainsborough had previous experience in this process of painting on glass from the glass panels he

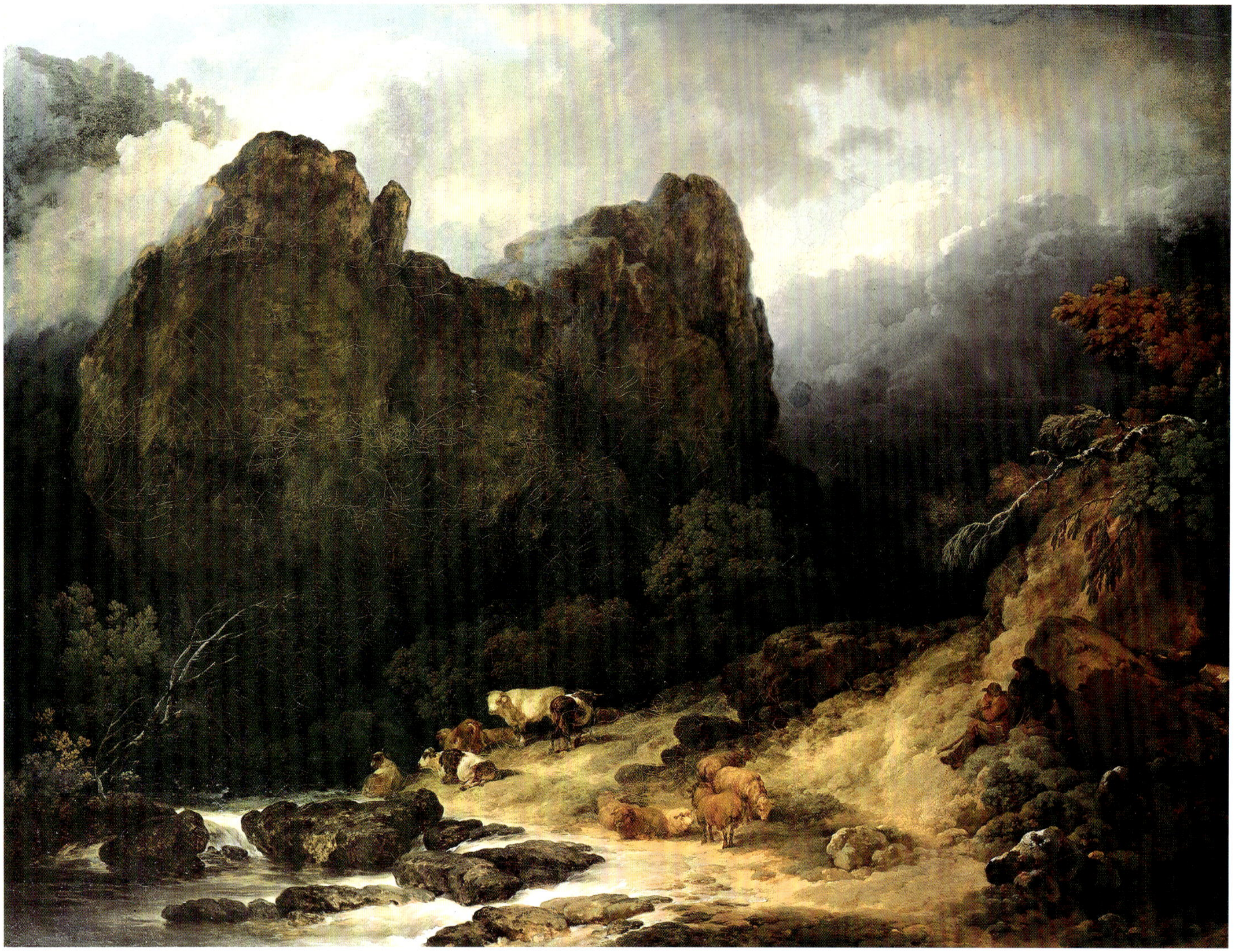

114 Philippe-Jacques de Loutherbourg, *Dovedale in Derbyshire*, 1784, oil on canvas, 97.8 × 129.5 cm (38.5 × 51 in.), York Museums Trust (York Art Gallery)

had painted for the concert hall of his friends Carl Friedrich Abel and Johann Christian Bach. But more importantly, the showbox is constructed as a private, rather than a public, experience. Only one person may peer into it at a time, and as one does one has the experience of viewing in complete solitude a landscape in a darkened interior space. As Martin Myrone rightly points out, it is a space in which the viewer could lose him or herself and which shows a serious exploration of a deepened aesthetic experience.[29] It is a corollary of this that the glass slides themselves are not painted with *trompe l'oeil* illusionism as de Loutherbourg's scenes were, but with the broad handling that makes brushstrokes visible and encourages one to engage in the "magical" point of transformation at which our mind switches from seeing paint marks to perceiving an image of a landscape (fig. 116).

The darkened private world of viewing that Gainsborough's showbox evokes suggests a further optical device, the camera obscura. Always more a device for study than the magic lantern, the camera obscura has been characterized

115 Gainsborough's "Showbox," c. 1781–2, wood and glass, 69.9 × 61 × 40.6 cm (27½ × 24 × 16 in.), Victoria and Albert Museum, London

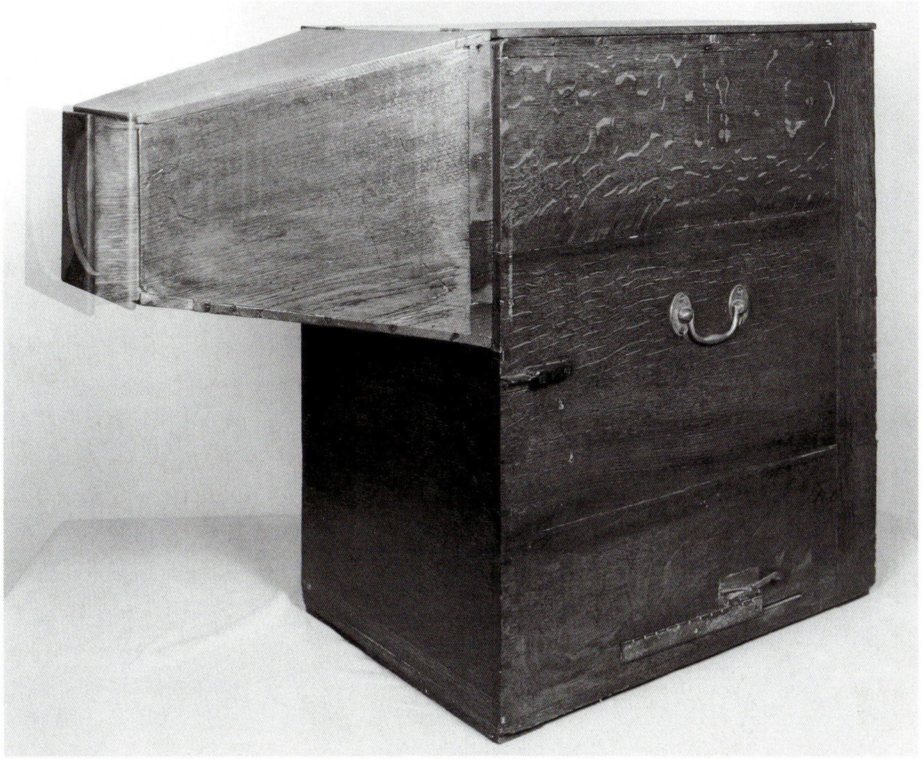

116 (*below*) Thomas Gainsborough, *Cottage Scene by Night*, c. 1781–2, oil on glass, 27.9 × 33.7 cm (11 × 13¼ in.), Victoria and Albert Museum, London

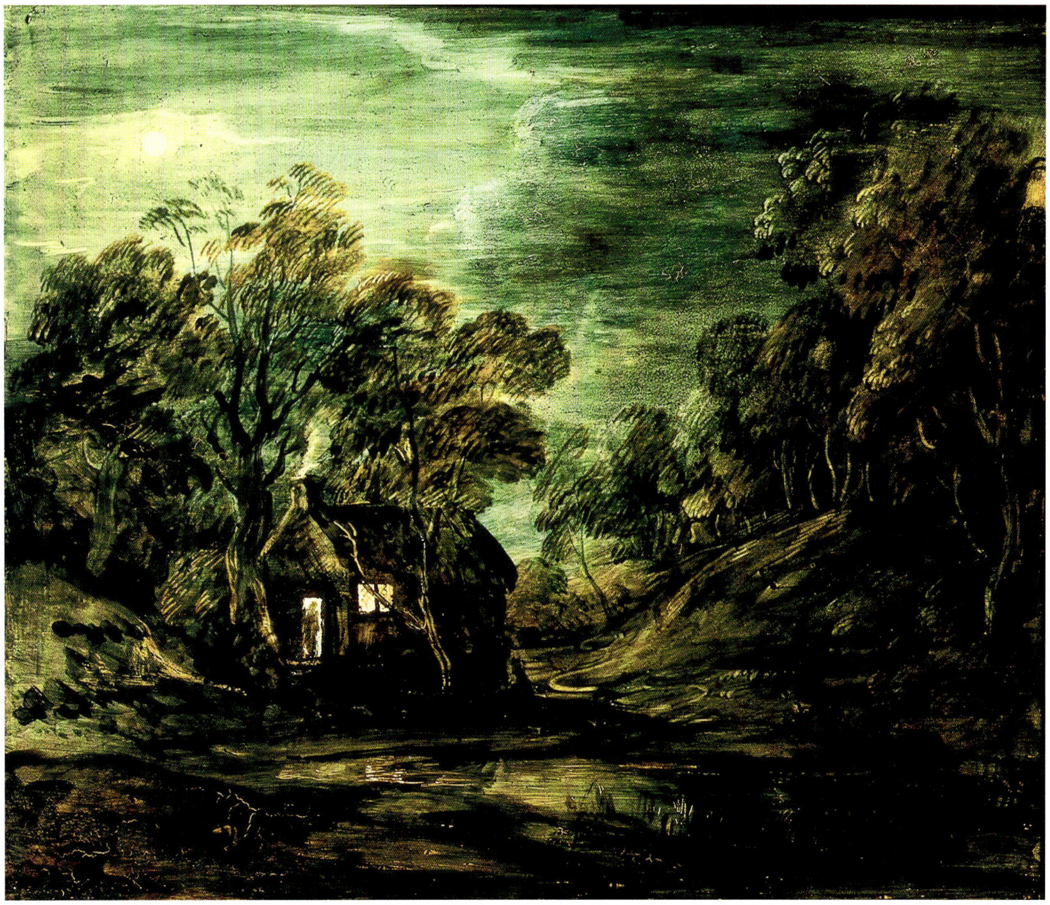

by Jonathan Crary as the "site of subjective individuation," and as such the initiator of modern optical experience.[30]

Gainsborough's showbox appears to represent a key moment in his development of a new kind of spectatorship for his art. Specifically, it encouraged him to increase the presence of broad painting and low illumination in his painting practice. Barbara Stafford has pointed out the way in which Gainsborough's "obsession with fluctuating illumination" in such pictures as *Peasant Smoking at a Cottage Door* related to his showbox experiments, which were "scientifically modelled after disembodying and re-embodying optical apparatuses that melted contoured figures into lambency only magically to coalesce them again."[31] This stress on the spectator's share in the perceptual process can be seen, as Stafford does, as an embodiment of George Berkeley's immaterialist theory of optics. Yet it is also a way of encouraging a new kind of reflectivity over the theme of the picture. By putting viewers into a meditative mood by his low-light broad-brush effects Gainsborough could let the urban viewer wistfully encounter a lost world of rustic virtues endowed with a sense of spiritual "otherness." It is worth recalling in this context how deeply religious Gainsborough was and how he adhered to the conventional Protestant view of the natural world as a sign of divine creation. His associations with Methodism, ably explored in relation to his late rural scenes by Marcia Pointon,[32] would have encouraged any tendency he had to stress the supernatural. In contrast to the established Anglican church, Methodists tended to retain a belief in magic and witchcraft as active signs of the supernatural at work. Wesley himself was emphatic on this point, insisting that "the giving up of witchcraft is, after all, the giving up of the Bible."[33]

It is a sign of Gainsborough's concern for the supernatural in landscape that his few excursions into history painting in the last decade of his life should also engage this theme. His *Hagar and Ishmael* of around 1788 (National Museum of Wates, Cardiff) shows the biblical pair at the moment when they are about to be rescued from death in the desert by being guided by the archangel Michael to a spring, a natural source of sustenance.[34] Something more in the nature of witchcraft can be encountered in his *Diana and Actaeon* (fig. 117), where transgression against the modesty of a supernatural being leads to death by means of a magical transformation. It shows the moment of metamorphosis, with Actaeon already sprouting antlers as the first stage in his transmogrification into a stag. Since the picture is unfinished, it is hard to know how far the sketchiness of its treatment was intended as an extreme example of the "kind of magick" whereby his paint marks assumed form. Yet this visual metamorphosis is certainly a particularly apt accompaniment to the thematic metamorphosis embodied in the subject.

As often with Gainsborough, the artist's own avoidance of discussion of such matters leaves one unable to push such arguments beyond the point of speculation. However, it is clear that the emphasis on the magical in pictorial representation and its role in stimulating the spectator's imaginative speculation became a key issue for theorists in the decades following Gainsborough's death. The clearest examples of such arguments can be found among the German Romantics. It was not Gainsborough but another British artist who provided the most celebrated example of such assertions. In 1799 the German critic August

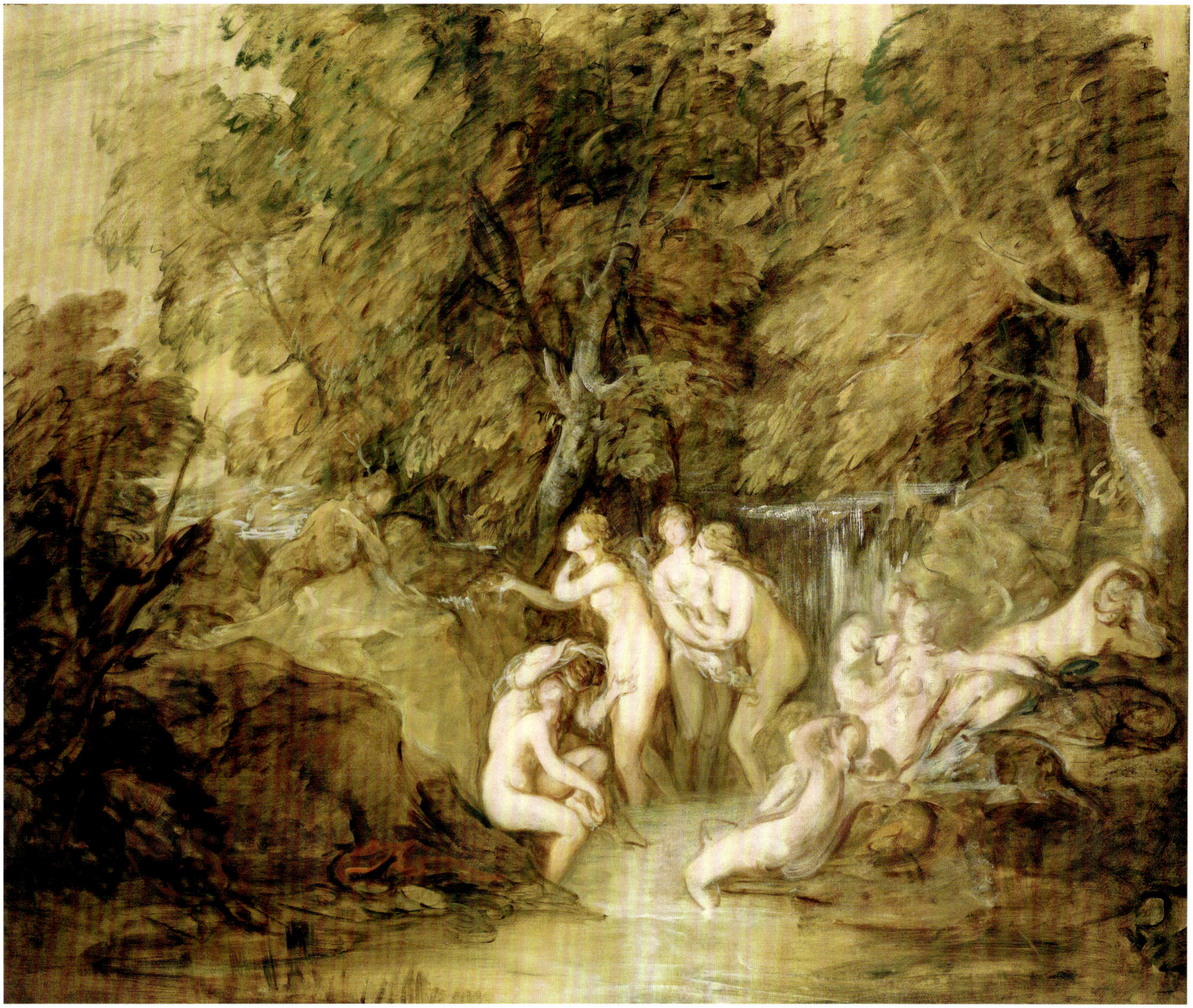

117 Thomas Gainsborough, *Diana and Actaeon*, c. 1785, oil on canvas, 158.1 × 188 cm ($62\frac{1}{2}$ × 74 in.), The Royal Collection, London

Wilhelm Schlegel wrote an important essay on the use of outline in the visual arts, in the form of a review of the celebrated "outlines" to Dante and Homer published by the British sculptor John Flaxman in 1793 (fig. 118). He published Flaxman's outlines in the magazine *Athenaeum* that he was then editing with his brother Friedrich. Schlegel felt that Flaxman's approach to outline had opened up a whole new possibility in the field of artistic expression. In classical aesthetics the outline was the means of defining form succinctly. In his third discourse Reynolds, for example, had spoken of how "a firm and determined Outline is one of the characteristics of the great style in painting" that led to the possession of "the knowledge of the exact form which every part of nature ought to have."[35] Schlegel, by contrast, considered outline as a means of allusion that could bring the visual arts into the same condition of symbolic succinctness as that enjoyed by poetry. Contrasting the outline method with the "prosaic"

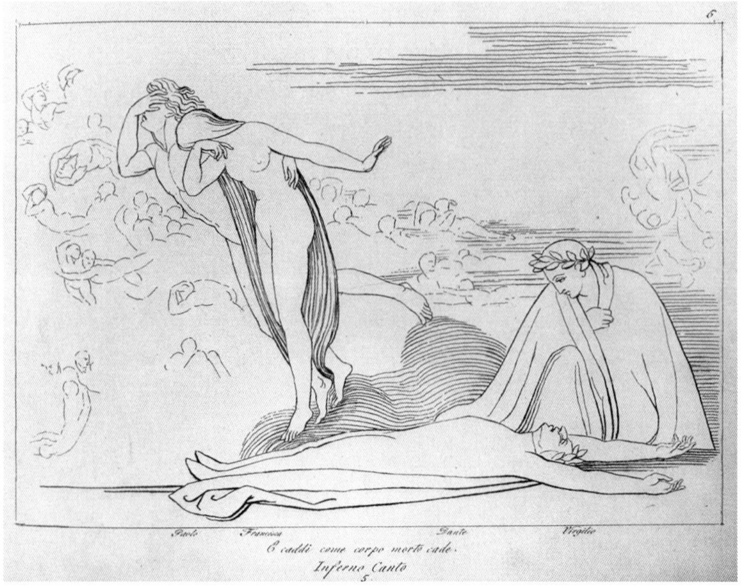

118 Thomas Piroli after John Flaxman, *Paolo and Francesca Leaving Dante* engraving from John Flaxman, *Compositions from the Hell, Purgatory and Paradise of Dante Alighieri*, Rome 1793, Yale Center for British Art, New Haven

elaboration of conventional depiction (as evidenced in the work of Hogarth and Chodowiecki) he said:

> Their signs become almost like hieroglyphs, like those of the poet. The imagination is incited to complete the picture and to continue to create independently according to the stimulation it has received. By contrast the finished painting holds it prisoner through its all too accommodating satisfactoriness. Just as the words of the poet are actually magic formulae for life and beauty (even if one does not observe their components or their secret power), so it appears to be true wizardry how, in a successful outline, so much soul can dwell in a few delicate lines.[36]

The analogy of outlines and poetry with magic can remind one of how these forms were seen to possess a supernatural element. This shift of focus to the allusive side of art is something that was soon developed further with far reaching consequences by August Wilhelm's brother Friedrich.[37]

The relocation of the supernatural to the studio and the garret, Roy Porter observes, has continued to inform the status of aesthetic experience in the modern world. Certainly both overt and covert allusions to the magical in pictorial practise continued to abound throughout the nineteenth and twentieth centuries and show no signs of diminishing. One only has to think of Jackson Pollock's ritualistic painting methods or Josef Beuys's re-invocation of the shaman to remember how much the image of the artist magician has remained a part of the modern art world. Yet this process has not been without its critics. Perhaps one of the strongest protestors in the twentieth century was the German Marxist critic Walter Benjamin, who saw the "mystification" of art by such processes as the cause of its ineffectiveness. In his seminal essay, *The Work of Art in the Age of Mechanical Reproduction*, Benjamin looked to the new processes of photography and film to rescue art from its "magical" impasse.[38] "Here the question is: How does the cameraman compare with the painter? To answer this we take recourse to an analogy with a surgical operation. The surgeon represents the polar opposite of the magician. The magician heals a sick person by the laying on of hands; the surgeon cuts into the patient's body."[39] "Magician and surgeon," Benjamin concluded, "compare to painter and cameraman. The painter maintains in his work a natural distance from reality, the cameraman penetrates deeply into its web."[40]

Benjamin's disdain for the magician artist forms an interesting contrast with his admiration for the magical practices of Count Cagliostro, probably the most notorious showman magician of the later eighteenth century. However, he celebrates Cagliostro's magical practices because of the unsettling effects these had in the years leading up to the French Revolution. Whether by design or accident, Cagliostro's role was a subversive one; paraphrasing Benjamin, McCalman hails him as "an underground messiah and a genius of disorder preaching creative irrationality in a repressive world."[41] By contrast, the modern artist magican is seen by Benjamin as forming part of the process of mystification whereby the established order maintains power in a capitalist world, and is therefore to be deplored.

Benjamin was a political visionary, who dreamed of a democratized art; one in which the "aura" of the masterpiece would have been undermined by the ubiquity of mechanical reproduction, and in which the "magic" of the painter would have given way to the analytical skills of the cameraman. As is well known, such a situation never came to pass. The use of technical processes, after all, depends on the priorities of the societies that manage them. In a prevailing commercial context, mechanical reproduction has come to enhance rather than destroy the mystique of the individual work of art. And the artist has remained as much a magician as ever – something richly born out by the increasing prominence of performance and paradox among contemporary practitioners. Some make a show of being surgeons, but the conditions of the art world are against them. The theater in which they practise is not one designed for surgical operations. It is a theater of magic, the transforming aesthetic space that emerged at the end of the eighteenth century and that is assiduously preserved in our institutions of art.

This may all seem a long way from Gainsborough's practise. Yet his insistence that the "work of the picture" involved engaging the spectator in the transformative powers of image-making can be seen as an early step in the use by artists of the invocation of the magical as a means of securing and enhancing the status of their practice in a modern commercial society.

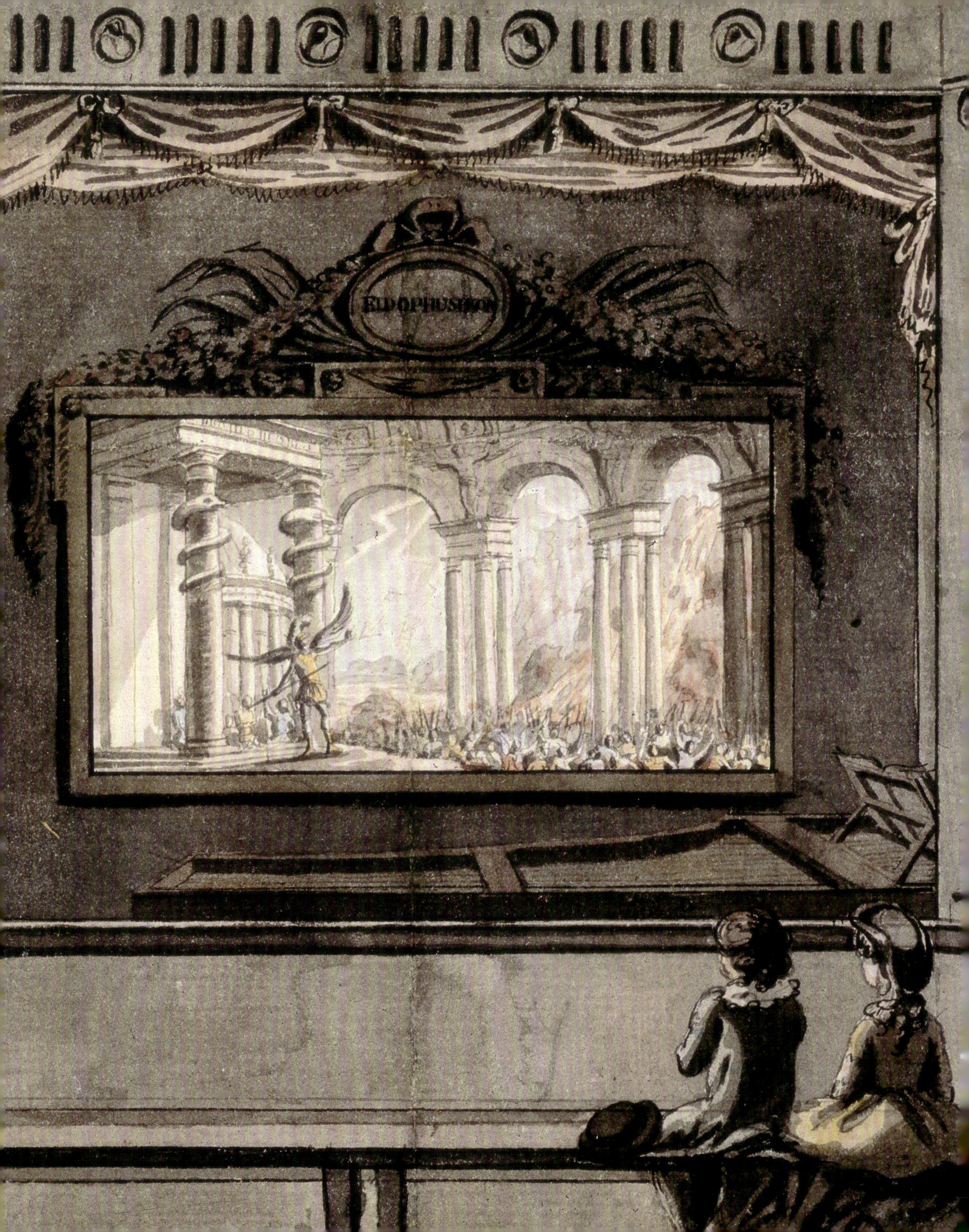

Iain McCalman

Magic, Spectacle, and the Art of de Loutherbourg's Eidophusikon

On 26 February 1781, sixty years before the invention of photography and a century before the first cinema, a moving picture show opened for business in a private house in Lisle Street, adjoining London's Leicester Square. Advertised under the name of "The Eidophusikon," the specially built miniature theater displayed what the *Public Advertiser* called "various imitations of Natural Phenomena, represented by moving pictures."[1] Its inventor and producer, an Alsatian-born, British-based artist called Philippe Jacques de Loutherbourg, unveiled a program of stunning natural effects using hidden lighting, magic lantern slides, colored silk filters, clockwork automata, three-dimensional models, painted transparencies, and a sophisticated sound system. The show projected a series of five natural wonders in action at moments of key change and transition. Awed viewers watched dawn creeping over the Thames at Greenwich, a view of Gibraltar at noon from the port of Tangier, the burning sun setting over the Bay of Naples, the moon rising over the Mediterranean, and a torrential storm wrecking a ship at sea. Four transparencies served as curtain drops, and Mr. and Mrs. Michael Arne entertained viewers with music and song in between acts.[2]

The Eidophusikon remains relatively little known outside specialist art history circles, yet it actually anticipated and influenced the Frenchman Louis Daguerre's celebrated Diorama of the 1820s as well as a host of subsequent spectacles of illusion. Indeed, the Eidophusikon's vivid three-dimensional program foreshadowed by a century the acknowledged birth of modern cinema when the French conjuror showman George Méliès opened his "cinema of attractions" in 1902. Like de Loutherbourg, Méliès aimed to create "astonishment" and wonder through images of "magical metamorphosis."[3] Neglect of the Eidophusikon probably owes something to France's longstanding dominance of the historiography of early cinema but it is also true to say that, compared with pioneering French illusionists of the period, de Loutherbourg's involvement with the revolutionary new show was relatively shortlived. He sold it after only three seasons and, despite pursuing an active and varied artistic career in England for a further thirty years, never returned to or developed his experiment.

Whatever the long-term influence of the Eidophusikon, there is no doubting that its early performances electrified London's chic art circles. Nothing quite like it had been seen before. The flaring rivalry between Sir Joshua Reynolds and Thomas Gainsborough showed only in the fervor with which they vied to praise the show and, perhaps, to debate its implications for the future of

facing page Edward Francis Burney, *The Eidophusikon showing Satan arraying his Troops on the Banks of a Fiery Lake with the Raising of the Palace of Pandemonium from Milton* (detail of fig. 124)

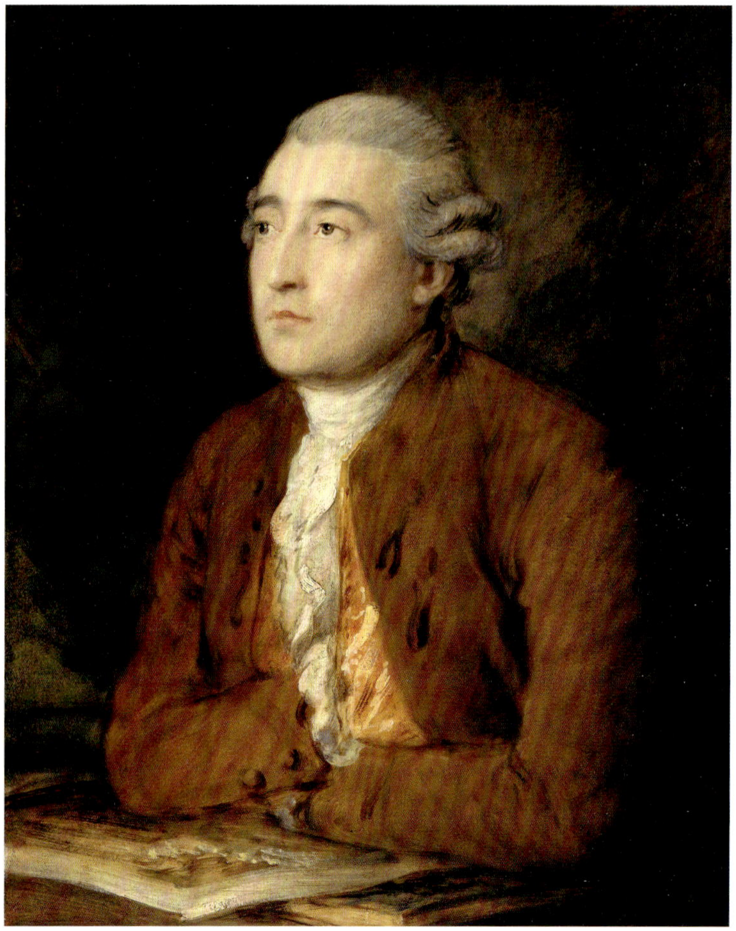

119 Thomas Gainsborough, *Philip James de Loutherbourg*, R.A. 1778, oil on canvas, 76.5 × 63.2 cm ($30\frac{1}{8} \times 24\frac{7}{8}$ in.), The Trustees of Dulwich Picture Gallery, London

painting. Gainsborough, a close friend of de Loutherbourg and a long-time experimenter with technologies of light, was especially smitten (fig. 119). He watched the program over and over, was "wrapt in wonder," spoke about "nothing else," and sometimes helped to operate the machinery. When comparing a virtual storm enacted by the Eidophusikon with a real-life one raging outside, he is said to have shouted out, "De Loutherbourg, our thunder's best."[4] Whether or not the show explicitly inspired his own showbox, which used moveable glass slides and a candle for exploring lighting effects, it undoubtedly informed several of his artistic experiments with model landscapes and transparencies.[5]

More pertinently, as Ann Bermingham and others have suggested, these lighting experiments influenced Gainsborough's subsequent work as a landscape painter, particularly, the artist's creation of a box for viewing transparencies, and his use of color and light in later works like *The Cottage Door*. Bermingham cites the Eidophusikon as prominent in a series of "popular landscape entertainments" that generated a "fertile cross-pollination" with the aesthetics and practices of *fin-de-siècle* British landscape art as a whole – all the more so because the crowded viewing conditions of Royal Academy painting hangs in Somerset House encouraged artists to make exaggerated use of scale and color in order to enhance the visibility of their paintings.[6]

There is no doubt that the Eidophusikon is a rich case study for exploring the interactions between art and popular spectacle, particularly because it brought into convergence de Loutherbourg's three different practices as a professional working within eighteenth-century visual culture – landscape and marine painting, theater scenography, and commercial optical spectacle. In this paper I argue, however, that an examination of what motivated the artist de Loutherbourg to take up spectacle technology in 1771, then to produce the Eidophusikon in its two different incarnations of 1781 and 1782, and, finally, to sell the show in 1786 suggests that risks, as well as rewards, could attend the intermixing of landscape painting and commercial spectacle. Trying to negotiate the socially engendered tensions between these different forms of visual culture forced de Loutherbourg to engage in a hazardous and delicate balancing act, and the costs proved high for his subsequent reputation both as an artist and as a pioneer of visual spectacles.

* * *

It is not enough – in the manner of many theater historians – to explain de Loutherbourg's invention of the Eidophusikon in 1781 as simply a natural extension of stagecraft innovations that he had initiated during his previous fourteen-year career as chief scenographer of the Drury Lane Theater, under the management first of David Garrick, then of Richard Sheridan.[7] To do so is to overlook the question of why he decided to work as a London theater scenographer in the first place: it was by no means an obvious or orthodox career move for a young, celebrated French Academic painter who was known to be acutely conscious of his artistic status. The letter of recommendation written to Garrick by his Parisian friend Jean Monnet, director of the Opéra Comique, described young de Loutherbourg as one of France's most distinguished painters who simply happened to be paying a recreational visit to England: it made no mention of his expertise or interest in working as a theater scenographer.[8]

Monnet was right that de Loutherbourg boasted impressive painting credentials. Born in Strasbourg, he had been trained from the age of fifteen in the Paris salons of Carle van Loo, Jean George Wille, and Francesco Casanova. In 1763, at the tender age of twenty-one, he had made a sensation with his first exhibition of paintings at the biennial Academy Salon.[9] France's foremost critic, Denis Diderot, hailed him as a young genius who could paint landscapes of a delicacy equal to Vernet, Berchem, and Wouvermans, vivid battle paintings that eclipsed those of Casanova, and pictures of banditti as wildly energetic as Salvator Rosa.[10] Three years later he had been appointed to the position of Peintre du Roi, and the following year he had been elected to the French Academy – its youngest ever member and technically still under the minimum entry-age. Over the next four years he had become a prolific Academy exhibitor and accumulated a string of noble patrons willing to pay good prices for his paintings. Why, then, should he have abandoned his glittering career in 1771 to work as a theater designer in England, a country where such people were classed more as jobbing artisans and craftworkers than elite professionals?

Theater historiography offers a plausible explanation. It was well known that David Garrick's lengthy visit to France in 1765 inspired the Drury Lane manager and actor to reform the lighting, costume, and stagecraft practices of his company. Despite piecemeal infusions of spectacular technique from itinerant Italian and French experts over many years, the stark lighting and stock stagecraft practices of British theater had nothing to compare with the subtle illumination and complex naturalistic spectacles of the Comédie-Française and the Paris Opéra. Using his friend Monnet as an advisor and agent, Garrick determined to rival the emphasis on spectacle at John Rich's Covent Garden by importing new French stage technology and know-how. The brilliant and versatile young painter, de Loutherbourg – doubtless also versed in French stage expertise gained from working with Parisian greats such as Giovanni Servandoni – happened to arrive on Garrick's doorstep at a peculiarly opportune moment. After viewing some examples of de Loutherbourg's painting, Garrick hired him initially to enhance the scenography of several of his existing pantomimes. The following year, de Loutherbourg followed up this initial success with a broad-based proposal to mastermind a sweeping new regime of scenography at the Drury Lane Theatre. Impressed, the normally parsimonious Garrick made young de Loutherbourg an offer he could not refuse – integrated control over the whole *mise en scène*, a generous budget for spectacle production and an impressive salary of £500 a year (close to that earned by the celebrated Servandoni in his British sojourn with Rich at Covent Garden).[11]

This is broadly the version of events that de Loutherbourg himself put out, but it was some way from the truth. In the first place there is no evidence that he possessed any prior expertise working on stage or other spectacles. Neither his own correspondence with Garrick nor his letter of recommendation from Monnet mentions any, and they had every incentive to do so. That said, he had trained in engineering and mathematics at Strasbourg University until the age of fifteen, and he was probably at least a regular and enthusiastic witness of Paris theatrical and public boulevard spectacle. And if he could not claim spectacle expertise personally, he knew someone who could: he arrived in London in 1771 with Giovanni Battista Torré, a pyrotechnics expert and impresario who also orchestrated mechanical and theatrical performances. Torré had both worked closely with the great Servandoni and had himself visited Britain as a spectacle expert on an earlier occasion.[12] Moreover, in 1771 he had been explicitly invited over to London by Garrick to demonstrate and apply his firework skills, and could thus provide his friend with an essential entrée to the theatre world. He also knew Monnet well and it was probably he who acquired an effusive reference for de Loutherbourg, who was not personally known to the Paris director.

It is equally important that Torré was acquainted with a key member of Garrick's circle in London, the fencing master Domenico Angelo, with whom the two Paris visitors first stayed on their arrival in London in November 1771. Angelo proved to be another crucial contact. For at least a decade he had been Garrick's informal local advisor on spectacle; he had introduced the Drury Lane manager (and Gainsborough, too, as it happens) to the idea of using colored moreen side slips in order to create varied lighting moods and also to the principle of constructing kinetic pasteboard models to simulate special effects that might later be translated to the stage.[13] (Significantly, de Loutherbourg immediately adopted both techniques as key aspects of his scenographic repertoire.) And it was while staying at Angelo's house in Carlisle Street that the young French painter was introduced to his future Drury Lane employer. In short, de Loutherbourg's visit was far from casual. It looks as if he arrived in London with a definite plan to gain employment with the Drury Lane manager by presenting himself as a prospective new Servandoni, and in the hope, as one of his cynical Parisian associates observed, "of finding an occupation and of filling his pockets with guineas."[14]

Both Torré and de Loutherbourg were actually in urgent need of some English guineas. The pyrotechnician had left Paris in frustration after having fallen victim to French court intrigue. Despite producing a magnificent fireworks spectacle for the marriage of Marie-Antoinette at Versailles, his commercial patent to exhibit fireworks in the boulevards had been given to a royal favorite.[15] De Loutherbourg's plight was worse: far from being a darling of the French Academy, he was actually fleeing Paris under a cloud of financial and social scandal. His star had begun to wane only a few years after the first triumphant exhibition of 1763. Although Diderot had initially enjoyed the young man's reputation for wild living and libertine sexuality, his chuckling indulgence had dissipated when this "furious boy who won't stay put" became an embarrassment to the Academy.[16]

In July 1764 an elderly East Indies merchant brought a legal charge that Philippe and his fiancée, a beautiful young widow called Barbe Burlat, had connived to milk him of money and gifts in return for Barbe's sexual favors. When this source had dried up, they allegedly resorted to outright theft. Eddies of gossip about this affair almost prevented de Loutherbourg's election to the Academy in 1767, but by 1771 they had become a torrent. In that year, de Loutherbourg's wife sought a formal separation of their finances; she charged that he had squandered her large dowry on reckless living and sexual profligacy, that he had failed to care for their five children, and had assaulted her on one occasion so violently that she had miscarried. To cap all this, he had vanished without warning to London, leaving her without any means of supporting their infant family. While Barbe was no paragon, as her subsequent record with the Paris police shows, it was a squalid story; and there was no disputing de Loutherbourg's reputation for being *déreglé* and for accumulating unpaid debts, including dues owed to the Paris Academy.[17]

His aesthetic standing had begun to slide in tandem with his social reputation. By 1771 Diderot's initial assessment of the young man's genius had soured: he routinely criticized his former protégé for churning out stock paintings and lingering in bed or the studio when he ought to have been out studying nature. He also observed that many of Loutherbourg's landscapes were marred by extremes of color, particularly a burning crimson, and by a forced and excessive theatricality.[18] De Loutherbourg was fortunate that his referee, Monnet, did not frequent Academy circles and had apparently heard nothing of Philippe's falling reputation. As with many Continental exiles, British insularity offered the young painter a chance to remake himself. The magisterial tone that he adopted in his proposal to Garrick for employment as a spectacle supremo on the same terms as Servandoni was actually pure bluff. In private, he wrote to Garrick's Austrian wife, Eva, begging her to intervene with her husband on his behalf because he had "nothing but the theater" to support him, was on the brink of losing his house, and – he claimed – had to maintain an infant in arms.[19]

When beseeching Eva's help, de Loutherbourg also offered an extra inducement to enhance his credentials as a spectacle expert. He and Torré presented themselves as learned practitioners of the occult sciences, an experimental realm that fascinated Eva and intrigued her husband.[20] Philippe wrote to Mrs Garrick at length explaining the significance of his friend Torré's convoluted and opaque experiments in alchemy and lending her his own favorite text on the subject. At the same time, he warned her that "there are sometimes things wich [*sic*] at first seem to be extraordinary, but you will find them to be right . . ."[21] Magical and mystical knowledge was intertwined with the experimental discovery in fixing and enhancing pigments that he claimed to have made as a boy in Strasbourg, and which he described to Garrick as "mon secret." By definition he could not and would not reveal on paper the precise nature of this secret, but he hinted at its implications in letters and in snippets of later conversation with friends and journalists.[22]

Born and educated in Strasbourg, long a hub of alchemical publishing, learned magic, and mystical freemasonry, de Loutherbourg had been steeped in occult theory and practice from an early age. His mother had hoped he would study theology and become a pastor, though mathematics, engineering, philosophy, then painting, had subsumed this ambition. In Paris, he seems to have spent a good deal of time and money on alchemical experiment, and it was probably there that he began to accumulate what became a formidable library of occult knowledge. Eventually it boasted most of the classics of sixteenth- and seventeenth-century European alchemy, as well as key works of Renaissance hermeticism, Rosicrucianism, Jewish Kabbalism, astrology, and Christian mysticism. Significantly, these occult tomes rubbed spines with up-to-the minute modern works on physics, chemistry, and practical technology (figs. 120 and 121).[23]

In short, Philippe de Loutherbourg and his friend Torré were heirs to a rich and creative occult scientific tradition, which, in Frances Yates's words, "expresses both the scientific outlook penetrating into new worlds of discovery, and also an attitude of religious expectation of penetrating into new worlds of religious experience."[24] Such an outlook reflected a fundamental belief in a vital world spirit that animated a multi-leveled universe and linked the large world of God with the small world of humanity – macrocosm and microcosm – through invisible forces of sympathy, antipathy, and correspondence. Yet for seekers of this kind, commitment to spiritual science seemed in no way incompatible with a methodology of rigorous empirical experiment and technological application. This magical-mystical "way of thinking" made de Loutherbourg and his friend Torré lifelong experimenters: they saw themselves as philosophers driven not only to discover the "stone" that would turn base metals into gold but also to deploy earthly and celestial knowledge in order to reveal and simulate the

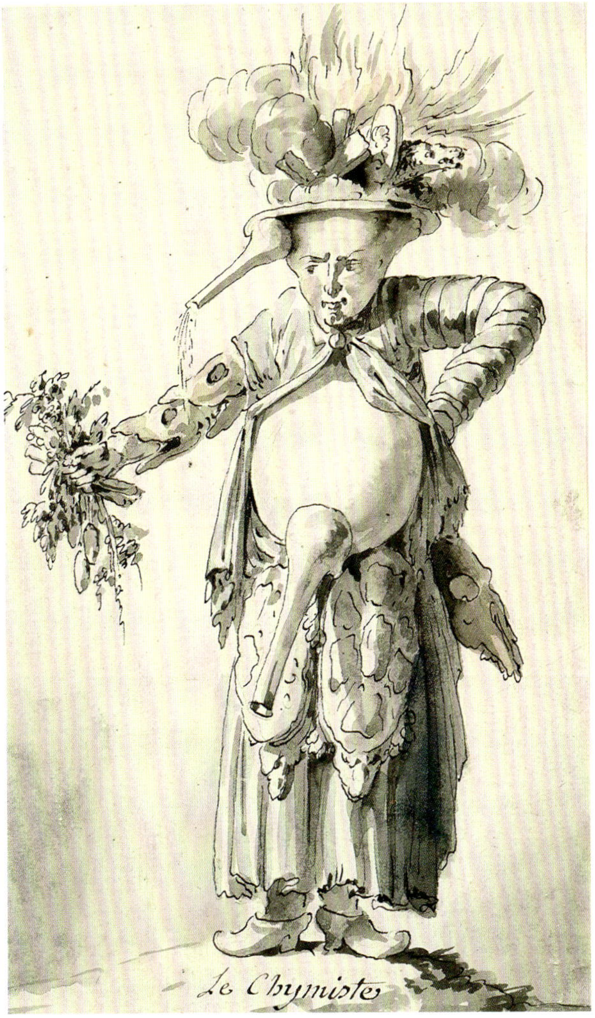

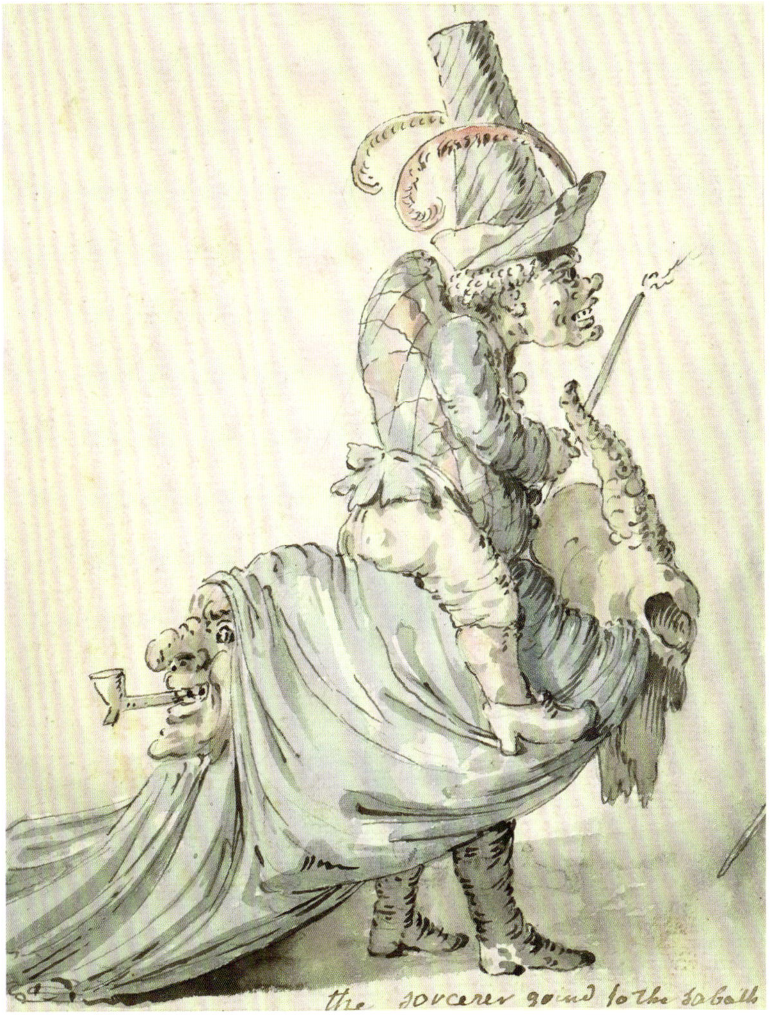

120 (*above left*) Philippe-Jacques de Loutherbourg, *Le Chemyste*, c. 1775, pen, ink, and watercolor washes, 19.0 × 11.2 cm ($7\frac{1}{2} \times 4\frac{7}{16}$ in.), Ashmolean Museum, Oxford

121 (*above right*) Philippe-Jacques de Loutherbourg, *The Sorcerer*, c. 1775, pen, ink, and watercolor washes, 18.1 × 14.6 cm ($7\frac{1}{4} \times 5\frac{3}{4}$ in.), Ashmolean Museum, Oxford

wonders of nature, whether through the medium of trance and vision or of paint, fireworks, chemicals, optical instruments, and rational machinery.[25]

For someone with practical and philosophical predilections of this kind, the work of theater scenography had much to offer. In effect, it promised to provide young de Loutherbourg with a practical laboratory for testing his magical-mystical artistic and scientific preoccupations. In particular, the knockabout theatrical form of adult pantomime or harlequinade suited his mix of talents. Pantomime's traditional repertoire of magical illusions, transformations, and metamorphoses seemed to mimic the larger cosmic processes of alchemical and spiritual transmutation whereby all things changed their form through a staged series of color transitions, from the black of primary matter to white, then citrine, through purple, culminating in the blazing red of successful projection – the very extremes of coloration that Diderot had begun to observe with distaste in the young man's paintings.[26] Realizing these proclivities, Garrick ensured from the outset that his new run of pantomimes of 1773, *Alfred*, *The Genii*, and *A Christmas Tale* would be written and produced as vehicles for demonstrating de

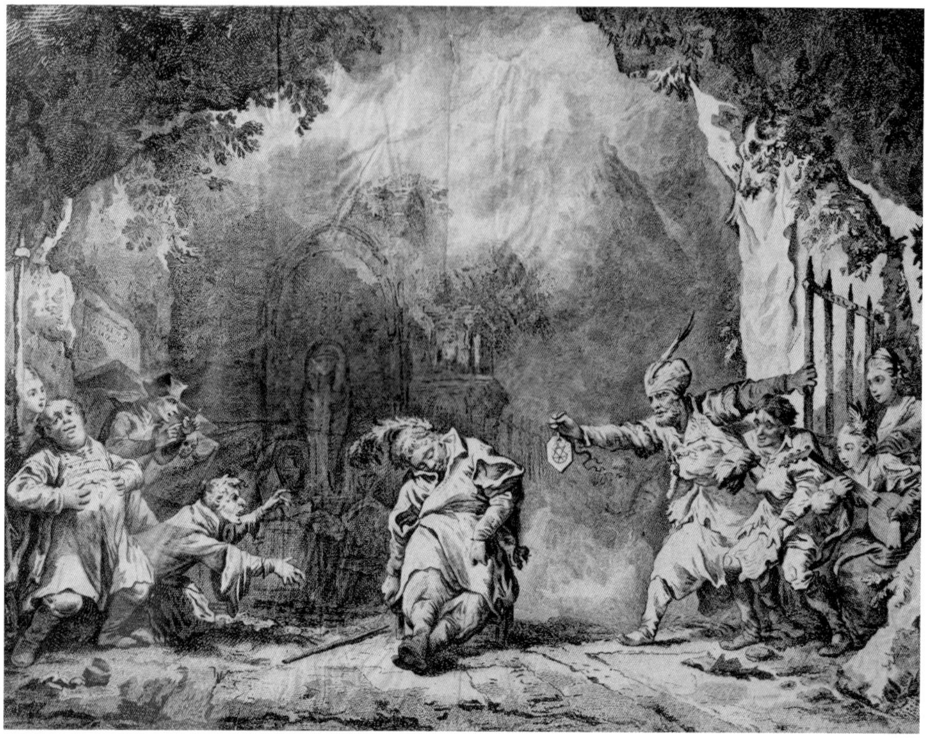

122 Philippe-Jacques de Loutherbourg, *Bonoro's Cell, A Scene from David Garrick's "A Christmas Tale,"* 1772, pencil, pen, and sepia, 23 × 31 cm (9 × 12 in.), Courtesy of the University of Bristol Theatre Collection

Loutherbourg's special talents in conveying mysterious and necromantic effects (fig. 122).[27]

And of all British theater's genres, it was the pantomime and the entertainment afterpiece that offered the greatest opportunities for pure spectacle. Feeble, predictable plots functioned as casings for pageants of topical events, displays of naturalistic scenery, cunning escapes, magical transitions, and demonstrations of natural wonders in action, such as storms, fires, volcanoes, and waterspouts. Here de Loutherbourg could work with his brush, pencil, cardboard models, and a tribe of supporting artists and technicians to fabricate fantastic alternative worlds that crackled with occult forces and exhibited the protean moods of nature, humanity and God working in synchrony and sympathy.

Finally, one should not underestimate the positive attractions of Garrick's London for talented and ambitious virtuosi with a hankering to find wealth and fame. True, Paris was still the acknowledged spectacle center of Europe, its proud tradition of theatrical display and royal spectacle having been galvanized by new social stimuli such as an Enlightenment-inspired growth in the status of useful mechanical arts, new technical inventions, a burgeoning of public spaces and boulevards, and a rapid growth in organs of publicity.[28] Yet from the mid-eighteenth century, London experienced accelerating trends of the same kind, increasingly challenging Paris's primacy as a hub of spectacle. Its much freer commercial conditions also meant that Torré was less likely to find himself blocked by court monopolies and noble privileges – here, money was king. It was not a royal prince but an independent theater entrepreneur and actor, Garrick, who brought Torré over from Paris to orchestrate a *fête champêtre* at his new house in Hampton Gardens. De Loutherbourg and Torré were also, of course, well aware that foreign virtuosi such as Servandoni, Devoto, and Ambrogio had acquired a special cachet in British opera and theater circles, and that London was a booming city where commercial opportunities abounded. Indeed, Garrick later secured Torré a position as fireworks expert in Marylebone Gardens, after which the pyrotechnician opened up his own bookshop from which he published de Loutherbourg's early engravings. With hindsight, one can see that the two men caught the first swell of what became a tide of visiting Continental performers, entrepreneurs, exhibitors, and spectacle experts. There was probably never a better time or place than London in 1771 for the young French painter to make himself into a second Servandoni.

* * *

Over the next fourteen years de Loutherbourg's work on twenty-nine productions for the Drury Lane Theatre enabled him to do exactly this. I need not rehearse the debate among theater historians as to whether his scenographic innovations were original or merely syncretic borrowings from elements that went back to the masques of Inigo Jones. It is enough to say in general that de Loutherbourg's scenography became legendary in its own time and brought him a status in Britain akin to Servandoni's. In pantomime, especially, de Loutherbourg's work became synonymous with new conceptions and practices of using theater space, new complexities and splendors of lighting, with naturalistic costuming, sublime and romantic set design, ingenious optical and mechanical illusions, and realistic perspective through the use of raked and broken wings and flats.[29] Ultimately, he, more than any other individual, was responsible for instantiating in British theater a new and enduring appetite for visual theatrical spectacle at the expense of its earlier emphasis on rhetoric, plot, and acting.

Why, then, did he leave Drury Lane in 1781 and launch the Eidophusikon? Most theater historians suggest that his new moving picture show was a logical development of earlier scenographic innovations – triggered at this particular time by personal differences with his employer, Sheridan, and frustrations at some of the inherent restrictions of contemporary stagecraft. There is much to support this view. De Loutherbourg's relationship with Sheridan had never been entirely comfortable and the Drury Lane manager's decision to cut his pay in 1781 certainly precipitated his formal resignation from the company. He had also long been fascinated with illusionist experiment – he claimed to have been working on the idea for twenty years; and his standard scenographic method of building small-scale models accorded well with developing a larger-scale miniature theater. Its small proportions – about 2 metres wide, 1 metre high, and 2.7 metres deep (6 feet wide, 3 feet high, and nearly 9 feet deep) – enabled him to control lighting sources far more precisely than on the massive barnlike stage of Drury Lane. His illusionist effects were greatly enhanced by displaying them in a framed looking box, rather like a peep show, which eliminated the front stage and raised the scene to the viewer's eye level, looking along the horizon line. He could also partially dim the interior, and his elimination of plot and actors further concentrated the audience's attention solely on the illuminated spectacle.[30]

Equally importantly, de Loutherbourg's private ownership of the theater enabled him to control the social bases and behavior of the crowd.[31] A relatively high five-shilling entrance fee and an imposing interior set the tone. Lacquered timber panels painted with festoons of flowers and ornamented with gilt enamelling, seats padded with crimson stuff, a genteel musical accompaniment, and the presence of a royal box were all designed to eliminate the usual boisterous involvement of theater audiences in the performing process.

There is no doubt, too, that much of the repertoire for the first program of the Eidophusikon had been borrowed and adapted from earlier scenographic work. Scenes of nature at transitional moments such as daybreak, sunset, and nightfall had been used in *Wonders of Derbyshire* in 1778.[32] Storms at sea and a sinking ship had been stock items of de Loutherbourg's paintings as well as his pantomimes and afterpieces (fig. 123). The prototype of the first Eidophusikon scene, the view of Greenwich Hospital with the Thames in the background, had first appeared in the pantomime *Queen Mab* in 1778.[33]

De Loutherbourg was at pains in 1781, however, to try to distance the Eidophusikon from obvious associations with theatricality or popular entertainment. The reason was simple: he knew that, unless carefully handled, the management of a commercial spectacle could endanger his fragile and freshly endowed standing as an elite British artist. Having successfully masked his Parisian disgrace, he had managed to cultivate a circle of respected artist friends in London, including Gainsborough and Reynolds. As one of the most prolific exhibitors at Royal Academy hangs, he had acquired a reputation as a highly accomplished landscape artist working in both the French and British picturesque styles, who also dabbled in a variety of other genres such as portraits, comic pieces, caricatures, and marine paintings. In 1780, the year he had begun working on the Eidophusikon in earnest, he had been elected an associate of the Royal Academy, and in the year of the show's debut he finally received the much-coveted invitation to become a full fellow. The icing on the cake was his election to the council of the Academy the following year. Yet, as he well knew from Parisian experience, a lofty standard of conduct was expected to accompany such an honor. At a time when the president, Sir Joshua Reynolds, was striving to elevate the status of Academy painters to the apex of Britain's hierarchy of aesthetic taste, de Loutherbourg could not afford to carry the taint of vulgar commercial showmanship.

He stressed to friends and newspaper critics that the Eidophusikon represented a refined development of his landscape and marine painting. As he explained to a journalist of the *European Magazine*, his motivation had been "to add motion to resemblance" because "the most exquisite painting represented only one moment of time in action . . ."[34] The ambience of the show's Lisle Street premises also hinted strongly of a painting salon or exhibition room. On first entering, visitors were greeted with the sight of de Loutherbourg's most celebrated landscape and battle paintings clustered on the walls of the foyer and waiting room. The program description implied that the show itself was a type of kinetic art exhibition. Instead of curtain falls, acts were punctuated by the lowering of transparencies featuring picturesque Alpine scenes taken straight from his easel paintings. The five major episodes of the show also hinted at artistic intertexuality.

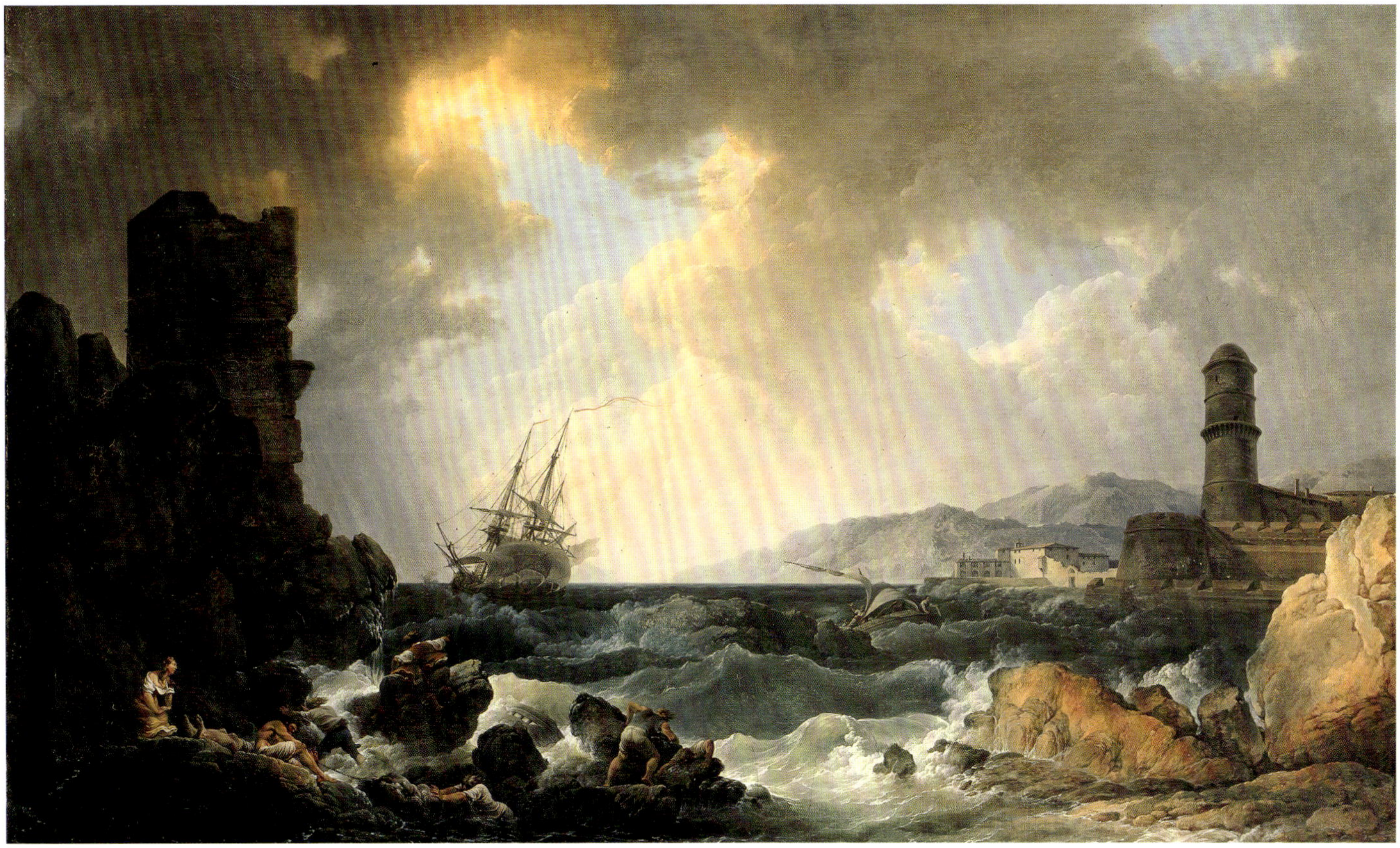

123 Philippe-Jacques de Loutherbourg, *A Storm at the Entrance of a Mediterranean Port*, 1768, oil on canvas, 67.2 × 160 cm ($38\frac{3}{16}$ × 63 in.), National Gallery of Ireland, Dublin

Critics commented approvingly on the resemblance between the "sunset at Naples" scene and related works of Joseph Wright of Derby, and the "Storm and Shipwreck at Sea" had several precursors among de Loutherbourg's own easel repertoire. Even the "moonlight in the Mediterranean" scene seems to have been an elaboration of his 1770 painting, *Pêcheurs au clair de lune*.[35]

To what extent de Loutherbourg actually cajoled or engineered the favorable reaction of both Gainsborough and Reynolds is impossible to know. There is no doubt, though, that such an enthusiastic response from Britain's two most distinguished artists proved germane in setting the tone and style of public commentary. Newspaper and journal reviewers commented on the show as if it were "a new species of painting" rather than a theatrical spectacle or entertainment. Consequently, as the *European Magazine* rhapsodized, "every person of taste in this metropolis beheld it with admiration."[36] The show's successful self-presentation as an elite art event also helped to avert a potentially damaging moment when an overzealous Westminster magistrate drew attention to underlying commercial realities by issuing a fine against de Loutherbourg for performing music without a licence. However, on representations from de Loutherbourg and others, the case was quashed.

Among the show's extensive and favorable publicity, no critic seems to have noticed the magical and theosophic vision that underlay de Loutherbourg's technical wizardry. Each of his delicate and violent natural illusions sought to simulate and evoke those invisible occult forces that could transfigure all material and spiritual life. By movement and illusion – through storms, sunsets, moonlight, and volcanoes in motion – he hoped to capture the fleeting evanescent moment of transmutation and metamorphosis when nature moved from one state into another, mirroring in the process the color transitions of alchemy and the emotional moods of the human spectators. It was, in short, a type of technomancy, an enchanting art show in every sense of the word.

* * *

After operating the Eidophusikon in 1781 for 59 successive performances, followed by a short further stint of eleven days, de Loutherbourg reopened on January 31, 1782 with a new program, whose significantly different content has attracted surprisingly little notice. Then it was no longer exhibited in his private home but in the premises of a well-known London commercial spectacle – Cox's museum in Spring Gardens, where his friends John Joseph Merlin and Henri-Louis Jacquet Droz displayed many of their dazzling and uncannily lifelike automata.[37] In the first act of the new show, sunrise on the Thames had been replaced by a more dramatic scene of the sun rising through fog in an Italian port; noon at Tangier had become the foaming cataracts of Niagara in North America (sometimes alternated with a topical spectacle of "Bringing the French and Dutch prizes into the Port of Plymouth"); and the storm and shipwreck was retained by popular demand. The second act presented three new scenes: "the setting of the sun after a rainy day near the cliffs of Dover," "the rising of the moon with a waterspout on the coast of Japan," and, the *pièce de résistance, Satan arraying his Troops on the Banks of a Fiery Lake with the Raising of the Palace of Pandemonium from Milton* (fig. 124).[38]

It would be an exaggeration to say that the painterly illusions of the Eidophusikon had been relinquished – indeed, in respect of topographical art they were enhanced. But the new program of 1782 exhibited a marked shift toward the theatrical and spectacular. It was much more recognizably a popular commercial show along the lines of the famous Patagonian puppets of the 1770s or Cox's exhibitions of ingenious automata and jewelry. The inclusion of Niagara, which de Loutherbourg had never actually seen, was a blatant appeal to contemporary tourist fascinations.[39] The waterspout scene had been pioneered in several pantomimes, though he had grafted on the completely fanciful setting of the Japanese coastline for exotic effect. The topical patriotic naval spectacle of prizes at Plymouth incorporated what had become a de Loutherbourg specalty at Drury Lane, famed for the minute accuracy of its ship models, sail settings, and tiny mechanical men rowing in synchronization.[40]

The key innovation of 1782, however, was the Pandemonium scene: not only was this a miniature theatrical narrative peopled with actors, albeit mechanical ones, but of its leitmotiv was also explicitly literary and occultic. According to one critic, its novelty derived from being "one of the most sublime spectacles ever produced by the hand of science."[41] W. H. Pyne's eyewitness description is well known but is worth quoting again: "Here in the foreground of a vista, stretching an immeasurable length to mountains, ignited from their bases to their lofty summits, with many-coloured flame, a chaotic mass rose in dark majesty,

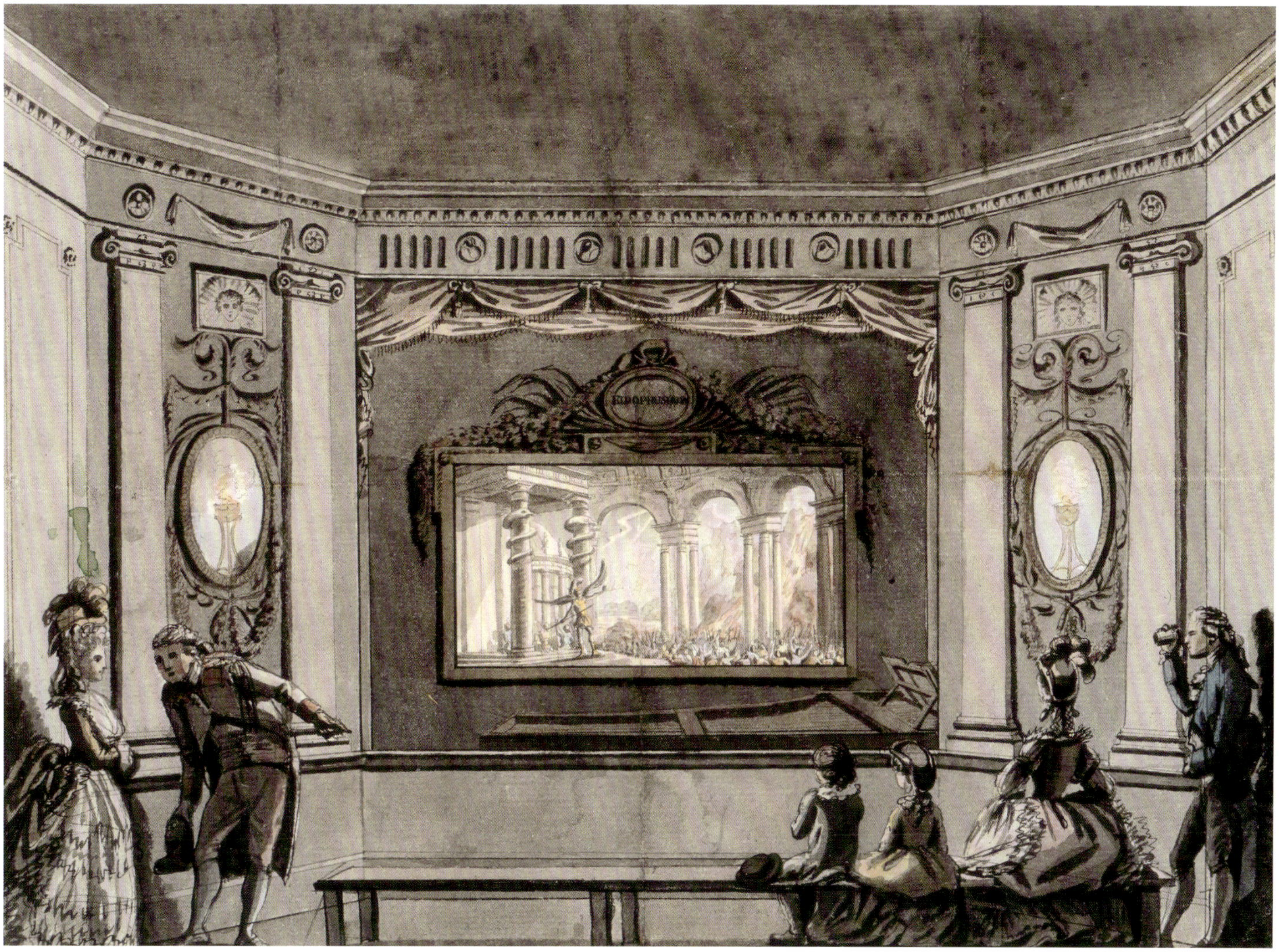

124 Edward Francis Burney, *The Eidophusikon showing Satan arraying his Troops on the Banks of a Fiery Lake with the Raising of the Palace of Pandemonium from Milton*, c. 1782, watercolor, 19.7 × 27.3 cm ($7\frac{3}{4} \times 10\frac{3}{4}$ in.), The Trustees of the British Museum, London, 1963-7-16-1

which gradually assumed form until it stood, the interior of a vast temple of gorgeous architecture, bright as molten brass, seemingly composed of unconsuming and unquenchable fire."[42]

There were probably both positive and negative reasons for the show's tilt toward openly spectacular and magical effects. On the negative side, de Loutherbourg must have experienced his first taste of the fickle attention span and voracious appetite for novelty of paying audiences. After around eighty performances at five shillings a head, he discovered that he had exhausted the appetite and pockets of London's art-minded audience (even of his most ardent fan, Gainsborough). Having successfully wooed the critics in 1781, the new program was designed both to renew the interest of tasteful art viewers and to extend his reach in the direction of less educated, more sensationally minded members of the public.

By 1782, moreover, the range of competition for spectacular London entertainments had suddenly increased. Within a small geographical radius, the Eidophusikon had to compete with such new drawcards as the necromantic, technological, and scientific "wonders, wonders, wonders" of Dr. Gustavus

Katterfelto and his spark-projecting black cats, and the still more alluring appeal of Dr. James Graham's Temple of Health, complete with magnetically charged bed for accomplishing sexual enhancements to the strains of the glass harpsichord.[43] The flock of fashionable and well-heeled crowds to both venues – in one of which, Schomberg House, he shared premises with Gainsborough – was a reminder both of the caliber of rival virtuosi and of the rewards that could be won from commercial spectacles.

Late in 1781, de Loutherbourg had also taken a private commission to mount a new spectacle for money, and this undoubtedly came to influence the shape and tone of the drawcard Pandemonium scene of the following year. He had been hired to produce an elaborate sound and light show at Fonthill-Splendens, the Wiltshire country house of William Beckford, a fabulously wealthy young aesthete and dabbler in the occult, who later had to flee to Portugal and Paris to escape charges of homosexuality. After visiting de Loutherbourg's house for a private showing of the Eidophusikon, young Beckford was entranced by his "experiments" and "deceptions."[44] He spoke to him about producing a multimedia and multi-sensual spectacle to entertain his most intimate friends. For three days over Christmas, de Loutherbourg's spectacles thus ravished the senses of Beckford's guests, including his boy lover William Courtenay, his equally besotted woman lover Louisa Beckford, and his own artistic mentor, the mysterious Russian-born landscape painter Alexander Cozens. According to Beckford, the "mystagogue" de Loutherbourg "poured his fervid imagination" into simulating Oriental scenes using magic lanterns and exotic scents, sensual tastes, and the haunting sounds of castrati singing, all blending to create "a realm of the Fairy, or rather, perhaps, a Demon Temple beneath the earth set apart for tremendous mysteries . . ."[45]

In all likelihood de Loutherbourg prepared transparencies, magic lantern slides, and tableaux developed in part from his earlier repertoire of Eastern settings in pantomimes such as *The Christmas Tale*, *The Sultan*, *Selima and Azor*, and *Semiramis*. All these had featured Oriental temples and seraglios, sometimes materializing out of lush gardens, sometimes catching fire and dissolving into sulphurous smoke.[46] The theme of a descent into the Islamic underworld of Eblis was a key feature of the Fonthill event, and was almost certainly prescribed by Beckford who had long been obsessed with this idea through Eastern texts he had translated.[47] So intoxicating were Philippe's spectral effects of this underworld that they were said to have triggered sex orgies among the guests. Perhaps more constructively, Beckford claimed the spectacle as the inspiration for triggering his own gothic literary masterpiece, *Vathek* (1786).[48] It may have been the literary-minded Beckford, too, who suggested that de Loutherbourg adapt the Eblis tableau into an Eidophusikon scene featuring the better known and more respectable Christian underworld theme of Milton's Pandemonium, especially since it was also suffused with alchemical references.[49]

When displayed early in 1782 the impact of this last scene exceeded anything the Eidophusikon had shown to date. Viewers and critics sensed that de Loutherbourg had crossed a new threshold of innovation. Although sudden and uncanny manifestations of exotic temples had been a stock feature of several of the magically themed Drury Lane pantomimes such as *The Christmas Tale*, critics were dazzled by the Pandemonium scene's evocation of a gothic mood of "magnificent horror" which "strikes terror and admiration on the mind."[50] The more powerful Argand lamps and elaborate sound effects of thunder, lightning, and boiling asphalt also grabbed attention. Pyne dubbed the last innovation a "picturesque of sound." Another critic summarized general opinion in saying of the scene: "It was a flight which only the genius of Loutherbourg could reach."[51] He had, in effect, produced a "phantasmagoria" – a miniature version of the type of spectral shows that the scientific entrepreneurs Paul Philipstal and Gaspard Etienne Robertson contrived for Berlin and Paris audiences some years later. By the end of the eighteenth century, magic lantern ghost shows of this kind were being staged by commercial showmen in all the major cities of Europe. Although de Loutherbourg's primacy is never acknowledged, the "phantasmagoria" has been seen by some cultural analysts as a foundational moment in the evolution of modern cinema and aesthetics.[52]

* * *

Why, given the critical and financial success of the Eidophusikon, did de Loutherbourg decide to close the show after the 1782 program and to cease experimenting with its stunningly original multi-media possibilities? When it eventually reopened in 1786, he had sold both the name and equipment to a former associate called Chapman, who seems to have retained and operated the show in London and the provinces well into the 1790s. De Loutherbourg has left no explanation for his abrupt action, and one can only guess at his motives. Perhaps he found the preparation of new repertoires exhausting, though one imagines he could simply have designed models for associates to construct. True, too, the mid-1780s brought him several new career distractions. A flurry of visits from foreign mystics caused him to become increasingly preoccupied with occult studies, a tendency further stimulated by the fashionable advent of mesmerism in London through the lectures of John de Mainauduc in 1785.[53] He was also lured out of retirement in the same year by a handsome offer from Covent Garden to plan and oversee the special effects pantomime of the century, *Omai, or a Trip Around the World*. During the mid-1780s, too, he seems to have discovered a fresh source of inspiration for landscape painting in the wild scenery and rich mythology of Derbyshire, Cumberland, and Wales, which he had first explored when sketching for the pantomime *Wonders of Derbyshire*.[54]

This last development may hint at why he decided to sell the Eidophusikon. It seems likely that by the end of 1782 de Loutherbourg realized that he had arrived at an aesthetic crossroads. If he were to continue to compete in the brutal hurly-burly of London's show world, his program would have to move in increasingly commercial and spectacular directions. Quite apart from any financial risks involved, this could entail serious social costs. Newspaper reports of 1783–4 revealed all too starkly the short shelf life of spectacle virtuosi like Katterfelto and Graham, both of whom were then routinely lampooned as charlatans, quacks, and empirics. Most worrying of all, the taint of showmanship was beginning to attach to de Loutherbourg's own work as an easel painter. By the mid-1780s he was experiencing a growing chorus of criticism from arbiters of

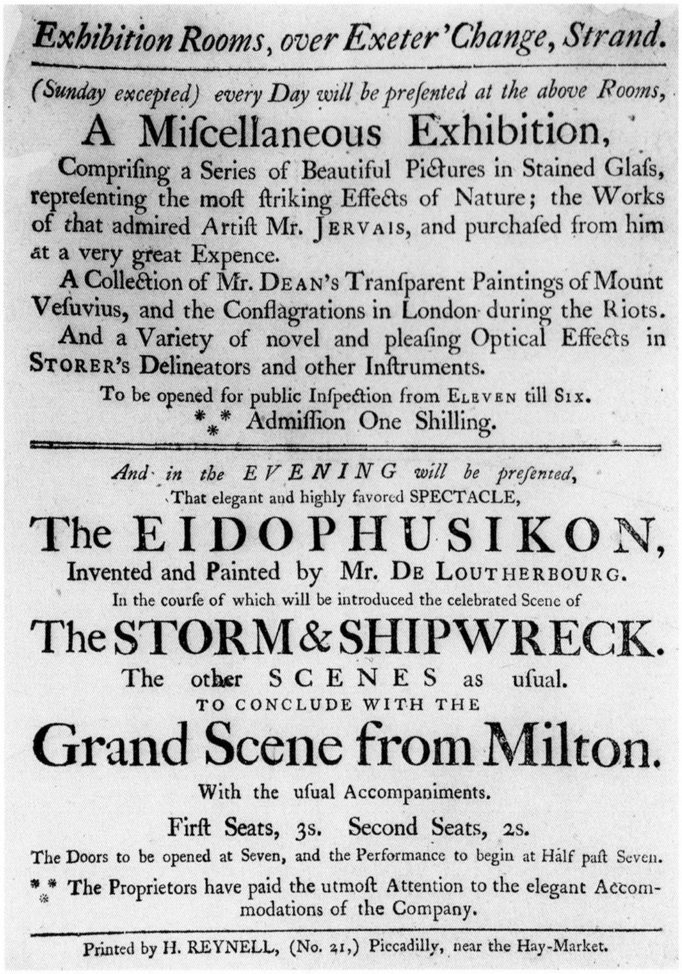

Exhibition Rooms, over Exeter 'Change, Strand.

(Sunday excepted) every Day will be preſented at the above Rooms,

A Miſcellaneous Exhibition,

Compriſing a Series of Beautiful Pictures in Stained Glaſs, repreſenting the moſt ſtriking Effects of Nature; the Works of that admired Artiſt Mr. JERVAIS, and purchaſed from him at a very great Expence.

A Collection of Mr. DEAN's Tranſparent Paintings of Mount Veſuvius, and the Conflagrations in London during the Riots.

And a Variety of novel and pleaſing Optical Effects in STORER's Delineators and other Inſtruments.

To be opened for public Inſpection from ELEVEN till SIX.

*** Admiſſion One Shilling.

And in the EVENING will be preſented,

That elegant and highly favored SPECTACLE,

The EIDOPHUSIKON,

Invented and Painted by Mr. DE LOUTHERBOURG.

In the courſe of which will be introduced the celebrated Scene of

The STORM & SHIPWRECK.

The other SCENES as uſual.

TO CONCLUDE WITH THE

Grand Scene from Milton.

With the uſual Accompaniments.

Firſt Seats, 3s. Second Seats, 2s.

The Doors to be opened at Seven, and the Performance to begin at Half paſt Seven.

*** The Proprietors have paid the utmoſt Attention to the elegant Accommodations of the Company.

Printed by H. REYNELL, (No. 21,) Piccadilly, near the Hay-Market.

125 Handbill for the Eidophusikon, 1786, letter press, City of Westminster Archives Centre, London

artistic taste such as Peter Pindar (John Wolcot), Horace Walpole, Henry Bate-Dudley, and Anthony Pasquin (John Williams).[55] They ridiculed the contrived theatricality of his themes and compositions, the heavy lacquering of his finishes, and the extreme bronze or vermilion coloring that suffused his landscapes.[56] The clear implication was that his practice as a spectacle expert had coarsened his taste and abilities.[57]

Whether or not this accusation was true is beside the point: it is equally possible that these critics were reacting adversely to the less chaste, more highly colored style characteristic of a French-trained landscape painter or to de Loutherbourg's covert inclusions of alchemical color transitions in many of his paintings. One or two of his friends also suggested that eyesight problems were contributing to the eccentricity of his coloration.[58] Whatever the truth, the implication that working as a spectacle monger was undermining his genius as a painter must have been devastating. There was even a danger that he might find himself squeezed altogether from the cherished republic of English painterly taste.[59] It is no wonder that he decided to sell the Eidophusikon and to embark simultaneously on a new mission to explore romantic British locales and landscape styles.

The Eidophusikon did not fail after its sale to Chapman, but there is no doubting the change in its status and audience when it reopened in 1786 as an explicitly commercial public performance located in the spectacle hub of the Grand Salon at Exeter Exchange (fig. 125).[60] It boasted a much larger seating capacity, graduated and cheaper pricing, more lurid advertisements, an increase in the numbers of topical spectacles, and a supporting program that included performing dogs and a 3 foot 3 inch guitar-playing dwarf from Poland (and, later still, an interlude of the magical deceptions of Sieur Comus).[61] By 1786, then, only five years after its inception, history's first moving picture show had formally gravitated from the elite art salon to the huckster world of popular showbusiness.

When Philippe de Loutherbourg thus relinquished his brilliant and original invention of a moving picture show, Britain undoubtedly lost the future fruits of a genius of special effects. Who knows where he might have taken his revolutionary visual spectacle had he continued to develop it during the remaining thirty years of his life? In the end, though, he should be granted a measure of historical respect for managing to maintain the delicate balance between his contending aspirations and talents as an eighteenth-century British artist, seeker, and showman.

Notes

INTRODUCTION

1 *Boswell's Life of Johnson; Together with, Journal of a Tour to the Hebrides; and, Johnson's Diary of a Journey into North Wales*, ed. George Birkbeck Hill, 6 vols, Oxford 1934–50, III, 176. Letter dated July 20, 1762. I am grateful to Anne K. Mellor and Sonja Steuber for this reference.

2 Quoted in *Thomas Gainsborough, 1727–1788*, exh. cat. ed. Michael Rosenthal and Martin Myrone, London 2002, 219.

3 Robyn Asleson and Shelley M. Bennett, eds, *British Paintings at the Huntington*, New Haven and London 2002, 112.

4 Uvedale Price, *On the Picturesque* (1794), ed. Thomas Dick Lauder, Bart., Edinburgh and London 1842, 393.

5 William T. Whitley, *Thomas Gainsborough*, New York and London 1915, 313–14, and Kenneth Clark, *English Romantic Poets and Landscape Painting*, London 1945, 3.

6 Sir Joshua Reynolds, *Discourses on Art*, ed. Robert Wark, New Haven and London 1975, 254.

7 William Hazlitt quoted in Ellis Waterhouse, "Gainsborough's 'Fancy Pictures'," *Burlington Magazine* LXXXVIII June 1946, 137.

8 Asleson and Bennett, *British Paintings*, 112

9 H. H. Kames, *Essays on the Principles of Morality and Natural Religion, In Two Parts*, Edinburgh 1751, 16

10 Adam Smith, *Theory of Moral Sentiments*, ed. D. D. Raphael and A. L. Macfie, Oxford 1976, 9.

11 David Hume, *A Treatise of Human Nature* (1739–40), ed. L. A. Selby-Bigge, Oxford 1888, 470.

12 In saying this I want to make clear that I disagree with the neo-conservative rewriting of British moral philosophy by Gertrude Himmelfarb, *The Road to Modernity: The British, French, and American Enlightenments*, New York 2004, which would have one believe that moral philosophers such as Shaftesbury and Smith anticipate the neo-cons' "sociology of virtue."

13 George Cheyne, *The English Malady: or, a Treatise of Nervous Diseases of all Kinds; as Spleens, Vapours, Lowness of Spirits, Hypochondriacal, and Hysteric Distempers, etc.*, London and Bath 1735.

14 On Cheyne and his relevance to sensibility see G. J. Barker-Benfield, *The Culture of Sensibility: Sex and Society in Eighteenth-Century Britain*, Chicago and London 1992, 6–36. On Cheyne and his relevance to Gainsborough see Susan Sloman in this book.

15 Vicesimus Knox, *Essays Moral and Literary*, 2 vols, London 1795, I, 2.

16 *Ibid.*, 7.

17 *Ibid.*, 3–4.

18 See Barker-Benfield, *Culture of Sensibility*, 351–95; Janet Todd, *Sensibility, an Introduction*, London and New York 1986; John Brewer, *The Pleasures of the Imagination: English Culture in the Eighteenth Century*, 120–22; and John Barrell in this book.

19 *The Letters of Thomas Gainsborough*, ed. John Hayes, New Haven and London 2001, 68, letter no. 40, Gainsborough to William Jackson, June 4 [year unknown].

20 *Ibid.*, 152, letter no. 91, Gainsborough to Sir William Chambers, April 27, 1783.

21 See Marcia Pointon, "Gainsborough and the Landscape of Retirement," *Art History* II (December 1979), 441–55; John Hayes, *The Landscape Paintings of Thomas Gainsborough*, 2 vols, Ithaca, N.Y. 1983, I, 149–56; Michael Rosenthal, *The Art of Thomas Gainsborough: "a little business for the Eye,"* New Haven and London 1999, 204–11.

22 Price, *On the Picturesque*, 408.

23 The only variation from this formula is the Scudemore painting, *Cottage Door with Girl and Pigs* (Ipswich, Suffolk), which shows a dejected young girl seated at the steps of a cottage observing a pig while a woman stands at the door with a broom. Reproduced here as pl. IV.

24 Sigmund Freud, "The Uncanny" (1919), in *Collected Papers*, ed. Joan Riviere, 4 vols, New York 1959, IV, 376–7, 399 and 403.

25 For a summary of other interpretations of these images see Hayes, *Landscape Paintings*, I, 148–50.

26 *Ibid.*, II, 156.

27 *Letters*, 40, letter no. 22, Gainsborough to William Jackson, August 23 [1767].

28 *Ibid.*, 39.

29 Lawrence Sterne quoted in Ann Jessie Van Sant, *Eighteenth-Century Sensibility and the Novel*, Cambridge 1993, 84.

30 Smith, *Theory of Moral Sentiments*, 1–13 and 113.

31 Knox, *Essays*, I, 261.

32 Roger de Piles, *The Principles of Painting*, trans. by a Painter, London 1743, 282–3.

33 Lomazzo quoted by Martin Kemp, *The Science of Art: Optical Themes in Western Art from Brunelleschi to Seurat*, New Haven and London 1990, 83.

34 Nicholas Hilliard, *A Treatise Concerning the Arte of Limning*, ed. R. K. R. Thornton and T. G. S. Cain, Ashington (Northumberland) and Manchester 1992, 57.

35 Michael Baxandall, *Patterns of Intention: On the Historical Explanation of Pictures*, New Haven and London 1985, 92.

36 Samuel Richardson, *Clarissa, or the History of a Young Lady*, Harmondsworth (Middlesex) 1985, 824.

37 *Letters*, 26, letter no. 13, Gainsborough to James Unwin, March 1, 1764.

38 On this subject and "vulgar Lockianism" see Baxandall, *Patterns*, 89–97.

39 Van Sant, *Eighteenth-Century Sensibility*, 83–91.

40 Reynolds, *Discourses*, 258.

41 St James Chronicle (1777) quoted in Rosenthal and Myrone, *Gainsborough*, 124.

42 Similar points are made by Asfour and Williamson in their important book *Gainsborough's Vision*, Liverpool 1991, 95–127, and by William Vaughan in this book.

43 Reynolds, *Discourses*, 258.

44 This report of "Nollekins" Smith is quoted by Whitley, *Gainsborough*, 247.

45 Asfour and Wiliamson, *Gainsborough's Vision*, 120–27.

46 Reynolds, *Discourses*, 259. For Locke on custom see Asfour and Williamson, *Gainsborough's Vision*, 16–17.

47 On the importance of process in sensibility see Northrop Fry, "Towards Defining an Age of Sensibility," *English Literary History* XXIII (June 1956), 144–52.

48 For a thorough account of music and its meaning for Gainsborough's art see Asfour and Williamson, *Gainsborough's Vision*, 128–62.

49 This image of Garrick as the "instinctual" actor is not unlike the image of Gainsborough (first propounded by Reynolds) as an instinctual painter.

50 Anon., *Garrick, ou, les acteures anglois*, Paris 1796, 23.

51 Denis Diderot, *The Paradox of Acting*, trans. Walter Herries Pollock, introduction by Lee Strasberg, New York 1957, 34–9.

52 Lillian Elvira Preston, "Philippe Jacques de Loutherbourg: Eighteenth-Century Romantic Artist and Scene Designer", PhD diss., University of Florida 1957, 46–9; Christopher L. Baugh, *Garrick and de Loutherbourg*, Cambridge and Alexandria, Va. 1990; and W. J. Lawrence, "The Pioneers of Modern English Stage-Mounting: Phillipe Jacques de Loutherbourg, RA," *Magazine of Art* XVIII, 1895. See too Austin Dobson, *At Prior Park and Other Papers*, London 1912; Ralph G. Allen, "The Eidophusikon," *Theater Design and Technology* VII (December 1966), 12–16; and Ephraim Hardcastle [W. H. Pyne], *Wine and Walnuts; or, After Dinner Chit-Chat*, 2 vols, London 1823, II, 281–304.

53 Henry Angelo, *Reminiscences*, 2 vols, London 1828, II, 326.

54 De Piles, *Principles*, 186.

55 Color and light were of essential importance to the science of perception, for once the eye was imagined as a Lockian *camera obscura*, the problem of focus (distinctness in depth) and acuity (distinctness across the visual field) emerged. How was it that the eye saw objects sharply and not simply as colored blots? The answer to this question and others depended on a better understanding of the anatomy of the eye – in particular, the lens, the iris, the crystalline humor, and the rods and cones – as well as on an understanding of light and the effect that various wave lengths of the spectrum had on perception. In most theories of perception color and light were important to the accurate perception of depth (acuity) and shape (focus). On this subject see Baxandall, *Patterns*, 75–104.

56 Lawrence, "Pioneers of Modern English Stage-Mounting," 174.

57 Rüdiger Joppien, *Philippe Jacques de Loutherbourg, RA, 1740–1812*, exh. cat., London 1973, n.p., section on"Theater."

58 *The Diary of Joseph Farington R.A.*, ed. Catherine Cave, Kenneth Garlick, Angus Macintyre, and Evelyn Newby, 16 vols, New Haven and London 1978–98, V, 1645, entry for March 28, 1804.

59 *Letters*, 107, letter no. 63, Gainsborough to David Garrick [1772].

60 On this subject see John Gage, *Colour and Culture: Practice and Meaning from Antiquity to Abstraction*, London, Boston, and Toronto 1994, 192.

61 Kemp, *Science of Art*, 292–6.

62 One cannot help but wonder if this fascination with colored light, arial effects in landscape and with transparency in pigments might not owe something to the general scientific preoccupation in the eighteenth century with atmosphere, that is, with the composition of air and the numerous experiments done with air pumps and other such devices. Such an interest looks forward to the arial effects of Turner and the tremendous interest at the turn of the century in the atmospheric and light effects achieved in watercolor.

63 Philippe de La Hire quoted in Gage, *Colour and Culture*, 192; also discussed in Baxandall, *Patterns*, 90.

64 Helen Glanville, "Gainsborough as Artist and Artisan," *A Nest of Nightingales: Thomas Gainsborough and the Linley Sisters*, exh. cat., London 1988, 24–5, and Rica Jones and Martin Postle, "Gainsborough in His Painting Room," in Rosenthal and Myrone, *Thomas Gainsborough*, 29.

65 Jones and Postle, "Gainsborough in His Painting Room," 36, and Whitley, *Gainsborough*, 368.

66 Reynolds, *Discourses*, 251.

67 Rosenthal, *Art of Thomas Gainsborough*, 113–16.

68 Kemp, *Science of Art*, 292; also De Piles, *Principles*, 211.

69 Reynolds, *Discourses*, 259.

70 Glanville, "Gainsborough as Artist and Artisan," 20–22.

71 Jones and Postle, "Gainsborough in His Painting Room," 30.

72 Mark Leonard, "Treatment Record," The J. Paul Getty Museum, Los Angeles, September 1999, and Jones and Postle, "Gainsborough in His Painting Room," 38.

73 Glanvillle, "Gainsborough as Artist and Artisan," 21.

74 For general accounts of early modern spectacles see Barbara Maria Stafford and Frances Terpak, *Devices of Wonder from the World in a Box to Images on the Screen*, exh. cat., Los Angeles 2001, and Richard D. Altick, *The Shows of London*, Cambridge, Mass. 1978. For an interesting discussion of Sir William Hamilton's mechanical model of Vesuvius, see Brent Sørensen, "Sir William Hamilton's Vesuvian Apparatus," *Apollo*, DVII (May 2004), 50–58.

75 *London Courant, and Westminster Chronicle*, 2 May 1781, 3.

76 Lawrence, "Pioneers of Modern English Stage-Mounting," 176.

77 Preston, *Philippe Jacques de Loutherbourg*, 200.

78 *Whitehall Evening Post*, 1 March 1781 quoted in Lawrence, "Pioneers of Modern English Stage-Mounting," 176.

79 Preston, *Philippe Jacques de Loutherbourg*, 208.

80 [Pyne], *Wine and Walnuts*, I, 295–6.
81 Rosenthal and Myrone, *Thomas Gainsborough*, 256.
82 As reported in Edward Edwards, *Anecdotes of Painters*, 1808, and cited by Hayes, *Landscape Paintings*, I, 142; Rosenthal and Myrone, *Gainsborough*, 256; and William Vaughan in this book.
83 Catalogue of W. B. Cooke's *Exhibition of Drawings*, 9 Soho Square, London, 1824, 14, quoted in Hayes, *Landscape Paintings*, I, 142.
84 Unfortunately, de Loutherbourg's transparencies do not survive. Given the fact that the Eidophusikon was a highly illusionistic spectacle and given the realism of de Loutherbourg's painting style, it is reasonable to suppose that his transparencies were similarly illusionistic.
85 William Vaughan, *Gainsborough*, London 2002, 188.
86 *The Diary of Joseph Farington R.A.*, ed. Catherine Cave, Kenneth Garlick, Angus Macintyre, and Evelyn Newby, 16 vols, New Haven and London 1978–98, IV, 1592, entry for 17 June 1801.
87 W. H. Pyne in *Somerset House Gazette*, II, (10 April 1824), 8.
88 This work is believed to be one of two cottage subjects (lot 78 or lot 69) offered for sale in the artist's posthumous sale at Shomberg House, March–May 1789. It is presently in the hands of Anthony Mould of Historical Portraits, Dover Street, London.
89 Gainsborough's transparencies appear to have been a further development of the art of transparency painting. Transparencies had been used in the theater as far back as Inigo Jones's court masks. However, later in the eighteenth century they appear to have come into vogue as a mode of domestic amusement and decoration. In his *Instructions for Painting Transparencies* (1799) Edward Orme explained to readers how to varnish watercolored prints so that they became transparent and could be viewed with light behind them. Gainsborough's work with transparencies seems to have involved a deeper exploration of color and light than what one finds in de Loutherbourg or Orme. His showbox had several slats in front of the candles. These slats could have been fitted with colored filters. This is a common feature found in commercially produced transparency boxes of the early nineteenth century such as John Heaviside Clark's Portable Diorama (1826). The filters would have colored the candlelight against which the glass slides were viewed. Such filters would have cast an overall hue or, depending on how they were painted, a variety of hues, against which the painted scene would have been viewed. The filters would thus have modulated the colors of the painted scene. By changing the filters Gainsborough could have change the light and mood of the image. When the filters were removed and the scene was viewed through candlelight alone the more vivid coloristic effects described by Pyne would have been clearly evident.
90 Hayes, *Landscape Paintings*, I, 150.
91 Douglas Hall, "Tabley House Papers," *Walpole Society* XXXVIII (1960–62), 70.
92 John Britton, *The Autobiography of John Britton, F.S.A., in three parts*, London 1849, 99.
93 *John Constable's Correspondence*, ed. R. B. Beckett, Ipswich (Suffolk) 1964, II, 73–4.
94 Christiana Payne, *Rustic Simplicity: Scenes of Cottage Life in Nineteenth-Century British Art*, exh. cat., London 1998, 60.
95 *John Constable's Discourses*, ed. R. B. Beckett, Ipswich (Suffolk), 1970, 67.
96 De Piles, *Principles*, 2–3.

"INNOCENCE AND HEALTH"

I am most grateful to the librarians of The Wellcome Institute for the History and Understanding of Medicine, London, London Metropolitan Archives, the London Library, and Bath Central Library and, personally, to Ann Bermingham for encouraging me to develop this theme.

1 *The Collected Works of Oliver Goldsmith*, IV, ed. Arthur Friedman, Oxford 1966, *The Deserted Village* (1770), 289, lines 57–62: "A time there was, ere England's griefs began, / When every rood of ground maintained its man; / For him light labour spread her wholesome store, / Just gave what life required, but gave no more. / His best companions, innocence and health; / And his best riches, ignorance of wealth."
2 Robyn Asleson and Shelley M. Bennett note the link between the "genteel fantasy of cottage life" and the contemporary literature of child-rearing in *British Paintings at the Huntington*, New Haven and London 2001, 116, n. 8.
3 William Cadogan, *Essay on Nursing and the Management of Children from their Birth to Three Years of Age*, London 1757 (7th ed., 1st ed. 1748), 25–6.
4 *Ibid.*, 42.
5 George Cheyne, *An Essay of Health and Long Life*, London and Bath 1724, 95.
6 Christiana Payne suggests that an observer of Gainsborough's paintings of poor children "might experience all the pleasurable emotions associated with sensibility, without any of its practical drawbacks"; Christiana Payne, *Toil and Plenty: Images of the Agricultural Landscape in England 1780–1890*, exh. cat., Nottingham and New Haven 1993, 50.
7 *The Letters of Thomas Gainsborough*, ed. John Hayes, New Haven and London 2001, 33, letter no. 17, Gainsborough to Percival Beaumont, 7 January 1765. On January 21 Gainsborough explained to his friend James Unwin that although he generally refused to work in London because of his poor health, he could not resist the Duke of Bedford's request; *ibid.*, 35, letter no. 18.
8 *Ibid.*, 23, letter no. 12, Gainsborough to James Unwin, from Bath, 30 December 1763.
9 *Ibid.*, 21, letter no. 10, Gainsborough to James Unwin, from Bath, 15 September 1763.
10 *Ibid.*, 25, letter no. 13, Gainsborough to James Unwin, from Bath, 1 March 1764.
11 *Ibid.*, 29, letter no. 14, Gainsborough to James Unwin, from Bath, 10 July [1764].
12 *Ibid.*, 58, letter no. 35, Gainsborough to David Garrick, from Bath, [August 1768]; William T. Whitley, *Thomas Gainsborough*, London 1915, 79.
13 *The Diary of Joseph Farington R.A.*, ed. Catherine Cave, Kenneth Garlick, Angus Macintyre, and Evelyn Newby, 16 vols, New Haven and London 1978–98, IV, 1152 (5 February 1799).
14 *Letters*, 23–4, letter no. 12, Gainsborough to James Unwin, from Bath, 30 December 1763.
15 *Ibid.*, 21, letter no. 10, Gainsborough to James Unwin, from Bath, 15 September 1763.

16 The Duke of Cumberland bought Cypron, an important broodmare, from Sir William St Quintin in 1755; see Richard Green, *Masterpieces from Yorkshire Houses*, exh. cat., York City Art Gallery 1994, 42, no. 5.

17 For Cheyne's relationship with Newton see A. Rupert Hall, *All Was Light: An Introduction to Newton's Optics*, Oxford 1993, 183–5, and Anita Guerini, *Obesity and Depression in the Enlightenment: The Life and Times of George Cheyne*, University of Oklahoma, Norman 2000, xiv–xv.

18 Quoted in Guerini, *Obesity and Depression*, 155.

19 *Ibid.*, 181.

20 George Cheyne, *The English Malady: or, a Treatise of Nervous Diseases of all Kinds; as Spleens, Vapours, Lowness of Spirits, Hypochondriacal, and Hysteric Distempers, etc.*, London and Bath 1735, 338. Samuel Johnson's Dictionary defines "hypochondriacal" as "melancholy; disordered in the imagination" and relates the condition to the two "hypochondres" regions below the ribs. Complaints of the bowels and hypochondria were believed to arise if the blood moved too slowly through the "hypochondres."

21 Cheyne, *Essay of Health*, 94 and 97.

22 Cheyne, *English Malady*, 262.

23 Cheyne, *Essay of Health*, 95; Cheyne, *English Malady*, 180.

24 Quoted in Guerini, *Obesity and Depression*, 163.

25 [Oliver Goldsmith], *The Life of Richard Nash, of Bath, Esq; Extracted principally from his Original Papers*, Bath 1762, 157–8.

26 *Letters*, 186, letter no. 131, Gainsborough to an unknown recipient, n.d. Hayes makes the point that the pun on "galloping" may refer to the artist's reliance on riding as healthy exercise; *ibid.*, 186, letter no. 4.

27 G. S. Rousseau, "Science Books and their Readers in the Eighteenth Century," in *Books and their Readers in Eighteenth-Century England*, ed. Isabel Rivers, Leicester 1982, 217 and 249, n. 99.

28 Clarence Tracy, *A Portrait of Richard Graves*, Toronto 1987, 49; William Falconer, *A Practical Dissertation on the Medicinal Effects of the Bath Waters*, Bath 1790, 164.

29 William T. Whitley, *Artists and their Friends in England 1700–1799*, 2 vols, London 1928, II, 293.

30 *Letters*, 21, letter no. 10, Gainsborough to James Unwin, from Bath, 15 September 1763.

31 Guerini, *Obesity and Depression*, 148.

32 Uvedale Price, *Essay on the Picturesque*, 2 vols, London 1796–8, II, 429–30.

33 Humphry's memoir is published in full in Susan Sloman, *Gainsborough in Bath*, New Haven and London 2002, 57.

34 *Ibid.*, 161.

35 *Letters*, 123–4, letter no. 72, Gainsborough to Giovanni Battista Cipriani, from Bath, 14 February 1774.

36 Ruth K. McClure, *Coram's Children: The London Foundling Hospital in the Eighteenth Century*, New Haven and London 1981, 230–31.

37 *Diary of Joseph Farington*, IV, 1153, entry for February 8, 1799.

38 Whitley, *Artists and their Friends*, II, 127–8.

39 David Tyler, "Gainsborough's Days in Hatton Garden," *Gainsborough's House Review 1992/93*, Sudbury (Suffolk) 1993, 27–32. Tyler documents Gainsborough's and the Foundling Hospital's occupation of Hatton Garden addresses through rate book entries and other contemporary sources.

40 Roy Porter, "Every Human Want," *Enlightened Self-interest: The Foundling Hospital and Hogarth*, eds Rhian Harris and Robin Simon, London 1997, 15, and John Orr and William Barnes, *The Story of the Thomas Coram Foundation for Children and its Art Collection*, London 1997, 12.

41 McClure, *Coram's Children*, 87.

42 *Ibid.*, 92.

43 Porter, "Every Human Want," 15; R. H. Nichols and F. A. Wray, *The History of the Foundling Hospital*, London 1935, 364. Hogarth was official inspector of nurses for Chiswick, Burgh for Chertsey.

44 London Metropolitan Archives, A/FH/MOI/103/125.

45 Sloman, *Gainsborough in Bath*, 178.

46 London Metropolitan Archives, A / FH / A10 / 3 / 7, Nursery Book No. 4, e.g., records children under Clutterbuck's care including child no. 15360, Mary Packer, sent to nurse Ann Hunt of Richmond on February 5, 1760.

47 London Metropolitan Archives, A / FH / A10 / 16 / 3, record of inspection of child no. 11183 on 15 January 1759.

48 McClure, *Coram's Children*, 90. Burgh was pursued by the Hospital between 1759 and 1763. He had been a governor since 1750: see Nichols and Wray, *Foundling Hospital*, 364. Burgh was already under suspicion of misappropriating funds from the Duke of Beaufort's estate, although the managers of the Foundling Hospital were evidently unaware of this. Gainsborough was still using him as a banker in 1759 but appears to have ceased contact with him after that date; see Sloman, *Gainsborough in Bath*, 27–9.

49 *Journals of the House of Commons from November the 11th, 1766 . . . To March the 10th 1768* (repr. 1803), XXXI, 248–9.

50 M. Dorothy George, *London Life in the 18th Century*, London 1930, 47.

51 Hugh Downman, *Infancy, or the Management of Children, A Poem in Three Parts*, London 1774–6, *Book the First*, 1774, 12 and 15.

52 John O'Keeffe, *Recollections of the Life of John O'Keeffe, written by Himself*, 2 vols, London 1826, I, 134–5.

53 John Yeoman, *The Diary of the Visits of John Yeoman to London in the Years 1774 and 1777*, ed. Macleod Yearsley, London 1935, 24. John Yeoman, a Somerset farmer and potter, was visiting his London cousin in April 1774.

54 O'Keeffe, *Recollections*, I, 135.

55 *Court and Private Life in the Time of Queen Charlotte: being the Journals of Mrs Papendiek . . .*, ed. Mrs. V. Delves Broughton, 2 vols, London 1887, I, 271.

56 *Ibid.*, 67–8, 130.

57 *Daily Advertiser*, no. 13713, December 2, 1774; *ibid.*, no. 13709, 28 November 1774.

58 *Ibid.*, no. 13698, 15 November 1774.

59 Anon., *The Good Nurse; or, Hints on the Management of the Sick and Lying-in Chamber and the Nursery*, London 1828, 271.

60 *Ibid.*, 273.

61 Ephraim Hardcastle [W. H. Pyne], *Wine and Walnuts or, After Dinner Chit-Chat*, 2 vols, London 1823, II, 223.

62 Nichols and Wray, *Foundling Hospital*, 363 (Clutterbuck), 357 (Hoare), 359 (Hayman), 368 (Ellis), 377 (Leycester), 383 (St Quintin), 383 (Bell), 387 (Piggott).

63 The portrait is still in the possession of the Marine Society; Ellis Waterhouse, *Gainsborough*, London 1958, 92, no. 665.

64 Ernest Caulfield, *The Infant Welfare Movement in the Eighteenth Century*, New York 1931, 159–60. Gainsborough was a friend of Dodd; see *Letters*, 120, no. 71.

65 Derek Hudson, *Sir Joshua Reynolds, A Personal Study*, London 1958, 90.

66 Unpublished letter dated December 24, 1762, from Richard Graves, probably to the poet Shenstone, Taunton, Somerset Record Office, DD/SK 281/1 letter 13.

67 Timothy Clifford, Antony Griffiths, and Martin Royalton-Kisch, *Gainsborough and Reynolds in the British Museum*, London 1978, 22, no. 70.

68 Quoted in Whitley, *Artists and their Friends*, II, 128. It has been noted that Gainsborough appears to have quoted from Reynolds's *Charity* in his *Charity Relieving Distress* (Martin Postle in *Thomas Gainsborough, 1727–1788*, exh. cat., ed. Michael Rosenthal and Martin Myrone, London 2002, 232, no. 129), but it is possible that both artists were referring to a common source.

SPECTACLES FOR REPUBLICANS

1 These paintings comprise (I give them the descriptive but dourly utilitarian titles provided by John Hayes in *The Landscape Paintings of Thomas Gainsborough: A Critical Text and Catalogue Raisonné*, 2 vols, London and Ithaca, N.Y. 1982) *Wooded Landscape with Family grouped outside a Cottage, Woodcutter returning, and Flock of Sheep* (*The Woodcutter's Return*), c. 1772–3, cat. 105 (Belvoir Castle); *Hilly Landscape with Peasant Family at a Cottage Door, Children playing and Woodcutter returning*, c. 1778, cat. 121 (Cincinnati); *Wooded Landscape with Peasant Family at a Cottage Door and Footbridge over a Stream* (*The Cottage Door*), 1780, cat. 123 (Huntington); *Wooded Landscape with Mother and Child and Housemaid outside a Cottage, Girl with Three Pigs at the Foot of the Steps, Cows, Shepherd and Scattered Sheep near a Pool, and Distant Buildings*, 1786, cat. 174 (Ipswich); *Wooded Landscape with Family grouped outside a Cottage, Mounted Peasant and Packhorses, and Distant Mountain* (*Peasant smoking at a Cottage Door*), 1788, cat. 185 (University of California, Los Angeles). There are also a number of drawings of cottage-door scenes, some illustrated in John Hayes, *The Drawings of Thomas Gainsborough*, 2 vols (London 1970).

2 *The Letters of Thomas Gainsborough*, ed. John Hayes, New Haven and London 2001, 68, letter no. 40, Gainsborough to William Jackson, from Bath, June 4 [year unknown], and see Ann Bermingham on Gainsborough's "cottage doors" as "idealized autobiography" (among other things), *Landscape and Ideology: The English Rustic Tradition 1740–1860*, Berkeley, Los Angeles, and London 1986, 105–8.

3 For an account of Gaisborough's landscapes as images of retirement (though of a more philosophical notion of retirement than I take them to be) see Marcia Pointon, "Gainsborough and the Landscape of Retirement," *Art History* II, no. 4 (December 1979) 441–55.

4 William Cowper, *The Task*, book I, lines 220–51.

5 Adam Smith, *An Inquiry into the Nature and Causes of the Wealth of Nations*, ed. R. H. Campbell, A. S. Skinner, and W. B. Todd, Oxford 1976, 869–70.

6 I offer a fuller version of my reading of these paintings in *The Dark Side of the Landscape: The Rural Poor in English Painting 1730–1840*, Cambridge 1980, ch. 2; see also (among many other discussions) Michael Rosenthal, *The Art of Thomas Gainsborough: "a little business for the Eye,"* New Haven and London 1999, 204ff.

7 Cowper, *The Task*, book IV, line 374.

8 Hannah More, *Tales for the Common People and other Cheap Repository Tracts*, ed. Clare MacDonald Shaw, Nottingham 2002, 67.

9 John Thomas Smith, *Remarks on Rural Scenery; with Twenty Etchings of Cottages, from Nature*, London 1797, 7–9.

10 Mary A. Favret, "Coming Home: the Public Spaces of Romantic War," *Studies in Romanticism* XXXIII (Winter 1994) 539–48.

11 John Thelwall, *The Peripatetic*, ed. Judith Thompson, Detroit 2001, 133–40.

12 William Paley, *Reasons for Contentment, addressed to the Labouring Part of the British Public*, in *Political Writings of the 1790s*, ed. Greg Claeys, London 1995, vol. 7, 224–6.

13 *The Happy Cottager* (London, 4 April 1794); *Virtue in a Humble Cott* (London, 22 July 1793).

14 The only examples I know of this pair of prints are separated now. *John Bull in his Glory* is in the Library of Congress (PC 2 – J [P&P]), Washington, D.C.; *Citizen CoupeTête in his Misery* in the British Museum, London; see Mary Dorothy George, *Catalogue of Political and Personal Satires preserved in the Department of Prints and Drawing in the British Museum*, London 1942, VII, no. 8293. Both prints are trimmed, with the result that *John Bull* has no details of artist, publisher, or date; *Citizen CoupeTête* bears the name T. Ovenden and the truncated imprint "[–]y 29 1793 by I. Downs, 240 Strand." George suggests that January was the month of publication, though it could possibly be May; February is out of the question, as 1793 was not a leap year. Both Diana Donald, writing of *John Bull in his Glory* in *The Age of Caricature: Satirical Prints in the Reign of George III*, New Haven and London 1996, 235–6, n. 106, and George, in her entry on *Citizen CoupeTête*, point out that each image required a pendant, but this essay is I believe the first occasion on which they are identified as a pair. Ovenden produced, also in 1793, an engraving "The End of Pain" (depicting Paine hanged from a lamp-bracket), probably commissioned either by the Association or by the government.

15 See John Keane, *Tom Paine: A Political Life*, London 1995, 337.

16 Lawrence Brown, *A Catalogue of British Historical Medals 1760–1960*. Volume III: *The Accession of Edward VII to 1960*, London 1995, 275.

17 *Ibid.*

18 More, *Cheap Repository Tracts*, 46.

19 Donald, *Age of Caricature*, 156.

20 *Ibid.*

21 *Ibid.*, 156–7.

22 Uvedale Price, *Essays on the Picturesque*, 2 vols, London 1796–8, II, 366–8.

GAINSBOROUGH'S COTTAGE DOORS

1 *The Letters of Thomas Gainsborough*, ed. John Hayes, New Haven and London 2001, 176, letter no. 110, Gainsborough to Sir Joshua Reynolds, from London, July 1788.

2 Sir Joshua Reynolds, *Discourses on Art*, ed. Robert Wark, New Haven and London 1975, 252.

3 For the *Woodman* see John Hayes, *The Landscape Paintings of Thomas Gainsborough: A Critical Text and Catalogue Raisonné*, 2 vols, London and Ithaca, N.Y. 1982, I, 80, II, cat. no. 185. On May 22, 1788 he wrote from London to Thomas Hervey of Catton Hall, near Norwich, that he could not "keep from working an hour or two of a Day, though with a great mixture of bodily Pain" (*Letters*, 174, letter no. 108.) from which one might infer that the *Cottage Door* was one of the pictures on which he worked.

4 Hayes, *Landscape Paintings*, II, cat. nos 24 and 58.

5 Reynolds, *Discourses*, 254.

6 *Ibid.*, 130 and 249.

7 *Ibid.*, 257–8. For the Vasari connection and Aglionby quotation, see Michael Rosenthal, *The Art of Thomas Gainsborough: "a little business for the Eye,"* New Haven and London 1999, 120.

8 [Joseph Holden Pott], *An Essay on Landscape Painting. With Remarks general and critical on the different Schools and Masters, Antient or Modern*, London 1782, 73–4.

9 William Jackson, *The Four Ages: together with Essays on various Subjects*, London 1798, 155–6.

10 Hayes, *Landscape Paintings*, I, 131.

11 Rosenthal, *Art of Thomas Gainsborough*, 86–93.

12 Hayes, *Landscape Paintings*, II, 439.

13 *Letters*, 112–14, letter no. 65, Gainsborough to William Hoare, from Bath, [1773].

14 *Ibid.*, 68, letter no. 40, Gainsborough to William Jackson, from Bath, 4 June [year unknown].

15 *The General Advertiser*, 30 April 1778.

16 Peter and Linda Murray, *A Dictionary of Art and Artists*, Harmondsworth 1968 (rev. ed.), 424.

17 Mark Leonard, "Treatment Record," April 1998, The J. Paul Getty Museum, Los Angeles.

18 David Solkin, cited in Robyn Asleson and Shelley M. Bennett, eds, *British Paintings at the Huntington*, New Haven and London 2001, 115.

19 Mark Leonard, "Treatment Record."

20 William Cowper, *Poems*, 2 vols, London 1814, II, lines 248–51.

21 For Gainsborough and the cult of sensibility, see Rosenthal, *Art of Thomas Gainsborough*, 219–46; *Thomas Gainsborough, 1727–1788*, exh. cat., ed. Michael Rosenthal and Martin Myrone, London 2002, 180–211.

22 Elisabeth Mention and Mark Leonard, "Treatment Record," September 1999, The J. Paul Getty Museum, Los Angeles.

23 For instance, the light through the trees in the *Vie near King's Bromley-on-Trent*, Philadelphia Museum of Art.

24 Hayes, *Landscape Paintings*, I, 178.

25 *Ibid.*, II, 568–9, quoting Bate-Dudley in the *Morning Herald*, 30 December 1786. Bate was reporting on the paintings in Gainsborough's studio, so it is feasible he had discussed them with the artist.

26 Reynolds, *Discourses*, 253.

27 *Letters*, 72, letter no. 43, Gainsborough to William Jackson, from Bath, [probably April 1770].

28 Hayes, *Landscape Paintings*, II, 439.

29 Oliver Goldsmith, *The Deserted Village*, London 1770, 22. For this subject in more detail, see Michael Rosenthal, "The Rough and the Smooth: Rural Subjects in Later Eighteenth-century British Painting," *Eighteenth-Century Life* XVIII, no. 2 (May 1994) 36–56; and Rosenthal, *Art of Thomas Gainsborough*, 183–207.

30 Maren-Sofie Røstvig, *The Happy Man: Studies in the Metamorphosis of a Classical Idea*, 2 vols, Oslo 1962 (2nd ed.). For Gainsborough and this tradition, see Marcia Pointon, "Gainsborough and the Landscape of Retirement," *Art History* II, no. 4 (December 1979) 441–55; Amal Asfour and Paul Williamson, *Gainsborough's Vision*, Liverpool 1999, 182–3, 186, 187 and *passim*. J. Dryden, trans., *The Works of Virgil*, 4 vols, London 1782, I, 318 (*Georgic* I, 659–60).

31 *Letters*, 68, letter no. 40, Gainsborough to William Jackson, from Bath, 4 June [year unknown].

32 Hayes, *Landscape Paintings*, II, 482–5.

33 Rosenthal, *Art of Thomas Gainsborough*, 107–10; Rosenthal and Myrone, *Thomas Gainsborough*, 142–3 (entry to cat. no. 60).

34 Martin Postle, in Rosenthal and Myrone, *Thomas Gainsborough*, 232 (entry to cat. no. 129).

35 Cited in William T. Whitley, *Thomas Gainsborough*, London 1915, 170.

36 Bate-Dudley, *Morning Herald*, June 7, 1781.

37 For an exemplary account of enclosure and the culture and economy of the commoners, see J. M. Neeson, *Commoners: Common Right, Enclosure, and Social Change in England, 1700–1820*, Cambridge 1993; for wood-gathering, see p. 40.

38 *Letters*, 43, letter no. 24, Gainsborough to William Jackson, from Bath, 14 September [1767]. See also Philip Thicknesse, *A Sketch of the Life and Paintings of Thomas Gainsborough, R.A.*, London 1788, 42–3.

39 Tobias Smollett, *Humphry Clinker* (1771), Harmondsworth 1967, 65–7. For the best general history of these issues see Dror Wahrman, *The Making of the Modern Self: Identity and Culture in Eighteenth-century England*, New Haven and London, 2004.

40 *The Gazetteer and New Daily Advertiser*, 20 April 1784.

41 John Hayes is categorical about the Watteau connection: see his *Landscape Paintings*, I, 134, and II, 516–20 (entry to cat. no. 148). For Watteau's *fêtes galantes*, see Thomas E. Crow, *Painters and Public Life in Eighteenth-century Paris,* New Haven and London 1985, 45–78.

42 For the Comte de Caylus's "Life of Watteau" (read at the Academy on 3 February 1748) see Charles Harrison, Paul Wood, and Jason Geiger, eds., *Art in Theory, 1648–1815: An Anthology of Changing Ideas,* Oxford 2000, 356–63. Reynolds, *Discourses*, 51.

43 Reynolds, *Discourses,* 41–53.

44 Louise Lippincott, "Expanding on Portraiture: The Market, the Public, and the Hierarchy of Genres in Eighteenth-century Britain," in *The Consumption of Culture 1600–1800: Image, Object, Text*, ed. Ann Bermingham and John Brewer, London and New York 1995, 75–88.

GAINSBOROUGH'S COTTAGE-DOOR SCENES

1 See George Boas and A. O. Lovejoy, *Primitivism and Related Ideas in Antiquity*, Baltimore 1935.

2 See John Hayes, *The Landscape Paintings of Thomas Gainsborough: A Critical Text and Catalogue Raisonné*, 2 vols, London and Ithaca, N.Y. 1982, II, cat. nos. 132, 134.

3 Quoted in William T. Whitley, *Thomas Gainsborough*, London 1915, 170.

4 John Britton, *The Fine Arts of the English School*, London 1812. Cf. Chauncey B. Tinker, *Painter and Poet: Studies in the Literary Relations of English Painting*, Cambridge, Mass. 1938; and Marcia Pointon, "Gainsborough and the Landscape of Retirement," *Art History*, II, no. 4 (1979), 441–55.

5 Written 1749–50, the poem was first published in 1788. Quoted from Roger Lonsdale, ed., *The Poems of Gray, Collins and Goldsmith*, London 1969, repr. 1980. All references are to this edition.

6 *The Letters of Thomas Gainsborough*, ed. John Hayes, New Haven and London 2001, 153, letter no. 92, Gainsborough to William Pearce, Summer 1783. See Whitley, *Gainsborough*, 170, and Hayes, *Landscape Paintings*, II, cat. no. 125.

7 Quoted from Lonsdale, ed. *Gray, Collins and Goldsmith*.

8 Pointon, "Landscape of Retirement," 451.

9 See Hayes, *Landscape Paintings*, I, 479.

10 See Amal Asfour and Paul Williamson, *Gainsborough's Vision*, Liverpool 1999, 88–94.

11 Quoted from Erwin Panofsky, "*Et in Arcadia Ego*: Poussin and the Elegiac Tradition," *Meaning in the Visual Arts*, New York 1955, 295.

12 Ellis. Waterhouse, "Gainsborough's 'Fancy Pictures'," *Burlington Magazine* LXXXVIII (June 1946) 134.

13 Hayes, *Landscape Paintings*, I, 569, referring to *Open Landscape with Two Woodcutters* (1787, National Trust, Stourhead) II, cat. no. 184.

14 See Asfour and Williamson, *Gainsborough's Vision*, 23–53.

15 See David Mannings and Martin Postle, *Sir Joshua Reynolds: A Complete Catalogue of his Paintings*, 2 vols, New Haven and London 2000, II, cat. no. 445.

16 See Panofsky "*Et in Arcadia Ego*," 298–304, and Paul Williamson, "Gray's *Elegy* and the Logic of Expression," in *Thomas Gray: Contemporary Essays*, ed. W. B. Hutchings and William Ruddick, Liverpool 1993, 39–72.

17 Henry Bate-Dudley, *Morning Herald*, May 9, 1788, quoted in Hayes, *Landscape Paintings*, I, 572.

18 See *ibid.*, 92–121.

19 See Asfour and Williamson, *Gainsborough's Vision*, 163–97.

20 Hayes, *Landscape Paintings*, I, 107.

21 Information on Malton is taken from the *Dictionary of National Biography*.

22 Gainsborough's copy was sold at Christie's in 1799. See Hayes, *Landscape Paintings*, I, 90, n. 59.

23 See Asfour and Williamson, *Gainsborough's Vision*, 103–12, and Martin Kemp, *The Science of Art*, New Haven and London 1990, 234–8.

24 Joshua Kirby, *Dr. Brook Taylor's Method of Perspective Made Easy*, Ipswich (Suffolk) 1754, I, 70.

25 Thomas Malton, *A Compleat Treatise on Perspective in Theory and Practice on the True Principles of Brook Taylor*, 2nd ed., London 1779, 94.

26 *Ibid.*, 95.

27 *Ibid.*, 13.

28 *Ibid.*

29 *Ibid.*, 95.

30 See Asfour and Williamson, *Gainsborough's Vision*, 163–82.

31 See James Ayres, *The Artist's Craft: A History of Tools, Techniques and Materials*, Oxford 1985, 63–9.

32 See Christopher Brown, *Making and Meaning: Rubens's Landscapes*, London 1996, 90, 59–60.

33 *Ibid.*, 86.

34 *Ibid.*, 63.

35 Walter S. Gibson, *"Mirror of the Earth": The World Landscape in Sixteenth-Century Flemish Painting*, Princeton, N.J. 1989, 84.

36 *Ibid.*, 83–4.

37 Cf. Asfour and Williamson, *Gainsborough's Vision*, 175–7.

38 See Hayes, *Landscape Paintings*, I, 142.

39 *Ibid.*, 183.

40 Cf. John Mullan, *Sentiment and Sociability: The Language of Feeling in the Eighteenth Century*, Oxford 1988, 18–56, and Asfour and Williamson, *Gainsborough's Vision*, 137–41.

41 Cf. *ibid.*, 145–62.

42 See Hayes, *Landscape Paintings*, II, cat. no. 185b.

43 See Whitley, *Gainsborough*, 323.

44 A larger version of the paiting is on loan to the Victoria and Albert Museum, London; the second, smaller painting (illustrated here) is at Lehigh University, Bethlehem, Penn. See Hayes, *Landscape Paintings*, II, cat. nos. 144–5.

45 Cf. Asfour and Williamson, *Gainsborough's Vision*, 250–51.

46 Ecclesiasticus, or The Wisdom of Jesus Son of Sirach, 25:22, 26:1, 26:7. Chapter and verse numbers given by Cats differ from those in the Authorised Version which Gainsborough would have used. Similarly, Dutch translations from the Greek sometimes diverge from the English. (The textual history of Ecclesiasticus is "exceptionally complicated." See *The Oxford Bible Commentary*, ed. John Barton and John Muddiman, Oxford 2001, 668.)

47 David Garrick's *Catherine and Petruchio*, "Alter'd from Shakespeare's *Taming of the Shrew*" (1756), e.g., or William Wallbeck's *Soctrates and Xantippe: A Burlesque Tale* (1786).

48 See Whitley, *Gainsborough*, 10. The epithet was used by Henry Angelo.

49 See Susan Legouix Sloman, "Mrs Margaret Gainsborough, 'A Prince's Daughter'," *Gainsborough's House Review*, Ipswich (1995/96), 47–58.

50 *Letters*, 130, letter no. 76; Gainsborough to Mary Gibbon, from Bath, December 26, 1775.

51 *Letters*, 131, letter no. 77, Gainsborough to Mary Gibbon, from Bath, June 10 [1776].

52 For Gainsborough and Cowper see Asfour and Williamson, *Gainsborough's Vision*, 235–7, 265–6.

53 See William Hayley, *The Life, and Posthumous Writings, of William Cowper, Esqr.*, 3 vols, London 1803–4, II, 415, and David Bindman, *The Complete Graphic Works of William Blake*, London 1978, cat. no. 399.

54 References are to *The Poems of William Cowper*, II, 1782–5, ed. John D. Baird and Charles Ryskamp, Oxford 1995. Begun in September 1783, *The Task* was first published in July 1785.

55 *Letters*, 130, letter no. 76, Gainsborough

to Mary Gibbon, from Bath, December 26, 1775.

56 Cf. Asfour and Williamson, *Gainsborough's Vision*, 182–7.

THE EARLY COLLECTORS OF *THE COTTAGE DOOR*

I am very grateful to Ann Bermingham for her valuable comments and suggestions on the draft of this essay and to Chin-Sung Chang for his help in collecting some of the references.

1 *John Constable's Correspondence*, ed. R. B. Beckett Ipswich (Suffolk) 1968, VI, 232, letter of 26 August 1827 from Constable to Fisher.

2 Sir John Leicester was ennobled as Baron de Tabley in 1826. The contents of the sale is available on the internet at the Getty Research Institute's Provenance Index Databases website, www.getty.edu.

3 *Morning Chronicle*, 9 July 1827.

4 *Ibid.*

5 John Hayes, *The Landscape Paintings of Thomas Gainsborough: A Critical Text and Catalogue Raisonné*, 2 vols, London and Ithaca, N.Y. 1982, I, 479.

6 Ellis Waterhouse, "Gainsborough's 'Fancy Pictures'," *Burlington Magazine* LXXXVIII (June 1946), 134.

7 W. T. Whitley, *Artists and Their Friends in England 1700–1799*, 2 vols, London 1928, I, 380.

8 For the provenance of the painting, see Robyn Asleson and Shelley M. Bennett, eds, *British Paintings at the Huntington*, New Haven and London 2001, 112. The only document confirming the early provenance of the painting is a receipt dated April 19, 1809 from Daniel Coppin to Sir John Leicester. See Douglas Hall, "Tabley House Papers," *Walpole Society* XXXVIII (1960–62), 70. The complete list of Sir John's collection is provided at the end of this indispensable source material.

9 For Harvey, see Francis Hawcroft, "Crome and His Patron: Thomas Harvey of Catton," *Connoisseur* XLVII (December 1959), 232–7.

10 Hall, "Tabley House Papers," 70.

11 *The Letters of Thomas Gainsborough*, ed. John Hayes, New Haven and London 2001, 174.

12 Trevor Fawcett, *The Rise of English Provincial Art*, Oxford 1974, 18–19.

13 Sir John's patronage and collecting of British art is the subject of my doctoral dissertation, "A History of the Leicester Family, Tabley House, and its Collection of Paintings," University of Manchester 2000.

14 Hall, "Tabley House Papers," 70.

15 Since the term "British" was used in many cases interchangeably with "English" in this period, I make no distinction between the two in this essay.

16 Hall, "Tabley House Papers," 70.

17 For a detailed account of the gallery, see Dongho Chun, "Public Display, Private Glory: Sir John Leicester's Gallery of British Art," *Journal of the History of Collections* XIII (2001), 175–89.

18 Giles Waterfield, "The Town House as Gallery of Art," *London Journal* XX (1995), 47–66.

19 C. M. Westmacott, *British Galleries of Painting and Sculpture*, London 1824, ix.

20 *Morning Herald*, May 12, 1818.

21 Fréderique Desbuissons, "A Ruin: Jacques-Louis David's *Sabine Women*," *Art History* XX, no. 3 (September 1997), 432–48.

22 In his letter of 17 December 1785 to his mother, written from Geneva while he was on the Grand Tour, Sir John says that he has become a "master of the French language." Chester, Cheshire Record Office, Leicester-Warren Papers, DLT/C9/14.

23 *Gentleman's Magazine*, September 1827, 273.

24 *Morning Chronicle*, 30 June 1827.

25 *The Times*, 4 July 1827.

26 *Morning Post*, 11 July 1827.

27 See the will and codicils of John Fleming Baron De Tabley, Public Record Office, London, PROB 11 /1728, LH 135–142, proved at the Prerogative Court of Canterbury in London on July 18, 1827 by Thomas Lister Parker.

28 J. A. Venn, *Alumni Cantabrigienses*, Cambridge 1951, IV, 167.

29 The second codicil made on 14 December 1826.

30 For biographical information about Parker, see Leslie Stephen and Sidney Lee, eds, *Dictionary of National Biography*, London 1922, XV, 283. Parker's collection is listed in Thomas Lister Parker, *Description of Browsholme Hall*, London 1815, 8–10.

31 Quoted in Guy Acloque and John Cornforth, "The Eternal Gothic of Eaton–II," *Country Life*, 18 February 1971, 360.

32 Guy Acloque and John Cornforth, "The Eternal Gothic of Eaton–I," *Country Life*, 11 February 1971, 304–7.

33 For the history of the house, see F. H. W. Sheppard, gen. ed., *Survey of London*, London 1980, XL, 239–50.

34 R. Windsor Liscombe, "Ellis, Welbore Agar", *The Grove Dictionary of Art Online*, Oxford University Press, accessed 1 June 2004, www.groveart.com.

35 *The Diary of Joseph Farington R.A.*, ed. Catherine Cave, Kenneth Garlick, Angus Macintyre, and Evelyn Newby, 16 vols, New Haven and London 1978–98, 1982, VII, 2720.

36 *Ibid.*, 2763.

37 *Ibid.*, VIII, 2803.

38 *Ibid.*, 3088.

39 David Cast: "Seguier, William", *The Grove Dictionary of Art Online*, accessed 1 June 2004, www.groveart.com.

40 Cheshire Record Office, Grosvenor Manuscripts, 9/13/3.

41 For Stafford's collection, see Giles Waterfield, *Palaces of Art*, London 1991, 74–5.

42 Sheppard, *Survey of London*, XL, 242.

43 Farington, *Diary*, IX, 3291.

44 *Ibid.*, 3307.

45 Sheppard, *Survey of London*, XL, 243.

46 William Young Ottley, *Engravings of the most noble the Marquis of Stafford's collection of pictures in London*, 4 vols, London 1818.

47 See Gervase Huxley, *Lady Elizabeth and the Grosvenors: Life in a Whig Family 1822–1839*, London 1965, 1–2.

48 See P. G. Patmore, *British Galleries of Art*, London 1824.

49 G. F. Waagen, *Works of Art and Artists in England*, 3 vols, London 1838, II, 301.

50 Huxley, *Lady Elizabeth*, 17.

51 *Manchester Gazette*, 14 July 1827.

52 W. T. Whitley, *Art in England*, Cambridge 1930, II, 137.

53 Cheshire Record Office, Grosvenor Manuscripts, 9/182.

GAINSBOROUGH'S *COTTAGE DOOR* IN SIR JOHN LEICESTER'S "TENT ROOM"

I am grateful to the following people who assisted me in preparing this essay: Dongho Chun, Peter Cannon-Brookes, and Brenda Folds of Tabley House, Liz Green of the Cheshire Records Office, Steven Kendall, Melinda McCurdy, Kelly Turner, Leslie Edwards, and Stephen Wingrave of HSBC.

1 *Morning Herald*, 12 May 1818. William Carey, *A Descriptive Catalogue of a Collection of Paintings by British Artists, in the Possession of Sir John Fleming Leicester, Bart.*, London 1819, 107; John Young, *A Catalogue of Pictures by British Artists, in the Possession of Sir John Fleming Leicester, Bart., with Etchings from the Whole Collection. Including Pictures in his Gallery at Tabley House, Cheshire*, London 1821, no. 18.

2 *Monthly Magazine and British Review*, July 1827, 99.

3 Chester, Cheshire Records Office, Leicester/Warren Papers, DLT/F/60, 1819, i.

4 Quoted from an 1819 anonymous catalogue of Sir John's pictures in the Cheshire Record Office, Leicester/Warren Papers DLT/F/60.

5 *Repository of the Arts*, 2nd series, XIII (June 1822) 359.

6 Quoted in Dongho Chun, "Public Display, Private Glory: Sir John Fleming Leicester's Gallery of British Art in Early Nineteenth-century England," *Journal of the History of Collections*, XIII no. 2 (2001), 181. I am very grateful to Dr. Chun for his generous help and for allowing me to read his doctoral dissertation, "A History of the Leicester Family, Tabley House, and its Collection of Paintings," University of Manchester 2004.

7 *Morning Post*, 20 February 1806, 2.

8 Chun, "Public Display, Private Glory," 185.

9 The sale document, drawn up by Mr. Phillips of Bond Street in 1805, describes it as a leaseshold of 39 years with a ground rent of £11.7s.6d per annum. It is believed that this document is among the uncatalogued Leicester/Warren papers in the Cheshire Records Office. I am extremely grateful to Leslie Edwards for alerting me to the existence of this document and for showing me a copy of it, and also for her help in suggesting where I might locate other documents related to the Hill Street house and its collection. I am also grateful to Dr. Peter Cannon-Brookes for sharing with me his extensive knowledge of the Tabley House collection and for putting me in touch with Ms. Edwards.

10 Mary Cathcart Borer, *Mayfair: The Years of Grandeur*, London 1975, 226–7.

11 *Ibid.*, 119.

12 Howard Colvin, *A Biographical Dictionary of British Architects, 1600–1840*, London 1978, 244–6. For Cundy's activities in Mayfair and around Berkeley Square see F. H. W. Sheppard gen. ed., *Survey of London: The Grosvenor Estate in Mayfair*, parts 1 and 2, London 1977 and 1980. The numbering of houses on Hill Street began in 1762. Before that the occupier's name was on a brass plate on the door. The houses on Hill Street were renumbered in the nineteenth century with the result that no. 24 is now no. 29. Until June 2004, the premises were occupied by the financial corporation HSBC, which extensively renovated the interiors of the building so that the original rooms are no longer intact.

13 An uncatalogued document among the Leicester/Warren papers, Cheshire Records Office.

14 *Ibid.*, DLT/4996, Box 29, 1805.

15 On the design and use of natural top lighting for galleries in this period see Michael Compton, "The Architecture of Daylight," *Palaces of Art: Art Galleries in Britain 1790–1900*, ed. Giles Waterfield, London 1991, 37–48.

16 It makes sense that the main gallery would have opened to the conservatory in that such a room would provide the gallery with more light, air, and seating. Given the large number of people visiting the main gallery daily during the spring months of the season, one imagines that the heat generated by the crowds in what was a windowless room would have been considerable. The conservatory would provide air circulation as well as extra seating, and when necessary its drapes could shade the area from the direct afternoon sun of the south-facing widows. Because many Mayfair houses had no back gardens conservatories were common features in them.

17 *Morning Chronicle*, 30 June 1827.

18 Cheshire Records Office, Leicester/Warren Papers, DLT/4996, Box 29, 1805.

19 *Ibid.*, DLT/C3/55 and DLT/C3/56, 1809. See too DLT/4996, Box 31, 1809. It is unclear if Sir John ever carried out Cundy's plans but it seems that some renovations were made to the ground floor over time.

20 John Morley, "The Age of Associations", *Country Life* CLXXXV (June 1991) 111.

21 Dorothy Stroud, *Henry Holland: His Life and Architecture*, London 1966, 79 and 84.

22 *The Diary of Joseph Farington*, ed. Catherine Cave, Kenneth Garlic, Angus MacIntyre, and Evelyn Newby, 16 vols, New Haven and London 1978–84, VII, 2745.

23 Thomas Hope, *Household Furniture and Interior Decoration*, London 1807, pl. 10. On the subject of tent rooms see Peter Thornton, *Authentic Décor: The Domestic Interior, 1620–1920*, New York 1984, 193–6; Morley, "Age of Associations," 110–12; John Fowler and John Cornforth, *English Decoration in the Eighteenth Century*, London 1974, 144–7.

24 The watercolor is undated but the paper is identical to other drawings at Tabley House watermarked 1801. I am grateful to the assistant curator at Tabley House, Brenda Folds, for this information.

25 *Oxford English Dictionary*.

26 In eighteenth-century France the boudoir was associated exclusively with women and was used discursively as the spatial antithesis of the public (i.e. democratic) Salon. On this subject see Jill H. Casid, "Commerce in the Boudoir," in *Women, Art, and the Politics of Identity in Eighteenth-Century Europe*, ed. Melissa Hyde and Jennifer Milam, New York 2003, 91–113. On the etymology of "boudoir" see Ed Lilley, "The Name of the Boudoir," *Journal of the Society of Architectural Historians* LIII (June 1994), 193–8. Lilley observes that the word derives from the French verb *bouder* meaning to sulk, and the room was understood to be a place to which a lady might retire when she was out of sorts.

27 Sheppard, *Survey of London*, part I, figs 9 and 24; part II, figs 36 and 47.

28 From the exterior brickwork of the house it appears that in Sir John's day the upper two floors (second floor and attic) extended back only about 18 feet from the front windows of the house. This allowed room for the lantern ceiling of the library on the first floor to project upward. The rooms on these two upper floors were described as bedrooms and garrets and given the fact that they face the front street they may have been reserved for servants. This suggests that the main bedroom was located on the first or ground floor of the house where it could be placed in the back away from the noise of the street. Thus the first-floor "boudoir" may indeed have been the main bedroom before 1818, unless the main bedroom was relocated to somewhere on the ground floor in one of the renovations. I am grateful to Steven Kendall for examining the Hill Street house for me and for taking pictures of its interiors, and to Stephen Wingrave, the archivist for HSBC, who shared with me his observations on the brickwork, and who gave me measured drawings of the interior of the house as it is today.

29 Chester Records Office, Leicester/Warren Papers DLT/4996, Box 34, 1818.

30 *Diary of Joseph Farington*, X, 3506, and Cheshire Records Office, Leicester/Warren Papers DLT/4667, Box 31, 1809.

31 Four anonymous watercolors at Tabley House show the four walls of the gallery with a diagram of the hang c. 1806–9. There is a pattern to the framing of the works in that gallery: largest works have wide moldings and foliated corners (presumably this was the kind of frame used for the *Cottage Door*), medium-size works have wide moldings but lack the decorative corners, and small works have simple narrow moldings.

32 Cheshire Records Office, Leicester/Warren Papers DLT/C33/128, 1818. I am very grateful to Liz Green of the Cheshire Records Office for this information.

33 Sir John purchased the painting for 200 guineas from Daniel Coppin in April of 1809; to make up the difference in the £400 asking price, Sir John also gave Coppin two paintings from his collection valued at £100 each. Douglas Hall, "The Tabley House Papers," *The Walpole Society* XXXVIII, (1962), 70.

34 I base this conjecture on the fact that the upholsterers were hired in April 1809 to make a cover for the pianoforte (Cheshire Records Office, Leicester/Warren Papers DLT/4996, Box 29, 1808–09), presumably because it was not being used, and the following April furntiure-removal men took the pianoforte away and began un-packing cases for Sir John and his new wife's spring visit to London (IBID., Box 31, 1811). *Diary of Joseph Farington*, X, 3833 and VI, 2331.

35 William Carey, *Some Memoirs of the Patronage and Progress of the Fine Arts, in England and Ireland, During the Reigns of George the Second and George the Third*, London 1826, 107.

36 *Ibid.*

37 *Ibid.*, 108.

38 *Ibid.*, 113.

39 William Carey, *The Artist*, 17 March 1807, 131.

40 Sir Joshua Reynolds, *Discourses*, ed. Robert Wark, New Haven and London 1959, 13.

41 Morris Eaves, *The Counter-Arts Conspiracy: Art and Industry in the Age of Blake*, Ithaca, N.Y., and London 1992, 25.

42 *Ibid.*, 26–7.

43 *Ibid.*, 84.

44 Carey, *Descriptive Catalogue*, x.

45 Linda Colley, "Whose Nation? Class and National Consciousness in Britain 1750–1830," *Past and Present*, no. 113 (November 1986) 97–117. On the politics surrounding the founding of the National Gallery in London see Carol Duncan, *Civilizing Rituals: Inside Public Art Museums*, London and New York 1995, 21–47.

46 Young, *Catalogue of Pictures*, n. p.

47 Hall, "Tabley House Papers," 111.

48 *Ibid.*

49 On this see Chun, "Public Display, Private Glory," 184–6.

50 Quoted in *ibid.*, 184.

51 From its debut at the Royal Academy in 1780 *The Cottage Door* was hailed as a great painting. Similarly, the reputation of Gainsborough as one of the leading masters of the British School was enshrined not only in Reynolds's fourteenth *Discourse*, delivered after the artist's death, but also in the 1814 exhibition of the British Institution of his work along with that of Reynolds, Zoffany, and Wilson, an exhibition that followed the previous year's celebration of Hogarth. *The Cottage Door* was exhibited in this exhibition and seven times after that in the nineteenth century, and always in the context of being one of the finest exemplars of Gainsborough's style and of British art.

52 *Morning Herald*, May 12, 1818.

53 Hall, "Tabley House Papers," 70, and Carey, *Catalogue*, 109.

54 Christie's, *Sale Catalogue of Pictures from the Collection of Sir John Leicester, Baron de Tabley*, London 1817, 8.

55 J. M. W. Turner quoted in Robyn Asleson and Shelley M. Bennett, eds, *British Paintings at the Huntington*, New Haven and London 2001, 112; *Farington Diary of Joseph*, X, 3506.

56 Anna Jameson, *Companion to the Most Celebrated Private Galleries of Art in London*, London 1844, 276.

57 This attention to the display of the work of art looks forward to James McNeill Whistler's display of his lithographs. A reconstruction of that display, including a tented room, was mounted at the Freer Gallery in Washington, D.C. ("Whistler in Paris: Lithographs from the Belle Epoque, 1891–1896," November 20, 2003–August 15, 2004).

58 On this subject see the essays published in *Art on the Line: The Royal Academy Exhibitions at Somerset House, 1780–1836*, ed. David Solkin, exh. cat., London and New Haven 2001, esp. his introduction, "The Great Mart of Genius: The Royal Academy Exhibitions at Somserset House, 1780–1836," 1–8, and Ann Bermingham, "Landscape-o-rama: The Exhibition Landscape at Somerset House and the Rise of Popular Landscape Entertainments," 127–43.

59 See his essay in this collection.

60 Waterfield, "Picture Hanging and Gallery Decoration," *Palaces of Art*, 49–50.

61 Jameson, *Celebrated Private Galleries*, xxxix–xl.

62 Turner quoted in Asleson and Bennett, *British Paintings at the Huntington*, 112.

63 Anon., "Conversations on the Arts,"

Repository of the Arts, 1st series, v (January 1811) 5.

64 Walter Armstrong, *Gainsborough and His Place in English Art*, London 1898, 225.

65 Reported in William T. Whitley, *Thomas Gainsborough*, London 1915, 248.

66 John Hayes, *The Landscape Paintings of Thomas Gainsborough: A Critical Text and Catalogue Raisonné*, 2 vols, London and Ithaca, N.Y,. 1982, I, 155.

67 Kay Dian Kriz, *The Idea of the English Landscape Painter: Genius as Alibi in the Early Nineteenth Century*, New Haven and London 1997.

68 Andrew Hemingway's meticulous examination of art exhibition reviews in the early nineteenth-century press makes this plain. See his *Landscape Imagery and Urban Culture in Nineteenth-Century Britain*, Cambridge 1992.

69 The tendency to view the cottage doors as fancy pictures persisted into the twentieth century to the degree that Ellis Waterhouse felt it necessary to set the record straight by excluding them from his list of fancy paintings by Gainsborough. Waterhouse limited his list to those works in which the figure is on the "same scale as if it were the subject of a portrait" and "which owe their inspiration directly to Murillo." See Ellis Waterhouse, "Gainsborough's 'Fancy Pictures,'" *Burlington Magazine* LXXXVIII (June 1946) 134–40.

70 Anon, *An Account of the Pictures Exhibited in the Rooms of the British Institution*, London 1824, 262–5.

71 Quoted in Whitley, Gainsborough 292, and in his *Art in England* 1800–1837, 2 vols., New York 1973, I, 228.

72 Carey, *Descriptive Catalogue*, 107–109

73 Thomas Hearne quoted in Asleson and Bennett, *British Paintings at the Huntington*, 114.

74 See John Barrell, "Gainsborough's Rural Vision," *The Listener*, May 12, 1977, 615–16, as well as his *The Dark Side of the Landscape: The Rural Poor in English Painting 1730–1840*, Cambridge 1980, 65–82, and his essay in this volume. See, too, Ann Bermingham, "The Simple Life: Cottages and Gainsborough's Cottage Doors," in *Land, Nation and Culture, 1740–1840: Thinking the Republic of Taste*, ed. Peter Da Bolla, Nigel Leask, and David Simpson, New York, 2005.

75 Young, *Catalogue of Pictures*, 19.

76 *Ibid.* There has been some question whether the Ward painting of *Phaeton* at Tabley House today (bought in 1808 from the artist) is the same painting that was sold at Christie's after Sir John's death. See Peter Cannon-Brookes, *Paintings from Tabley*, London 1989, 64.

77 Carey, *Descriptive Catalogue*, 146.

78 *European Magazine*, 1823, 204.

79 Hall, "Tabley House Papers," 121–2. Ward was also a great favorite of Sir John's. In addition to the *Fall of Phaeton*, Carey lists three paintings by Ward at Hill Street: *Landscape with Figures and Cattle, Landscape with Figures*, and *View of Tabley Park*; and at Tabley House he lists *Dogs of the Dalmation Breed*. The more complete inventory of paintings by Douglas Hall lists eight paintings by Ward in Sir John's possession; Hall, "Tabley House Papers," 121. Only the eleven paintings by Turner owned by Sir John exceed this number. On the development of the collection at Tabley see Cannon-Brookes, *Paintings from Tabley*.

80 Bermingham, "The Simple Life," 2005; and John E. Crowley, "Picturesque Comfort: The Cottage," *The Invention of Comfort: Sensibilities and Design in Early Modern Britain and Early America*, Baltimore and London 2000, 203–29.

81 On David's use of a mirror to fuse the Parisian public with his *The Intervention of the Sabine Women* and metaphorically with an ideal of the post-Thermidor French nation, see Ewa Lajer-Burcharth, "David's Sabine Women: Body, Gender, and Republican Culture under the Directory," *Art History* XIV, no. 3 (1991) 397–430. In fact, it was not unusual at this time to exhibit works of art in draped and mirrored rooms. Thomas Hope exhibited John Flaxman's sculpture of *Aurora visiting Cephalus on Mount Ida* in a heavily draped room in his Duchess Street house. An illustration of this room appeared in Hope's *Household Furniture and Interior Decoration* (1807), Showing a draped room with a coved ceiling. The drapery was parted so as to reveal the Flaxman group reflected in three mirrors placed opposite to each other on the side walls. As a result of this arrangement, David Watkin notes, "the eye is pleasingly confounded by this device into supposing for a moment that the room contains not one but three pieces of sculpture"; David Watkin, *Thomas Hope and the Neo-Classical Ideal*, London 1998, 110. The use of mirrors was also adapted by Sir John Soane, who installed them throughout his house at 12 Lincoln's Inn Fields to amplify the appearance of the rooms as well as to show off his collection and to help illuminate it. See also Kriz (*Idea of the English Landscape Painter*, 1997, 39) on the use of mirrors in the decoration of Carlton House.

82 Reynolds, *Discourses*, 258.

83 Jameson, *Celebrated Private Galleries*, xix.

MAGIC IN THE STUDIO

1 Sir Joshua Reynolds, *Discourses on Art*, ed. Robert Wark, New Haven and London 1959, Discourse XIV (1788), 258.

2 Keith Thomas, *Religion and the Decline of Magic*, London 1971.

3 In Marijke Gijswijt-Hofstra, Brian Levack, and Roy Porter, *Witchcraft and Magic after the Witch Trials: The Eighteenth and Nineteenth Centuries*, London 1999, 250.

4 Iain McCalman, *The Seven Ordeals of Count Cagliostro*, London 2003, 161–73. See also his essay in this book.

5 Michael Rosenthal, "Gainsborough's *Diana and Actaeon*," in *Painting and the Politics of Culture: New Essays on British Art 1700–1850*, ed. John Barrell, Oxford and New York 1992, 167–94.

6 Reynolds, *Discourses*, 258.

7 *Ibid.*

8 For Gestalt psychologists this process was explained by the concept of isomorphism, which assumed the pre-existence of forms within the mind. This theory is now largely discredited and most perceptual psychologists would agree with R. L. Gregory that there remains "a problem in how the mosaic of retinal stimulation gives rise to the perception of objects"; R. L. Gregory, *Eye and Brain*, London 1966, 8.

9 Michael Rosenthal, *The Art of Thomas Gainsborough: "a little business for the Eye,"* London and New Haven 1999, 100–01.

10 *The Letters of Thomas Gainsborough*, ed. John Hayes, New Haven and London 2001, letter no. 97, Gainsborough to the Hanging Committee of the Royal

Academy, from London, 10 April 1784.

11 Osias Humphry, "Memoir," London, Royal Academy Humphry Papers HU 1/20–40 fol. 36; see Rosenthal, *Art of Thomas Gainsborough*, 62–3.

12 "Vous venez à temps, Chardin, pour récréer mes yeux. Vous revoilà donc, grand magicien, avec vos compositions muettes" [Salon de 1765], Denis Diderot, *Oeuvre esthétiques*, Paris 1965, 485.

13 See David Mannings and Martin Postle, *Sir Joshua Reynolds: A Complete Catalogue of his Paintings*, 2 vols, New Haven and London, 2000, II, cat. no. 1282.

14 Reynolds, *Discourses*, 94–5.

15 *Ibid.*, 94.

16 *Ibid.*, 95.

17 For citations of these, esp. in the poems of Richard Graves and Daniel Webb, see Susan Sloman, *Gainsborough in Bath*, New Haven and London 2002, 117, 161, 166.

18 John Newman, "Reynolds and Hone: *The Conjuror* Unmasked," in *Reynolds*, ed. Nicholas Penny, exh. cat., London 1986, 344–54.

19 For a recent discussion of this debate see John Hope Mason, *The Value of Creativity: The Origins and Emergence of a Modern Belief*, Aldershot 2003, 135–56. See esp. ch. 7 "Intuition and Judgement."

20 Thomas Warton Jr., *Verses on Sir Joshua Reynolds's Painted Window at New College, Oxford*, London 1782, 4, lines 63–70.

21 Edmund Burke, *A Philosophical Enquiry into the Origin of our Ideas of the Sublime and Beautiful* (1757), ed. James T. Boulton, London 1958, 119, Part 3, section XII.

22 Barbara Maria Stafford and Frances Terpak, *Devices of Wonder from the World in a Box to Images on a Screen*, with an object list by Isotta Poggi, exh. cat., Los Angeles 2001, 175–7.

23 Jean-Jacques Rousseau, *Emile, ou de l'éducation* (1762), Paris 1967, Book III, 194–7.

24 For a discussion of Sandby's critique of Hogarth see Ronald Paulson's preface in William Hogarth, *The Analysis of Beauty*, ed. Ronald Paulson, New Haven and London, 1998, xliii.

25 Immanuel Kant, *Critique of Practical Reason* (1787), trans. T. K. Abbott, New York 1996, 22.

26 For the most extensive discussion of the Eidophusikon in recent decades see Christopher Baugh, "Philippe James de Loutherbourg and the Early Pictorial Theatre: Some Aspects of its Cultural Context," in *Themes in Drama*, ed. J. Redmond, IX, Cambridge 1986, 99–127.

27 Quoted in Mark Hallett, "'The Business of Criticism': The Press and the Royal Academy Exhibition in Eighteenth-Century London," in *Art on the Line: The Royal Academy Exhibitions at Somerset House 1780–1836*, exh. cat., ed. David H. Solkin, New Haven and London 2001, 69.

28 Rosenthal, *Art of Thomas Gainsborough*, 257–8.

29 *Thomas Gainsborough, 1727–1788*, exh. cat., ed. Michael Rosenthal and Martin Myrone, London 2002, 256.

30 Jonathan Crary, *Techniques of the Observer: On Vision and Modernity in the Nineteenth Century*, Cambridge, Mass. 1990, 3.

31 Stafford and Terpak, *Devices of Wonder*, 82.

32 Marcia Pointon, "Gainsborough and the Landscape of Retirement," *Art History* II, no. 4 (December 1979), 441–55.

33 John Wesley quoted in Gijswijt-Hofstra, Levack, and Porter, *Witchcraft and Magic*, p. 239.

34 Repr. Rosenthal, *Art of Thomas Gainsborough*, 282, fig. 291.

35 Reynolds, *Discourses*, 52.

36 August Wilhelm Schlegel, *Athenaeum* II, Berlin 1799, 204 (my translation).

37 Werner Busch, *Die notwendige Arabeske: Wirklichkeitsaneignung und Stilisierung in der deutschen Kunst des 19. Jahrhunderts*, Berlin 1985.

38 Walter Benjamin *Illuminations*, ed. H. Arendt, London 1970, 235–6.

39 *Ibid.*, 235.

40 *Ibid.*

41 McCalman, *Cagliostro*, 245. See also Jeffrey Mehlman, *Walter Benjamin for Children: An Essay on his Radio Years*, Chicago and London 1993, 52–8.

MAGIC, SPECTACLE, AND THE ART OF DE LOUTHERBOURG'S EIDOPHUSIKON

1 Richard D. Altick, *The Shows of London*, Cambridge, Mass. 1978, 121.

2 *Ibid.*, 117–25.

3 Tom Gunning, "An Aesthetic of Astonishment: Early Film and the (In) Credulous Spectator," in *Viewing Positions*, ed. Linda Williams, New Brunswick, N.J. 1995, 118.

4 Austin Dobson, *At Prior Park and Other Papers*, London 1912, 116; Ralph G. Allen, "The Eidophusikon," *Theater Design and Technology* VII (December 1966), 12; William T. Whitley, *Thomas Gainsborough*, London 1915, 369–70; Isabelle Worman, *Thomas Gainsborough: A Biography 1727–1788*, Lavenham (Suffolk) 1976, 99.

5 Edward Edwards, *Anecdotes of Painters*, London 1808, 141; Rüdiger Joppien, "Die Szenenbilder Philippe Jacques de Loutherbourg, eine Untersuchung zu ihrer Stellung zwischen Malerei und Theater," PhD diss., University of Cologne, 1972, 346–7; Michael Rosenthal, *The Art of Thomas Gainsborough*, New Haven and London 1999, 258; Jack Lindsay, *Thomas Gainsborough*, London 1981, 149–51; Malcolm Cormack, *The Paintings of Thomas Gainsborough*, Cambridge and New York 1991, 25; John Hayes, *The Landscape Paintings of Thomas Gainsborough: A Critical Text and Catalogue Raisonné*, 2 vols, London and Ithaca, N.Y,. 1982, I, 140–42.

6 Ann Bermingham, "Landscape-O-Rama: The Exhibition Landscape at Somerset House and the Rise of Popular Landscape Entertainments," in *Art on the Line: The Royal Academy Exhibitions at Somerset House, 1780–1836*, ed. David H. Solkin, exh. cat., New Haven and London 2001, 127–43. See also her introduction to this volume.

7 Sybil Rosenfeld, "The Eidophusikon Illustrated," *Theatre Notebook* XVIII, no. 2 (1963), 52–4; Sybil Rosenfeld, *A Short History of Scene Design*, Oxford 1973, 87–93; Sybil Rosenfeld, *Georgian Scene Painters*, Cambridge 1981, 4–35; Allen, "Eidophusikon," 120–27; B. Allardyce Nicoll, *The Garrick Stage*, Manchester 1980, 116–19, 137–41.

8 Christopher L. Baugh, *Garrick and Loutherbourg*, Cambridge and Alexandria, Va. 1990, 29–30.

9 See Geneviève Levallet-Haug, "Philippe Jacques Loutherbourg," *Archives alsaciennes* 16 (1948), 77–134; H. Stein, "Quelques particularités de la vie du peintre Philippe-Jacques Lauterbourg," *Bulletin de la societé de l'histoire de l'art français* (1915–17), 85–6; Joppien, "Die

Szenenbilder," 1–17; Dobson, *Prior Park*, 96–100.

10 Denis Diderot, *Salons*, ed. Jean Seznec and Jean Adhémar, 4 vols, Oxford 1957–67, (Salon of 1763), I, 186–7, 225–7, 243; (Salon of 1765) II, 38–9, 123, 165–71. See also Else Marie Bukdahl, *Diderot, critique d'art*, Copenhagen 1982, 2, 186–7, 292–3.

11 See *A Biographical Dictionary of Actors, Actresses, Musicians, Dancers, Managers & Other Stage Personnel in London, 1660–1800*, ed. Philip H. Highfill, Jr., Kalman A. Burnim, and Edward A. Langhans, 16 vols, Carbondale, Ill. 1973–93, IV, 300–14; Nicoll, *Garrick Stage*, 116–19.

12 W. W. Wroth, *The London Pleasure Gardens of the Eighteenth Century*, London and Basingstoke 1896, 105–8.

13 Henry Angelo, *Reminiscences*, 2 vols, London 1904, I, 8–12.

14 Diderot, *Salons*, (Salon 1767) III, 116, 257–64; Dobson, *Prior Park*, 100.

15 *The Letters of David Garrick*, ed. David M. Little and George M. Kahrl, 3 vols, Oxford 1963, II, 761–3, 809.

16 John Goodman, ed., *Diderot on Art*, 2 vols, New Haven and London 1995, (Salon 1767) II, 248. See also II, 230–49.

17 Levallet-Haug, "Loutherbourg," 80–85; Stein, "Quelques particularités," 87–97; J. Guiffrey, "Philippe Jacques Loutherbourg et sa femme," *Revue de l'art française* IV (1888), 204–9.

18 Diderot, *Salons*, (Salons of 1769, 1771, 1775, 1781), IV, 35–6, 99–100, 142, 189–93.

19 P. de Loutherbourg to Eva Maria Garrick, n.d., Garrick Correspondence, 1712–81, Folger Shakespeare Library, Washington, D.C., MS W.b. 486–9, fol. 45.

20 Torré had offered to teach Garrick the secrets of the Kabbalah and how to harvest "the celestial manna"; Frank A. Hedgecock, *David Garrick and His French Friends*, London 1912, 394.

21 P. de Loutherbourg to Eva Maria Garrick, n.d. [1772], Garrick Correspondence, MS W.b. 486–9, fol. 44. The book he recommended was from the Cosmopolite, the name given to a seventeenth-century Scottish alchemist and adventurer called Seton. However, it might equally have come from the Polish alchemist Michael Sendivogius with whom Seton was often confounded.

22 See esp. "Anecdotes of Mr Loutherbourg," *European Magazine* I (1782), 181.

23 [P. Coxe], *A Catalogue of all valuable drawings, sketches, sea-views and studies of that celebrated artist, Philip James de Loutherbourg*, London, 1812, esp. 7–16.

24 Frances A. Yates, *The Rosicrucian Enlightenment*, London and New York, 1986, 226.

25 For the two most insightful analyses of this occult scientific outlook, see Hillel Schwartz, *The French Prophets: The History of a Millenarian Group in Eighteenth-Century England*, Berkeley, Los Angeles, and London 1980, 238–50; Allen G. Debus, "Scientific Truth and the Occult Tradition: The Medical World of Ebenezer Sibly (1751–1799)," *Medical History* XXVI (1982): 259–78. With the exception of the excellent discussion of Baugh, *Garrick and de Loutherbourg*, 28–9, 48–9, most of the secondary sources which discuss de Loutherbourg's magical and mystical interests focus on the later part of his career when these predilections surfaced in public. A good general example is Joscelyn Godwin, *The Theosophical Enlightenment*, Albany, N.Y. 1994, 100–06, 132–3. For the best discussion of the influence of de Loutherbourg's occultism on his art, see John Gage, "Loutherbourg: Mystogogue of the Sublime," *History Today* XIII (1963), 332–9, and his *Color in Turner: Poetry and Truth*, New York 1969, 136–9, 181–2, 229. See also, Stephen Daniels, "Loutherbourg's Chemical Theatre: *Coalbrookdale by Night*," in *Painting and the Politics of Culture: New Essays on British Art, 1700–1850*, ed. John Barrell, Oxford 1992, 195–230.

26 This is interesting because Gainsborough too objected to what he saw as de Loutherbourg's overuse of these colors in his scenography. Writing to Garrick in 1772 he joked: "When the streets are paved with Brilliants, and the Skies made of Rainbows I suppose you'l be contented, and satisfied with Red blue & yellow – It appears to me that fashion, let it consist of false or true taste will have its run"; *The Letters of Thomas Gainsborough*, ed. John Hayes, New Haven and London 2001, 107, letter no. 63. Rather than curb de Loutherbourg's brilliant effects, Garrick encouraged him to produce his most spectacular pantomime to date, *A Christmas Tale*. Gainsborough appears to have become reconciled eventually to the new stage of de Loutherbourg.

27 Joppien, "Die Szenenbilder," 55–77.

28 Paul Metzner, *Crescendo of the Virtuoso: Spectacle, Skill, and Self-Promotion in Paris during the Age of Revolution*, Berkeley, Los Angeles, and London 1998, 1–12, 213–97.

29 The three most comprehensive and judicious assessments by far of de Loutherbourg's scenographic achievements can be found in Baugh, *Garrick and de Loutherbourg*, *passim*, Christopher L. Baugh, "Philip James de Loutherbourg and the Early Pictorial Theatre: Some Aspects of its Cultural Context," in *The Theatrical Space*, ed. James Redmond, Cambridge 1987, and Joppien, "Die Szenenbilder," *passim*.

30 Joppien, "Die Szenenbilder," 349–50.

31 See William T. Whitley, *Artists and their Friends in England, 1770–1799*, 2 vols, London 1928, I, 353–4.

32 Ralph G. Allen, "The Wonders of Derbyshire," *Theatre Survey* II (1961), 54–66.

33 Highfill, *Biographical Dictionary*, IV, 306.

34 Philippe de Loutherbourg to the *European Magazine*, quoted in Frederick Burwick, "Romantic Drama from Optics to Illusion," in *Literature and Science: Theory and Practice*, ed. Stuart Peterfreund, Boston 1990, 170.

35 Joppien, "Die Szenenbilder," 354–5, ill. 145.

36 Allen, "The Eidophusikon," 180.

37 Altick, *Shows of London*, 119. On his friendship with Merlin and Jacquet Droz, see Angelo, *Reminiscences*, II, 249.

38 Allen, "The Eidophusikon," 14.

39 See Joppien, "Die Szenenbilder," 359.

40 Ralph G. Allen, "Topical Scenes for Pantomime," *Educational Theatre Journal* XVII, no. 4 (1965), 289–300.

41 Whitley, *Artists and their Friends*, II, 352.

42 Ephraim Hardcastle [W. H. Pyne], *Wine and Walnuts or, After Dinner Chit-Chat*, 2 vols, London 1823, I, 302–3.

43 See Patricia Fara, "An Attractive Therapy: Animal Magnetism in Eighteenth-Century England," *History of Science* XXXII (1995), 127–77; Roy

Porter, "Sex and the Singular Man: The Seminal Ideas of James Graham," *Studies on Voltaire and the Eighteenth Century*, no. 228, ed. H. T. Mason, Oxford 1984, 4–22; Simon During, *Modern Enchantments: The Cultural Power of Secular Magic*, Cambridge, Mass. 2002, 247–52; Barbara Maria Stafford, *Artful Science: Enlightenment Entertainment and the Eclipse of Visual Education*, Cambridge, Mass. and London 1994, 14–16, 74–6.

44 Cyrus Redding, *Memoirs of William Beckford*, 2 vols, London 1859, II, 38, 42.

45 Guy Chapman, *Beckford*, London 1937, 92–9.

46 Ralph G. Allen, "The Stage Spectacle of P. J. De Loutherbourg," PhD diss., Yale University 1960, reproduced by University of Michigan Microfilms, 1969, 69–88, 147–61.

47 Timothy Mowl, *William Beckford: Composing for Mozart*, London 1998, 7–89; Chapman, *Beckford*, 60, 87, 92.

48 J. W. Oliver, *The Life of William Beckford*, London 1932, 159–83; Chapman, *Beckford*, 92–9; Nigel Leask, "Wandering through Eblis: Absorption and Containment in Romantic Exoticism," in *Romanticism and Colonialism: Writing and Empire, 1780–1830*, ed. Tim Kitson and Peter J. Fulford, Cambridge and New York 1998, 170–71.

49 Joppien, "Die Szenenbilder," 362–3, also points out that Servandoni had presented a spectacle on the same theme at the Tuileries theatre in Paris in 1758, but de Loutherbourg, if he saw it, would have been only eighteen at the time.

50 Allen, "The Eidophusikon," 15.

51 *Ibid.*, 14.

52 Terry Castle, "Phantasmagoria: Spectral Technology and the Metaphorics of Modern Reverie," *Critical Inquiry* (Autumn 1988), 26–61; Barbara Maria Stafford and Frances Terpak, *Devices of Wonder from the World in a Box to Images on a Screen*, with an object list by Isotta Poggi, exh. cat., Los Angeles 2001, 82–7; During, *Modern Enchantments*, 97–106.

53 See Godwin, *Theosophical Enlightenment*, 100–33; Fara, "An Attractive Therapy," 127–56.

54 William Vaughan, *Gainsborough*, London and New York 2002, 187–93.

55 Dobson, *Prior Park*, 99–100. Significantly, the influential ex-painter and satirist John Wolcot launched his first bout of ridicule against de Loutherbourg in 1782; see "Lyrical Odes for the Royal Academicians for 1782" in *The Works of Peter Pindar*, 2 vols, London 1816, I, 28–9. For the mounting chorus of newspaper criticisms of de Loutherbourg's gaudy style, see Anne Puetz, "Foreign Exhibitors and the British School at the Royal Academy, 1768–1823," in *Art on the Line*, ed. Solkin, 233–4; Pasquin's printed criticisms were later but are mostly retrospective from the earlier period. Anthony Pasquin, *A Critical Guide to the Exhibition of the Royal Academy for 1796*, London 1796, 13; on Bate-Dudley, see Whitley, *Artists and their Friends*, I, 366.

56 This may also lie behind Lawrence's contemporary assessment that de Loutherbourg "was at the top of the ingenious men but went no further." *The Diary of Joseph Farington*, ed. James Grieg, 8 vols, London 1923, II, 237.

57 For a discussion of the views of modern art historians who hold this same view, see Nancy J. D. Hazelton, "'Green to the very door': Painted Landscape on the Nineteenth-Century Stage," *Theatre History Studies* XXII (2002), 115–36.

58 This was the view, especially, of his friend and former pupil Sir Francis Bourgeois; *Diary of Joseph Farington*, III, 151; V, 84.

59 See John Barrell, *The Political Theory of Painting from Reynolds to Hazlitt: "The Body of the Public,"* New Haven and London 1986, *passim*.

60 The Exeter Exchange had also hosted the Patagonian puppet theater; see Joppien, "Die Szenenbilder", 346–7.

61 See advertisement, *Morning Herald*, April 28, 1786; Altick, *Shows*, 125; *The Times*, 28 May 1793, I.

Photograph Credits

© Alte Pinakoteck, Munich, 6; Art Resource, New York, 7; Ashmolean Museum, Oxford, 41, 120, 121; The Bridgeman Art Library, London/New York, plate I, 2, 43, 61, 91; By permission of the British Library, 54, 55; © Copyright The Trustees of the British Museum, 30, 49, 50, 53, 56, 57, 113, 124; From the Castle Howard Collection, 5; Cincinnati Art Museum, plate II, 34, 40, 64; City of Westminster Archives Centre, London, 125; Conway Library, Courtauld Institute of Art, 42; By Permission of the Trustees of Dulwich Picture Gallery, London, 13, 119; © English Heritage Photo Library, Photographer: Jonathan Bailey, 1, 67; Reproduction by permission of the Syndics of Fitzwilliam Museum, Cambridge, 39, 75; Photograph © The Frick Collection, New York, 71; Courtesy of Gainsborough's House, Sudbury, Suffolk, 58, 68;Glasgow City Council (Museums), 31; Research Library, Getty Research Institute, Los Angeles, 112; Guildhall Library, Corporation of London, 33, 38; The Huntington Library, Art Collections, and Botanical Gardens, San Marino, California, plate III, 8, 27, 32, 72, 73, 104, 105; Ipswich Borough Council Museums and Art Galleries, Ipswich, plate IV; Lehigh University Art Galleries LUP 60 5003/Museum Operation, 82; Library of Congress Prints and Photography Division LC-USZC42898, 48; London Metropolitan Archives, 36; Los Angeles County Museum of Art, Photograph © 2005 Museum Associates/LACMA, 4; Kunsthistorisches Museum, Wien oder KHM, Wien, 60; Photograph © 1986 The Metropolitan Museum of Art, 8; © The National Gallery, London, 10, 11, 63, 66, 76, 81, 103; © Board of Trustees, National Gallery of Art, Washington, D.C., 65; © The National Gallery of Ireland, 111, 123; National Museums & Galleries of Wales, Cardiff, 26; National Portrait Gallery, London, 12; The Nelson-Atkins Museum of Art, Kansas City, Missouri, Photo Credit: Jamison Miller, 96; Philadelphia Museum of Art, 22, 28; © Robert Poulter, 15; © Photo RMN, 69; The Royal Collection © 2004, Her Majesty Queen Elizabeth II, 108, 109, 117; Royal Holloway College Art Gallery, University of London, 29; © Stephen Saitas Designs, New York, 100; © Tate, London 2004, 3, 70, 110; Courtesy of the University of Bristol Theatre Collection, 122; Collection of the University of California, Los Angeles, Hammer Museum. Photo by Lou Meluso, courtesy of the J. Paul Getty Museum, Los Angeles, plate V, 44, 78, 79; University of Manchester (Tabley House Collection), 85, 86, 87, 89, 92, 94, 95, 98, 99, 101, 102, 107; V&A Images/Victoria and Albert Museum, London, 14, 16, 17, 18, 19, 20, 25, 90, 115, 116; Reproduced by kind permission of the Trustees of The Wallace Collection, 77; Wellcome Library, London, 34; Yale Center for British Art © Richard Caspole, 23, 24, 45, 74, 80, 83, 84, 88, 97, 106, 118; York Museum Trust (York Art Gallery), 114

Index

Page numbers in *italics* refer to illustrations

Index by Margaret Binns